THIS DAY THAT YEAR

Memory down the lane of hindi movies of Late **60'S** and Early **70'S**

K V Laxminarayan
aka LAX

BLUEROSE PUBLISHERS
India | U.K.

Copyright © K V Laxminarayan aka LAX 2024

All rights reserved by author. No part of this publication may be reproduced, stored in a retrieval system or transmitted in any form or by any means, electronic, mechanical, photocopying, recording or otherwise, without the prior permission of the author. Although every precaution has been taken to verify the accuracy of the information contained herein, the publisher assumes no responsibility for any errors or omissions. No liability is assumed for damages that may result from the use of information contained within.

BlueRose Publishers takes no responsibility for any damages, losses, or liabilities that may arise from the use or misuse of the information, products, or services provided in this publication.

For permissions requests or inquiries regarding this publication,
please contact:

BLUEROSE PUBLISHERS
www.BlueRoseONE.com
info@bluerosepublishers.com
+91 8882 898 898
+4407342408967

ISBN: 978-93-5819-749-5

Cover design: Muskan Sachdeva
Typesetting: Rohit

First Edition: January 2024

ABOUT THE AUTHOR

K V Laxminarayan aka Lax aka Laksh

Hello & Greetings

This is Laxminarayan aka Lax aka Laksh, an IT Professional from 1976 and moved out of the corporate world as a Senior Professional in 2011 from a Big IT player called **ORACLE**. I was always fascinated by Hindi Movies/Music and Cricket and was blessed with decent memory to recall about movies, songs and cricket matches. During my professional days too I could connect any situation at work with a movie, music or cricket and people around used to get surprised and amazed at this quality of mine. I used to share some information as a child about movies and matches with friends and they have always liked them and encouraged me.

Having a fairly good memory always helped me both in Professional and Personal lives. In most of the organizations I worked for, they had internal magazines and I used to contribute there too and once Facebook became known and there was no looking back. Here was a platform where I could express my experiences of anything be it movies, music or cricket. I could talk about events, conduct quizzes and write about cricket matches that generated a lot of interest among the friends community. I could also comment on other posts on similar subjects with value add.

Post retirement while people always wondered and worried with the question of What Next, nothing like that bothered me, as I was already into Facebook from 2009 after Orkut wrapped up. The forum was good to share a review of a musical event or a movie that I saw or about any cricket match with lots of details, and this really kept me busy and the best part of social media coming up was to get reconnected with people and make new friends. My strength has been people and social media gave me the opportunity not only to reconnect with people who had vanished from my radar, but it also helped me to expand the circle of friends and ex-colleagues.

I am naturally a relaxed person with a decent disposition and armed with some early training in music and penchant to entertain, I decided to add the objective of

Spreading Happiness and with this book, I hope to reach out to more people and expand my friendship base. I would like to thank some of the people who coaxed me into publishing and they are:

Dilip Apte, Balakrishnan Narayan, Viswanathan Krishnan - my good friends

Viswanath Iyer, my nephew

Manjunath, my late friend

My school friends – cannot name all

I will await your valuable feedback on reading my book and you can reach me out at "lax2402tdty@gmail.com" and please note that the dates mentioned of release of the movie are from my memory and may have errors. Hence E&OE

THE EXCESS OF INCOME OVER EXPENDITURE FROM THE SALES OF THIS BOOK WILL BE DONATED TO SOME OF THE CHARITABLE INSTITUTIONS, I AM ATTACHED WITH & ALL WHO BUY WILL BE ALSO MAKING A CONTRIBUTION FOR A GOOD CAUSE.

Cheers

Lax

FORWORD

Hello Reader

This is BS Narayan, a close friend of the author of this book for over six decades. We have grown up together and I have been his "Partner in Crime" most of the times. I have known him as a person with a fair amount of knowledge about Bollywood and as we grew up and found our own paths and in different cities, we stayed in touch always and in the last decade plus thru his daily column on social media called "This Day That Year". The write up week after week could take me to those days when we didn't have enough money to see a new release and if I had seen the movie then this was a platform for me to share my experiences about the same movie. In no time, we found many common friends who could relate to that era and started commenting on the thread with their own experiences. People in general started looking forward to this column and relived those golden moments.

As a well-wisher of Lax, I felt his experience needs to reach a larger audience and since 2013, I have been cajoling him to publish his experiences and finally after almost a decade the time has arrived. Lax has a very simple way of articulating his thoughts and in a way that most of the people who grew up in the 50s, 60s & even the next decades can relate to. I have personally read all the experiences that he has shared in the social media and found them interesting as he has good memory to recall all those incidences related to the movie in question and has the ability to put it across in an interesting manner.

I wish the best for my friend who has been gifted with good memory and the ability to involve everyone with his lucid way of writing

Regards

Balakrishnan S Narayan

FORWORD

Hello Reader

This is Dilip Apte, a close friend of the author of this book for over a decade. I have known him as a person with a good amount of knowledge about Bollywood and got to know him thru his daily column on social media called "This Day That Year". The write up week after week could take me to those days when we didn't have enough money to see a new release and if I had seen the movie then this was a platform for me to share my experiences about the same movie. In no time, we found many common friends who could relate to that era and started commenting on the thread with their own experiences. People in general started looking forward to this column and relived those golden moments.

As a well-wisher of Laksh I felt his experience needs to reach a larger audience and since 2013, I have been cajoling him to publish his experiences and finally after almost a decade the time has arrived.

Laksh has a very simple way of articulating his thoughts and in a way that most of the people who grew up in the 50s, 60s & even the next decades can relate to. I have personally read all the experiences that he has shared in the social media and found them interesting as he has very good memory to recall all those incidences related to the movie in question and has the ability to put it across in an interesting manner.

I wish the best for my friend who has been gifted with good memory and the ability to involve everyone with his lucid way of writing

Regards
Dilip Apte

CONTENTS

"EK BECHARA & EK HASEENA DO DIWANE" 1
"PYASI SHAAM" 2
"VICTORIA NO. 203" 4
"DAMAN AUR AAG" 7
"HUMRAAZ" 9
"DO CHOR" 12
"VAASANA" 14
"ANJAANA" 16
"SEEMA" 18
"SAMADHI" 20
"KAHANI KISMAT KI" 23
"HUMSAYA" 26
"SATYAKAM & SHART" 28
"ALBELA" 31
"MERA NAAM JOKER" 33
"KHOJ" 35
"TANHAAI" 36
"AABROO" 37
"UPAHAAR" 39
"NAYA RAASTA" 41
"DO GAZ ZAMEEN KE NEECHAY" 43
"HEERA" 45
"EK KALI MUSKAYEE" 47
"DO YAAR" 49
"PARAYA DHAN" 50
"KHAMOSHI" 52
"DO RAASTE" 54
"BLACKMAIL & DHARMA" 56
"SADHU AUR SHAITAN" 59
"GOPI" 62
"KAL AAJ AUR KAL" 65
"ROOP TERA MASTANA & SHEHAZADA" 67
"NAMAK HARAM & MANCHALI" 70
"NANHA FARISHTA" 74
"JOHNY MERA NAAM" 75

"EK NARI EK BRAHMACHARI"	78
"RAJA JANI"	81
"AA GALE LAG JAA"	83
"SAATHI"	85
"MERE HUMSAFAR"	87
"HANGAMA"	89
"MUNIMJI"	91
"YAADON KI BAARAAT"	93
"AULAD"	96
"ARADHANA & JIGRI DOST"	98
"SEETA AUR GEETA & GAON HAMARA SHEHAR TUMHARA"	102
"JWAR BHATA"	106
"BAAZI"	108
"ITTEFAQ"	110
"BACHPAN & JAHAN PYAR MILEY"	112
"CARAVAN"	115
"KASHMAKASH"	118
"NIGHT IN LONDON"	120
"HOLI AYEE RE"	121
"RAJA SAAB"	123
"RAM AUR SHYAM"	125
"SANGHARSH"	129
"PYAR HI PYAR"	132
"BIKHRE MOTI & BUDDHA MIL GAYA"	134
"MASTANA & ISHQ PAR ZOR NAHI"	137
"KOSHISH"	140
"JOSHILA"	142
"JUARI"	144
"UMANG"	145
"PHAGUN"	147
"DIWANA"	149
"SAMAJ KO BADAL DALO"	151
"HULCHAL"	153
"MERE JEEVAN SAATHI"	155
"RICKSHAWALA "	157
"ZINDAGI ZINDAGI"	157
"WARIS"	159
"PAVITRA PAAPI & PUSHPANJALI"	163
"GUDDI"	166
"SHOR"	169

"BOBBY" 171
"AANKHEN" 174
"RAKHWALA" 176
"GEET" 178
"PRATIGGYA" 180
"JOROO KA GHULAM" 183
"NAINA" 185
"AANSOO BAN GAYE PHOOL" 187
"BHAI BHAI" 189
"KATHPUTLI" 191
"JHEEL KE US PAAR" 193
"KISMAT" 195
"SAWAN BHADON" 197
"CHOTI BAHU" 199
"RIVAAJ" 201
"JAISE KO TAISA" 202
"PYAR KA SAPNA & October 17 1969 ANMOL MOTI" 204
"YAADGAR" 206
"NADAAN" 208
"ZAMEEN AASMAN" 210
"AAJ KI TAAZA KHABAR" 212
"TAMANNA" 214
"TUM HASEEN MAIN JAWAN" 215
"AAP AAYE BAHAAR AAYEE" 217
"BAWARCHI" 219
"CHALAK" 221
"BADI DIDI" & "CHANDA AUR BIJLI" 222
"SHOLAY" 224
"MAHAL" 228
"MERA GAON MERA DESH" 230
"RAMPUR KA LAKSHMAN" 233
"KUCHHE DHAAGE" 236
"GAURI" 238
"PRINCE" 240
"SAFAR" 243
"NAYA ZAMANA" (NZ) 245
"BE-IMAAN" 248
"JUGNU" 250
"SAJAN" 252
"JEEVAN MRITUE" 254

Title	Page
'EK NAZAR'	256
"ABHIMAAN' & "GEHARI CHAAL"	258
'YAKEEN' & 'VISHWAS'	260
"PARWANA"	262
"DARPAN"	264
"SANGAM"	265
"TANGEWALA"	267
"SAMJHAUTA"	269
"DHADKAN"	271
"AMAR AKBAR ANTHONY"	273
"JAWAN MOHABBAT"	275
"SHARAFAT"	277
"MADHAVI"	279
"JAI SANTOSHI MAA"	279
'SHAREEF BUDMASH'	281
"HASEENA MAAN JAYEGI"	282
"ABINETRI" "ROOTHA NA KARO"	284
"HAATHI MERE SAATHI"	286
'BHAI HO TO AISA' & 'BANDAGI'	288
"CHUPA RUSHTAM"	290
'SHIKAR"	291
"CHIRAG"	292
"PEHCHAAN"	294
"PARAS" "PYAR KI KAHANI"	296
"PIYA KA GHAR"	298
"ZANJEER"	299
"BRAHMACHARI"	301
"HUMJOLI"	303
"ELAAN"	305
"EK PHOOL DO MALI"	307
"ANHONEE"	309
"APNA DESH"	310
"SACHHA JHOOTA"	312
"ANDAZ"	314
"Mom Ki Gudiya" "Mangetar" & "Shararat"	316
"DAAG" - a Poem of Love	318
"JEENE KI RAAH"	319
"BANDHAN" & "MAA AUR MAMTA"	321
"MAIN SUNDAR HOON" & "PARDESI"	323
"APRADH" "SHADI KE BAAD"	326

Title	Page
'GAAI AUR GORI' 'ANOKHI ADA'	329
'HUMSHAKAL'	332
"SAMBANDH"	333
"HEER RANJHA"	335
"HIMMAT"	336
"HAAR JEET"	337
"DOST"	338
"CHUPKE CHUPKE "	340
"INTEQAM"	342
THE TRAIN & KHILONA	343
"LAKHONE MEIN EK"	345
"DASTAAN"	347
"ANURAAG"	349
"MANORANJAN"	351
"ASHIRWAD"	353
"DEVI"	355
"UPAASNA" "MELA"	357
"ANITA"	359
"Lal Pathar", "Annadaata" & "Wafaa"	361
"BANARASI BABU"	364
"KHOTE SIKKAY"	365
'SUHAAG RAAT"	367
"LAGAN"	369
"HANSTE ZAKHAM"	370
"CHOR MACHAYE SHOR"	372
"DHARTI"	374
"PARDE KE PEECHAY"	376
"MEMSAAB"	378
LOAFER	380
SHATRANJ	382
"MAN KI AANKHEN"	384
"ANAND"	386
PANCH DUSHMAN	388
Mere Huzoor	389
JAWAB	391
SAAS BHI KABHI BAHU THI	392
BOMBAY TO GOA	393
HEERA PANNA	395
SAPNON KA SAUDAGAR	396
AADMI AUR INSAAN	398

HASEENON KA DEVTA	400
SANJOG	401
DHUND	403
WAPAS	404
SACHAAI	405
GAMBLER	407
EK NANHI MUNNI LADKI THI	409
MERE APNE	411
DO RAHA	413
BANDHE HAATH & GORA AUR KAALA	414
DUNIYA	416
RAHAGEER	418
PREM PUJARI	421
"PYASI SHAAM"	423
PAAKEEZAH	425
IZZAT	427
PAGLA KAHIN KA PYAR KA MAUSAM	429
KATI PATANG	431
AMAR PREM	433
DIL AUR MOHABBAT	435
DOLI (53 Years ago)	436
HARE RAMA HARE KRISHNA	437
BHAI BEHAN	439
AAN MILO SAJNA	440
GANGA TERA PANI AMRIT	442
RASTE KA PATHAR	443
PADOSAN	444
TEESRI KASAM	446
TALASH	448
JOHAR MEHMOOD IN HONG KONG	450
DUSHMAN	452
SARASWATICHANDRA	454
DO BHAI	456
AANSOO AUR MUSKAN	457

March 10th 1972

"EK BECHARA &.
EK HASEENA DO DIWANE"

51 Years Ago two movies of Jeetendra released and both did not do well. They are **Ek Bechara & Ek Haseena Do Diwane** both had Jeetu and Vinod Khanna as the common factors while Rekha was the sought after one in EB and Babita in EHDD

Both movies had decent hummable music. With First Year College exams round the corner and also with limited pocket money had to give the movies a pass and wait for April 22 1972 for the exams to get over!!! By then these movies were out of the main halls.

I would request knowledgeable people to talk about these 2 movies - here are the song links:

Ek Bechara

https://www.youtube.com/watch?v=QFl873v86uw ;

https://www.youtube.com/watch?v=N20ajOGyC3A ;

https://www.youtube.com/watch?v=Zekk5IZM240 ;

https://www.youtube.com/watch?v=xlc0JKCDMwM ;

https://www.youtube.com/watch?v=7Do7IhjemVk ;

Full movie Link - https://www.youtube.com/watch?v=G3lgj99Z3UE

Ek Haseena Do Diwane

Song List Link - https://www.youtube.com/watch?v=vK30bDcYtT8 ;

Cheers

Lax

February 05, 1971

"PYASI SHAAM"

Dear Friends:

It was 52 years ago today i.e. on Feb 5 1971, this flop movie called "PYASI SHAM" released made by Kewalji Productions who had earlier made a better movie in "Mere Humdum Mere Dost" but this one was a disaster. All I recall, this was curfew period for me wrt seeing movies as a class XI student and the movie did not last long enough for me to see it once my exams got over in 1.5 months after the release. So, just feel happy with the poster and envy Sunil Dutt who hugs Sharmila Tagore. The other thing I recall is the wedding of my Amma's Marathi student's brother at Tamil Sangam on this day and I did attend the Muhurtam and went to school – here I must tag my Amma's student V Narasimhan, who later became my colleague in P&G. The movie and the music could not recreate the magic of the banner's earlier movie but this had a couple of hummable songs like "YE KAISA GUM SAJNA PYASA DIN PYASI SHAM", "AWARA MAAJI JAYEGA KAHAN" & "DUNIYA MEIN DILWALE HONGAY HAZARON". But, a Big Box Office Disaster and here is the star cast:

- Sunil Dutt
- Sharmila Tagore
- Feroz Khan
- Om Prakash
- Manmohan Krishna
- Dhumal
- Anjali Kadam
- Kamal Kapoor &
- Birbal

Since I have not seen the movie till now, I have no option but to talk to people and gather the data but I will request some of the more knowledgable folks to share about the plot and the movie. All I can say is it is a triangular plot with 2 good friends i.e. the Hero and the side Hero who get the Hero's sister married and then both fall for the Heroine Sharmila. Naturally there is going to be a fair amount of misunderstandings and till the side Hero realises that the Heroine too is fond of Hero ahead of him & then things get sorted out. Nothing much to rave about the performances I suppose. Friends – plese help me with more dope on the plot. Here are the songs for you.

- https://www.youtube.com/watch?v=ljFOVuEjPJg ;
- https://www.youtube.com/watch?v=riecuME48cY ;
- https://www.youtube.com/watch?v=DD2tQ6v-Tyc ;
- https://www.youtube.com/watch?v=QQ5AYQ9g4Bk ;

Cheers

Laksh KV

December 08, 1972

"VICTORIA NO. 203"

Dear Friends:

It was today, 51 years ago on December 8, 1972, this hit movie from the banner Dynamo International, Produced and Directed by Brij called "VICTORIA No. 203" released. I have good memories of this movie as a great entertainer and the thespians Ashok Kumar and Pran had some great timing and had meaty roles. Though, I did not see it as soon as it was released as I was not too impressed with the Hero but as the movie picked up, I could not help but go and see at Rivoli Cinema bunking college. It was not Ameen Sayani for the advertisements and radio program but it was Ehasan Rizvi (I hope I got the spelling right) and the ads were very funny "ABHI ABHI KHABAR MILI HAI KI EK FILM BANKAR TAYYAR HI – NAAM HI VICOTRIA No. 203" in his typical voice and inimitable style. Some impact scenes for me are listed below:

- Saira Banu as a man riding the Victoria
- The enticing dress during the song "Thodasa Theharo" filmed on Saira Banu
- Ashok Kumar seen as an incorrigible flirt
- Deadly duo of Ashok Kumar and Pran escaping from a drowning boat with Pran using his teeth to cut the ropes tied on Ashok Kumar's wrist & Ashok Kumar trying to do the same despite free hands
- When they read the news about the robbery of diamonds, while sipping tea at a tea stall, first they check and feel safe that they were in the jail. Then, they crib about what is offered by the tea stall "Thandi Chai, Soday Mein Makhi"
- The wild ghoose chase with the key without a lock. The lovely song by KK and MK filmed on the thespians and with Helan and my English teacher Luku Sanyal too coming on screen

- Mohan Choti as ward boy, has a favourite number that was 6 or 8 – someone can help me
- Anwar Hussain telling Pran to kill his son played by Navin Nischal and collect 20K when Pran calls for a huge ransom amount running in lakhs in lieu of his son's life.
- Anwar Hussain trying to torchure his adopted son Navin Nischal and asking him "KUMAR HEERAY KAHAN HAIN?"
- Now I can also say how the 1994 cult movie "Andaaz Apna Apna" used the climax of this movie regarding the diamonds!!!

Our neighbour and good friend Kumar Harihar – was rechristened as "Heera" and the name got imprinted with the release of the movie "Heera" in December 1973!!! Kalyanji Anandji's music was quite interesting and helped the movie to become a huge money spinner in that year. The star-cast of the movie is as under:

- Ashok Kumar
- Navin Nischal
- Saira Banu
- Pran
- Anwar Hussain
- Ranjeet
- Chaman Puri
- Anup Kumar &
- Mohan Choti

The plot was quite intriguing with a set of people from Anwar Hussain's gang trying to locate the stolen Diamonds that were hidden in the lamp of the Victoria No 203. A typical KA Narayan story that had son and dad (Navin Nischal & Pran) getting separated, a wronged Saira Banu, takes over her dad's Victoria and dresses up as a man to earn a livelihood and Navin Nischal who has roving eyes settles for Saira Banu & then we have Anwar Hussain and his gang trying to get hold of the stolen diamonds. The way it gets tracked right from the Bandra fly-over (East to West) to the locker at VT station that has a chit indicating where the diamonds are hidden is really a wild chase for those who are after it. Overall a great entertainer and when remade later it could not capture the magic. Enjoy the songs here:

- https://www.youtube.com/watch?v=ybg2YqfJ46c ;
- https://www.youtube.com/watch?v=CDv_8RmNGvE ;
- https://www.youtube.com/watch?v=axZtA9kL5Wg ;
- https://www.youtube.com/watch?v=QweyQJQgnu8 ;

Cheers

Laksh KV

January 19, 1973

"DAMAN AUR AAG"

Dear Friends:

It was today 50 years ago on Jan 19th 1973, this flop movie called "Daaman Aur Aag" released. I recall seeing it on Saturday 3 PM show at Rupam mainly as it had some leg display of Saira Banu – and I saw it all alone just to show my support for Shankar Jaikishan who had composed the music for the movie. All I can recall of the movie is major overacting of Anwar Hussain who plays a Christian character Pinto and turns from a bad to good man. The movie barely did run for 5 weeks and declared a big flop. The main characters of the movie are:

- Saira Banu
- Sanjay (Khan)
- Balraj Sahani
- Madan Puri
- Anwar Hussain
- KN Singh
- Sanjana
- Sundar
- Mukri &
- Rajendranath

The plot revolves around Balraj Sahani (BS) who is a very honest guy and loses his wife when she delivers but BS wants to give a good life to his son, educates him but circumstances forces him to get into wrong business but that enables him to send his son Sanjay Khan abroad and returns as a polished guy back home. Soon he falls in love with Saira Banu and Sanjay holds his dad in very high esteem and wants to be a good man and needless to say he is part of police and realizes that his dad with his 2 cronies Anwar Hussain and Mukhri is doing something wrong. Now, the movie takes a turn for the son to go against his father once he realizes that his dad is the guy who runs illicit liquor business for Madan

Puri and good has to prevail and evil needs to be punished. Balraj Sahani has done a decent job while others are passable and Anwar Hussain has big time over acted. Music by SJ was just about decent but the classical song "Tirkha Badan Tu Geeton Ke" sung by the Lata Asha duo is simply outstanding. Here are the songs for you.

- https://www.youtube.com/watch?v=H9zx1STiweI ;
- https://www.youtube.com/watch?v=5_NDgl8hwPI ;
- https://www.youtube.com/watch?v=N0IFrTpAL8o ;

Cheers

Laksh KV

December 29, 1967

"HUMRAAZ"

Dear Friends:

56 years ago i.e. on Dec 29, 1967, this big banner hit movie from the famous film makers Chopras (BR Chopra) called "HUMRAAZ" was released. It had all components for a hit movie that comprised of great settings, good photography, good music, lovely star cast, suspense, and murder besides of course the court scenes. My recall about this movie is that, my parents had kept it as a guarded secret and we had a surprise when we had coffee at Hanuman Coffee House Sion and then went inside the Cinema hall Rupam – "S row" was second from front but was flabbergasted at seeing a new movie all five of us ufff... what a feeling!!! Just a few days before that, me and my 2nd brother saw Upkar at Rupam that had long "Q" and while he stood in one Q (Upper Stall) I was at the Balcony Q and there was one gentleman who came and gave me Rs. 10/- and told me to book tickets as "Sunday 2nd show 3 tickets" – I realized I was in the same show as I did the booking for that gentleman. I could see my elder brother getting excited as Raj Kumar and Vimmi were shown in each others arms with lovely location in the background and the song "Ye Neelay Gagan Ke Talay". Overall, a great feeling during X'mas vacation for a class VIII student. The star cast of the movie is as under:

- Raj Kumar
- Vimmi
- Sunil Dutt
- Balraj Sahani
- Mumtaz
- Iftikahr
- Anwar Hussain
- Madan Puri
- Sarika
- Helan
- Manmohan Krishna
- Jeevan

- Achla Sachdev

The plot of the movie:

Sunil Dutt plays a stage actor in Bombay, who performs plays along with Mumtaz. While on a trip to a beautiful hill station, he meets and falls head over heals for the Heroine played by Vimi, who is the daughter of a rich Businessman, reprised by Manmohan Krishna. Soon, Sunil Dutt and Vimmi tie the knot and return home. Some years later, Vimi's dad passes away after telling her something that he had kept disreetly.

Sunil Dutt notices that Vimmi stops accompanying him for his stage shows, and claims to be sick. He finds evidences that suggest that his wife is meeting somebody else on the sly. Sunil Dutt now suspecting his wife, engineers a trip, with a new look and name as S.N. Sinha, checks into a hotel. Then he proceeds to his home, and finds the main door open, and is in for a rude shock as he hears a gunshot. When he enters his room, he finds Vimmi dead.

Angrily, he decides to take police help, but soon it dawns on him that he will be caught in the murder, as his fingerprints are available on the pistol used to kill. So he returns to the hotel instead, and being upset smokes many cigarettes. To investigate the case, Balraj Sahani is called and the next day, when Sunil Dutt comes home officially, the Policeman observes that Sunil Dutt knew which room the body is in, despite none updating him.

There is a coconut seller near our Hero's house who says that he saw a bearded man in the area the night of the murder and the owner of the hotel which the Hero had checked into calls the police, saying that a bearded man had checked into their hotel. The cigarette buds that he had smoked were retrieved, and handed over to the Police. When the Policeman visits the Hero at his house later, the Hero offers him the same brand of cigarette that enhances the suspicion. More evidences point fingers at the Hero to be the culprit.

In a hurry, Sunil Dutt, our hero decides to vanish from the growing suspicion of Inspector. He has a lawyer friend, in Iftekhar, who says that he will definitely be implicated as the murderer of his wife. He finds a clue about the suspected killer from his home, a key with room number of a hotel. Sunil Dutt visits the room as a last attempt to clear things before being captured. There, he meets Raj Kumar who calms him down and tells him that neither of them is the killer. He tells Sunil

Dutt that he is his wife's first husband, who was supposedly dead in a war, and that he had the honourable intentions of taking care of their illegitimate baby, Sarika, because she wouldn't be able to raise a child born out of wedlock.

Raj Kumar tells Sunil Dutt that whoever the killer is, he was seen by Sarika because she was present in the room where her mom died as both mom and baby was playing and their activities were being recorded by a video camera. Together, they both decide to track the girl, and locate her at Ooty. Balraj Sahani continues to track these 2 men and they both are nabbed by him with the help of Ooty Police. Sunil Dutt explains his case, and updates the Police that the child is in the custody of Madan Puri, who tries to run away from there. The video tape is retrieved and its clear as to who is the culprit – but then Madan Puri does his last minute bit to hold the child to ransom but the real dad (Raj Kumar) of the Baby saves her and ends up dying.

Sunil Dutt is not very keen to continue his profession but Mumtaz persuades him and also shows that the young child is occupying her mom's seat and things settle down. Here is the song link for you.

- https://www.youtube.com/watch?v=KflXlB0_27Y ;

Cheers

Laksh KV

December 29, 1972

"DO CHOR"

Dear Friends:

It was today 51 years ago (Dec 29 1972) this Raj Khosla comedy movie called "DO CHOR" released. It did decent business and had a fair amount of entertainment. What stands out in my memory is Tanuja as a Boy called "Bob" – despite best of efforts, it was very clear that it was a female donning the bhes of a man. Good memory for me is also of the Hippy song "Yari Hogayee" filmed with a lot of phirangs. Those days, it was quite common to have an exhibition where some valuable stuff would be displayed and the Heroes (mostly Dharam Paji) will rob it despite the best of security and we can expect our dear Iftikar as a Police Officer getting upset at the chori. Good songs laced with slick editing made the movie quite watchable and since it was Xmas vacation and money no more an issue thanx to my job at Pentagon, I could see the movie without any pressure. The other interesting aspect of the movie was that, Tanuja's real life mom Shobhana Samarth playing her mom and those scenes between the mom and daughter were in Black & White. The cast of the movie included:

- Dharmendra
- Tanuja
- KN Singh
- Dhumal
- Trilok Kapoor
- Bhagwan
- Sajjan
- Shobhna Samarth
- Murad
- Viju Khote
- Jagdish Raj &
- Laxmi Chaya

The plot was very simple - A series of mysterious Chori takes place at the homes of four rich men. The burglar takes a single piece of jewellery from each of the men, but not touching the cash and other jewellery, and leaving behind a card of a swastik. The police suspect Tony (Dharmendra) generally known in the community as a thief, but he pleads innocence. He tries to find out who the real Chor is and sees Sandhya (Tanuja) stealing from one of the wealthy men. She tells him that she is taking back what is really her inheritance, as these items belong to her mother (Shobhana Samarth) since these four men swindled her mother after her father's death. Her mother is now in a mental institution. Tony and Sandhya fall in love. He helps her recover all her items and put the wealthy men behind bars. Sandhya's mother is well again. Tony and Sandhya decide to start a fresh life together once they are done with their short jail stints. Songs are as under:

- https://www.youtube.com/watch?v=r1rvar9IaAY ;

Cheers

Laksh KV

December 27, 1968

"VAASANA"

Dear Friends:

It was today 55 years ago i.e. on December 27, 1968, this movie called "VAASNA" released. It did average business though I felt it should have done better. Good music by Chitragupta was well received by people. Again for me it was the same thing – X'mas vacation and going to Uncle's place and seeing a movie and this time my uncle and self went for the night show. This time round, we got balcony tickets and I recall since it was winter, my uncle wore a blazer that had golden buttons and very proudly displayed it to my aunt and said "People will look at the golden buttons and would say 'Some Big Shot'". He was such a fun loving and jovial guy – still miss him though he left us suddenly in 1994. The movie started and soon there was Helan dancing and singing "JEENEWALE JHOOM KE" and I, for a minute felt how come Sharmila Tagore!! Then, I soon realized that it was not her. There was one Akash Deep too who gets drunk in this song and reaches home to get a mouthful from Padmini (his mom I guess). She then tells her about his dad how drink really took a toll on his life. I simply loved the movie and also the music – all songs were superb. Enjoyed the movie and felt proud to tell all that I had indeed seen the movie on release, especially to my good friend Bedi who was big fan of Raj Kumar. The star cast included:

- Raj Kumar
- Padmini
- Biswajit
- Kumud Chugani
- Sayeeda Khan
- Tiwari
- David
- Laxmi Chaya
- Helan

- Manorama &
- Rajendranath

The plot revolved around a businessman Raj Kumar, who is successful and his wife Padmini who is a busy socialite and their child gets a bit ignored. Both of them play the 'blame game' when the child is hurt and at some point some decisions need to be taken if career/business is more important or the child/family. The mother decides to focus on the child and as luck would have it, Raj Kumar's thriving business also undergoes a big loss and he takes to drinking and everything that can go wrong goes wrong. Raj Kumar's sister is played by Kumud Chugani and falls for Biswajit who is a Doctor. Drinking ensures Raj Kumar dies and Padmini narrates the story to her son about her dad and ensures he does not follow his dad's foot-steps. Over all the songs were immensely hummable. Here are the songs for you.

- https://www.youtube.com/watch?v=OJBx7AQMoQ8;
- https://www.youtube.com/watch?v=iLnGBuB-PO4 ;
- https://www.youtube.com/watch?v=271aTR4BYvM ;
- https://www.youtube.com/watch?v=dgnWoKFZ3lk ;
- https://www.youtube.com/watch?v=hW_z7XwZPN4;

Cheers

Laksh KV

December 26, 1969

"ANJAANA"

Dear Friends:

It was today 54 years ago i.e. on the 26th of December 1969, this movie made by the banner called EMKAY Films and produced by Mohan Kumar called "ANJAANA" released in Mumbai. This movie just about did average business and was blessed with some great songs from the duo of Laxmikant Pyarelal. This was during my X'mas vacation and those days the ritual was to go and stay with my uncle in Thane and see one movie and get back home. On one side I was tempted to see "Shart" which had entered its 2nd week at Prabhat Cinema Thane but the movie with a bigger star value was released today in 1969 and I opted for that. While the higher class tickets were sold out, only the lower stall tickets were kept for current booking and then to top it only one ticket per head was given. My uncle had told me to go ahead and do the booking and that he would join me but I got only one ticket and in a while he came and I told him my plight. He very graciously told me to carry on and return home after the movie on Sunday evening of the movie's release. May His soul be in peace! The excitement of seeing a movie within the first 3 days and also having seen Satyakam before the year ended, made me feel proud to have seen 2 new movies on release – one up on the others of my class and building!!! Though, it was an ordinary movie, these nostalgic thoughts make me see the movie again and again when it comes on TV. Some good songs also make it watchable. Otherwise it was a very routine triangular plot with property issues, illegitimate kid etc. The main cast of the movie included:

- Rajendra Kumar
- Babita
- Pran
- Prem Chopra
- Nirupa Roy
- Sundar
- Nazima

- TunTun &
- Jr. Mehmood

The plot revolved around Rajendra Kumar a poor guy living with his mom falls for a rich Babita but not acceptable to Pran who is her guardian and he wants his son Prem Chopra to marry her. Pran then goes and insults our Hero's mom and now the Hero decides to avenge this, with his uncle played by Sundar, as they decide to trick Pran and succeed too as our Hero comes as a rich Prince & succeeds in turning things around only to be foiled towards the end. With a lot of fights and chase, the movie ends on a happy note with both Hero and the Villain who are actually half brothers. Overall everything is predicitble. Here are the songs for you.

- https://www.youtube.com/watch?v=P0JKTXHdv4A ;

Cheers

Laksh KV

December 24, 1971

"SEEMA"

Dear Friends:

It was today 52 years ago i.e. on December 24th 1971, this average movie called "SEEMA" released. The Bangladesh war had just ended and needless to say it had its share of impact due to black out and other issues the movie had limited success. Kabir Bedi was just establishing himself as the handsome hunk and was acting with a slightly senior looking Simmi as his heroine – it was quite similar to Simmi with Rishi Kapoor in Karz. But my recall of this movie, though I have not seen till today is my good friend Balakrishnan Narayan aka Bedi who told me in Tamil "Kabir Bedi Shattu Kadappan Da"... meaning "Kabir Bedi lies dead". The movie was released soon after the great music director Jaikishan died and the music by the duo of Shankar Jaikishan was really great and top of the chart was "JAB BHI YEH DIL UDAAS HOTA HI" sung by Mohd Rafi and also by Sharada. The star cast of the movie:

- Simmi Garewal
- Kabir Bedi
- Rakesh Roshan
- Bharati
- Padma Khanna
- Chand Usmani
- Abhi Bhattacharya &
- Sulochana

The plot revolved around a complex character played by Simmi who has this feeling that anyone who comes close to her dies and hence becomes a negative minded person with all efforts not to love any one or also fall in love – but in comes Kabir Bedi and despite all attempts to be away from him she gets drawn to him and they fall in love and quietly get married in a temple. Needless to say, Simmi gets pregnant quickly and Kabir Bedi meets with an accident and dies and then

Simmi delivers a boy who grows into Rakesh Roshan and is brought up by Simmi's maid and he grows into a very Happy Go Lucky man and finds his lady love in Bharati. Now, at this point I recall the radio ad "MA MAHAL MEIN AKELI, BETA JHOPDIYON MEIN MAST" followed by the song "DIL MERA KHO GAYA, PYAR AB HO GAYA". Eventually, this superstation of Simmi has to get killed and she embraces Rakesh Roshan and things end happily. Here are the songs for you.

- https://www.youtube.com/watch?v=NL83GRm5bjQ ;
- https://www.youtube.com/watch?v=_NCNE60b-v0 ;
- https://www.youtube.com/watch?v=jf4GBj77F3k ;
- https://www.youtube.com/watch?v=uApE4fOB5R8 ;
- https://www.youtube.com/watch?v=8tG3ImDXq7I ;

Cheers

Laksh KV

December 22, 1972

"SAMADHI"

Dear Friends:

51 years ago, i.e. on December 22, 1972, a Dacoit movie called "SAMADHI" was released which was produced under the banner of Sangam Arts International & directed by Prakash Mehra. The movie had Dharam Paji playing dual role – one as a Dacoit with a Heart of Gold and the other was his son another young handsome hunk. The movie did reasonably well at the Box Office since it ran for 15 weeks. This was the time when I was in Inter Commerce and the college took sympathy towards all the film-loving people and had all important and good lectures between 8.15 and 11 am and after that it was languages and we were always ready to see the first day 1130 show at any of the halls. This one, I saw at Neptune all alone and loved the movie and since I was also learning shorthand those days (ambition to be a good steno – a typical Madrasi trait) and kept writing "Fantastic" in shorthand... There were some touching scenes in the movie – especially during the song "JAB TAK RAHE TAN MEIN JIYA" Dharam Paji with his broad shoulders and massive Chest on full screen was a treat to watch. The other point was how well our Hero could play Jaya Bhaduri's boy-friend – he really pulled it off well despite the age difference of 13 years. The senior Dharam did justice to his role and the songs by RD Burman are still quite popular as we do hear people perform them on stage these days. The main cast of the movie is as under:

- Asha Parekh
- Dharmendra (dual role)
- Jaya Bhaduri
- Abhi Bhattacharya
- Madan Puri
- Ram Mohan
- CS Dubey
- Keshav Rana

- Master Satyajeet
- Dulari &
- Tun Tun

The plot is that of a Dacoit with a heart of gold. Dharam Paji plays a dacoit and during one of the loots, falls for Asha Parekh – while his partners take the money and jewellery, our Hero takes the Heroine with him. Normally, the loot is shared by the partners but not this one and the partners are unhappy, but our Heroine is a Sherni and she shoots the Hero with his bandook and our man is so impressed with her that he wants to escort her back to her village. On reaching they overhear the conversation where her people express happiness over her being missing and that the property would come to them etc and that is when our Heroine feels the Hero is genuinely in love and they get married in a temple. Dharam Paji gives up all the bad activities and starts living in a village with a new identity and does hard work and leads a happy singing life with his wife who eats imli and indicates that she is pregnant. But soon his dark past would come and trouble him some way – now they have a 3 year old son and the heroine is now troubled by cancer and needs a fair amount for her surgery. So the local money lender Randhir refuses and while returning home, Dharampaji sees Master Raju playing in the lawn and gets into the act of getting a ransom from the rich dad Abhi Bhattacharya by kidnapping the kid. The poor dad goes with the money to take charge of his son but in his excitement of getting money & also to see his wife in a hurry, Dharampaji loses his balance with Master Raju in his arms and the child falls off the cliff and dies. Poor dad tries to get hold of our Hero but fails and leaves and his shocked wife passes away. Dharam Paji burries the child and still worse things follow as he goes home to see his wife Asha Parekh dead – completely crestfallen, he goes back with his 3 year old son to the dacoit world and is welcomed by his partners. However, he does not want his son to follow his footsteps and does everything to protect him – a chance encounter in the same place where he buried the child some 5 years ago, he happens to see Abhi Bhattacharya still hoping for his kid visit the same place and now Paji gets the idea to position his own son as Abhi's and convinces him about it. He also surrenders and goes thru imprisonment for about 17 years. When he returns, there is his son who has now grown up as another Dharam and is in love with Jaya Bhaduri. Abhi Bhattacharya gives shelter to the senior Dharam in his house as he has been now reformed. But it is a matter of time when the younger one develops some kind of hatred towards the senior Dharam and feels he is too interfearing and so on. Finally it ends with some sacrifice and demise of senior Dharampaji, whose Samadhi is built to be respected by his next generation. Not very realistic, as it is so easy to see the resemblance between the Senior and Junior except for the characters in the movie. Here are the songs for you which have also made an impact with some remixed versions...

- https://www.youtube.com/watch?v=wJ1mqmbngO0 ;
- https://www.youtube.com/watch?v=F3pqRMJobto ;
- https://www.youtube.com/watch?v=vlgpI0OSTWc ;
- https://www.youtube.com/watch?v=1ISaz5Kgpl8 ;
- https://www.youtube.com/watch?v=FjqA-aD2P88 ;
- https://www.youtube.com/watch?v=wcg257F_AzY ;

Cheers

Laksh KV

December 21, 1973

"KAHANI KISMAT KI"

Dear Friends:

Its 50 years since this big hit movie called "KAHANI KISMAT KI" released in Mumbai on December 21, 1973 under the banner of Kapalaeshwar Films – maker being Arjun Hingoorani – the man who had a penchant for making movies with alpha "K" like "Kab Kyoon Kahan", "Katilon Ke Katil" & "Khel Khiladi Ka". Ever since "Kab Kyoon Kahan" became a big hit, we were waiting for the next one which took good 3+ years to come i.e. from July 1970 to December 1973. The big difference for me personally was being financially independent from June 1972 – thanx to my part-time job at Pentagon which became a full time job from November 1973. This movie was in my agenda but could not see it on the first day as I had an important wedding to attend and then decided to see it on Sunday 3 PM show at Sahakar. I booked one extra ticket for my good friend M Ganesh who now lives in the US of A. He lived in Ghatkopar near Odeon Cinema and I had to communicate to him about this ticket I picked up for him. I knew his dad's office number and so I dialled on Thursday – number 296400 – the Operator said "Hindustan Lever – Good Morning", I said extension 250 please & the call got connected to the extension and I heard the voice that said "Mahadevan Here" – then I said "Mama, Namaskaram, I am Laxminarayan, classmate and friend of Ganesh, I have booked a ticket for him for Sunday 3 PM show for the movie Kahani Kismat Ki at Sahakar Cinema, please tell Ganesh to come as I will be waiting for him" & he said "Wait a minute" & the organized man that he was he started making notes "Sunday Dec, 23rd a? 3 PM Show va? Kahani Kismat Ki ya?" I said "Aamam Mama" – He said he would inform Ganesh accordingly. So, as planned I was at the Cinema Hall around 230 PM and Ganesh landed soon and we were in good time to see the movie right from the "No Smoking" slide. We both were quite amused at what we saw – the ultimate was Dharam Paji jumping across buildings from one roof top to the other – at times from lower to higher ...hahaha! For money Dharam Paji fights a round of KHUSHTI with a professional wrestler and of course the role of the Producer

Director who irritates Ajit no end with his standard lines "KYA SAMJHE? NAHI SAMJHE?" is quite funny... Another interesting line was Ajit asking Dharam Paji "Tumhara Naam Kya Hai?" & gets the response "AJEET" – sounds Ajeet to Ajeet!!! The scene where Police give a chance to check a film that is supposed to prove the innocence of Dharam Paji but end up seeing an ad of Coca-Cola – but then there is always a faithful DOG that very cleverly hides the film from the villains and provides it at the nick of time to have our hero freed and above all none of us can forget the hilarious song "ARRE RAFTA RAFTA DEKHO AANKH MERI". Well, can't forget as 6 years later in Sept 1979, during the sing song session of our marriage, this was one of the songs I sang with a modification as "AANKH JISSAY LADHI HAI WOH PAAS MERE BAITHI HI" instead of "KHADI" hi!!! The cast of the movie is as under:

- Dharmendra
- Rekha
- Ajit
- Abhi Bhattacharya
- Rajni Sharma
- Arjun Hingurani
- Sulochna
- Ashoo
- Jayashree T
- Bharat Bhushan
- Shetty
- Leena Das &
- Rajendranath

The plot revolves around Father and Son (Abhi Bhattacharya & Dharmendra respectively) both are into organized robbery and at one point post the dad's demise, Dharam gets jailed and comes out 2 years later and wants to lead a reformed good life. But not that easy however, he meets a nice businessman (Ajit) who has a dark past and gets constantly blackmailed for this by none other than the maker of the movie Arjun Hingurani. In fact Ajit has acquired all his wealth thru Rekha who plays his daughter. It is now expected that Dharam Paji and Rekha would fall in love and some surprise scene as though Ajit is unhappy takes over and finally the drama is over when Ajit says that he was doing mazaaq. Ajit employs Dharam paji in his company and at an appropriate time frames him for the murder of Arjun Hingurani. Then the balance of the movie is the struggle for Dharam Paji to prove that he was innocent all along. Some interesting songs composed by Kalyanji Anandji really did a world of good to the movie in making it a money spinner. Here are the songs for you.

- https://www.youtube.com/watch?v=qs01Ox2rkyE ;
- https://www.youtube.com/watch?v=1XNQAhLaBdo ;
- https://www.youtube.com/watch?v=-meMABQenN0 ;
- https://www.youtube.com/watch?v=ISuAWTegxRw ;
- https://www.youtube.com/watch?v=SrB2r2KeC9A ;

Cheers

Laksh KV

December 20, 1968

"HUMSAYA"

Dear Friends:

It was 55 years ago on this day i.e. on Dec 20th 1968, a very well publicized and hyped movie released which was the debut of Joy Mukherji Productions – yes, I am talking about the movie "HUMSAYA" which Joy Mukherji himself produced & directed. Joy had a good start with some great hit movies aided by lovely songs but slowly he started declining in the later part of 60s and to salvage his image, he made this movie with the war backdrop of India & China - I guess must have been 1962 war that he tried to depict. Well, I am yet to see the movie though on TV have seen in bits and pieces but the movie was a huge disaster and moved Joy from "A" grade Hero to lower "A" and higher "B" grade Hero – after this he had movies like "Dil Aur Mohabbat", "Inspector", "Kahin Aar Kahin Paar" and "Mujrim" - the last 3 were clearly "B" grade movies. Now coming back to "Humsaya", I recall the jingle on the radio

"BAAR BAAR DEKHIYE,
HAZAAR BAAR DEKHIYE,
DEKHNE KI CHEEZ HAI,
LAAKH BAAR DEKHIYE,
JOY MUKHERJI KA HUMSAYA, DEKHIYE.
MALA, SHARMEELA AUR JOY KO
EK SAATH DEKHIYE
JOY MUKHERJI KA HUMSAYA, DEKHIYE"

I just wish FB had an easy method of recording audio files and uploading along with my write up the way I can do in Watsapp... but be that as it may... I think the message was loud and clear to Joy that his days as a Hero were almost over – despite that he commenced the movie "Love in Bombay" in the early 70s with big stars including himself which took 40 years to release, well after our Hero was dead and gone. However, when realization dawned on him, he became producer and salvaged a bit as "CHAILA BABU" *ing Kaka did decent business. But the movie in question despite being a failure, had hit music by maestro OP Nayyar with Asha Bhonsle dominating with lilting numbers like "OH KANHAYYA", "WOH HASEEN DARD DE DO", "AAJA MERE PYAR KE SAHARAY" & "KITNA HASEEN HAI YEH JAHAN" – a lovely duet with Mohd Rafi "MUJHE MERA PYAR DE DO" & of course not to forget the hit Rafi solo 'DIL KI AWAZ BHI SUN" – absolute bliss these songs have been. Here is the star cast for you.

- Joy Mukherjee (dual role – as Indian and Chinese)
- Mala Sinha (Joy's Chinese Partner)
- Sharmila Tagore (Joy's Indian Partner)
- Madan Puri
- Rehaman
- Sapru
- Gajanan Jagirdar &
- Polson

The plot revolves around Joy Mukherji who is stripped off his rank/position for a murder. It was all the doing of Madan Puri who frames him and then he takes him to Indo-China border with a strategy in mind. Joy overhears the conversation between Madan Puri and the look alike Chinese officer Joy Mukherjee. The plan was to impersonate the original and be the spy in India and pass on the information. However, our Hero kills the Chinese Joy and continues to impersonate and gets into a lot of complications as both had their girls in Mala Sinha (Chinese) & Sharmila Tagore (Indian). After a lot of trouble the task gets completed and Mala Sinha goes back to China while Sharmila and Joy get back to each others arms. Well, I am sure it must have been tough for people to sit thru this saga but for the good music. Here are the songs for you.

- https://www.youtube.com/watch?v=1OrdsBNMKK4 ;
- https://www.youtube.com/watch?v=1OrdsBNMKK4 ;
- https://www.youtube.com/watch?v=28ikCFBKffM ;
- https://www.youtube.com/watch?v=4lz-4LEgRZ0 ;
- https://www.youtube.com/watch?v=_rGWnBVNcDU ;
- https://www.youtube.com/watch?v=j_Nq-Hq0sNo ;

Cheers

Laksh KV

December 19, 1969

"SATYAKAM & SHART"

Dear Friends:

54 years ago 2 movies released and both belonged to completely different categories – while one had a strong message and deep-rooted philosophy, the other was a suspense thriller – I am talking about Hrishikesh Mukherjee's "SATYAKAM" & Rajkumar Kohli's "SHART". While "Shart" failed big time at the Box Office, "Satyakam" did 15 weeks run. Let me take it up one by one.

SATYAKAM – I recall seeing this movie on 31st Dec 1969 at Rivoli Cinema – 11 am show along with my brother KV Radhakrishnan. As big Dharam Paji fans, we wanted to see and it was some kind of a ritual we used to follow in the 70s to see a movie on the last day of the year. Both ways we walked crossing thru the "Z" Bridge that took us from East to West Matunga and stood in the "Q" for Re. 1/- ticket – the cheapest – it was a heavy movie for both of us but we loved it though it was far away from the "He-man" image of Dharam who used to bash people up – but here he fought the system, and dies of cancer and never takes bribe and does not grow in the organization. In no way the movie was entertaining but Manmohan had a repeat of Aradhana act where he once again raped Sharmila Tagore here but there was no Master Chikku to kill him. Both of us maintained that it was a great movie and also was acclaimed by critics and later we read that this was the maker Hrishida's most favourite movie like Raj Kapoor had "MNJ". During our walk back in the sun, we stopped over at Mishraji's sugar cane juice shop opposite to Shankaramatham and that was heavenly experience as we gulped down multiple glasses of cane sugar juice. The movie had the following main actors:

- Ashok Kumar
- Dharmendra
- Sharmila Tagore
- Sanjeev Kumar
- David
- Tarun Bose

- Manmohan
- Baby Sarika &
- Asrani

The plot revolved around Dharam Paji an honest person with strong ideals and views in life. Armed with an Engineering degree, he gets into a job where he finds that people do not share his view point and becomes very difficult with everyone around as his "Honesty" comes in the way always. Due to guilt pangs, he marries Sharmila Tagore who is a victim of rape (Manmohan the doer) & gives his surname to the child but has no relationship with his wife. He continues to change jobs and everywhere he meets with the same fate while his contemporary played by Sanjeev Kumar, moves up the value chain as he is street-smart. Dharam Paji is attacked by the dreaded disease cancer and gets hospitalized and is on his death bed. That is when one of the contractors who had done a shoddy job, wants him to approve some project and promises him that he will give enough money to take care of his wife and kid. Very reluctantly, he signs the documents and hands over to Sharmila who tears it and throws it away – that brings a broad smile on our Hero's face. Dharam Paji's Guruji is played by Ashok Kumar who was very upset with his disciple as he did not take his approval before getting married to Sharmila Tagore who had a dark past. When Dharam Paji dies, the last rites are to be performed and Ashok Kumar, does not agree to Sarika (playing Sharmila's son) doing the last rites citing the age factor. But the child retorts saying that since he was not Dharam Paji's son, he is not eligible to do and this truth shocks Ashok Kumar and he accepts both the kid and Sharmila and they walk away to the Ashram. Very poignant and touching bit!!! Not too many songs in the movie but were pretty decent composed by LP. Here are the links for you:

- https://www.youtube.com/watch?v=SotyhvcQbDA ;
- https://www.youtube.com/watch?v=QJIClg9dzIk ;
- https://www.youtube.com/watch?v=tGDNB8xuaEg ;

SHART:

This movie had the "Pull" factor of Mumtaz in swimming pool and I very much wanted to see the movie – now could not openly put it across and those days during vacation, it was very common for me to go and stay with my late uncle at Thane. See a movie or two and return home (KRA achieved!!!) – so here I was at Thane with my uncle and while "Shart" was being screened at "Prabhat" Cinema in Thane, "Anjana" released on Dec 26th 1969 was screened at "Ashok" Cinema – so I was given a choice and I opted for the newer movie "Anjana" – but my uncle used to pull my legs by saying "SHIRT" is to be worn not seen in a movie hall... He had an uncanny sense of humor and his daughters Anjali, Akhila and Anu will agree with me. So missed Shart then but saw it much later at Rupam in a matinee show when it was running at reduced rates. I and my good friend Bedi went to see the movie and as we were walking towards the hall, we heard someone call us from behind and we turned back and it was our friend from Jaggar Niwas – CS Ganesh who too was heading to see the same movie. We were at Rupam in good time and afforded "Samosas" during the interval and during the break I told them that I suspect "Ramesh Deo" to be the culprit as he was shown as a very good man and yes, I was right. The movie was rank stupid and quite boring and we had a good laugh at the way it was made. Songs were pretty OK again by LP duo. The main star cast of the movie is as under:

- Sanjay (Khan)
- Mumtaz
- Ramesh Deo
- KN Singh
- Kumud Chugani
- Shammi
- TunTun &
- Rajendranath

The plot was pretty confusing where our Hero Sanjay Khan would bet (Shart) on anything and everything. Then there is a female Kumud Chugani, who is shown dying several times and comes back every now and then – to create some suspense. There are murders and as expected the suspect is our Hero and he takes it upon himself to clear his position and get the wrong doers to the police. Mumtaz plays his lady love but the intriguing role was that of Kumud Chugani. Nothing much to talk about but the songs were decent and here are the links for you:

- https://www.youtube.com/watch?v=3Q5iIZMTaBg ;
- https://www.youtube.com/watch?v=7kI6gXixXtQ&t=1s;

Cheers
Laksh KV

December 17, 1971

"ALBELA"

Dear Friends:

The movie that released 52 years ago on Dec 17, 1971 besides KHOJ, is "ALBELA" that had a truckfull of comedians and no one person as a Hero... I recall, my classmate Churi (K Suryanarayan – not in FB) used to talk of this movie while we were still in school that "Albela" is in the making and has almost all the comedians of the Hindi film Industry. But sadly the movie did not do well and I could not see it on release and saw much later some time in 1999 on TV when we had moved to Bangalore and the screen name of Mehmood sounded funny to all of us "Maheshchandra Nangdu"... not "Phunsukh Vangdu". Here is the cast of the movie:

- Mehmood
- Aruna Irani
- IS Johar
- Rajendranath
- Achla Sachdev
- Leela Mishra
- Lolita Kumari
- Anwar Ali
- Gajanan Jagirdar
- Ramesh Deo
- Dhumal
- Mukri
- Asit Sen
- Moolchand
- Mohan Choti &
- Johny Whisky

Very limited recall of the plot for me though seen in 1999 at home but the focus was not so much as it is when one goes to the hall. All I recall is that Mehmood is a stage artist and while performing gets the news of his dad's illness but leaves the stage after that and meets his dad before he kicks the bucket. He promises to his dad that his sister will be married to a well to do person who would be from a rich family. So the search is on and his friends identify a bachelor Prince and to ensure nothing goes wrong, being from the stage gets the attire of a King and calls himself a King from some unknown place as "Maheshchandra Nangdu"... Then, one after the other a lot of funny situations arise – however, all that could not salvage this movie and the music by Shankar Jaikishan (SJ) was very average and did not help the cause of the movie. Here are the songs for you.

- https://www.youtube.com/watch?v=ZGoS0s9ZDws ;
- https://www.youtube.com/watch?v=g0Vl4Qyw7d8 ;

Cheers

Laksh KV

December 18th 1970

"MERA NAAM JOKER"

Folks:

It was exactly 12 years ago on Dec 18th 2011, I started this column called "This Day That Year" when I was in Chennai to celebrate my friend Meena Sinha's daughter's Birthday and felt this will be a good exercise in sharing things. . So, what you see below is what I wrote 12 years ago and I feel I need to embellish it a little more and that I have added at the end. So this is a very significant moment for me and hence doing it a bit differently.

Cheers

I thought I will start the "Theme of This Day That Year" with a Miserable Flop Movie

53 years ago on this day i.e. Dec 18 1970, Raj Kapoor Saab released his "Closest" to the heart movie "Mera Naam Joker". Those days the advance booking counter used to open on Mondays for a Friday release the- tickets were issued on a Monday for Friday, Saturday and Sunday. Then on Tuesday, they would add Monday and so on. Hence on 15th Dec 1970 it was mad rush for booking tickets. Maximum demand would be for Sunday evening show and then Saturday night show then the first show on Friday.

MNJ was a long movie with 2 breaks showing 3 phases of a Joker's life - Childhood to old age. After the initial euphoria the movie slumped. People found it tough to sit thru a long movie. Raj saab's contemporaries Dev Anand & Dilip Kumar had their movies released around the same time - November 20 1970 saw the release of "Johny Mera Naam" that was a big money spinner & one week later on November 27 1970 was the release of "GOPI" *ing the Husband wife couple of Dilip Kumar & Saira Banu which too did reasonable business. But RK Films could not keep up its standard & MNJ resulted as a Huge Flop making things very difficult for the showman.

However, in 1973 RK films made up with BOBBY everything that it lost by way of Mera Naam Joker.

Silver lining, the length of the movie MNJ was good for school going kids like me then to stay away from school and go home after the movie.

Wait for the next during the week
Cheers
Lax

So, my friends – today it is 53 years of the release of the movie. With Prelims in progress, there was only chance of seeing the movie during X'mas vacation and luckily for me I had approval of my parents to see the movie and in my Maasi – Kamla Narayan, I found a good company to see the movie at Rupam where it had started its 2nd week. Given the length of the movie the show started at 10 am and what was sad to me was virtually empty cinema hall – probably only 20% occupancy – very sad state – my Amma had a friend who worked as a Nurse in Sion Hospital and dropped in home and asked my Amma with all concern in Tamil "Is it true that Raj Kapoor is going to start begging? I want to give my Rs. 2/- to him" That was the discussion those days and I was eagerly waiting for some of those scenes that were talked about like the following:

- Simmi Garewal's fall in the pond followed by her undressing
- Raj Kapoor kissing the Russian actress Kseniya Ryabinkina
- Padmini's exposure – "Upthrust in water" – this term we studied in Physics and could relate to in MNJ...

The showman assumed that the movie will be a big hit and tells the audience "JAYIYEGA NAHI –YEH EK MADHYANTAR HI" & the movie ends saying "POSITIVELY NOT THE END" – but that was an unfulfilled desire of the maker to make a sequel. The movie was star-studded with some great songs by Shankar Jaikishan (SJ) duo. At least a couple of songs were deleted to manage the length of the movie and one of them was the "Heer" song by Mohd Rafi (a bit rare for RK – but suited as RK did resemble SK in this song) and even the Quwali "Daag Na Lag Jaaye" was removed after the initial screenings. In the recent past I have been in touch with some SJ fans headed by Sand Deep, who along with his team has put together all the songs of SJ in a hard copy form and in a big ceremony on November 4th 2018 handed over 5 volumes of 1,400 plus songs to Director of National Film Archive of India (NFAI) – Mr. Prakash Magdum located in Pune. Songs were exceptional in this movie and here are the links for you:

- https://www.youtube.com/watch?v=kT9eExGqm6Q ;

Cheers
Laksh KV

December 17, 1971

"KHOJ"

Dear Friends:

It was exactly 52 years ago today, the low budget offering from Jugal Kishore called "KHOJ" released. This movie was not in my agenda to see for (a) it was not released in Rupam & (b) Budget constraints played a big role those days. However, I have very few recalls about this movie coming from Jugal Productions. It had music by Usha Khanna and these were times, when the great Mohd Rafiji was going thru a very lean patch and KK was dominating. People in general were busy creating rumours about the fight between these 2 singers and who is better and so on and so forth. This movie had the song 'HALKA HALKA SA, RANG GULABI SA" where the 2 great singers joined hands and sang to put to rest all the misunderstandings – well, but people were not too convinced and still tried to find fault and argued on who did better – this drew the conversation to the solo from "Pyar Ka Mausam" – "Tum Bin Jaaoon Kahan" and the hit song of Andaz "Zindagi Ek Safar Hi Suhana"... these fights were never ending. All, I can say about "Khoj" was it bombed at the Box Office. The star-cast of the movie is as under:

- Shatrughan Sinha
- Farida Jalal
- Jayashri T
- KN Singh
- Deepak Kumar or Dheeraj Kumar (someone help me solve this)
- Jr. Mehmood

No website gives any idea about the plot and would request anyone who has seen the movie to share the same. The songs of the movie are as under:

- https://www.youtube.com/watch?v=IWAXj8m3tOA ;
- https://www.youtube.com/watch?v=jJf_qAJMPEk ;
- https://www.youtube.com/watch?v=N4HKPiByJBw ;
- https://www.youtube.com/watch?v=5BQqpRoGGvg ;

Cheers
Laksh KV

December 15, 1972

"TANHAAI"

Dear Friends:

It was today i.e. on the 15th of December 1972 – 51 years ago this flop movie called "TANHAAI" released. Those were the days Anil Dhawan & Rehana Sultana made an impact mainly after "Chetna" – to complete the triangle there was also a Shatrughna Sinha in the movie. But he was not eyeing for Rehana in this movie. I had seen it in the very first week with lots of expectations but the movie did not meet my expectations – yes there was a rape scene though but nothing much to talk of. I recall that the Heroine is shown as working in a shop next to Bandra Talkies and when I used to go to college, I used to feel happy seeing that shop – name unable to recall but sounded like "Ansons" – The movie had decent music by Usha Khanna and top of my mind is "BHEEGI HUI AANCHAL" by KISHORE KUMAR – all said and done, the movie did show the exploitation of working women and so on. I have very limited recall of the movie and here are the actors who played key roles in the movie:

- Anil Dhawan
- Rehana Sultan
- Shatrughan Sinha
- Laxmi Chaya
- Iftikar
- Lolita Kumari
- Jagdish Raj &
- Jankidas

I am unable to locate the plot on any of the websites and hence would request those who have seen it to share the same. However, here are the songs for you.

- https://www.youtube.com/watch?v=UQX20_OAREI ;
- https://www.youtube.com/watch?v=E1I9s4ujfjw ;
- https://www.youtube.com/watch?v=1E92znPhVXc ;
- https://www.youtube.com/watch?v=rj1OIZLTQzY ;

Cheers
Laksh KV

December 13, 1968

"AABROO"

Dear Friends:

It was today 55 years ago on December 13, 1968, this movie from Rawal Bros called "AABROO" released. It was a Box Office disaster – this banner had earlier made, probably their launch movie "DIL NE PHIR YAAD KIYA" which did well at the BO. It had higher star cast than "Aabroo" as this movie introduced a new hero called "Deepak Kumar". I was in class IX and all we used to do is to discuss the radio ad on Vividh Bharti next day at school – the dialogue on radio was "AGAR MANISH MERA BHAI HAI, TOH CHANDAR MERA DOST HAI" – probably delivered by Ashok Kumar. The other was the jingle of the ad towards the end "AA GAYEE AABROO MERE YAAR, CHALO DEKHENGAY DEEPAK KUMAR". Finally, in the Times of India on the day of release a personal message from the debutant Deepak Kumar was published which was more of an appeal to all the readers from him saying that every one makes a beginning and that he too wanted the blessings and best wishes from all the "Janata Janardan". The music director duo of Sonik Omi had made their debut with this banner's earlier movie and had some great songs in that as well as in this movie in question. On top of my mind are "AAP SAY PYAAR HUA, AAP KHAFAA HO BAITHAY", "HAR CHEHARA YAHAN CHAAND" & the Mukesh number 'JINHE HUM BHOOLNA CHAHAY WOH AKSAR YAAD AATEN HAIN". Well, all said and done, I am yet to see this movie and just do not have the bandwidth to see it on YouTube. The starcast of the movie is as under:

- Ashok Kumar
- Deepak Kumar (Debut)
- Vimmi
- Rehaman
- Jeevan
- Shashikala

- Nirupa Roy
- Lalita Pawar
- Sundar &
- Mukri

I gathered that Ashok Kumar is an advocate & his wife Nirupa Roy & his younger brother Deepak Kumar, who has obtained his medical degree from abroad live together. Deepak meets Vimmi during holidays in Kashmir & needless to say falls for her. Rehaman, a friend of Ashok Kumar lives with his wife Leela Naidu who also happens to be Vimmi's elder sister. Deepak gets a job in a hospital and waits for a job in Mumbai but all of a sudden the childless Leela Naidu dies after being at the receiving end of her MIL played by Shashikala and much against his wishes Rehaman marries Vimmi who too is unhappy. To make things more difficult, Lalita Pawar's relatives Jeevan and Shashikala too land up to live with them and ensure that Leela Naidu was troubled a lot and then it continues for Vimmi too. Rehaman has no interest in Vimmi. When Deepak Kumar finally gets a job in Mumbai, till he settles is advised by Ashok Kumar to stay with Rehaman, who is his friend. Here, Deepak gets the shock of his life when he sees his girl as Rehaman's wife. Then Jeevan ensures that he exploits the past of the two and spreads the news about an affair etc. Rehaman gets to know of the affair and gets upset and the Hero is supposed to be treating him as a Doctor. Unfortunately for our Hero, Rehaman dies and the blame is on him and then follows a court scene where Ashok Kumar is at his wits end as if Deepak is his brother, Rehaman is his friend & eventually all the games by Jeevan & co comes out and all is well in the end. Here are the songs for you.

- https://www.youtube.com/watch?v=OO4HEoV_5EI... ;

Cheers
Laksh KV

December 10, 1971

"UPAHAAR"

Dear Friends:

It was today 52 years ago (Dec 10 1971), yet another family entertainer from the banner of Rajashri Productions hit the screen – this movie was called "UPHAAR". The story of the movie was written by the great Rabindernath Tagore. This movie had some element of contradiction about being the debut movie of Jaya Bhaduri while "GUDDI" was released on Sept 17th 1971 ahead of this and lot of us thought Guddi was her first movie. But later, I gathered that GUDDI won the race of getting released earlier though this was the movie which was supposed to introduce her. Another story going around those days (more from our Gujju friends like Chikkoodi & Gotu) that the hero of the movie Swroop Dutt was another Guru Dutt in the making but we never heard about him later though he acted exceptionally well in this movie. Another highlight of the movie was the music by LP duo that had some real lilting numbers and during the rough days of Mohd Rafi, here he got to sing a good one "MAIN EK RAJA HOON, TU EK RAANI HI"... There was another beautiful Mukesh number "MAAJI MAIYYA" was well received by people while the other 2 songs of the movie were by Lataji "HAATHON MEIN MEHANDI" & "SOONI RE NAGARIYA"– again Bongla Desh war impacted the movie to some extent but being a fairly low budget movie, it made good money in terms of bottom line. My recall is only what I have written above as I did not get a chance to see it on release and much later I did see on DD on a Sunday in bits and pieces. Here is the cast of the movie:

- Jaya Bhaduri
- Swaroop Dutt
- Suresh Chatwal
- Nandita Thakur
- Nana Palshikar
- Leela Mishra

- Kamini Kaushal &
- Younis Parvez

The plot revolves around Jaya Bhaduri, who despite growing up does not leave her childish attitude. Swaroop Dutt, who is a law student in Calcutta, and is slated to get married to a girl selected by his mom but he insists on meeting the girl. He goes to meet the bride to be, but gets hooked by the childish Jaya Bhaduri instead and returns home saying that he would only get married to JB. Things are accepted and the marriage takes place and once JB moves to our Hero's home, she continues her playful attitude and has no capabilities that are expected of a Bahu of a movie. She does not know what marriage entails and when the time comes for Swaroop Dutt to get back to Calcutta, JB refuses to join him and also refuses to stay with his mother. So she is promptly dropped back at her maika with her mom. Now, here is where her transformation takes place as she starts missing Swaroop and learns things that a wife needs to do and soon enough realizes her love for her hubby and tells her mom that she wants to go to her "Piya Ka Ghar" and does well all the household activities and gets accepted by her mother-in-law very well. But Swaroop Dutt does not come during vacations too as he sees no value addition and eventually the MIL realises the requirement and plans a visit to Calcutta where hear daughter Nandita Thakur & her SIL Suresh Chatwal reside. The visit does the trick and the young couple unite and everything is Happy Happy after this. Nice and simple story line. This did appeal to the crowd at large. Here are the songs for you from the movie:

- https://www.youtube.com/watch?v=CfdOgQScT9Y ;
- https://www.youtube.com/watch?v=zxRvPREpXkE ;
- https://www.youtube.com/watch?v=pI09ucDL0yc ;
- https://www.youtube.com/watch?v=XJs_WEH_QXg ;

Cheers

Laksh KV

December 11, 1970

"NAYA RAASTA"

Dear Friends:

53 years ago today was the day i.e. on 11th Dec 1970, this movie "NAYA RAASTA" made by Nadiadwala under the banner of Pushpa Films hit the screens in Mumbai. It did not create any magic at the box office as it was dragged for 10 weeks those days and that does not make it a success story. For me as a class XI student, with Prelims round the corner, there was no hope of seeing it for in one week's time besides the exams, Mera Naam Joker was to release and there was money only for one movie.... so you know what would be my choice!!! However, it did not dampen my spirits to go and check at Rupam Cinema as to what was going on and I found that on Friday 6 PM tickets were available in current booking – so I said "Flop Hi Bhai!!!" - While, those were the days when the music directors like SJ, LP & KA were dominating and here was a movie that had music by N Dutta and a couple of songs stood out and on top of my mind is the song by Mohd Rafi saab 'POCHKAR ASHQ APNI AANKHON KA" – reminds me of my bench mate "M Ganesh" who was very fond of this song and now lives in the USA & the second one again by the legend "MAINAY PEE SHARAAB, TU NE KYA PIYA" filmed on Balraj Sahani. Not to forget the song by Asha Bhonsleji "JAAN GAYI MAIN TON JAAN GAYI" & the duet "CHUNAR MORI KORI". Well, this is all I recall about the movie that had the following main star cast:

- Asha Parekh
- Jeetendra
- Balraj Sahani
- Farida Jalal
- Sujit Kumar &
- Lalita Pawar

Not having seen the movie, I had to only resort to what I could gather from the various sources & what I got looks far from complete as I do not see anything about Balraj Sahani's role.

Jeetendra plays a criminal lawyer & decides to settle down in a village to look after his property that he inherits after his father's demise. He practices the progressive ideas and educates the workers and he gets accepted as one of them. During this exercise, he falls in love with a village girl played by Asha Parekh. The villagers and also Asha Parekh's mom do their bit to convince Jeetendra not to marry her. Needless to say Jeetendra is upset but he is determined to win his love rather than sulk. On the other hand, Asha Parekh, is married to Sujit Kumar into another family and is in trouble as she is not accepted by her in-laws. In the meantime, Jeetendra's younger sister essayed by Farida Jalal gets married in the same village and her husband, Kishan Mehta is a drunkard. But Farida decides to correct her husband and also tries to settle Asha Parkeh's position in her house, with Sujit Kumar, Asha Parekh's hubby is convinced of his wife's virtues but not the mother-in-law. Consequently, Sujit decides to live with his wife and Thakur who has evil designs on Asha Parekh gives them shelter in his house. Asha Parekh kills the wrong doers with the same spear which had taken her husband's life and she was charged in the court for both the murders. Rest of the story is whether she is proved innocent or not.

Here are the songs for you.

- https://www.youtube.com/watch?v=zgMnYoWYHXU ;
- https://www.youtube.com/watch?v=6-WXvdpM5lU ;
- https://www.youtube.com/watch?v=T0YbIXpQCzo ;
- https://www.youtube.com/watch?v=-NUXRi3lwAs ;
- https://www.youtube.com/watch?v=78SlWJFi7F4 ;

Cheers
Laksh KV

December 15, 1972

"DO GAZ ZAMEEN KE NEECHAY"

Dear Friends:

It was today 51 years ago, this horror movie from the "Ramsay" clan called "DO GAZ ZAMEEN KE NEECHAY" released – Ramsay brothers were famous for their brand of horror movies that they presented from time to time in the 70s and 80s – as one of the famous Marathi stand up speaker called "Shirish Kanekar" in his item called "Fillumbhaji" spoke about Ramsay Bros and was very keen to meet the family – in fact he further adds saying that there are so many in the family that it would fill up a class room – FU Ramsay, Gangu Ramsay, Shyam Ramsay, Tulsi Ramsay and so on.... By the way the same guy also had another item on cricket called "Phatkebhaji" which was very interesting too. But now coming to this horror movie, though I saw it in the 2nd week at Basant Cinema behind RK Studios – Chembur, I have almost no recall of the movie. The banners and posters were very inviting and promised to have a lot of sleaze and steamy scenes and but none from my gang wanted to see the movie. We had a driver in our building called Babu, who joined me to see the movie. While, I was disappointed with the steamy scenes, it did have some scenes where the audience really got scared and the driver sitting next to me though much elder to my 17 yr frame, was shivering when the dead man comes back to punish the wrong doers. Nothing more except Imtiaz Khan (Amjad Khan's elder brother and Jayan's elder son) played a key role in the movie – rest of the cast was unknown to me. Here are the names of the cast as shown picked up from various sources:

- Surender Kumar
- Pooja
- Imtiaz Khan
- Satyendra Kappu
- Helan &
- Dhumal

I have limited memory and hence giving details from what I have gathered from multiple sources:

A rich scientist rescues a woman and marries her. She exploits her hubby to fulfil her uncle's demands for money all the time. Though unhappy, he helps. It dawns on him that his marriage is a complete disaster as his wife and her uncle are around only to milk him. On another occasion, the Scientist rescues another lady and brings her home in a state of unconsciousness. With a lot of care and with the help of domestic help this new lady gets back to normalcy. However, the 2 ladies cannot get along and the senior one insults the new one and also the scientist.

This results in the Scientist becoming a workaholic and is in his lab that he has made as home. He accidently consumes milk that had a few drops of chemicals and his health suffers. While his wife is not bothered the other lady is, and now the scientist is handicapped as he can't walk. However, the sympathetic lady nurses him and prays for the scientist's help. While admitting the scientist to the hospital, he is killed by his wife and only claims that she would locate a Doctor who can handle this case. In the meantime the wife meets her old flame and with the aid of the grave digger burries the Scientist. But the money minded people realise that the body is buried with the key without which they cannot get the money. Then starts the Ramsay's Special part – the scientist returns as a zombie to avenge and finishes them off

Here are the songs for you:
- https://www.youtube.com/watch?v=x9eBnZDctrI ;
- https://www.youtube.com/watch?v=KpLDlwPcnvY ;
- https://www.youtube.com/watch?v=JmRrvGIwAAA ;

Cheers
Laksh KV

December 7, 1973

"HEERA"

Dear Friends:

It was today 50 years ago i.e. on the 7th of December 1973, a dacoit saga made by Sultan Ahamad called "HEERA" released and did well at the Box Office. Sunil Dutt had his career revived in the early 70s and Heera helped him quite a bit. I have some very odd memories of this movie – I had started working full time in a company called Pentagon and attended college in the mornings. So my standard practice was to see Friday 6 Pm or 9 PM shows but invariably around 2.30 – 3 PM, I used to walk back home for snacks as my office was not more than 10 mins walk from our home those days. The best part was I had to pass thru Rupam Cinema and gauge what is happening. This was a disaster for those who had tickets for 3 PM show on the first day – "FDFS" was the acronym for "First Day First Show" – though Matinee was the 1st show at 11 am and normally first show was the one that would start after lunch between 1.30 to 3 PM. So, as I was walking home for my food, I saw heavy duty police around Rupam and all the glass panes were broken – the reason being the show was cancelled due to non-arrival of the "Print" and there was a long "Q" to get refund but they could not be accommodated for another show before Sunday as it was already booked in advance. People got violent and pelted stones – the worst hit were people who bought tickets in black as they received only Rs.2/- back from the counter. Our good friend "Kumar Harihar" was one of the sufferers due to this and we soon started calling or referring him as "Heera". However, the 6 PM show was on and people who had booked were lucky but I really do not know what the 1st show guys did – I am sure they would have seen it later. Well, I was not too inclined to see the movie and I gave it a pass and ended up seeing on TV on February 7th 1999 on TV – all alone sitting in front of my new 29" SONY TV in Bangalore – family was yet to move from Bombay. Now, how do I recall Feb 7 1999, well, that was the day India defeated Pakistan at Ferozsha Kotla Delhi and Kumble took 10/74 in that match. After the match, I had a quick walk of 100 mins feeling thrilled at our win and then plonked myself in front of the TV with nothing much to do and remembering my college days but by that time, my daughter had started going to college!!! Well, the movie did well and had some powerful lines for both the lead actors Sunil Dutt and Shatrughan Sinha. The star cast is as under:

- Asha Parekh
- Sunil Dutt
- Shatrughan Sinha
- Farida Jalal
- Helan
- Kanhayalal
- Anwar Hussain
- Nasir Hussain
- Sulochana
- Tabassum
- Tun Tun &
- Mukri

The plot revolved around Sunil Dutt playing the title role of Heera who lives happily with his parents – Nasir Hussain & Sulochana in a small town in a rual area. He falls in love with Asha Parekh who is the daughter of the money-lender in that area and they both decide to get married but fate does not allow as murder takes place and Sunil Dutt is arrested and found guilty as all the possible evidences are against him. He is jailed for the murder he never committed and just waits for the opportunity to escape from the jail and nab the areal culprit and prove himself innocent. So, he escapes from the jail and becomes a bandit and manages to avenge by finding out that it was all the doing of Shatrughan Sinha. Eventually all ends well – songs were average in the movie and here are the songs for you.

- https://www.youtube.com/watch?v=3WRfODavzOY ;

Cheers
Laksh KV

December 6, 1968

"EK KALI MUSKAYEE"

Dear Friends:

It was today 55 years ago i.e. on December 6th 1968 a flop movie made by Vasant Joglekar called "EK KALI MUSKAYEE" released and needless to say it was a big disaster at the Box Office. The director Mr. Vasant Joglekar, introduced his daughter Meera Joglekar as the Heroine of the film and to my knowledge, that was her last Hindi movie – I am open to correction. I recall seeing in a filmy magazine called "Picture Post" the ad of this movie where Meera in shorts with a hockey stick in her hand is shown as a sports girl. In my view, the only plus point in the movie was its music by Madan Mohan – really good melodious numbers and the combination of Lataji with Madan Mohan can't be matched easily. When she sings the lines "AA GAYE AA GAYE MUSKURANE KE DIN" antara of the song "KAUN ROKEGA AB PYAAR KA RAASTA", I remember my late uncle SD Iyer (Anu's dad) – he loved this part of the song so much and we together enjoyed it at his house in Thane in the late 60s. I have not seen the movie till date and I don't find anything regarding the plot and would like help from those who would have seen this movie. The cast of the movie is as under:

- Ashok Kumar
- Joy Mukherjee
- Meera Joglekar
- Nirupa Roy
- Lalita Pawar
- Nana Palshikar
- Om Prakash
- Mallika &
- Mehmood

Regarding the plot – please help or the other option for me is to sit thru the movie on YouTube and that would mean sitting for 150 mins!!! Bit tough – hope my good friends can dig out something and share. Here are the songs for you.

- https://www.youtube.com/watch?v=XPAQfH_bxVU ;
- https://www.youtube.com/watch?v=PUu-BiFtGmw ;
- https://www.youtube.com/watch?v=Xf0ZK748iRk ;
- https://www.youtube.com/watch?v=DQg-xj7hi6A ;

Cheers

Laksh KV

December 1, 1972

"DO YAAR"

Dear Friends:

51 years ago, it was today i.e. on Dec 1, 1972 a flop movie called "DO YAAR" was released. This was in the wake of "Mere Apne" which had the same combo of Vinod Khanna and Shatrughan Sinha playing "YAAR" though unknowingly unlike in "Mere Apne" where they turn into foes from being good friends. Well, this movie has very little memories for me except that it was released on this day and I was in no mood to see the movie. It was produced by Kewal Mishra with music by Sonik Omi and no songs did anything great to the movie. Here is the cast for you.

- Rekha
- Vinod Khanna
- Shatrughan Sinha
- Birbal
- Nazima
- Ram Mohan &
- Kundan

Not having seen the movie till date, I drew a blank from various sources. I and would request my friends who might have seen the movie to share their thoughts about the movie.

All I know is that Vinod Khanna and Shatrugan Sinha are friends by fate while they actually are not aware that both are trying to settle score against each other. Looks very predictable and things in the end would have fallen in place.

Here are the songs for you:

- https://www.youtube.com/watch?v=s35va0_tHtw... ;

Cheers

Laksh KV

December 3, 1971

"PARAYA DHAN"

Dear Friends:

52 years ago, today – i.e. on the 3rd of December 1971, this average heroine-centric movie called "PARAYA DHAN" released. Rajendra Bhatia was the director of the movie which released in the midst of Bangla Desh war and it had its own impact on the box office. Unlike most other movies, here it was not Bedi who accompanied me but it was Venkacham aka Kundoti and Venkatramani aka Veeru who were with me and when we reached Rupam Cinema at 2 PM for the first show on the very first day we saw the huge "House Full" board and black marketers were making merry, despite a relatively new Hero in Rakesh Roshan, Hema Malini had the capacity to "Pull" crowd to the cinema hall. We were at our wits' end but were lucky to get extra tickets for all 3 in a good location of the hall. We felt funny inside the hall as were not used to last row... but once the movie started, we had a hearty laugh when a small baby is shown burning in fire – it was very evident that it was a doll!!! Some other good memories are as under:

- Rakesh Roshan's first meet with Hema Malini who is like a fearless Nadia
- Rakesh Roshan's encounter with another lady when he goes to see Hema at her home and mistakes that lady to be the girl
- Hema Malini's duplicate who is shown in Bikini (short hair)
- Om Prakash reading newspapers for the benefit of people in the village "MASHHOOR CHOR HIRALAL JAIL CHODKAR BHAAG GAYA" – headlines in the news paper and to this he adds by saying "YEH CHOR BHI AJEEB HOTE HAIN, HAMESHA BHAAGTE HI REHATE HAIN"
- Father, Daughter duet with no lip sync for father in the song "AAO JHOOME GAAYEN"
- The climax fight between Hema Malini and Ajit
- Good songs in the movie.

Here is the star cast for you:
- Hema Malini
- Rakesh Roshan
- Balraj Sahani
- Ajit
- Abhi Bhattacharya
- Chaman Puri
- Jayashri T
- Krishankant &
- Om Prakash

The plot revolved around dacoits Ajit and Balraj Sahani – at some point, Balraj Sahani decides to leave it all and become a good man and helpful one. This turn around happens when during one of the loot attacks of a rich man, the rich man's wife gets killed and he is left with a lot of jewllery and a small baby girl – the dying mom's eyes says it all and the change of heart takes place and while the police nabs Ajit, the reformed dacoit goes to Kulu Manali and brings up the girl (Hema Malini) as his own daughter. The jewellery's custodian is Balraj Sahani and has not informed anything about his past to his daughter and one day Ajit escapes from jail and wants to retireve the booty and tries to get it from Balraj Sahani but ends up in the death of Balraj Sahani and soon Ajit lands up at Balraj's Sahani's house as a relative. Its a matter of time for Ajit, as he is on the lookout for the booty and Hema realises something is wrong and like a strong "Jhansi Ki Rani" fights with Ajit and the skill she attains to fight with stick at school stands her in good stead. Rakesh Roshan as the one who falls for her has virtually no role in the movie. Another wasted role is for Om Prakash who just reads out news paper for the village folks. Good songs by RD Burman helped the movie and here are the songs for you.

- https://www.youtube.com/watch?v=VXOg3MzDHik ;
- https://www.youtube.com/watch?v=nRQIF5ttHoQ ;
- https://www.youtube.com/watch?v=uxvD7OZ7ndg ;
- https://www.youtube.com/watch?v=eI5fCsCzutw ;
- https://www.youtube.com/watch?v=YdHIMSiwsEo ;

Cheers
Laksh KV

December 4, 1970

"KHAMOSHI"

Dear Friends:

53 years ago, today i.e. on December 4 1970 a very different, off-beat and unique movie called 'KHAMOSHI" was released. In the days when over 95% of the movies were in colour, this was one B&W movie that made a big impact – though commercially not a very big hit, it had critic's support in a very big way. As a class XI student, I could only envy my elder brother, late Vaidya V Raj who was a college student and went to see the movie with his college friend Kandi aka John whose original name was Moorty. On a Saturday both of them went from the college to Broadway Cinema and saw the movie and came back home raving about a great movie. He was a great fan of Manoj Kumar and my second bro and myself were Dharam Paji fans and when my late bro mentioned that he felt that Dharam Paji also had a small role in the movie, we both wanted to see but with no money and with prelims round the corner – "Perish the thought" was the verdict at home. Eventually, when both, me and my dear friend Bedi saw the movie at Rupam when it came for matinee show (cost of ticket Re.1.25) we really enjoyed the movie and felt bad that we could not see it earlier. The figure of speech "IRONY", we understood very well after seeing the movie. The last scene when Lalita Pawar calls the name of the patient who was a nurse earlier was very touching indeed... Here is the cast for you:

- Waheeda Rehaman
- Rajesh Khanna
- Lalita Pawar
- Nazir Hussain
- Iftikar
- Deven Varma
- Anwar Hussain
- Snehalata &

- Dharmendra in a Special Appearance

The plot revolves around Waheeda Rehaman who nurses Dharmendra and falls in love with him but once he recovers, he says bye and leaves her and needless to say, the nurse in love is crestfallen – soon enough yet another patient Kaka aka Rajesh Khanna comes to get nursed by her though she initially avoids but relents eventually. When she starts nursing, her memories with her earlier love flashes on and off. Now, here she is very scared to go thru the experience all over again though Kaka too has fallen for her but the fear becomes so acute that she ends up as a lunatic in the end – what an "Irony"!!! – Superb music by Hemant Kumar helped the movie to become immensely watchable – though Box Office Collections were kind of average but 2 heroes (never in the same frame) in this B&W movie during the color arena; it had to have something to make it an impacting movie. Here are the songs for you.

- https://www.youtube.com/watch?v=Iiobymr_yq4... ;

Cheers
Laksh KV

December 5, 1969

"DO RAASTE"

Dear Friends:

It was today 54 years ago on Dec 5, 1969, yet another huge hit movie of Rajesh Khanna aka Kaka saw the light of the day – early days of a Super-star in the making – yes, I am talking about Raj Khosla's "DO RAASTE" – in this movie Khosla & co moved from suspense thrillers to a decent family melodrama that had a quiet start at the booking counters and did pick up as days passed and the word of mouth and review helped it – besides of course the foot-tapping music of Laxmikant Pyarelal that played a key role in the movie. I remember very well that for the first day 6 PM show at Rupam Cinema, tickets were easily available in current booking and I felt this movie would not do much and that Khoslas should continue with suspense movies – but I was proved wrong. The other big memory for me is my dear friend Arun Balakrishnan aka Naseeba, who was the first one from our gang to see this movie and was raving about it and he would only talk about how great a movie it was – he made a valiant attempt to sing the song "MERE NASEEB MEIN HAI JO" but the tune was evading him and he kept emphasising on the word "NASEEB" that we started addressing him as "Naseeba". The movie picked up steam and people went berserk when the songs came on screen!!! – But, somehow, I felt the Mukesh number/title song did not fit the club dance bit "DO RANG DUNIYA" but must have appealed to people though for a family audience, it looked a bit out of place in my view. There was no chance for me to see this movie on release as a class X student but 7 months later in July 1970 it came for a re-run after doing its silver jubilee run at Rupam and I booked my ticket in advance and saw the movie and was well aware that yet another sexy looking actor was there in the movie known as Bindu who played Prem Chopra's wife. Despite the prejudice against Kaka, I saw the movie and liked it then and acknowledged Naseeba for his judgement of a good movie and he was on cloud 9 and kept saying he knew what to expect in a movie blah blah... Here is the star cast for you.

- Rajesh Khanna
- Mumtaz
- Balraj Sahani

- Kamini Kaushal
- Prem Chopra
- Bindu
- Veena
- Asit Sen
- Jayant &
- Jr. Mehmood

The plot was that of a lower middle class family consisting of 3 brothers played by Balraj Sahani, Prem Chopra and Rajesh Khanna – though, Balraj Sahani is the step brother, he took care of his siblings very well. However, when Prem Chopra gets married to rich Bindu, it turns into a major adjustment issue for her and slowly the brothers tend to disintegrate. The youngest brother is unable to tolerate his Bhabhi while the elder one has a large heart. Kaka falls for his college friend Mumtaz who looks to blend better with the middle class values. Bindu continues to disrupt the peace in the family. There are people ready to exploit the poor family and after a lot of tears the family comes back to its united self. Lovely songs made things interesting for all. Here are the songs for you:

- https://www.youtube.com/watch?v=G7aDwcowd3Q ;

Cheers

Laksh KV

November 30, 1973

"BLACKMAIL & DHARMA"

Dear Friends:

It was today 50 years ago i.e. on November 30, 1973 2 movies released – one with heavy starcast, great names, good production house & everything required including good music to make a hit movie as thought by the makers but alas it became a disaster & that is Vinod Doshi & Vijay Anand movie "Blackmail" and the other one sounded more like a "B" grade movie with no big names and limited publicity but that became a runaway hit and here I am talking about SK Kapur's "DHARMA". While my good friend Balakrishnan Narayan was feeling happy about "Namak Haram" doing well released just one week prior, me and my brother kept saying wait for "Blackmail" & out there we have a winner in 2 great actors etc etc. With all that in my mind, I had done advance booking at Rupam Cinema for Friday 6 PM show after my office and went inside with a lot of enthusiasm. Great names, great banner, great music and a sure-shot formula we all thought but the Samosa during the interval was a welcome relief – the plot was triangular and nothing novel about it – it also looked a lot unreal that Shatrughan was a good friend yet a guy who betrays the hero. Rakhee was his girlfriend and soon Dharam takes over – very unbelievable!!! There was some "Eureka" scene when Madan Puri discovers the formula to generate electricity from sun and when he realized what he has done, he runs all over wearing almost nothing like the famous scientist did. Overall, a big disappointment despite all ingredients and the movie barely ran for 10 weeks and hence a flop. The only unique thing besides the solar energy is the background music of dog barking used during the interlude of the song "Mile, Mile Do Badan" picturized on Rakhee and Dharmendra when the dogs chase them. The star cast is as under:

- Dharmendra
- Rakhee
- Shatrughan Sinha
- Madan Puri

- Iftikar
- Kamal Kapoor
- Jagdish Raj &
- Keshav Rana

Madan Puri a scientist, who discovers solar energy and that threatens Iftikar and his business and foresees to go bankrupt. Shatrughan and Rakhee (Iftikar's daughter) have been seeing each other and in love but the 2 gentlemen plan to get Rakhee married to Dharam Paji, who happens to be Madan Puri's nephew and find a way to inherit the property. Then the Hero and Heroine get married but not all is well as our hero suspects something fishy about Rakhee's past and it takes almost the end of the movie for Dharam Paji to find out that it was none other than Shatrughan troubling her. Eventually things get cleared – music was outstanding and here are the songs for you from one solitary link:

- https://www.youtube.com/watch?v=qkhP7reeOqo ;

The second movie is "Dharma" which had almost zero expectations for people and it exceeded all the expecatations in a very big way and celebrated silver jubilee. In fact, the initial draw was low given that a big name and movie was released alongside but this movie picked up steam on a daily basis and though we friends felt that it was a B grade movie, we avoided it for a long time but when it came back for re-run at Rupam during the movie's 10th week or so, we did visit and saw and felt funny at times as to how the crowd lapped it up – especially when Bindu and Pran do the jugalbandi in the song "ISHARON KO AGAR SAMJHO, RAAZ KO RAAZ REHNAY DO"... The friendship of Ajit and Pran – for a change Ajit was the good man as a Cop while Pran had a dual existence in most part of the movie – should say triple act – as Dacoit Dharama, Chandan and Sikandar. Navin Nischal played the romantic hero who falls for the fallen woman Rekha who gets adopted by Pran – the do-gooder. The star cast for you is:

- Pran
- Navin Nischal
- Rekha
- Ajit
- Madan Puri
- Ramesh Deo

- Mohan Choti
- Sonia Sahani
- Rajan Haksar
- Jayashree T &
- Murad

Pran plays Dakoo Dharama who kills Rajan Haksar who is his trusted man as he betrays him and in a police encounter ensures that while escaping Pran's wife and son get separated from him due to the Police officer Ajit. Pran assumes the name of Chandan Singh in a different area. Now, Chandan Singh takes revenge by kidnapping Ajit's wife and daughter – while the wife is killed in an accident, the daughter is rescued by a prostitute. After many years, now Chandan has twin identity – Dakoo Chandan and Sikandar who is a good friend of the promoted IG Ajit. Rekha is now a dancer and Navin Nischal who is Pran's right hand man is in love with Rekha. Lot of game playing happens between the Police and Sikandar as it is almost clear to the IG that Pran is playing double game. In the end, the kids find their parents and all is well that ends well. Songs were well received in the movie and here are the songs for you:

- https://www.youtube.com/watch?v=UHpIkRhwzgk ;
- https://www.youtube.com/watch?v=5b0aCcIFkqc ;
- https://www.youtube.com/watch?v=YubvrTkSmgM ;
- https://www.youtube.com/watch?v=Vp-Ri2qqDzc ;

Cheers

Laksh KV

November 29, 1968

"SADHU AUR SHAITAN"

Dear Friends:

It was today 55 years ago on the 29th of November 1968, the hit comedy movie called "Sadhu Aur Shaitaan" released – it was out and out a comedy movie with a whole lot of comedians thrown in – part time, full time, guest artists and what not. I was in class IX and needless to say the only time we could see the movie was during vacations & luckily Christmas Vacation was not far off. But my good friend Narayan Balakrishnan aka Bedi had not only seen the movie on release but had witnessed the shooting of the scenes where Mehmood freaks out on seeing Pran's dead body in his taxi. He explained to us as to how it was and how all the students from his school enjoyed the shooting. It took some few weeks before, we 3 brothers managed to see the movie at Broadway when it was well into its 4th week. We had heard about the movie and all of us knew that it was a remake of a Tamil movie called "Sadhu Mirandal" with Nagesh reprising the cab driver's role that Mehmood too did with aplomb. Some of the memories of the movie for me are as under:

- The wait outside the Broadway cinema for the matinee show to get over
- The first song "Nandlaal Gopal" sung by Om Prakash's kids
- Tangewale Ka Sapna – the play by Mehmood for his Taxi Drivers' Union
- Lalita Pawar playing Mehmood's wife in that play
- The 2 Pandits gossiping always and getting disappointed when Om Prakash forgets to do Namashkar to the Gods in the temple
- Fluent English spoken by Mehmood to shock the Heroine Bharati
- Excellent acting of Kishore Kumar and his musical Mandali
- Pran cheating Mehmood as Sher Khan
- Anwar Hussain playing a good Police Officer

- A whole lot of guest artists coming on and off
- Climax scene of a whole lot of taxi drivers going to support Mehmood in trouble

The star cast of the movie :

- Mehmood
- Om Prakash
- Pran
- Bharati
- Kishore Kumar
- Nasir Hussain
- Anwar Hussain
- Mukri
- Keshto Mukherjee
- Janki Das
- Tun Tun
- Dulari
- Sunil Dutt
- Jeevan
- Shubha Khote
- Ashok Kumar
- Dilip Kumar
- Mumtaz
- Lalita Pawar
- Nirupa Roy &
- Anwar Hussain

The story revolved around a sincere Bank employee played by Om Prakash, with Nasir Hussain as his Boss and Pran as his friend who cheats him. Mehmood, a taxi driver has sympathy towards Om Prakash and his 2 kids and their teacher Bharati on whom the taxi driver has his eyes set and her brother is played by Kishore Kumar. Pran wants to take advantage of the position of his friend Om Prakash and has a plan to loot the bank where he works. He manages to make a duplicate key of the bank locker by feigning illness and then manages to loot the bank but the 6th sense of Om Prakash ensures he goes to the bank only to find his friend doing the damage – then the 2 friends have a fight and they go and sit inside Mehmood's cab and continue the fight and in doing so, Om Prakash kills Pran and manages to retrieve the bank money and wants to go to the police but the situation does not support. Then there are a lot of hilarious scenes as many guest artists hire the cab and during their journey they see Pran's dead body and react in different fashion but Mehmood gets to know of it only in the end. Finally, things fall in place and Mehmood marries Bharati. Laxmikant Pyarelal had given decent music that helped the movie to run for 25 weeks. Here are the songs for you.

- https://www.youtube.com/watch?v=mwyevT_vgTI ;
- https://www.youtube.com/watch?v=Ue2qW9Gglo0 ;
- https://www.youtube.com/watch?v=1x8Jmgjz92w ;
- https://www.youtube.com/watch?v=vle5D3F8gdo ;
- https://www.youtube.com/watch?v=ylxxQrzh6Fc ;
- https://www.youtube.com/watch?v=N4daYmYF9hE ;

Cheers
Laksh KV

November 27, 1970

"GOPI"

Dear Friends:

It was on November 27th 1970 – 53 years ago – just one week after the Big Hit by Dev Anand called "JMN" – this movie called "GOPI" got released and it was a reasonable hit – nowhere compared to Dev Anand's block-buster and certainly did much more business than the other contemporary Raj Kapoor's "MNJ" did that released 3 weeks later. As usual I had to feel happy listening to the radio program aired by Vividh Bharati and looking at the posters at Rupam Cinema in Mumbai. The advertisements had some dialogues from the movie "MAIN HANUMAAN KA BHAKT, MERE BAARE MAY KAISAY KAISAY VICHAR KARTE HO, AISAY BAATEN SOCHO TOH PAAPA LAGEGA" all coz he explains that he was present when he personally saw the delivery... and innocently gives the feeling to all around that it was that of a baby and not a calf delivery that he actually saw. Then Saira Banu's line "BEECH MEIN GOPI RAJA, AUR CHARON TARAF GOPIYAN". The movie ran for 2 weeks at Rupam and in the 2nd week on the last day i.e. on a Thursday evening, I had taken a round and saw our dear "Hariharan" Sir from our school, who had a neat hair cut near the cinema hall and went to see the movie – he smiled at me and I felt "Kya Majja Hi, he has the money to see the movie!!!" But, I had no such luck. Then a couple of weeks later, my elder brother Radhakrishnan and my Maasi Kamala Narayan saw the movie at Rivoli Cinema – both seated at the lower stall and came back happy from the movie. I was in class XI and having failed in Hindi, I had very limited chance of getting a nod from parents – waiting till Christmas meant going far off to see the movie while "MNJ" & "JMN" too were in the agenda!!! So had to skip "Gopi" then. Eventually, I saw the movie on DD on a Sunday evening in the 80s and simply loved the movie and have seen it several times and every time I see it on Zee Classic, I go back to my school days. I loved the first song "HEY RAMACHANDRA KEH GAYE" where the 2 brothers played by Om Prakash and Dilip Kumar come across as 2 really affectionate guys and with Nirupa Roy as our Hero's Bhabhi who almost considers the Hero as her son. For a change it was not Naushad's music but it was Kalyanji Anandji who provided the musical score for this movie. There was a Bhanjan song "SUKH KE SAB SAATHI DUKH MEIN NA KOI" the only song sung by Mohd Rafi as most of the songs were sung by Mahendra Kapoor including the funny 'GENTLEMAN GENTLEMAN GENTLEMAN" – again brought a lot of camaraderie between the 2 brothers. Here is the star cast of the movie:

- Dilip Kumar
- Saira Banu
- Om Prakash
- Nirupa Roy
- Durga Khote
- Farida Jalal
- Sujit Kumar
- Pran
- Mukri
- Lalita Pawar
- Tiwari &
- Johny Walker

The story was about 2 step-brothers Om Prakash and Dilip Kumar who lived together along with Nirupa Roy who played Mrs. Om Prakash & Farida Jalal – the kid sister of our Hero. Our Hero is a good hearted rascal, who does all odd jobs for his home but does not have any source of income while the elder brother sculpts a lot of statues and sells it to a local Zamindar played by Pran who gives him a pittance for all the hard work and sells it and makes supernormal profits. At some point, our Hero realizes that there is exploitation here and when Om Prakash goes for his share of money, he is thrown out by Pran and hence our Hero takes it upon himself to recover the money and he does it in style but gets into trouble by none other than Pran so much so that the 2 brothers go apart from each other – and then it is all hardship for the elder couple while the younger bro and his sister end up at Durga Khote's kothi and her son played by Sudesh Kumar falls for Farida Jalal. When things get better, Dilip Kumar returns to his village only to find his bro talking ill of him and sister in law has sympathy for him.

Later the elderly couple have to leave the village and are in dire straits and eventually they land up in the same place where Dilip Kumar has made a decent life and all of them meet in some tough conditions and all ends well. The movie though predictable, I found good and will continue to watch for some good acting and songs and pure nostalgia. Here are the songs for you.

- https://www.youtube.com/watch?v=IArMXG2Ywz8 ;
- https://www.youtube.com/watch?v=cewJDl8hDog ;
- https://www.youtube.com/watch?v=8IqfmiZRhoo ;
- https://www.youtube.com/watch?v=_n_XyS_4g0E ;
- https://www.youtube.com/watch?v=GWAk6uPxu0g ;

Cheers

Laksh KV

November 26, 1971

"KAL AAJ AUR KAL"

Dear Friends:

It was today 52 years ago i.e. on November 26, 1971, the movie that launched Randhir Kapoor by his dad Raj Kapoor called "Kal Aaj Aur Kal" was released. It was a saga of 3 generations – post the failure of "Mera Naam Joker", the showman went ahead and launched his eldest son who made a fairly good impression but the movie at an overall level was an average grosser and at the same time senior RK gave the role of direction to the debutant son Randhir Kapoor and had his heroine as his girl-friend Babita with whom he tied the knot. It really needed guts to make movies after the spectacular failure of Joker and with my sympathy towards RK and Shankar Jaikishan I wanted this movie to do well and I did see the movie alone at Nandi Cinema at Bandra. The movie had hardly about 40% occupancy but I did observe that on Saturday 6 PM show at Rupam was going "Full" and lot of people were looking for extra tickets and I was just observing and did not have the money to buy tickets. But there was one bald Tamilian who had a few extra tickets was hounded by people and he thought I was keen to see and he told people that I was known to him but since I did not have money he had to take someone else. The movie had some interesting situations and some of them on top of my mind are:

- Raj Kapoor asking Randhir re: Babita "Airportwali?"
- Babita referring Prithviraj Kapoor as "Maali"
- Raj Kapoor slipping when he joins the youngsters on a dance floor
- Prithviraj Kapoor selecting "Rukmini" as the Bahu for Randhir Kapoor
- The famous scene on the stairs of the house with 3 men forming triangle and argueing
- "Dynamite" the term used by Raj Kapoor to bring the grandpa and grandson together

Well, the star cast to the movie is as under:
- Randhir Kapoor

- Babita
- Prithviraj Kapoor
- Raj Kapoor
- Achla Sachdev
- Tiwari
- Roopesh Kumar
- Narendranath
- David &
- Iftikar

The plot revolved around the communication gap across 3 generations – the middle one is sandwiched between his father and son. The real life members play on the screen their real life roles. The major difference of opinion comes between the granpa and grandson with the dad sandwiched not knowing whom to support. Eventually a very strong stand taken by the middle generation brings the youngest and oldest together and all is well and this cycle continues life long as "Kal Aaj Aur Kal". The music played a good role for the movie and with this movie ended the long-standing relationship of RK with SJ. This movie ran for 12 weeks at Novelty and was extended by another 2 weeks but, did not make it to 100 days and hence not a hit movie. Here are the songs for you:

- https://www.youtube.com/watch?v=ocZ_gUUOvhw ;

Cheers
Laksh KV

November 24, 1972

"ROOP TERA MASTANA & SHEHAZADA"

Dear Friends:

It was today 51 years ago i.e. on the 24th of November, 1972, two BIG movies released and both BOMBED. I am talking about "ROOP TERA MASTANA" & "SHEHAZADA" – both movies with good star value, good music and nice settings, produced lavishly – but could not hold the audience. Well, my memories are that I was keen to see RTM & avoid Kaka movie as those days I was in that mode but in case of RTM – I had gathered that, it was the last movie of Pran as a Villain and has a rape scene with Mumtaz – so that was a must and this movie was branded and hyped heavily and the ad on the radio with Ameen Sayani's voice said "SANSANI BHENT CHAKACHOUND – ROOP TERA MASTANA"followed by the song "Dil Ki Baaten, Dil Hi Jaanay". So it was a Friday that afforded me to step out of the college at 11 am and walk to Neptune Cinema at Bandra and my dear friend Balakrishnan Narayan aka Bedi was with me and both of us were very disappointed at what was offered – We loved the passionate number "Haseen Dilrubah Kareeb Aa Zara, Ke Abhi Dil Nahi Bhara"... Mumtaz had a dual role or double act – now I don't recall but very well recall that the movie closed out after 4 weeks – the main theatre was Ganga at Tardeo – read in the paper "4th & Last Week" – big loss for the makers for they had put in a lot of money in making this movie. After a long time, it was Asad Bhopali who got a chance to write the songs for Laxmikant Pyarelal – the song "Bade Bewafa Hain Husnwaale" made an impact and the costumes of all was just outstanding but what a miserable flop!!! Uff... here is the cast of the movie:

- Jeetendra
- Mumtaz
- Pran
- Brahmma Bharadwaj
- Leela Mishra
- Birbal

- V Gopal &
- IS Johar

Pran, assistant to Princess Mumtaz gets rid of her and brings in her look alike – a poor Mumtaz. Pran's idea is to capture the property and forces the poor girl to work for him. The poor princess now meets Jeetendra who is a Prince himself and falls in love – but how long can the reality be hidden – it comes out and with a lot of issues things get sorted out with fights, chase, rape and what not. Over all no impact just that songs were effective and here are the songs for you.

- https://www.youtube.com/watch?v=a-9tKVYD4o4 ;
- https://www.youtube.com/watch?v=_u-nPPn1yMI ;
- https://www.youtube.com/watch?v=hivltN99Cbk ;
- https://www.youtube.com/watch?v=RzgBzN69kCc ;

SHEHAZADA:

Kaka's decline had started from "Dil Daulat Duniya" in July 1972, and "Jhoroon Ka Gulam", "Bawarchi" & "Mere Jeevan Saathi" did not help much – this one too had good advertisements and publicity on the radio but looks like people did not accept Kaka as a Truck Driver as probably people felt he was more suited for romantic roles with his special winks that really ensured the girls missed a beat. Here he was trying to teach a lesson to his rich grandma who has wronged our hero's mom. I saw this movie in bits and pieces on TV just a couple of years back and felt that it was after all not such a bad movie but that was not a great time for Kaka. Here is the cast of the movie:

- Rajesh Khanna
- Rakhee
- Veena
- Karan Dewan
- Pandharibai
- Sundar
- Madan Puri
- Jairaj &
- Mohan Choti

Pandari Bai gets married to Karan Devan but Veena the MIL is not happy with the alliance and during riots, she loses her hubby and Veena the strict MIL feels it is all because of the new DIL Pandari Bai and drives her away and her hubby also witnesses the whole thing helplessly and then Pandari Bai goes and lives with her dad who too passes away and she delivers our hero Kaka. Kaka is a truck driver and is advised by his mom to go and meet his dad who lives a very happy and comfortable life. His grand mom wants him to move over to the palace which he refuses and that is not taken well by the old lady. She continues to trouble Pandaribai and after a lot of drama, jail going by Kaka etc things fall in place and all is well. RD Burman's music had a role to play in salvaging the movie that could run for 10 weeks those days and hence not considered a hit. Here are the songs for you.

- https://www.youtube.com/watch?v=SkdCV-ijVIc ;
- https://www.youtube.com/watch?v=np6G3T8cNbk ;
- https://www.youtube.com/watch?v=vF43ZY7279A ;
- https://www.youtube.com/watch?v=CQIbuuAlXS0 ;

Cheers
Laksh KV

November 23, 1973 & January 4, 1974

"NAMAK HARAM & MANCHALI"

Dear Friends:

It was exactly today 50 years ago on November 23 1973, & on January 4th 1974, 2 hit movies were released – the first one was "NAMAK HARAM" & the second one "MANCHALI" and both did good business at the Box Office. Let me take it up in alphabetic order – so it is:

"MANCHALI" – a light hearted comedy film that had very catchy songs composed by Laxmikant Pyarelal (LP) – Unfortunately for me this movie did not release at Rupam my usual hideout and it took a while for me to find an opportune moment to go to a slightly distant cinema hall and it did come when the movie was well into its 4th week and was declared a hit. My elder brother had already seen the movie and was going gaga over it mainly for LP as he was a great LP fan and I too thought to myself once my exams were over well before X'mas will find a window of opportunity to see the movie, and I took some time off from my work (remember, I was a working student) and reached Bijli Cinema for a 615 PM show. The top memories for me are – Sanjeev Kumar at the Railway station keeps irritating Leena Chandawarkar. When Sanjeev Kumar starts flirting with Leena's best friend Nazima, Leena does not like it and tells him to stop and Sanjeev Kumar replies saying that "this clause is not in the agreement" – Leena gets more irritated – the ability to win over her parents by Sanjeev Kumar was portrayed beautifully. Some of the songs that are on top of my mind "GUM KA FASANA BAN GAYA ACHHA" – this one has Leena speaking some lines in the song, "MILE KAHIN DO AJNABI" – if I recall it is the last song of the movie and here SK really looked a polished man and did a brilliant job. The title song "OH MANCHALI KAHAN CHALI" had all the fun elements. Raja Nawathe produced this movie and the cast is as under:

- Sanjeev Kumar
- Leena Chandavarkar
- Nazima

- Nirupa Roy
- Krishankant &
- Shrikant Moghe

The plot was about a rich spoilt girl Leena (LC) refuses to marry and the issue is as per the will she would not get the property till she marries. She rejects all cases and since the pressure builds, she with her friend gives an ad in the matrimony column of a daily and shortlist a candidate and get disappointed to see an old man who had a younger photo sent. Dejected, Leena is on her way and at the platform meets a ruffian Sanjeev Kumar (SK) who shows his willingness to help the Heroine and agrees to play her hubby in front of her parents and the agreement has terms and conditions. So in walks SK and soon wins over her parent's hearts and even Leena's close friend is fond of him. SK also starts demanding more and more money from LC and she is shocked when she finds that her parents have added him as a joint holder in the property. Well, all this is done by SK to teach a lesson to LC and everything falls in place at the end. Good music helped the movie to do good business too and here are the songs for you.

- https://www.youtube.com/watch?v=7o1UL7_GXCI... ;

"NAMAK HARAM" – brilliant work by the director Hrishikesh Mukherjee & producers Rajaram, Satish Wagle & Jayendra Pandya, who joined the first 2 names for this movie. Earlier the duo had made "Pyar Hi Pyar" & "Yaar Mera" which were in a different league but "Namak Haraam" became a cult movie. Since Kaka, had a whole lot of flops in 1972 and also in the beginning of 1973, I started feeling sympathetic towards him and started seeing his movies and stopped the earlier attitude of not giving my revenue to a Kaka movie. This was the time my late uncle had come along with the family i.e. aunt and their 3 daughters (Anjali, Akhila & Anuradha) for their first vacation after they moved to Singapore in 1970. We were looking forward to their arrival and for some strange reasons, they could not join me for this movie and I happened to see the movie alone at Rupam. (We, all did see Bobby – 13 of us! at Bandra Talkies as they chose Bobby over Namak Haram!!!). Having seen Anand earlier and developed a fondness towards AB, I felt Hrishda reversed the roles in this movie – in Anand Kaka did all the talking but here it was AB who was given the punch lines – 'KIS SALENE SOMU PE HAATH UTHAYA BOLO, KAUN HAI WOH MAI KE LAAL, AGAR MAA KA DOODH PIYA HAI TO AAJAO SAAMNE" !!! Till I saw the movie, I could not believe that AB can deliver such lines with total comfort. I liked the role of Manmohan who plays a "KHABARI" and keeps informing the management for money and there is once he makes an exception and says that he will not charge for his services... I felt bad that I was alone in this movie and would have loved my friends like Bedi to be with me as I had Samosas during the interval. The movie again has Kaka die at the end like Anand but here it was a planned murder to look like an accident. "BANDHU" is the term used by Raza Murad as he refers to Kaka and they made a good pair in the Basti. Lovely songs by RD Burman helped the movie further. It was very timely in the 70s when there were strikes in mills and unemployment in a big way and showed how exploitations would take place then. I recalled the definition that I learnt in college that said "Scientific Management is a clever way of exploiting the labourers" and I felt it was very relevant here. Well, coming to the cast of the movie:

- Rajesh Khanna
- Rekha
- Amitabh Bachhan
- Simmi Garewal
- Asrani
- Raza Murad
- Om Shivpuri
- AK Hangal
- Durga Khote
- Jayashree T &
- Manju Asrani

The plot revolves around 2 thick friends Kaka and AB, Kaka a poor guy & AB a rich guy. When AB's dad - Omshivpuri falls sick, he fills in and handles the factory and has a major showdown with the union leader AK Hangal that results in a strike by the workers. He has a massive ego but as advised by his dad apologises and the strike is called off but he confides in his good friend Kaka how badly he has been hurt. Now, the good friend that he is, Kaka wants to help his friend teach the union leader a lesson and moves to Calcutta and joins the same factory and wins the confidence of the people with some quick wins (planned by AB and Kaka) and replaces AK Hangal and becomes the Union Leader. Now this goes on but slowly Kaka in the midst of poor people starts empathising with them and tries to change AB and a rift builds between the 2 and the one to take advantage is the industrialist dad of AB and eventually Kaka is killed and AB who had felt that his friend had betrayed him (Namak Haram) realises that his dad was very scheming in the entire thing. Very well made movie that did good business plus good music by RD Burman ensured a BIG HIT. Here are the songs for you.

- https://www.youtube.com/watch?v=lCCNzfW7l80... ;

Cheers
Laksh KV

November 21, 1969

"NANHA FARISHTA"

Dear Friends:

It was today 54 years ago i.e. on November 21, 1969, this movie called "NANHA FARISHTA" released. It did not have a hero or heroine – there was a cute little girl who was the central character. It was produced by Nagi Reddy and directed by T. Prakash Rao. I had not seen this movie on release nor was very keen as it was a hopeless situation for me to try when money was just not available – movies would be only during vacations. The memories are of 2 main songs "OH NUTKUT NANHI LAADLI" & "BACHHA HAI MAHAN" – the second song was filmed on Pran, Ajit and Anwar Hussain who are the 3 negative characters in the movie and this young girl who is kidnapped by them changes them and that is the main theme of the movie. I had seen the movie much later in matinee at Rupam cinema. The dad of this young girl was played by Tamil Hero Ravichandran – this is what someone told me – I am open to correction. Padmini also played a key role as the governess of the kid. Anyone who has more details of this movie, kindly share.

The plot revolved around the 3 criminals Pran, Ajit and Anwar Hussain (Hindu, Christian & Muslim respectively) who kill a rich man and kidnap his young daughter. This girl has her own charm and brings about a change in the hearts of the 3 criminals – when the kid falls ill, she tells them to get her governess Padmini and she realizes that the kid needs the attention of a Doctor and insists on calling a Doctor but these 3 are worried of getting exposed as they still have control over the kid and Padmini. Eventually things fall in place. Here are songs for you.

- *https://www.youtube.com/watch?v=nqhjPd4qmAo* ;
- *https://www.youtube.com/watch?v=Ge223BVPcQg* ;
- *https://www.youtube.com/watch?v=giOX9d959bQ* ;

Cheers
Laksh KV

November 20, 1970

"JOHNY MERA NAAM"

Dear Friends:

It was today exactly 53 years ago the biggest hit of 1970 was relased... Yes, I am talking about the movie "JOHNY MERA NAAM" released on November 20 1970 – made by the banner called Trimurty Films, Produced by Gulshan Rai and directed by Vijay Anand. This turned out to be a big hit at the Box Office, very crisply edited movie and people lapped it up from the word go. Black Marketers made a killing and Friday 6 PM show was not just "House full" but the ticket of stalls costing Rs. 2/- was being sold at Rs. 5/- so imagine the premium was 150% and my classmate Suryanarayan aka Chury wanted to see it under any circumstances. He used to attend Maths classes very close to Rupam Cinema with KRK sir and that day he managed to get the required money and I had the privilege of seeing him off inside Rupam Cinema and felt, one day I too will have that kind of money to see movies. The entire Rupam area was so crowded and people were in a hurry to go inside and needed some kind of major discipline to get the people inside. On the following day when I met Chury at school, he could not stop talking about the movie and was fully fida – the emphasis was on Padma Khanna's dance and her attire – so I guess he too was a normal guy like us!!! I did not have the guts to ask for money and see the movie but did read the review in TOI on Sunday and realized that this movie will run and it is a "must see" during X'mas vacation. The main reason I could not ask for money was the fact that I had failed in Hindi in the terminal exams and whenever I asked anything in that manner, all 4 members of the house would attack me reminding me of my failure!!! I did see the movie with my late brother during X'mas vacation after seeing "Mera Naam Joker" at Rupam, on the following day saw at "Kohinoor" Cinema where it was still running to packed houses. My brother never liked to stand in "Qs" and I decided to get the cheapest ticket but unfortunately they were giving only one ticket to an individual – so I told him that I got only 1 ticket, but he very smartly went and bought a ticket for himself from the Upper Stall Quota where the cost of the ticket was Rs.2.50, full Re.1/- more than lower stall. He was seated in the centre of the hall and me in the corner of one of the front rows. Lots of memories of this movie for me – my Senior duo Shivram and Manikkyam who stayed in the next building to our school, had seen the movie and kept saying it was 100% entertainment – all this, when I did not have the warewithall to see the movie. Even the seniors in our area who were playing over-arm cricket on road, used to talk of the movie and do some "Boxing" stunts like the 2 brothers Dev Anand and Pran. The condition of the mother Sulochana of the 2 school going boys called Sohan and Mohan was pitiable – when they were in the boxing ring, she would feel bad as if one hit the other, it was her sons always at the receiving end. Premnath's extravagance, the stylish English that he spoke during the exhibition of rare jewellery was simply amazing. Jeevan looked really smart as a lawn tennis player carrying the racquet in style. As mentioned earlier, Padma Khanna's dance was exciting and how Premnath the strong man first asks "Zaleel Ladki Tere Paas Hai Kya" & Padma says "Kuch Toh Hoga" – Randhawa, as her boyfriend who is willing to betray his boss for a good life ahead loses out. The support Dev Anand gets from Police dept to get closer to Hema Malini looked stupid but still interesting. We had an overdose of IS Johar – 3 of them – Pehalay, Doojay & Teejay Rams. In the climax ISJ plays the transistor that says "AB SUNIYE MOHD RAFI KO MAHENDRA KAPOOR KI AAWAAZ MEIN" – The fight scene between the grown up brothers starting with Pran asking "BOL KYA NAAM HI TERA?", & Dev Anand responds saying "JOHNY MERA NAAM HAI". This goes on for 3 times and after some heavy duty boxing they discover that they are long lost brothers & join hands to finish off the villains - Kalyanji Anandji was in full form in this movie with some great songs that touched everyone. Hema Malini looked gorgeous in the movie. The main star-cast of the movie included:

- Dev Anand
- Hema Malini
- Pran
- Premnath
- Sulochna
- Iftikar
- Jeevan
- Sajjan

- Dulari
- Randhava
- IS Johar
- IS Johar &
- IS Johar.

The plot was interesting – a police officer has 2 sons – Dev Anand and Pran who are good at boxing and regularly win joint trophies at school as young kids. Premnath's man kills the Police officer and the young Pran is a witness of the event and he follows the killer and kills him and escapes from the eyes of police by sitting in the boot of the car and gets separated from his family. The kids grow up and while Pran becomes part of Premnath's gang, Dev Anand becomes a police officer who solves cases by taking up different guises. He then takes the name of Johny as a petty thief and gets into a jail where he gets pally with Jeevan and escapes from the jail and gets to the root of the problems with the help of Hema Malini who has her dad under Premnath's control. Lots of actions, fights and entertainment later the movie has a happy ending!!! Here are the songs for you.

- https://www.youtube.com/watch?v=eEkdAL7P2C4... ;

Cheers

Laksh KV

November 19, 1971

"EK NARI EK BRAHMACHARI"

Dear Friends:

It was today, 52 years ago i.e. on November 19, 1971, the hit movie "EK NARI EK BRAHMACHARI" saw the light of the day. This was clearly a remake from South Indian movie I felt when I saw it on the very second day, night show. Earlier, my late brother and my cousin had accompanied me to see the same pair in September for a movie called "Katputli" and I had started liking Jeetendra from then and Caravan in the next month added to my liking – so I also wanted not just to see this movie for Jeetendra, but also for its music by SJ and really was praying hard for the movie to do well. My benchmark would never be the collection or "House full" board on the first 3 days but what happens on Monday – and I was happy when I saw the Monday and Tuesday shows too had the "House full" board intact. So, it was on Saturday night we went to see the movie and found that the movie looked quite lavish with a palatial bungalow and was a bit different than the standard triangular themes that we had got used to by then. Here the influence of the Hero to remain single or "Brahmachari" was so strong on me that, I had decided to remain a bachelor lifelong but ironically, in less than 8 years of seeing the movie, I was in a hurry to tie the knot jumping "Q" and leaving my elder brother behind. Some of the other memories are –Shorab Modi's heavy voice really was scary and it looked authentic when he ordered his son Jeetendra to get married. Jagdeep did heavy overacting as the batch mate and all the guys shown as college students clearly indicated that all of them were overgrown for playing collegians or should I say that they looked right as guys who failed regularly in college. The curly haired baby reminds me of our 10 month old Grandson Rudra only due to the curly hair. This I felt more as recently this movie was on Zee Classic – the most unforgettable song for me was the song by Sharada "AAP KE PEECHAY PAD GAYI MAIN" where Mumtaz tries hard to entice an unwilling Jeetendra. Shatrughan Sinha makes an impact guest appearance & exhibits his style. The main cast of the movie is here under:

- Jeetendra

- Mumtaz
- Shorab Modi
- Durga Khote
- Mukri
- Mohan Choti
- Keshto Mukherjee
- Birbal
- Polson
- Brahmchari
- Mallika
- Shatrughan Sinha (Special Appearance)
- Aruna Irani &
- Jagdeep

The plot was that of a well do Chowdhary family headed by Shorab Modi, who had 2 sons Shatrughan and Jeetendra. While Shatrughan was married and well settled, Jeetendra was still a student in a college where Mumtaz also was his classmate. The Senior Chowdhary was unhappy that his elder son despite being married for several years was yet to have a kid and the younger one had decided to remain "Brahmachari" or single – so no chance of heir for the family. The boys somehow manage to create situations where by the Hero and Heroine were made to look like lovers and a photo clicked makes it look genuine. When the dad visits the hostel he sees the snap where his son Jeetu and Mumu are in each-other's arms, he feels they should get married. Then all of a sudden Mumtaz lands in the palatial house of Chowdhary with a toddler in her arms and claims that the little one was the heir of the family. Automatically it is felt that Jeetu is the father and he continues to decline such claims and DNA test is done and it comes out that the child belongs to Chowdhary clan. The hidden story is that the child belongs to Mumtaz's elder sister Mallika and Shatrughan Sinha and once the mother of the kid dies, Mumtaz wants the child to be entrusted to the right family. Shatrughan Sinha eventually admits to be the dad and all things end up well and also our Hero decides to kick his "Celibacy" thoughts and ties the knot with Mumtaz. Some good songs by SJ did help the movie and here are the songs for you:

- https://www.youtube.com/watch?v=JnMFc58NE-g ;
- https://www.youtube.com/watch?v=MsmaERL41EA ;
- https://www.youtube.com/watch?v=kE7keybgWAQ ;
- https://www.youtube.com/watch?v=23dHSi7cE18 ;
- https://www.youtube.com/watch?v=_7cBROPfqhs ;

Cheers

Laksh KV

November 17, 1972

"RAJA JANI"

Dear Friends:

It was today 51 years ago one of the biggest box office hits called "RAJA JANI" released. It was made by the same banner that offered us "SHARAFAT" earlier with the same hit lead pair of Dharam Paji and his wife to be, Hema Malini. Good action, hit music, crisp editing made the movie interesting and there was no song on the Hero. That morning, we set off to our college with all excitement and while in Inter Commerce, I used to have the lectures from 815 am on Fridays and the main lectures would get over at 11 and the last 2 sessions would be languages – so I always thanked my college authorities for giving such a lovely time table where I never felt guilty of bunking some language sessions and go for 1st day Matinee show – mostly 1115 or 1130 or 12 noon shows. The routine was for me to get ready first and go to the other side of the building and make my traditional sound and my dear Balakrishnan Narayan aka Bedi would come to the balcony and wave at me and I would wait for him to come. In the mean time we had one Arun (aka Annu) Khanna in the next building called Kamal Kunj and he asked "KYOON PAAPA, AAJ KAUNSA PICTURE JAANEKA IRADA HI?" & I confidently told him "Raja Jani" & he approved our decision. In a hurry we finished our lectures and were out of the class by 11 am and had to reach Badal Cinema – since I was earning in Pentagon a princely salary of Rs. 75/- pm, I told we will hire a cab and reach Badal in good time from Bandra close to Pamposh hotel. Bedi agreed and we reached the hall and we had done the tickets in advance. The movie was running packed and we reached inside, and the movie had just started the titles with the background song by Kishore Kumar "JAANI-O-JAANI" – felt very odd when Johny Walker opened the door for his Malik Dharam Paji and had made Biryani which he too had consumed in his sleep!!! The other big memory for me was the dance steps of Prem Chopra in the song "KITNA MAZAA AA RAHA HI" – it was to make Dharam Paji jealous and with Johny Walker's help who wanted the couple to come together while our He-man had other ideas. Another unforgettable thing for me was

Bhushan Tiwari wearing Dharam Paji's mask and talks in the Hero's voice (obviously dubbed). Well, a good value for money movie and we had many repeat sessions later and even now when it comes on Zee Classic, I enjoy it. The star cast for you is here:

- Dharmendra
- Hema Malini
- Premnath
- Prem Chopra
- Durga Khote
- Sajjan
- Nadira &
- Johny Walker

Plot was hovering around identifying a Raj Kumari who was lost in her childhood and the Raani maa played by Durga Khote wants her located. Her Diwan is Premnath & his son Prem Chopra are keen to get the property in their names. Premnath meets Dharam Paji who partners him to get a female in her 20s, train her up with all possible information and data that he has collected and eventually present her as the Rajkumari. So he identifies Hema Malini who is a street dancer but has all the ingredients to be presented as the fake Rajkumari – with the clear objective that she would get the keys of the safe and hand it over to him and then both Premnath and Dharampaji would share it 50% each. Things go differently as first and foremost Hema is the genuine Rajkumari & our hero falls in love with her. Premnath has a different agenda to finish off our hero and take the 100% loot. But like all good entertainers, during the climax the Rani Maa shows her trust on Dharam Paji and finally manages to get rid of the Diwan & his son gets shot accidentally by his dad and things end well. Great music by LP helped the movie complete its 25 weeks run. Here are the songs for you.

- https://www.youtube.com/watch?v=7RVtijLPr8g... ;

Cheers
Laksh KV

November 16, 1973

"AA GALE LAG JAA"

Dear Friends:

It was today i.e. on the 16th November 1973 (50 Years Ago), this hit movie from Manmohan Desai Banner called "AA GALE LAG JAA" released. It celebrated silver jubilee those days and was handled well by the makers – it had all ingredients for a hit movie – a popular star pair as lead, an impactful Shatrugan Sinha in a key role & coincidences and close misses galore – great songs and good acting by most actors – Master Tito showed a lot of promise too who played the role of a crippled child. My late brother and self saw it at Rupam on Saturday night since I had done advance booking. Shinde bros were busy selling tickets "DO KA CHAAR BOLO DO KA CHAAR" and made 100% super-normal profits. We two bros went to see the movie with no expectations and probably we ended up liking the movie though things went in a very expected fashion like the Hero-Heroine couple winning the competition without knowing each other. When Shashi Kapoor saves a freezing Sharmila Tagore by giving his warmth, we all knew she will get pregnant and her dad Om Prakash will be upset about it. When Shatrughan Sinha almost comes to blows with the crippled boy and a very serious looking Shashi Kapoor goes to him as though to beat him but thanks him for his son could walk a few steps. Another thing is that of Shatrughan's younger sister played by Roohi (resembling Jaya Bhaduri) would fall for Shashi Kapoor All these are expected things. Songs were very good in the movie and standing out were the 2 songs "TERA MUJHSE YE PEHALAY KA WADA" & "WADA KARO NAHI CHODOGI TUM MERA SAATH". The main cast has been covered above but still reiterating below:

- Shashi Kapoor
- Sharmila Tagore
- Shatrughan Sinha
- Om Prakash
- Sulochna

- Jagdeep
- Shubha Khote
- Gajanan Jagirdar
- Roohi Berede &
- Master Tito

The story revolved around a Dr. in the making – Sharmila Tagore meets Shashi Kapoor who is an amateur skater and after some initial tiff, they both fall in love and decide to tie the knot. Due to freezing cold in the hilly region, Sharmila Tagore once loses her consciousness and Shashi Kapoor saves her by giving his warmth to her and in the bargain makes her pregnant. But her dad Omprakash is unhappy with the boy as he has identified another Dr. Shatrughan Sinha as his Daamad to be and creates evidence where by Sharmila feels that Shashi Kapoor was after her money and though disappointed accepts reality and gets ready to marry Shatrughan. As the Doctor goes for higher studies to Germany, the heroine and her dad get to know of her pregnancy. Now, our Heroine wants to deliver the child while her dad wants her to abort but the decision to give birth by the Heroine stays and guess where they plan to have the child delivered – in a remote place where the Hero lives. The Heroine is told that she delivered a still born baby and the child is handed over to the legitimate dad i.e. the Hero. The Hero then comes to Mumbai where he starts teaching skating and earns his livelihood and again meets the heroine in an engagement function and feels that her man has been married and has a son. Now, Shatrughan Sinha sees the kid and feels he can cure the boy & shouts "YEH MANGNI NAHI HOGI!!!" He wants to ensure the child is normal and then get married. But the truth comes out and Om Prakash accepts all the wrong things he did and all is well in the end and our Hero also saves the Dr's sister from the wrong people. Manmohan Desai knew to entertain people and this movie too was well received by the audience. Here are the songs for you.

- https://www.youtube.com/watch?v=VBJEqhyPb8c ;

Cheers
Laksh KV

November 15, 1968

"SAATHI"

Dear Friends:

It was today, i.e. on November 15, 1968 – 55 years ago, a much hyped and successful Tamil movie "Palum Pazhavumum" that was remade in Hindi as "SAATHI" by a big south based banner called "Venus Pictures" released – but this remade movie could not match the success of the Tamil version. It just about managed to be dragged for 15 weeks but was expected to be a bumper hit. I was still in school but my late brother was in college and he, my maasi Kamala Narayan and my Amma went to see the movie at Rupam but I felt very upset and my second brother too who was also equally unhappy for not getting a chance to see the movie. To compensate, my Maasi did take me for a movie called "Tarzan & the Great River" at Aurora one night and the good thing about that movie was each one got a small packet of "Bournvita" mix which I finished off in the hall itself while my cousins religiously took it back home. Another great recall for me is the statement made by my good friend Balakrishnan Narayan aka Bedi on the previous Sunday before the movie was released. I am sure all of us hate that Sunday evening time as the next day is a school/college or office day and no one (normal people) likes it. It was November 10th evening when Bedi and myself were having our customary evening stroll and as we crossed Tamil Sangam and passing thru the park adjoining to the hall, a frustrated Bedi told "PAAPA, SAATHI DEKH KE MAR JANA HI YAAR!!!" – He also mentioned something more that I cannot share and when he said that I imagined something and needless to say that too cannot be shared!!! The start cast of the movie is as under:

- Rajendra Kumar
- Vyjantimala
- Simmi Garewal
- David
- Pahari Sanyal
- Veena

- Ram Mohan & Special Appearnces by
- Shashi Kapoor & Nanda shooting for Raja Saab in Kashmir

The movie had music by Naushad and strangely the songs were sung by Mukesh and not Mohd Rafi and in my personal opinion the music did not meet the expectations of a normal Naushad movie where the standard combination of Shakeel, Naushad and Rafi would have created magic – it sounded strange to me though. Be that as it may – let me move to the plot.

It had Rajendra Kumar playing a Surgeon who tries to help a poor lady Vyjantimala's mother by performing a surgery but unfortunately the lady dies and the Hero feels guilty and gets married to Vyjantimala. But his mentor is upset with the Hero's decision as he was planning to have his daughter Simmi Garewal married to the Hero. The Hero is so much besotted with his wife and after their Honeymoon in Kashmir, he shows very little interest in his research work to eradicate cancer. On one particular day, the Head Doctor visits him and reminds him as to how good he was earlier and how he has now become so indifferent. This also opens the eyes of the couple and our Hero gets so involved with his work that the Heroine starts feeling neglected and falls ill and she does not want to come in the way of the progress of the project, one day she walks out on him. Then our Hero tries hard to search his wife but fails and eventually learns that she dies in a train accident and our man is devastated. Simmi's dad takes ill looking at her one-sided love towards the Hero and to save his life, very reluctantly, our Hero marries Simmi but he still continues to see his late wife in every possible living minute. Now, it is Simmi's turn to feel neglected and confronts him one day about it and in doing so loses his eye sight and there ends his cancer research project. Now in comes Sanjeev Kumar from USA and is ready to perform a surgery on our Hero so that his vision can be retrieved. In the meantime while our Hero is in the hospital, the supposedly dead Vyjantimala comes back as a nurse with a different identity and does all the seva. Now listening to her voice, our Hero thinks of his wife and tries to tell the eye Dr. Sanjeev Kumar to marry her. Eventually, Simmi sacrifices and Vyjantimala is restored to Rajendra Kumar – our Hero. No wonder, the film did not do too well. Some songs did become hit or were made artificially as hit songs. Here is the link for you consisting of all the songs.

- https://www.youtube.com/watch?v=DK64x1BBGyU ;

Cheers
Laksh KV

November 13, 1970

"MERE HUMSAFAR"

Dear Friends:

53 years ago it was today i.e. on November 13, 1970, (probably the only time Jeetendra and Sharmila Tagore came as a lead pair) this movie "MERE HUMSAFAR" released and which was a very average grosser at the Box Office. All I recall about this movie is that it was released after our Diwali vacation got over and there was no hope of seeing this movie as I was sure it will not be at the close by halls during Xmas vacation. So just felt happy looking at the posters and reading the reviews. The title song of the movie was a well-received one by all though I felt Mukesh singing for Jeetendra was not done but the melody was simply amazing. The main cast of the movie is as under:

- Sharmila Tagore
- Jeetendra
- Balraj Sahani
- Laxmi Chyaya
- Jagdeep
- Suresh
- Jeevan
- Sundar
- Shammi &
- Keshto Mukherjee

The Hero - Jeetendra is called a "Junglee" by everyone in the village except his dad and a jail convict and then tragedy strikes when our Hero's dad kicks the bucket and there is a huge liability for him to handle. So he decides to go to Mumbai and make money to buy a couple of bullocks and then handle the business in his village. He gets no support from anyone as he moves out of the village and with no money, he somehow gets into a truck that transports fruits and commences his journey to the Big Land of Opportunities and is surprised to find a gypsy girl – Sharmila Tagore, who too has run away from her home and now anyone can guess, these both fall in love and have all the good intention of getting married and at some point they have to change their mode of transport and land into a goods train that is heading towards Mumbai but as expected they get separated and lead their individual lives. After some time, our Hero gets to know that his wife to be has become an actress and has full trust in her and tries to reach out to her. But he is not allowed to do that and gathers the information that she is married to Balraj Sahani. He is very disappointed and there is more misunderstanding that follows and eventually the gentleman that Balraj Sahani is, he ensures the 2 lovers meet and also hands them over a couple of bullocks at the end of the movie. Kalyanji Anandji composed some good songs in this movie and here are some of the songs for you.

- https://www.youtube.com/watch?v=IIutlVFZ4zM ;
- https://www.youtube.com/watch?v=z9mSFlBWiEY ;
- https://www.youtube.com/watch?v=OlY9tui6hmQ ;
- https://www.youtube.com/watch?v=V32OKv4AgS0 ;

Cheers

Laksh KV

November 12, 1971

"HANGAMA"

Dear Friends:

It was today 52 years ago i.e. on the 12th of November 1971, this comedy movie called "HANGAMA" released with a lot of fan-fare but the movie could not hold the audience interest despite the presence of some great names who are good at comedy. The movie also had a recently introduced Heroine (in Hulchal) Zeenat Aman, who once again went almost unnoticed in the midst of big names but in a matter of few months' time she created a different "HANGAMA" in her next release "Hare Rama Hare Krishna" – all 3 movies she starred – the titles were with "H"!!!!. Well, I have some memories of this movie about my attempt to see the movie at Paradaise Cinema at Mahim. We had a Maharashtrian wedding of one of our family friends to attend at Shivaji Park. So my second brother, our Amma and self, went for the wedding as it was a working day for my dad and late brother. After having heavy lunch that included Shrikhand, Puri, Muttha, Jilebi, Masala Bhat etc. while Amma decided to go home, we 2 brothers got her concurrence to go to see the latest release at Paradise – it was not possible to see the matinee show since by the time we were done with lunch it was 130 PM. So, we both walked to the Cinema Hall called Paradise at Mahim and it was around 215 PM and the next show was at 3 PM. There was a "Q" for the cheapest ticket which was sold only on current booking while the other tickets were sold out. So we both stood in the "Q" and once the gate opened, there was a mad rush to get closer to the ticket counter. One had to go thru some real narrow path to reach the counter with the idea of people unable to overtake and still the crowd was so bad that I started sweating and felt giddy and dropped the idea of going for the movie. We both just went to the adjoining hotel Naaz had Irani Chai and took the bus # 315 to return back home. Later got to know that it was not all that great a movie and till date have not seen it. My friend Chintya only told that it had Johny Walker and Kishore Kumar as real misers who get a challenge of spending a big amount in a short time and when they try to lose money in horse race, they end up doubling and multiplying their holdings. A couple of songs did appeal to me like

"WAH REE KISMAT" & "KACHI KALI KUCHNAARKI". The star cast of the movie is as under:

- Kishore Kumar
- Mehmood
- Johny Walker
- Vinod Khanna
- Zeenat Aman
- Aruna Irani
- Helan
- Fariyal
- Dhumal &
- Mukri

The plot revolved around 2 miserly brothers who had a spend-thrift nephew and they wanted to control things by getting him married but he escapes and meets his soul-mate during his time away from his uncles. Now, the 2 misers get a court order to pay off Rs. 50 lakhs in the next 6 months or else the money would go to a charity trust. So, here is where they want to spend the large amout in quick time and whatever they try to do, the money only grows – giving them a problem of plenty!!! I will request anyone who has seen the movie to share more about the storyline. Music by RD Burman - though not all songs were hit some did catch the imagination of the audience. Here are the songs for you

- https://www.youtube.com/watch?v=uQIKZM0LnDs ;
- https://www.youtube.com/watch?v=pWZbFRFd5DY ;
- https://www.youtube.com/watch?v=q75neUU4CCs ;
- https://www.youtube.com/watch?v=Fe2Q4YYN2_o ;

Cheers
Laksh KV

November 10, 1972

"MUNIMJI"

Dear Friends:

After talking about some big block-busters like "Seeta Aur Geeta", "Aradhana" & "Yaadon Ki Baaraat", it is my turn to talk about a very insignificant release that happened today 51 years ago i.e. on November 10, 1972 – made by Jugal Kishore under the banner of "Jugal Productions" – the flop movie "MUNIMJI". Very limited recall about the movie for me except for the following 2 points:

1. There were some scenes on the posters of Yogita Bali with a torn blouse
2. Jayashree T swimming & singing "PAANI MEIN JALAY"

The above 2 points were good enough for me to convince my brothers to go for a night show after the week end of the movie's release. The movie was such a disappointment for all 3 of us though Usha Khanna had given some good songs in the movie. "Paani Mein Jalay" was so funny to watch wherein probably they used a large fish tank as a background and showed Jayashree T swimming along – so funny!!! The other memory is that of Anil Dhawan acting as an aged Accountant aka "Muneemji" and constantly saying "Hoon Hoon" like "Hmm". I also recall Ramesh Deo having a key role but if I can guess (no memory about it), he must have been a bad man for sure. Anyways, nothing more to talk – here is the star-cast for you:

- Yogita Bali
- Anil Dhawan
- Ranjan
- Ramesh Deo
- Jayashree T
- Nazir Hussain
- Leela Mishra
- Chandrasekhar

- Maruti
- Jr. Mehmood

With regard to the plot, I would request anyone who can help to share it as I do not recall the storyline nor am I able to get it from the other sources. So may be Ambarish or Amitabh or Dilip Apte can help. However, here are the songs for you:

- https://www.youtube.com/watch?v=o3SYKNOrzbg ;
- https://www.youtube.com/watch?v=PaZHLTjRHU0 ;
- https://www.youtube.com/watch?v=S91zylfe4Ro ;
- https://www.youtube.com/watch?v=dTMJTqHphwk ;

Cheers
Laksh KV

November 09, 1973

"YAADON KI BAARAAT"

Dear Friends:

It was today, 50 years ago i.e. on November 09 1973, one of the big blockbusters called "YAADON KI BAARAAT" released. Coming from the house of hit film maker Nasir Hussain, the film had a great draw, good publicity, excellent following for Dharam Paji and superb music by RD Burman. Yet another hit for our favourite Dharam Paji. I have lots and lots of memories about this movie and countless number of times that I have seen this movie and on occasions the song "OH MERI SONI" was edited and the noise we made at Aurora Cinema was something to be seen. I loved Dharam Paji in black and was quick to stitch a pair and used to tell my close friends like Bedi, Naseeb and JKB – 'BLACK PANT, BLAK SHIRT, BLACK BELT, BLACK SHOES" and all of us would have a hearty laugh – just imagine, the persona of Dharam Paji and compare with a dark guy like me who had just started to put on weight. Well, saw the movie regularly at various cinema halls and the best memory for me is when I saw it at Novelty 11 am show once. It so happened that when I used to work for Pentagon from 1972-1976, we had a customer FOURESS ENGINEERING located in Mahalakshmi Chambers. There was a fair amount of outstanding that was due from them and I used to chase the customers for money and dodge the suppliers those days very efficiently. Since this amount had grown too huge, one day my Director Mr. Rajninath Surendranath Kale, spoke to the director of FOURESS & literally begged for clearing the outstanding in my presence. This was on a Friday and Kale Saheb told me "Go to Mahalakshmi Chambers on Monday morning and do not return without the cheque". I said "Yes Sir" and on Monday I took bus number 63 from Jain Society around 745 am and was at the venue just before 9 am and the office was yet to be opened. I was made to sit at the reception and saw people trickling in – nice posh office and I felt, one day I too should work in such big office – I kept waiting for one Mr. John (who was a Malayalee) and he showed up at 10 am. I told him that I cannot go back to my office without the cheque and that I would wait at the reception thru the day. He felt odd at my stand and requested me to come by 3 PM and that the cheque would be ready – he also mentioned that it is pending for signature and once signed, it will be handed over. I said that I cannot leave the premises and insisted on waiting at the reception. He said it will be very odd for all the people to see someone wait at the reception for over 6 hours and that I should come back by 3 PM – may be go out. I said I will do that but insisted on seeing the unsigned cheque and he obliged. So around 1030, I decided to go and see a movie and chose this very movie "Yaadon Ki Baaraat" – so took a cab and reached in good time and walked into Novelty Cinema and enjoyed the familiar scenes as under:

- The Family song which is the title song of the movie
- Ajit playing Shakhaal and killing Nasir Khan and his wife Ashu but the 2 elder sons escape while the youngest one (Master Amir Khan) joins his governess Sanjana.
- Satyen Kappu shows sympathy towards the 2 boys and allows them to escape from Shakhaal
- The most familiar scene of the 2 elder sons getting separated due to the speed of the goods train is very touching.
- Dharam Paji jumping on top of a goods train from a bridge
- Shetty sporting a wig gets beaten up by Dharam Paji – but successfully opens the soda bottle with his thumb
- Ajit with his special brand of dialogues and also foot wear of different numbers on his feet
- Imtiaz trying to woo Zeenat and failing
- Vijay Arora and Zeenat having fun at the cost of 2 fatsos who take a dip before their lunch and exclaims "What a cold water, what a fine weather!!!"
- Dharam Paji saying "BADLA BADLA BADLA"
- Brothers keep meeting each other without knowing their relationship and still help each other
- The Grand reunion in the end with Dharam Paji in a helpless state looking at his younger siblings

- Supariwala as "Raabat" who comes to the "Khoofia Hawaai Adda" and is willing to buy the Natraj Ki Moorti for "Chaalis Laakh Dallar"
- Neetu Singh just grown up to start her heroine avatar – though Rikcshawala released earlier – we still felt her to be Baby & Ravindra Kapoor as Usman Bhai Batliwala makes an impact like he did in the earlier movie Caravan
- Finally the train running over Ajit in white & his son Imtiaz (Roopesh on screen) seated dejected.

The above memories suggest not talking about the star cast of the movie. But what baffled me was the acceptance levels of audience for a similar plot written earlier by the same duo for "Zanzheer" which released about 6 months before this and the movie was still running and crossed silver jubilee and YKB too completed its silver jubilee – though similar plots, the treatment was different – if one points out that Seeta Aur Geeta too did bumper business as female version of Ram Aur Shyam – but here the gap was of 6 years while between YKB and Zanzheer it was only 6 months. Excellent songs helped the movie in a big way.

The plot was very straight forward and well known. Parents of 3 boys get killed and the 3 boys get separated and only the elder one wants to take revenge on the person who killed his parents. That is his single minded obsession. All 3 grow up in different situations and the family song helps them to come together and finish off the man who killed the parents of the 3 boys. Overall a very well made movie with interesting situations in the movie – e.g. the fight between Shetty and Dharam Paji is one sided – all he says is "Martin Ladki Ko Chod Do" & Shetty says "Chup Bay Gochu Baitkar Daaru Pee" & just 8 punches from Dharam Paji completely baffles Shetty who is on the floor. Song situations are also very interesting with an unknown character sings one line "I love you" in the "Oh Meri Soni" song & the background music when some stones roll from the mountain down – captured beautifully. Here are the songs for you.

- https://www.youtube.com/watch?v=YuqQ0WgNM0o... ;

Cheers
Laksh KV

November 08, 1968

"AULAD"

Dear Friends:

It was today i.e. on the 8th of November 1968, 55 years ago, this Kundan Kumar's movie called "AULAD" released – the movie did average business and not considered a hit. I recall seeing this movie during X'mas vacation of the same year at KOHINOOR Cinema Dadar – which was a very ordinary cinema hall with no AC but stall ticket was priced at a princely sum of Rs. 2.50 per ticket. We 3 brothers have seen quite a few movies in this hall that includes "HUM SUB CHOR HAIN", "GUIDE", "JOHNY MERA NAAM", "SHAGIRD" & 'ANARI" to name a few. It was next to the main cinema halls (not in terms of distance) and many movies have celebrated Silver Jubilee runs. We loved the movie though it was very predictable and at that age Mehmood made a big impact on us – he acted as a foreign returned character "Chamanlal Charlie Singapori" that falls for a village girl played by Aruna Irani. Chitragupt's music was very pleasing and the one on Mehmood and Aruna Irani was very good "JODI HAMARI JAMEGA KAISAY JAANI" – Chitragupt brand of music normally is very pleasant & soothing. The main cast of the movie is here under:

- Jeetendra
- Babita
- Sujit Kumar
- Mehmood
- Aruna Irani
- Nasir Hussain
- Manmohan Krishna
- Manmohan
- Jeevan
- Sulochana
- Achla Sachdev &

- Helan

The plot revolved around a rich Zamndiar Manmohan Krishna whose son gets lost and to avoid the shock for his wife, he approaches a poor villager – Nasir Hussain who has 2 sons – to save his wife's life, he parts with his younger son who grows to become Jeetendra. The elder brother while growing goes to meet his younger brother and both enjoy Diwali but the elder one is mistaken for a petty thief and is beaten up by his own dad and he runs away. Once, the kids grows up, slowly Jeetendra gets to know that he is not the real son and he in fact belongs to a very poor family. There is Jeevan, who tries to exploit the situation and position Manmohan to be the original lost kid. Everything gets sorted out and the wrong doers get punished. The soulful music was the real highlight for music lovers. Here are the songs for you.

- https://www.youtube.com/watch?v=qUCcUcCsLfw ;
- https://www.youtube.com/watch?v=SDEM9iddWZE ;
- https://www.youtube.com/watch?v=fdPfeX4nJtk ;
- https://www.youtube.com/watch?v=Jwpsn9GzL0A ;
- https://www.youtube.com/watch?v=1ZSvfQkVqd0 ;

Cheers
Laksh KV

November 07, 1969

"ARADHANA & JIGRI DOST"

Dear Friends:

It was today 54 years ago – i.e. on November 07, 1969 – a new era began – a phenomenon was recognized and what a Super-stardom he achieved is something that we folks who grew up in the 60s and 70s have seen – the younger generations can only read about it and look at the archives. Yes, it was a BIG day for "Rajesh Khanna" aka Kaka whose one of the biggest hit movies called "ARADHANA" that spiralled him into a different world was released. Though, a few weeks ago another hit movie of Kaka called "ITTEFAQ" was released and paved the way for his super-stardom, it was Shakti Samanta's "Aradhana" that really gave the impetus and push for a young, handsome actor to make a mark in the film industry. And the foot-prints he left allow us to recall and relive those golden days over and over again. "Pahadi" raag specialist SD Burman da created some great magic in the songs department with songs like "KORA KAAGAZ THA YEH MANN MERA", "ROOP TERA MASTANA", OH MERE SAPNON KI RANI KAB AAYEGI TU" "GUNGUNA RAHE HAIN BHAUREN", "BAAGON MEIN BAHAAR HAI", "CHANDA HAI TU" & above all "SAFAL HOGI TERI ARADHANA". The treatment given by the makers and directors of this movie was simply outstanding and it touched the entire nation and this movie ran and ran never to stop almost – just imagine it did 100 weeks run in place like Madras (called that way then) where the majority of the crowd was not comfortable with the language. That was the impact the movie created. The hero was relatively new – not exactly unknown given that "Raaz", "Baharon Ke Sapne", "Aurat" & "Ittefaq" had already happened. He did not look like a cute chocolate faced hero, nor was a strong "He-man" kind of a Hero, in fact he looked different and nice notwithstanding the pimples that had subsided from his cheeks leaving some marks but the way he could wink and raise his eyebrows – enough for all the female hearts to miss a beat. That was the impact – some of you may be wondering how I am praising Kaka when I was not a big fan of his then – that is the maturity that has come in over a lot of years and having seen closely how this phenomenon took the industry by storm, it would be unjust on my part if I do not share what I know. However, at a personal level there was no agenda to see this movie at my level though it was Diwali vacation time – the attitude was when a bigger movie is releasing the same day called "JIGRI DOST", who will go to see an odd pair? Be that as it may, that very day me and my brother had gone to visit our cousins in Thane and then from there we went to meet our Maasi at Mulund and were surprised to find our Maasa had taken off and was helping our Maasi to make "Diwali" sweets – we both felt we were at the right place at the right time and had the opportunity to taste all the good stuff that were getting prepared. Lovely day having met a lot of people that day, we both took a Harbour line train to Koliwada then (now Guru Tej Bahadur Nagar) around 930 PM post dinner at Maasi's place. It was a bit chill in the train and there was a Maharashtrian family in the train travelling with a tiny tot who was just a few month old kid sleeping in the lap of his mom. Suddenly, all the movents of the kid stopped and all the family members started weeping and were doing their bit to revive the kid. My brother felt that the kid was struggling in the cold and just got off his seat and went and started rubbing the child's foot vigorously – that generated some warmth due to friction and slowly the child woke up – that family was eternally thankful to the 2 of us as soon I too joined my brother. I am sure the kid must be a big man somewhere at the age of 54+!!! Well now coming to the cast of Aradhana:

- Ashok Kumar
- Sharmila Tagore
- Rajesh Khanna
- Sujit Kumar
- Madan Puri
- Farida Jalal
- Ashit Sen
- Manmohan
- Master Chikkoo (same kid who acted in Sadhu Aur Shaitan)
- Pahadi Sanyal
- Abhi Bhattacharya &
- Dulari

The plot revolved around one Air force Pilot played by Kaka who falls in love with Sharmila Tagore and they decide to get married and do so in a temple and there is a photographer who clicks them. Later during one rainy night, "ROOP

TERA MASTANA" happens and to Sharmila's bad luck, her Hero goes on a mission and his flight crashes and he dies. To top it Sharmila is in the family way – thanx to that one rainy night – our Heroes and Villains hit the Bull's eye almost always at the first attempt!!! More misfortune awaits our Heroine as her dad dies out of shock and then she finds a Good Samaritan who helps her to have the child delivered and also places the child into an "Anath Ashram" for just one day and wants to do the adoption formally on the following day. But unfortunately for her, someone else picks that child and with some luck on her side, our heroine manages to be the governess of that child in that rich house-hold. Then years roll and "CHANDA HI TU, MERA SURAJ HI TU" happens – but then there is an unwelcome guest in the house who happens to be the Maalikin's brother – Manmohan, who eyes our heroine. He finds an opportue day and does his job but the little boy who returns from school breaks open the door and comes inside and with his scissors kills Manmohan and the real mother of the child takes the blame on herself and goes thru a life sentence. Once she comes out, she gets the shelter from the jailor who has a chirpy daughter Farida Jalal and the 2 ladies hit it off very well. Now, this young girl is in love with another pilot from Air force – no prizes for guessing – it is Kaka again and Sharmila sees a lot of her hubby in him and the situations keep repeating. Eventually, the son manages to lay his hand on his mom's diary and gets to know the reality which his mom did not want him to know. The finale is when the son gets an award and invites his mom to the stage to receive the same from her and Ashok Kumar feels very familiar to see young Kaka whose dad he knew. A good movie that really helped Kaka in a big way and Shakti Samanta commenced making more meaningful movies. I saw this movie much later during summer vacation at Broadway along with my 2 brothers and loved the movie. Here are the songs for you in one solitary link:

- https://www.youtube.com/watch?v=ql1-jjEPErw... ;

The second movie is 'JIGRI DOST" – produced by Dhoondy and Sunderlal Nahata & directed by Ravikanth Nagaich – the movie had pretty peppy music by Laxmikant Pyarelal & was launched as a big banner movie that guaranteed success and all components in the movie – but this movie was very average as it ran for 14 weeks where as a Silver Jubilee was expected. I did not see this movie when released but did see on TV in bits and pieces – honestly it could not hold my interest for too long. As an SJ fan, I used to fight with my brother who was an ardent LP fan – but here I kept saying that SD Burman was better etc. My classmate Easwar was again a big fan of LP and Jeetendra, who used to be my good friend and then he himself started saying "We both are Jigri Dosts". The star cast of the movie is as under:

- Jeetendra in a dual role
- Mumtaz
- Komal aka Poonam Sinha
- Agha
- KN Singh
- Jagdeep
- Nirupa Roy &
- Aruna Irani

The plot was kind of predictable that happens when we have dual role by the Hero – confusion, exchanging places or too much of misunderstandings and so on. This is exactly why the movie could not do the desired business. However, songs were well received by people and here are the songs for you.

- https://www.youtube.com/watch?v=l9ySNwff7SM ;

Cheers
Laksh KV

November 03, 1972

"SEETA AUR GEETA & GAON HAMARA SHEHAR TUMHARA"

Dear Friends:

It was today 51 years ago on November 03 1972, two contrasting movies released – one a super-duper hit and the other a big flop. I am talking of "SEETA AUR GEETA" (the super-hit movie from the Sippy Khandan) & of "GAON HAMARA SHEHAR TUMHARA" (the big flop from the shop Rajendra Kumar household).

We friends of Jagdish Niwas, had a ritual on every Diwali day to see a movie & both these movies were released on Diwali day. The ritual used to be get up early morning, have Ganga Snaan, wear new dress, eat Diwali goodies and flaunt our new dress with all in the building and around in that area. This would be pretty early and being all Madraasis, we would have very limited crackers to burst and 50% would have been done the previous night and the next morning the balance. After finishing, we all would look for the unburnt crackers from the serial lot for us to fire with an Agarbatti in one hand and throw the little cracker in the air. By 915 all of us would get back home for a quick or an early lunch and be done with by 10 am.

Then all the boys of our building would go walking to some cinema hall and in this particular year, it was a walk from Sion Koliwada to Badal Cinema via Matunga Atheletic Club, to the "Z" Bridge and go to the western side of Matunga and then walk for another 10 minutes to reach Badal, Bijlee, Barkha Cinema halls. While Badal had heavy crowds for "Seeta Aur Geeta" the neighbouring hall Bijli was going almost empty as it was screening "Gaon Hamara Shehar Tumhara". So about half a dozen of us had a nice walk and were happy that we had done advance booking and in we went to see the movie which started on time (no tension like the maker's next movie Sholay where multiple halls shared one print on day 1) and as we saw all of us said "Arre – this is female version of Ram Aur Shyam" and still people were lapping it up. When Hema Malini rescues a boy who loses money by playing cards – we felt it was the same "Z" bridge which we crossed over to reach our destination. Post Guddi, we had all become big Asrani fans and he had a small role of a Doctor who tries to help the delivery of the twin girls and the delivery happens before he reaches the venue. Still money is offered to him and his instant reaction "Haaa... Iski Kya Zaroorat Thi!!!" he takes the money & immediately changes "Haaa.. Iski Toh Bahut Zaroorat Thi!!!". Satyen Kappu plays the henpecked husband of Manorama and when she asks in her authoritative voice "Aaj Ek Tarreq Hai?"...the response from Kappu "Haan... kal ikattis tha toh aaj Ek hi hoga"... Sanjeev Kumar sees a smart Hema Malini in his rear view and waves at her & realizes she is inside the car and applies emergency break out of shock and there is this Parsi Bava who did not have any indication of this shock treatment and bangs his car from behind... and gets into an argument ... Bava's name is Rushtom and in that cameo role he fights with Sanjeev Kumar and his wife from inside advises him to just ignore and move on as not much damage to either of the vehicles and their youngest kid is with Rushtom – Sanjeev Kumar listens to all the blah blah of the Bava and then just shows some affection towards the lil kid and the Bawa retorts "MARO NALLO RUSHTOM CHAY" in typical Bawa style. Then the confident Hema Malini comes in and argues with Rushtom and makes one basic point that "We applied break in our Car and not yours!!!" and indicates to Sanjeev Kumar to move on. Once back in the car, Sanjeev Kumar having seen a meek Hema, now is flabbergasted at the confident girl sitting next to him and starts questioning about his previous meeting with her look-alike and he gets spontaneous responses from the confident girl and he exclaims "AAPKA JAWAB NAHI" & she retorts "PAR AAPKE BAHUT SAVAAL HAIN"!!! You have Rupesh Kumar in his elements yelling "DAAMODAR KEERTI" & when he goes to the vegetable market he asks pointing towards Baingan asks "YEH KYA HAI?" The vendor (who too played dual role in the movie – which we discovered during our subsequent visit to see the movie) says 'BAINGAN HAI" – so Roopesh says "BAINGAN AISA HOTA HAI?"... in the climax scenes Dharam Paji says "SHER KA BAAP AAGAYA" and hammers Shetty in his den. The dialogue by Roopesh Kumar "BAK NAHI RAHA, FARMA RAHA HOON"... I was reminded of the lines from "JEEVAN MRITUE" where one of the unknown faces says the same lines. Loved the way Dharampaji said "PIYUNGA NAHI TOH JIYUNGA KAISAY" - It was a very entertaining movie though we knew what was coming but it was the treatment to the script by the talented Sippy – somehow, my personal feeling is that both movies "Seeta Aur Geeta" &

"Sholay" from the same banner had just about average music wrt songs though the background music in the latter was outstanding. The star cast of the movie is:

- Dharmendra
- Hema Malini
- Sanjeev Kumar
- Manorama
- Roopesh Kumar
- Satyen Kappu
- Kamal Kapoor
- Master Ravi etc

The plot was about twin girls separated at the time of birth – one meek and one smart and due to situations, they get exchanged when grown up as adults and that creates a lot of hilarious situations and all the wrong doers get punished. But it can't sustain for long and the cat has to come out of the bag but everything is settled well in the end with the theory of "Truth Prevails"... Here are some of the songs for you from "Seeta Aur Geeta"

- https://www.youtube.com/watch?v=LJfISoHC6Ac ;
- https://www.youtube.com/watch?v=foMaO-Kwdno ;
- https://www.youtube.com/watch?v=j0oYdTHZhyQ ;
- https://www.youtube.com/watch?v=z8yx5iJlOcQ ;
- https://www.youtube.com/watch?v=8Jzyd6EY15A ;
- https://www.youtube.com/watch?v=KGzdhOZ2IzA ;

"GAON HAMARA SHEHAR TUMHARA" – let me talk about this movie – as I did go and see the movie all alone at Bijli Cinema – next to Badal where "Seeta Aur Geeta" was still going full. Ticket was easily available and I went as a cinema buff – having seen earlier movies like "Pehchan", "Ek Bechara" etc. Where a Dhoti clad hero - Rajendra Kumar, comes to a city and how tough it is for him and this one was no different and how his relatives treat him like a servant. I knew exactly what was coming – all the people of the house are tough with him except the maid played by Rekha who has sympathy towards the hero who is in deep trouble. The song "EK PYAR KARNE WALE NAY EK PYAR KARNE WALE SAY, YE POOCHA KE PYAR KAHAN

REHTA HI" is very melodious – but as expected in the movie suddenly things turn around for our Hero as he possesses a Lottery ticket that has won the first prize and one can see how the entire family lobbies around him and makes things good for him. Our Hero still does not see the cunning people around him but the maid who is sympathetic towards him educates him and eventually, he fights them and leaves them happily to be with his love. Nothing new and fresh was offered in this movie. Rajendra Kumar's decline had started already and there was no pull factor. The golden wig with a closed crop look did not help and it looked completely out of place for a Gaon Ka Chora. Nothing much to write about except that having seen the movie, I could see how Dharam Paji had been so consistent in his position and the Jubilee Kumar had slid by then. The songs are here for you.

- https://www.youtube.com/watch?v=MiKVgJs9N48 ;
- https://www.youtube.com/watch?v=duu3grr1Oiw ;
- https://www.youtube.com/watch?v=BZyh_HwfZm8 ;
- https://www.youtube.com/watch?v=IpjbOZQKjck ;

Cheers
Laksh KV

November 02, 1973

"JWAR BHATA"

Folks:

It was today 50 years ago, i.e. on November 02, 1973, one of the average grossers called "JWAR BHATA" released. It was not a super-duper hit but just about passed muster. For all Dharam Paji fans it was fun watching the movie and given that I was an 18 year old employed student, money was no more a constraint and Rupam Cinema was my favourite hideout – I entered the Cinema Hall on my way back from my office on the very first day for 615 PM show. Though, I was not an LP fan, I still liked the music in this movie and was very keen to see if the movie does well. But it was a bit slow on the uptake but Dharam paji had a pull factor though in that era Saira Banu was considered a bit of a "Panwati" and the movies of Saira Banu with almost all heroes did not do well from 1973. Pocket Maar, Saazish, International Crook, Chaitali & later Zameer, Daman Aur Aag – all did not do well at the Box Office. This movie Jwar Bhata, I really enjoyed though it looked odd for a 38 year old hero having some kid sisters and then claiming to be 27. That apart, songs like "DAL ROTI KHAO PRABHU KE GUN GAAO" & "TURU RURU TURU RURU TERA MERA PYAR SHURU" were very enjoyable. Here is the star cast for you:

- Dharmendra
- Saira Banu
- Nazir Hussain
- Sujit Kumar
- Jeevan
- Shammi
- Sundar
- Jayshri T
- Meena T
- Randhir
- Baby Guddu

- Baby Pinky
- Baby Sabira
- Shivraj &
- Rajendranath

The plot was that of a rich sethji – Nasir Hussain who objected to his son getting married to a poor girl and the son dies soon after his poor wife delivers a son. This boy grows up to become the Hero Dharam Paji who calls himself Billu Seth... He runs a small time dhaba kind of joint where he feeds people "Daal Roti". When the rich Sethji gets old, he tries to search for his son and fails but gets a secretary Saira Banu to look after him. She connects with Dharam and they fall in love and you guessed it right, Dharampaji is the grandson of Sethji. But there is a "Chandal Chowkdi" that wants to take advantage of the ailing Sethji and tries to play games to evict the Hero and Heroine so that they can take over the property. But good has to prevail and all is well in the end. Here are some songs for you:

- https://www.youtube.com/watch?v=fT7vHxsluMM ;
- https://www.youtube.com/watch?v=8jKWOZev09w ;
- https://www.youtube.com/watch?v=AiN-eAB9rGw ;
- https://www.youtube.com/watch?v=nE7pJsNwnJo ;

Cheers

Laksh KV

November 01, 1968

"BAAZI"

Dear Friends:

It was today November 01 1968 – 55 years ago the average grosser "BAAZI" saw the light of the day. It was directed by Moni Bhattacharya and music was composed by Kalyanji Anandji – it was in the category of "Murder Mystery Thriller". Since, I have till date not seen the movie, I have nothing much to say except that as a Dharam Paji fan, I wanted the movie to do well but it only ran for 12 weeks and hence not considered a hit and since it ran for over 10 weeks, it was considered an average grosser. All I know about the movie is Dharam Paji played a Police Officer and also the song "AA MERE GALE LAG JAA" which was a hit number. Needless to say as a class IX student... there was no money for seeing such movies – only poster gazing was allowed for us. Here, I would invite my friends who have seen the movie to enlighten all about this movie. The cast of the movie is:

- Dharmendra
- Waheed Rehaman
- Nasir Hussain
- Chand Usmani
- Helan
- Ulhas
- Shammi
- Manmohan
- Keshto Mukherjee
- Pinchoo Kapoor
- Jagdish Raj &
- Johny Walker & Mehmood

The plot is as under:

This was a suspense thriller where in Dharmendra plays a cop and solves a mysterious case where his sweetheart played by Waheeda Rehaman is also a suspect. It is quite a Masala entertainer wherein a dead body buried is missing when it is reopened. Very predictable indeed.

- https://www.youtube.com/watch?v=X3qx56ZblFc ;
- https://www.youtube.com/watch?v=KAFFBRy8bIo ;
- https://www.youtube.com/watch?v=xsw715O1g6Q ;
- https://www.youtube.com/watch?v=xsw715O1g6Q ;
- https://www.youtube.com/watch?v=ni841X11GDE ;
- https://www.youtube.com/watch?v=zGUFPI20h7s ;

Cheers
Laksh KV

October 10, 1969

"ITTEFAQ"

Folks:

"ITTEFAQ" – released today 54 years ago on October 10 1969. Though people say that it was "Aradhana" that commenced Kaka's career skywards, I would say almost one month before "Aradhana" this off-beat movie from the BR Chopra banner with direction by Yash Chopra set the ball rolling for the Supersatar to be. Kaka built a great relationship in later years with Yash Chopra. The movie was not the standard one and hence termed off-beat – movie was "Song less" and the foundation for a big career was laid on this day 54 years ago and the way Kaka grew was something only people who were part of that era can empathize with. Relatively unknown, but the Chopra banner had the pull to attract crowd and they did it even after a decade when they made "Insaaf Ka Tarazoo" with 2 new actors in Deepak Parashar and Raj Babbar – and still got a hit for the difference they could bring on to the table. Ittefaq – means coincidence and I guess the Chopras were fascinated by this word, for in their earlier movie "Aadmi Aur Insaan" this term had a big place – every time Mumtaz bumped into the Hero Dharminder, she would say "Ittefaq" and the song "Zindagi Ittefaq Hai" was a legendary one. Well folks, as a class X student and no pocket money, there was no hope of seeing this movie but my friends Balakrishnan Narayan and Viswanathan Krishnan did see this movie and went ga-ga over it. I eventually saw as a college student when this movie had its re-run at Bandra Talkies, to make my good friend Bedi happy, I saw the movie and simply loved it. Exceptionally handled everything – be it the narrative, screen play, the suspense element and the eventual decision of ending her life by Nanda was just outstanding. Sujit Kumar too made a great impact in this movie and when he took the lighter from the table and put in his pocket, proved to be his biggest error & he got trapped. The main actors of this movie were:

- Rajesh Khanna
- Nanda
- Bindu
- Iftikar
- Sujit Kumar &

- Madan Puri

The plot revolves around an unhappy couple, where the hubby is a painter and married to a rich lady and they have their tiffs and once she spoils her hubby's painting & the enraged hubby screams at her that he would kill her for this act. Totally disturbed, he steps out of the house and returns to find his wife dead and he is the prime suspect and his sister-in-law Bindu claims that she was aware of their fights and only Kaka could have killed her sister. He claims that he did not kill her and during trial, they find that he needs some psychological examination and is retained in jail. But he escapes one night and lands in Nanda's house at gunpoint. She is scared and gives him shelter and the police continue their hunt of Kaka. At some point, Kaka feels bad for Nanda and they commence to talk like friends and when policemen come to her house, Kaka hides himself but finds a dead body in the loo. He realizes that Nanda's hubby is dead while she claims that he had gone to Kolkotta. The Inspector and his senior continue to hang in there and at some point by mistake the Inspector takes the cigarette lighter left behind by Kaka in the sitting area and keeps in his pocket. Now Kaka realizes that there is some foul-play wrt the death of Nanda's hubby and he gets a chance to prove the involvement of the Police Inspector and Nanda in the murder of her hubby and the police inspector goes to jail and Nanda kills herself. In the mean-time Kaka's wife actually gets killed by her own sister Bindu and that is found by the senior cop wherein he finds a piece of jewellery stuck in the painting. Overall, a lovely movie that did over 100 days of successful run in Mumbai. No songs to share!!!

Cheers

Laksh KV

October 30, 1970

"BACHPAN & JAHAN PYAR MILEY"

Folks:

It was today i.e. on October 30 1970 – 53 years ago, 2 movies released and both were average grossers. Going in alphabetic order they are "BACHPAN" & "JAHAN PYAR MILEY". Again it was during Diwali vacation but the catch was that I was in class XI, so had limitations and having not done well in the first terminal exams, it was tricky asking for money to see movies. Still I wanted to see "JPM" for 2 reasons – first for the Heroine – Hema Malini and second for the music composers Shankar Jaikishan. So, let me go thru the movies one by one – memories are that I wanted JPM to be a hit and was indifferent about Bachpan.

"Bachpan" had the following actors playing pivotal roles:

- Sanjeev Kumar
- Tanuja
- Keshto Mukherjee
- Mukri
- Sachin
- Jr. Mehmood &
- Master Alankar

The movie had good music by the duo Laxmikant Pyarelal with some catchy numbers and the plot revolved around Sanjeev Kumar, who loses his entire family in an accident and takes to drinking but to make a living, he continues to sell toys and sing the popular song "AYA RE KHILONE WALA, KHEL KHILONE LEKE AAYARE". The three Masters, Sachin, Jr. Mehmood and Alankar are fond of Sanjeev Kumar and there is Tanuja who sells flowers & is in love with Sanjeev Kumar silently. Sanjeev Kumar gets the blame for killing someone that he never did by a smuggler who takes advantage of the fact that the hero was drunk and had no recall of what happened earlier. But the 3 kids are aware of his innocence and help him come out clean and our hero realizes that there is no point in living a life only thinking of past and eventually gets ready to settle down with Tanuja. Here are some of the songs for you.

- https://www.youtube.com/watch?v=_TsWSQbHtvM ;
- https://www.youtube.com/watch?v=oa5rg6LHKv0 ;
- https://www.youtube.com/watch?v=vY4lOxmc2Do ;
- https://www.youtube.com/watch?v=ewc_04h6DVg ;
- https://www.youtube.com/watch?v=uqZmtiKeRhY ;

"Jahan Pyar Miley" – this was the name that came to my mind when I got to know about the director of the movie "Lekh Tandon's" demise six years back. This movie, I saw at Rupam Cinema on the very first day but 6 PM show and managed to get an extra ticket on par i.e. Rs. 2/-. I was thrilled and was waiting for the movie to start but was seated in the 2nd row from front and would see a bit of compressed heads of all the characters as the seat also was towards the corner and not in the middle. But who cared... it was important to see the movie and as the movie started I was excited and right in the beginning, we have our hero travelling by train and in no time there is an accident and many die but our Hero loses memory but he gets back to normal soon. Well, there are people who claim that the hero belongs to their religion – Hindus, Muslims and Christians – the thing I vaguely recall is that the Hero though, does not recall anything is able to read French and gets kicked about it. I did feel it had the theme of National Integration – combined with some great songs composed by the SJ duo really made my Diwali that year as a SSC student. The main actors of the movie were:

- Shashi Kapoor
- Hema Malini
- Nazir Hussain
- Nadira
- Jeevan
- Helan
- Zeb Rehman
- Naaz &
- Anjali Kadam

Here are the songs for you :

- https://www.youtube.com/watch?v=_HHb2kqDOcg ;
- https://www.youtube.com/watch?v=2EK1UmrLQCI ;
- https://www.youtube.com/watch?v=u0Y5GmQxvFI ;
- https://www.youtube.com/watch?v=AN0hCeK_MHw ;
- https://www.youtube.com/watch?v=f2tkBVdurj4 ;
- https://www.youtube.com/watch?v=HDH7T2ZJ984 ;

Cheers

Laksh KV

October 29, 1971

"CARAVAN"

Dear Friends:

The hit movie from the year 1971 – released today i.e. on October 29 1971 – 52 years ago – made under the banner of TV Films – Tahir Hussain – Yes, I am talking about "CARAVAN" – top entertainer and big time money spinner – has a lot of lovely memories for me. I was in college as FY student and studying in Bandra had its own advantages. From the station to college was a good walk for about 15 minutes and as we used to pass Bandra Talkies on the linking road side, we would walk a bit slow and wait to see if some foreign brand cars would pass by and invariably it would be some big star inside. It was very interesting for us those days to see who can be seen!!! When this movie released it was vacation (Diwali) time and for me as an energetic NCC student and who qualified to be an Under Officer, it was religion to go for parade during winter – early in the morning and thanx to my employed brother (who is sadly no more now) who worked for Asian Paints, he would give me a monthly pocket money of Rs. 10/- that was a lot then. So, we all had decided to see the movie that was also running in Rupam. But my brother had a bit of a problem to reach Rupam in time for the evening show and he suggested we see the movie at Sahakar that was easier for him to reach for a 615 PM show while at Rupam it was 545 PM show. So the tickets were done well in advance, and I was very excited on that day. My bro had also told us to book one extra ticket for his friend Mahadevan by name. So my second brother and me were at Sahakar Cinema by 530 PM and were waiting for these 2 colleagues from Asian Paints to arrive and they did come by 610 PM and we had the habit of seeing from the first slide of "No Smoking" but could not take panga with the guy who gave the princely sum of Rs.10/- as pocket money. Well, we entered and soon the movie started and after the initial lines "PHANOOS JISKI HIFAZAT HAVA KAREN, WOH SHAMMA KYA BHUJE JISE ROSHAN KHUDA KAHAY" started the banner TV Films... uffff... soon my 2nd brother exclaimed, this scene is from Teesri Manzil, when the car has a fall from the hill top and I said "No bro, filmy people will not re-use and are not knajoos" – but he was right. Every song was a treat and every character was brilliant in this movie – take Jeetendra as Mohan, Asha Parekh as Sunita (Sunita was the common name of the heroine in this banner) -, Aruna Irani as Nisha, Madan Puri as Meethalal Totha, Ravindra Kapoor as Johny, Kishan Mehta as Rajan & Mehmood Jr. As Monty....not to forget Anwar Ali as Bhola (looks so much like Mehmood). Madan Puri for a change was not a negative character but when he shows a snake from his "Pithara" and says "ISKA KAATA PAANI NAHI MAANGTA"... we thought he has come into his own but were mistaken. With a lot of punch he says "NISHA NAACHEGI TUB NA?" – Ravindra Kapoor saying 'SACHI BAAT KEHNAY MEIN JOHNY BHAGWAN SAY BHI NAHI DARTA"... The climax scene had a red van with number 354 (and at times it used to pass thru our road in Sion and we all would feel good filmy van on our road) – the error in the movie – the bus "Toofan Mail" that Jeetendra drove had the number "5159" but in one scene it had "2191" and I felt happy finding this error!!! Anwar Ali played the admirer of Aruna Irani and looks abnormal and when a stranger (Subodh Mukherji – Theatre Wala) comes to meet Madan Puri who is the head of the Caravan – he somehow meets Anwar Ali first, who suspecting him to be some negative person throws a knife at him which he defends with a shuttle bat – this is followed by a question from Anwar Ali "AAP KAUN THA?" and Subodh Mukherji responds by saying "MAIN THA NAHI MAIN HOON, AGAR YE CHAKOO LAGTA, TO THA HO JATA"... wow lots of memories – not just that once the college re-opened after the vacation, it was very tough to pass thru Bandra Talkies without entering and seeing the movie spending Re. 1/- - the movie ran for 100 days at Bandra Talkies. During the interval on the day of release, the lovely Samosas were heavenly & I had it for the first time, simply loved the experience. Till then we only used to have mini samosas in Irani Hotel with sauce – 6 of them in a plate for 30 paise – very tiny patti samos predominantly with onion fillings or Uduppi Samosas that were a bit big, but it had fillings including poha – but Punjabi Samosa – wah – developed the taste after this movie. Then we were regular at Sion Gurukripa from where the supply went to cinema halls like Rupam, Sharda, Sahakar and Broadway. It was a small shop which now is a restaurant for over 30 plus years. Extraordinary memories for me regarding this movie.

The plot is as under:

The movie is an out and out an action filled thriller. The plot revolves around a young woman, Sunita (Asha Parekh), her dad Mohandas (Murad) who detects out that his trusted employee, Rajan (Krishen Mehta), has been swindling money from him. On confrontation, Rajan kills him by throwing him out of the window of a multi-storied building but the entire thing is positioned as an accident or suicide. Rajan plays the confidence trick and manages to wed Mohandas's only daughter, Sunita. Sunita in a weaker moment agrees to the alliance with the "wrong" man, Rajan. Soon enough, Sunita finds out the truth. She realises that Rajan has hatched a plan with his girlfriend Monica (Helen) to get her out of the way. So she flees from the scene to find her father's old friend who can be trusted to be of help. On the way she finds safety with a group of performing nomadic community. She meets Mohan (Jeetendra), who is part of the nomadic clan and she is inclined towards him for support. But there is Nisha (Aruna Irani), who loves Mohan, and is ready to kill Sunita. Rajan continues to follow Sunita and eventually after some fights where police makes a delayed yet a timely entry to kill Rajan and all is well. Here are the songs for you.

- https://www.youtube.com/watch?v=OmLF3vNEH74... ;

Cheers
Laksh KV

October 26, 1973

"KASHMAKASH"

Dear Friends:

It was today 50 years ago i.e. on 26th October 1973, this average grosser called "KASHMAKASH" released. The movie created a lot of excitement for the people and belonged to the category of Murder Mystery. The banner was Delux Productions and directed by Feroz Chinoy – it was positioned as a slightly hot movie with some steamy bedroom scenes and that was enough for a Jr. B.Com, employed college going guy like me. It was a must see for me and I could exercise my influence and get both my brothers to join for a night show at Rupam. It was not easy for me for I had to go to college at 6 am (Morning College for employed) but the priorities were very clear. So on my way back from my office (Pentagon) which was also close to Rupam Cinema, I booked the tickets for the 3 of us and post dinner reached Rupam well in time in fact ahead of time as the previous show was still on. Finally, we parked ourselves in our seats and waited for the INR documentary to get over. The wait was always frustrating and all we were thinking of some steamy scenes... We brothers were totally fida over Shatrughan Sinha who actually sang in his own voice – the song "NA TU ITNI AAKAD CHAL RAASTA PAKKAD" with Asha Sachdev. Over all, we 3 were happy at the end of the movie but we knew it will not be a big hit. The star cast of the movie is as under:

- Feroz Khan
- Rekha
- Shatrughan Sinha
- Asha Sachdev
- Rehaman
- Padma Khnna
- Ramesh Deo
- Zeb Rehaman
- Ranjeet &
- IS Johar

The plot was interesting – Feroz Khan (FK) is happily married to Rekha and did not miss an opportunity to display his hairy chest with the hope of attracting the female audience but we guys were only looking at Rekha or Padma Khanna. At some point of time, Rekha leaves him alone to pay visit to her ailing mom who lives in a different city. Now FK is alone at home and in comes his friend Ramesh Deo and realizes his weakness and promises him total paisa vasool and in a weaker moment, FK succumbs and is about to spend the night with Padma Khanna (PK) who is a cabaret dancer – but as luck would have it, even before he can think of doing anything major to PK, he finds her murdered. Now FK is worried but there is IS Johar who wants to make the most out of the situation and blackmail whoever he can. The prime suspect to start with is Ranjeet who had an affair with PK and they decided to part ways but with a threat from Ranjeet that he would kill her. Now, here enters Shatrughna Sinha (SS) as the Police Officer who is entrusted the task of solving the mystery. SS continues to investigate and clears Ranjeet now all evidences point towards FK and also Rehaman who had given his flat to PK to stay. SS has his style and mannerisms and finally cracks the mystery and FK is cleared and is advised that not to fall prey to such things especially when he has such a good wife. The songs were very average by Kalyanji Anandji duo. Here are the songs for you.

- https://www.youtube.com/watch?v=Z3d99bdG6iI ;
- https://www.youtube.com/watch?v=JQ6i0vGvfmo ;
- https://www.youtube.com/watch?v=6eFjMSgt1EM ;
- https://www.youtube.com/watch?v=yzduLjcmOqc ;

Cheers

Laksh KV

October 25, 1968

"NIGHT IN LONDON"

Dear Friends:

It was today 55 years ago the flop movie "Night in London" released that was directed by Brij. All I can recall as a class IX student is, there was no hope of seeing the movie but my bench-mate A. Vijayan had seen this movie and kept telling how Biswajeet wore tight trousers and was going ga-ga over the songs – I would agree, the movie had some very catchy numbers but that probably could not help the movie to do good business. While I had a lot to write about the movie released one week before this "SUNGHARSH", but nothing much for this one. The star cast of the movie is as under:

- Mala Sinha
- Biswajeet
- Johny Walker
- Helan
- Madhumati
- Anwar Hussain &
- Shetty

Regarding plot, read on

Much against her wishes the Heroine, Mala Sinha leads a life of a criminal as her dad is in captive with some wrongdoers. She finds Biswajeet, another criminal and needless to say that they fall in love and then join hands to nab the wrongdoers and free up Mala Sinha's dad. Here are the songs for you in one single link:

- https://www.youtube.com/watch?v=Uct9rlsstrg

Cheers

Laksh KV

October 23, 1970

"HOLI AYEE RE"

Dear Friends:

It was today 53 years ago i.e. on October 23, 1970, a very average movie called "HOLI AYEE RE" released. When I had gone to see "Mastana", I saw the trailer of this movie at Rupam and what stood out for me were the songs – be it "MERI LOTTERY LAG JAANE KI BAARI HI" on Rajendranath or 'MERI TAMANNA", "HOLI AYEE RE" "TERE HASEEN BADAN MEIN" or "GIRNA NAHI HI GIRKE SAMBHALNA HI ZINDAGI" – well composed by Kalyanji Anandji. The movie was not a big hit but most people felt like seeing the movie after seeing the trailer mainly for the acting of Balraj Sahani and Mala Sinha. The star cast of the movie is as under:

- Mala Sinha
- Balraj Sahani
- Premendra
- Kumud Chugani
- Kanhaiya Lal
- Janki Das
- Dulhari
- Shatrughan Sinha &
- Rajendranath

Shatrughan Sinha was yet to make his mark in the industry but prior to this he did make an impact in "Khilona" where he played Bihari. Here he played a Police Officer and there was this Manoj Kumar look-alike in Premendra who had one more release "Duniya Kya Jaane" – may be a handful of more but did not make it big in the industry.

The plot was about Mala Sinha being ditched by a rich Zamindar's son (unknown actor to me) after making her pregnant. The rich Zamindar's son is approached by Balraj Sahani who plays Mala Sinha's brother to tie the knot but he refuses and they end up fighting and accidentally the rich son gets killed. Now, Mala Sinha loses her hubby to be and also her brother is behind the bars and to top it she is pregnant. Now, she has some exploiters, some sympathizers and eventually lands up as a Nurse at Premendra's hospital and brings up her son Shatrighan Sinha. Balraj Sahani after serving his sentence becomes a cycle rickshaw puller and earns the sympathy of Premendra. Eventually, all the loops are closed and all people meet and for comedy relief there is Rajendranath with his weakness for Lottery. Of late we don't hear the name of "Impala" car but in the Lottery ticket song there is a line "CAR-ON-MEIN EK CAR SUNI HAI CAR SUNI IMPALA" and this line was constantly sung by my class-mate KK Chandrasekhar aka Sekhar Krishnan – not sure if he recalls this. So here are the songs for you:

- https://www.youtube.com/watch?v=gI-bynT4W64 ;
- https://www.youtube.com/watch?v=2nHl9DCHMVM&t=14s ;
- https://www.youtube.com/watch?v=c2p8BJYzwp8 ;
- https://www.youtube.com/watch?v=udx1Wjqy7YY ;

Cheers
Laksh KV

October 24, 1969

"RAJA SAAB"

Dear Friends:

It was today 54 years ago i.e. on October 24 1969, this flop movie "RAJA SAAB" was released. It came with high expectations as the earlier movie by the same banner "JAB JAB PHOOL KHILEN" was a huge hit and the director repeated the same leading pair but this time they were not lucky enough. It was again Diwali vacation for me studying in class X, and me and my brother had gone to see "Arzoo" at Chitra for a matinee show and at that time we saw the trailer of "Raja Saab" and very much wanted to see the movie due to the earlier hit movie and also good songs. That was the time when Bill Lawrey's Australian team had come to India and on reaching home we got to know that Australians were doing very well in one of the local games and I think it was Indian University boys had to majorly do the leather hunt. Suraj Prakash was the Director of this movie which barely ran 7 weeks in Mumbai. The cast of the movie is as under:

- Nanda
- Shashi Kapoor
- Kamal Kapoor
- Shammi
- Agha
- Naaz &
- Rajendranath

The plot revolves around an orphan played by Shashi Kapoor who dreams to be a Prince, well depicted in the title song "RAJOO KA HAI EK KHWAAB, RAJU RAJA RAJA SAAB". He gets thrown away from the orphanage as he misbehaves with a Princess Nanda but falls in love with her big time - and he finds a job with a rich Prince – Kamal Kapoor. The Prince is so impressed by Shashi Kapoor that he tells the youngster to impersonate him and his Dream is about to come true. But in this role, he is expected to be difficult and insult the same Princess whom he loves. Like most Hindi movies, I would expect this one to have a happy ending with people expecting good to prevail. The movie had really some good songs composed by the duo of Kalyanji Anandji and here are the songs for you in one single link.

- https://www.youtube.com/watch?v=-wFOnKnMWJA

Cheers
Laksh KV

October 20, 1967

"RAM AUR SHYAM"

Dear Friends:

Fifty Six Years ago – wow – really long period it was today on the 20th October 1967, the mega-hit movie "Ram Aur Shyam" released. The movie was produced by B. Nagi Reddy and directed by Chanakya. It was earlier made in Telugu as "Ramudu Bheenudu" with NTR in the lead and later it was made in Tamil as "Enga Veettu Pillai" *ing MGR playing dual role. It was a hit in all 3 languages and coming to "Ram Aur Shyam", I have some memories and I will certainly share it. This movie too was around Deepawali that year and on October 18th we left for Bangalore by train – the 5 of us that included my parents and, we 3 brothers. We boys were to get off at Guntakkal where my Grandpa (Mom's dad) was to come to pick us up and take us by another train to Bangalaore. I still recall the telegram that my dad sent to my grandpa which read "Leaving Bombay 18th Janata, Meet Gundakkal Certain". So as planned our Grandpa was there to receive us and the train reached at some odd hour in the night and we said Bi to our parents who were heading to Madras and were to join us after a couple weeks. We brothers noticed Amma giving Rs. 300/- to my grandpa for any expense and also allow some movies, cricket matches etc. We had a long wait at Guntakkal for the Bangalore connecting train was to come only around 10 am in the morning and we had to find a bench where all of us could sit and spend the time. My grandpa found one gentleman wearing dhoti and occupying one full bench and was peacefully sleeping. So he woke him up and the man got up with a shock on his face and said "I just came at 1 O'clock" but somehow, my grandpa, a result-oriented man that he was, made him also sit with us and commenced conversation with him. He inquired about his family – he had 2 daughters one aged 9 and the other 2 and when he said that my grandpa said "Good Gap". After a long wait and sleeplessness, it was around 10 am we got into a train heading towards Bangalore and we had another old couple with their 5 year old grandson occupying the opposite seats. Again the chat commenced and my grandpa asked the man if that was his grandson and he proudly said yes and the next logical question he asked how many grand kids he had and the answer was "2".

With pride my grandpa said "Add 15 to it that is the number of grandkids I have and here are 3". That man gave a smile and the journey went on as we had "Puliogarai" that was homemade etc and by the time we reached it was around 5 PM and we were in Bangalore Central. But we had to reach Kengeri and that meant another few hours of wait to get the connecting train and by the time we got into that train and reached our home at Kengeri it was past 9 in the night. I was excited to meet my 2 year old cousin Bala Ganesh who was with his mom and his mom had delivered a baby girl Revati just a month plus back. So we were 5 grandkids with our grandparents in that small house but we were all looking forward to it. Grandpa kept the money given by Amma carefully in the cupboard. Soon there was a Duleep Trophy cricket match that was being played between Central Zone and South Zone. We boys told our grandpa that we wanted to see the match but he resisted saying it is very costly and there is no money etc. But, we were not going to take it that way and pointed out that Amma has given money for our expenses. So very reluctantly, we were taken on the first day of the match. Jaisimha was the captain of South Zone team while Hanumant Singh was the skipper for Central Zone. South Zone commenced batting after winning the toss with Kundaran and Rajgopal opening with Kailash Ghatani bowling tirelessly thru out the day. Both openers scored 50 plus and one down Abbas Ali Baig came he made 40+ followed by skipper Jaismiha who took a lot of time to walk from the dressing room to the crease. Played with a lot of style and hit a six of Joshi and eventually got out to him for a stylish 47. Subramaniam struggled to put the bat to the ball but hung around and managed 46 and South Zone folded for 331 with Joshi taking 4 wickets and Ghatani 3 but Durani went wicket-less while skipper Hanumant Singh scalped one. Central Zone scored 157 all out with Durani making 61 – well but we saw only the Day 1 when South Zone were 250 + for 6 wickets. We had carried food and had some fruits too. The ticket cost Rs.2.50 and my grandpa announced that Rs. 10/- daily and train fare etc is not affordable – so no question of seeing the match on the remaining days. Unfortunately, there was no radio commentary too – only some time slots were there for commentary in Kannada – so it was a struggle but we realized that there were a lot of common words with Marathi. Be that as it may South Zone won the match on the basis of their lead in the first innings while the match ended in a draw.

Now, we rebel boys were insisting on seeing movies and grandpa was very smart, he took us to a nearby tent one night and we were seated on benches and we all saw some Tamil movie that had KR Vijaya and had no idea about the actors and the cost of per person ticket was 50 paise here. But we were not satisfied and we demanded that we all go to see "Ram Aur Shyam" and my late brother pointed out that the movie was running in "Sangam" Cinema near Bangalore station. Luckily here our Maasi Vijaya Ganeshan too wanted to join us for the movie and when she too requested my grandpa had to relent and so one day we all decided to go 5 grand kids, one Maasi and 2 grandparents – we set and from Kengeri to Bangalore Central by train and then a walk to Sangam Cinema – now the 2 kids 1 of 2 yrs and the other of 40 days did not need tickets but the 2 year old Bala Ganeshan occupied one seat till someone claimed that seat and then my younger bro shared my seat – wah and today Bala Ganeshan is a 6feet plus 58 year old man living in the US of A. During the movie he slept off and fell off the chair and I got fired by my Maasi but from that point I was more careful. But all of us enjoyed the movie thoroughly and I vividly recall my Maasi saying during the movie itself "Fimfare Award" when Shyam came on screen and acted with confidence totally opposite to the character of Ram. Well, she was so right and the award did go Dilip Kumar's way. We also loved Pran's acting besides the huge leg piece of Chicken that Dilip Kumar ate and topping it with Rasgullas. The hangover of the movie was so strong that on way back I felt Dilip Kumar had entered inside me and was trying to rattle some dialogues of Dilip Kumar like "गजेंद्र बाबू मुझे मत मारो" – Lovely memories of the movie that again had good songs penned by Shakheel and composed by Naushad with assorted singers like Mohd Rafi, Mahendra Kapoor, Lata and Asha. We also realized much later that one song by Lata Mangeshkar "मैंने कब तुम से कहा था की मुझे प्यार करो" was not part of the movie but we, the loyal listeners of Vividh Bharti on return to Bombay heard this song on radio and that was exactly the time Vividh Bharti became commercial and the first ad we heard was "Phillips Milk of Magnesia Ki Goliyan"… lots of memories and the most funniest was we created a story that this movie is being made in English called "John & George" & it is still being made !!!! – Now the movie had good performances from most of the actors and the names are as under:

- Dilip Kumar in a dual role
- Waheeda Rehaman
- Mumtaz
- Pran
- Nazir Hussain
- Mukri

- Leela Mishra
- Baby Farida
- Nirupa Roy
- Kahaiyalal &
- Raj Kishore

The plot revolved around identical twins with totally opposite characteristics separated at birth and growing up in different locations but at some point they both get exchanged and create a lot of action, drama and comedy. Eventually the good wins over evil and that results in some real good entertainment – so much so there were multiple movies in Hindi after this and all of them did decent business – the biggest hit was the female version "Seeta Aur Geeta" followed by "Chaalbaaz" while "Jaise Ko Taisa", "Kishan Kanhayya" too were very similar. Ram Aur Shyam grossed a lot of money. Here are the songs for you

- https://www.youtube.com/watch?v=MujG3nc-EXw ;
- https://www.youtube.com/watch?v=1uSf6xk8v8Q ;
- https://www.youtube.com/watch?v=e7gQo8Y0Qts ;
- https://www.youtube.com/watch?v=BiDIwdAIrGE ;
- https://www.youtube.com/watch?v=AN2-Byj2j40 ;
- https://www.youtube.com/watch?v=SKgHhwN9kYo ; (Not in the movie)

Cheers

Laksh KV

October 18, 1968

"SANGHARSH"

Dear Friends:

It was on October 18th 1968 – 55 years ago, this movie called "SUNGHURSH" released in Mumbai and I have some very unique memories of this big banner, heavy star-cast movie that did not do well at the Box Office though Wikipedia says it did well commercially. Let me go back in time as a school boy who had only the ability to go to Rupam Cinema, glance at the posters and check how is the black market doing. As a class IX student with no source of income I could only watch the state of affairs. Friday was not possible for me to take a walk to the cinema hall but I made it on Saturday evening i.e. on Oct 19th 1968 and was in for a BIG SHOCK. "Black Market" turned into "White Market" – Rs. 2/- tickets were easily available for buyers at par though the "House Full" board was very much present. So tickets were easily available for people to see and as the time elapsed the first shock came to me as the Indian News Reel (INR) had almost ended and the price was dropped to Rs. 1.50 per ticket and then it went down systematically till it reached 25 paise. Uffff – 2nd day 2nd show tickets sold in "White Market" at 4 annas – can you beat this? Well, I did not have even that to see this movie and came back to tell my friends the fate of this movie. In my view it was a huge disaster and I skipped the movie not out of choice but had no warewithall to see the movie. But I loved the music of Naushad with brilliant songs like:

"मेरे पैरों में घुंघरू बंधा दे तो फिर मेरी चाल देख ले",
"जब दिल से दिल टकराता है मत पूछिए क्या हो जाता है",
"मेरे पास आओ नज़र तो मिलाओ",
"इश्क़ दीवाना हुस्न भी घायल",
"तस्वीर-इ-मोहब्बत",
"छेड़ो न दिल की बात"

All the above songs had the great stamp of Shakeel-Naushad combo and frankly I felt bad that the movie was heading towards a big disaster. Much later during my college days, I saw the movie with my good friend Balakrishnan

Narayan aka Bedi at Gaiety Cinema where it was on a re-run. We actually liked the movie and felt it did not deserve to fail in such a big way. People had also mentioned that Sanjeev Kumar was better than Dilip Kumar etc (कचरा कर दिया) but very frankly I loved Dilip Kumar's acting – subdued where needed, free and full of fun during the song "मेरे पैरों में घुंघरू बंधा दे तो फिर मेरी चाल देख ले" & full of intensity & passion "जब दिल से दिल टकराता है मत पूछिए क्या हो जाता है" – I loved his performance and so did Bedi unlike in "Dil Diya Dard Liya". I am also sure my good friend Bharat Varma, one of the biggest Dilip Kumar fans would be happy reading praises of his idol. Bharat Bhai, wait for 20th October for John and George – Bedi समझ गए ना... Well, now coming back to the movie and away from nostalgia the movie had the following actors performing pivotal roles:

- Dilip Kumar
- Vyjantimala
- Jayant
- Iftikar
- Sapru
- Sanjeev Kumar
- Balraj Sahani
- Ulhas
- Anju Mahendru
- Durga Khote
- Deven Varma &
- Padma Khanna

Movie had excellent music and I will never get tired of talking about this for the great job done by the Mastero Naushadji and all songs penned by Shakheel Badayuni and great singing by Mohd Rafi Saab and the legendary sisters Lata Mangeshkar and Asha Bhonsle.

The story was about a powerful priest played by Jayant and in the city of Kashi he managed to loot rich people who stayed in his guest house and also kill them and offer that as sacrifice to the Goddess. His son Iftikar did not approve of his dad's ways and decided to separate with his wife and 3 kids but Jayant insisted and managed to hold back Dilip Kumar to continue the existing practice but again our Hero was not in favour of that. Jayant mysteriously kills Iftikar who is his son and puts the blame on his arch rival Sapru who happens to be his nephew. Sapru has 2 sons Balraj Sahani and Sanjeev Kumar and both want to avenge the death of their dad and they target to finish off Dilip Kumar and for that they take the help of Vyjantimala who is expected to seduce the Hero and help the process of Dilip Kumar's elimination. But these two (Hero & Heroine) fall in love and also recall that they knew each other from childhood. Now, Sanjeev Kumar decides to finish off Dilip Kumar and ironically gets killed by the Hero and now Dilip Kumar wants to end the feud and wants to serve Balraj Sahani who is the elder brother of Sanjeev Kumar by changing his identity and then he realizes that Balraj Sahani too is in love with Vyjantimala and wants to make her his 2nd wife. Eventually all the confusions get cleared – and at the end there is a general heaviness for the spectator. But songs are the saving grace and here are the songs for you.

https://www.youtube.com/watch?v=SfQ_2pdIMhI ;
https://www.youtube.com/watch?v=zbqyf75dES0 ;
https://www.youtube.com/watch?v=Sg-yzhSblYU ;
https://www.youtube.com/watch?v=qDRy7fsbbOQ ;
https://www.youtube.com/watch?v=Hda24Kq-DLw ;
https://www.youtube.com/watch?v=3vygAiSGtaY ;

Cheers
Laksh KV

October 17, 1969

"PYAR HI PYAR"

Dear Friends:

54 years ago today i.e. on October 17, 1969 one of the hit movies called "PYAR HI PYAR" was released. It was produced by Rajaram and Satish Wagle & Directed by Bhappi Sonie with lovely songs composed by Shankar Jaikishan – the movie did very good business then. Still in class X, no money syndrome continued and needed to feel happy with seeing posters at Rupam Cinema and also the wooden "House Full" board. Eventually, saw the movie at Broadway during my college days when it was running in matinee at reduced rates – enjoyed the songs and distinctly recall in one scene, Dharam Paji sits in an auditorium and after eating throws the paper behind which falls on the head of his dad or uncle and in the same scene he clearly abuses and the lip movement clearly indicated what he said and here I cannot write for it is unprintable. The star cast is as under:

- Dharmendra
- Vyjantimala
- Pran
- Mehmood
- Helan
- Dhumal
- Raj Mehra
- Madan Puri
- Sapru
- Manmohan
- Salim Khan (Salman Khan's dad)
- Sulochana &
- Jr. Mehmood

The plot is as under:

Vijay played by Dharmmendra grows up in an orphanage and is adopted by a wealthy man played by Raj Mehra and takes him as his long lost son. Vijay then joins Police department and his dad is not too happy about it. Vijay is given the job of finding the missing father of Vyjantimala and our man flips for her and is besotted with her and this justifies the title of the movie. Then there is some confusion regarding if Dharmendra is the real son or not as Manmohan is positioned as the real son – it takes some while and effort to clear till everything falls in place.

The movie's songs were popular and hit at that time. Mohd Rafi sang for Dharmendra and Mehmood in the same film. Gogo ageya was for Mehmood and remaining songs for Dharmendra. Mein Kahin Kavi and Dekha hai Teri aankhon mein of Mohd Rafi were huge hits. Here are the songs for you in one link:

https://www.youtube.com/watch?v=nH-xeQXkBXM ;

Cheers
Laksh KV

October 15, 1971

"BIKHRE MOTI & BUDDHA MIL GAYA"

Dear Friends:

52 years ago today i.e. October 15th, 1971 twin releases took place – one with a fairly established and hit couple and the other with relatively new entrants into the industry. While the established couple gave a flop, the new comers gave a hit movie. I am talking about "BIKHRE MOTI" & "BUDHA MIL GAYA".

Let me talk about "Bikhre Moti" first – my sympathy towards Jeetndra pulled me towards this movie as a college student and that too during Diwali vacation – also recall seeing that Jeetu played a cricketer in the movie and hence felt like seeing. Now with limited resources I had to decide between this movie and a Tamil movie of MGR at Rivoli – tickets for which was booked by a worker in a provision store who supplied groceries and this guy was the delivery boy and he was very pleased to know that I was an MGR fan too (though it was artificial since I did not like Sivaji Ganeshan). Now, I somehow wanted to avoid the Tamil movie and my 2 good friends Balakrishnan Narayan and Viswanathan Krishnan went to see Buddha Mil Gaya at Minor Cinema – part of Ambar Oscar those days. I skipped the Tamil movie and walked towards Rupam to see Bikhre Moti and found tickets easily available and as I was feeling a bit feverish, decided not to see the movie and came back home. Some how, did not have the inclination to see the movie and till date have not seen and I don't think I have missed anything in life. The star cast included:

- Jeetendra
- Babita
- Sujit Kumar
- Nazir Hussain
- Kamini Kaushal
- Helan

- Murad &
- CS Dubey

The plot is as under:

The plot revolves around 2 brothers who get separated as their mother tries to save the life of another girl. However, the girl is a millionaire's daughter and when her dad dies, he makes the mother of the 2 separated boys as the guardian. The 2 boys grow up as Jeetendra a cop and Sujit Kumar a criminal and fate makes them to fight against each other as both of them are in love with the girl who has now grown up to be Babita who is being taken care of by the mother of the 2 warring brothers. Now you can guess what happens in the end as good has to prevail over evil. Here are the songs for you:

https://www.youtube.com/watch?v=a9Lc0ckkr6w ;

https://www.youtube.com/watch?v=A0gkYt5LGP4 ;

https://www.youtube.com/watch?v=cmNICok1h2w ;

The next movie I am talking about is "BUDDHA MIL GAYA" – which did decent business and completed 100 days run with relatively new actors in the main lead:

- Navin Nischal
- Archana
- Deven Verma
- Om Prakash
- Sonia Sahani &
- Aruna Irani

Being not very impressed by Navin Nischal, I did not have the inclination to see the movie and the only pull factor was the Manna Dey song "AAYO KAHAN SAY GHAN SHYAM" but the feverish feeling continued for a while and what little thought came my way to see the movie also vanished and I was waiting for "CARAVAN" that was due for release in 2 weeks time and that was going to be a sure shot hit I felt. So conserved my resources, but I recall both my friends loved the movie and my late brother too saw and recommended that we see it. All he mentioned to me was that OmPrakash kills some of the people who wronged him and then after every murder, he would sing the Manna De number!!!... In all fairness, the movie did well and apparently had the stamp of

Hrishda in the treatment of the plot. Good music by RDB certainly helped the movie to do well. The plot is as under:

Deven Verma and Navin Nischol are unemployed and see an advertisement in the paper about an elderly man played by Om Prakash who is missing. This man is very rich in reality and these 2 unemployed youth locate him in a Park and start addressing him as uncle. The three of them move into an apartment despite unaffordable rent. The old man has a fondness towards Navin Nischol's sweetheart played by Archana. There are some murders that take place and all the clues point towards the 2 unemployed guys to be involved in it – but some bit of suspense for the crowd is interesting with the Manna De song thrown in at a frequency that is event-driven. Well, here are the songs for you.

https://www.youtube.com/watch?v=jFYlChHSdzo ;
https://www.youtube.com/watch?v=r1hWkp6umX8 ;
https://www.youtube.com/watch?v=9zxjUNb56ZI ;
https://www.youtube.com/watch?v=nm5jX2pAzdM ;
https://www.youtube.com/watch?v=LfoaH7j3X7Q ;

Cheers
Laksh KV

October 16, 1970

"MASTANA & ISHQ PAR ZOR NAHI"

Dear Friends:

53 years ago today i.e. October 16 1970, 2 movies released – one was with 2 Heroes and the 2nd one with a Character actor in a central role. The bigger star cast movie "ISHQ PAR ZOR NAHIN" was a failure but the Mehmood starrer "MASTANA" did well at the Box Office. I have memories of both – while one had my favourite Hero-Heman, the other had my favourite comedian and Diwali was round the corner and there was opportunity for me to see both movies – but the closer to home movie got the priority and that was "Mastana" at Rupam. So, let me talk about Mastana first – though in class XI, I used to wear Half pants mostly as I had only one full pant and having failed in Hindi in the first terminal exams, I did not have the guts to ask for a full-pant and fortunately my parents sympathized with me and thru one of the family friends having a shop at Jogeshwari allowed me to buy a pant piece for stitching a full trouser. I thanked Raghavan Mama for ever for selling this for Rs. 77/- and I had given this pant to stitch on this very day. But the tailor needed time to stitch and promised to give in 10 days and I knew this movie will last only one week in Rupam – so one more movie to be seen in the only full pant I had. I did not check with any one about joining me and I managed to see the movie on the following Monday and loved the movie. Some highlights or memory points for me are listed below:

- Vinod Khanna turning into a positive character
- Vinod Khanna and Bharti pairing up and came together in Purab Aur Paschim later
- Padmini playing Mehmood's Heroine
- Ramesh Deo opening up to Padmini as she seduces him singing "Peelay Peelay"
- Wonder Child Bobby playing a very good role that of a girl who sympathises with a poor Mehmood

- Mehmood going to bank to deposit money on behalf of Bharti and sees the board "Spit Here" and thinks it is mandatory to spit before depositing the cash – only to be cheated by Raj Kishore.
- The merging of Western and Indian music from a club to Nandlala
- Mehmood telling the audience to leave at the end of the movie

The cast I have almost covered – need to add only Rehaman, Shyama, Manorama and Mukri. Pretty decent music by Laxmikant Pyarelal also helped the movie.

Plot revolved around a Hanuman Bhakt bachelor played by Mehmood who acts as an errand boy for Bharati/Vinod Khanna while his main job is to reach food to working people and that includes the wonder child Bobby to whom he reaches food at her school. Padmini who is from the same place is in love with Mehmood but our man wants to remain a bachelor for ever but there are people like Ramesh Deo who has his eyes on Padmini. There is a Police Inspector played by Vinod Khanna & Mehmood ensures that he falls in love with Bharati. Wonder child Bobby is a neglected kid as her parents Rehman and Shyama have no time for her and she befriends Mehmood and then the question is how a rich girl can be good to a poor man. Ramesho Deo adds poison into her lunch box and the same is handed over by Mehmood and then police takes over. Finally the culprits are caught and all is well. Here are some songs for you:

https://www.youtube.com/watch?v=tU1rG3EElzw ;
https://www.youtube.com/watch?v=dMwU7aG6hgI ;
https://www.youtube.com/watch?v=pWLTvS0ojs0 ;
https://www.youtube.com/watch?v=H2QcSQ4ZmQQ ;
https://www.youtube.com/watch?v=zcaWbulK2Nw ;
https://www.youtube.com/watch?v=ZFAF7TZYnqM ;

The next movie I am talking of is "ISHQ PAR ZOR NAHI" – this movie was not running close to our house – closest was Rivoli – Matunga and the vacation was yet to start. Very keen to see the movie during vacation but it should run till the schools close which was going to happen only around October 24th and good possibility the movie would vanish from Rivoli – and vanish, it did. So during vacation I could not see the movie as it was only running in the main cinema halls that were far off and it ran only for 4 weeks to top it. The movie had all possible ingredients – Directed by Ramesh Saigal with Sadhna, Dharmendra and Biswajeet in the main roles – lovely music by SD Burman with great songs – the song 'YEH DIL DIWANA HI" though sounds very monotonous it was still refreshing – the title song 'SACH KEHTI HI DUNIYA, ISHQ PAR ZOR NAHI" was truly romantic, Romantic poem comes in the form of "MEHABOOBA TERI TASWEER" and the one with pathos was "TUM MUJHSE DOOR CHALAY JANA NA, MAIN TUMSE DOOR CHALI JAAOONGI". All this could not save the movie from being a flop and a loyalist of Dharam paji in me could do precious little and ended up seeing it on TV DD in the 80s and still can't forget the scene when totally upset, Dharam paji crushes a glass by his hand.

Nothing much to talk about the triangular plot of 2 friends – one rich and one poor falling for the same girl – standard complications between the 2 friends and eventually one friend (Biswajeet) sacrifices for Dharam Paji. Here are the song links for you.

https://www.youtube.com/watch?v=a3a_PO-XxqM ;
https://www.youtube.com/watch?v=ap9UZoeUHW8 ;
https://www.youtube.com/watch?v=whZgqBwq_BQ ;
https://www.youtube.com/watch?v=PF7er5ELgX0 ;
https://www.youtube.com/watch?v=1BtKstla6zg ;
https://www.youtube.com/watch?v=wExZqPgdghI ;
https://www.youtube.com/watch?v=_wjTnS6aH3o ;

Cheers
Laksh KV

January 12, 1973

"KOSHISH"

Dear Friends:

50 years ago today i.e. on January 12, 1973 released an off-beat movie "KOSHISH" that may not have done wonders at the Box Office but was accepted by critics and also the class audience – masses may not have taken a liking to it for it was not on the beaten track. I, for one, was a Masala Movie freak and was not keen to see a movie that had both the Hero and Heroine not talking and only using their hands and fingers to communicate. I did not see the movie when released but did see in the 80s when it was shown on DD. At that point I regretted my decision of not seeing when it was released. The performances by Sanjeev Kumar and Jaya Bhaduri were outstanding. I vaguely recall Sanjeev Kumar communicating his name as "HariCharan" by keeping a Green (Hari) chillie next to his feet (Charan). What I found it tough to accept was the parents could not figure out their first child going out of the house as I feel the people who have some senses low, have some others over-compensated. Another point was Sanjeev Kumar's expression of disappointment with his grown up son towards the end of the movie, indeed incredible it was. The movie was made by Romu and Raj Sippys' and directed by Gulzar. The cast included:

- Sanjeev Kumar
- Jaya Bhaduri
- Om Shivpuri
- Seema Deo
- Asrani
- Deepa Phatak &
- Dilip Kumar in a Special Appearance

The plot revolved around the fight of a disabled couple who could not speak and hear but wanted to live a normal life but for the fact that things were not easy for them. Sanjeev Kumar, who is deaf and dumb, lives a poor life as a news paper delivery man. He accidentally encounters Jaya Bhaduri who too has the same handicap like him and they decide to marry and live together – the silver lining for them is the birth of a normal son. In an unfortunate turn of events, the child dies and that makes life very tough for the couple. Sanjeev Kumar changes his profile by becoming a shoe polisher and in a while another son is born to the couple who too is a normal child. As parents, they do everything to educate the child so that he can find a good job and then as the couple grow old, what happens to their son – what he does and his attitude and learning makes the rest of the movie that has many touching situaions.

https://www.youtube.com/watch?v=SSxNnT3XCT0 ;

https://www.youtube.com/watch?v=T-P4_dFmlmU ;

The above links are the songs from the movie composed by Madan Mohan

Cheers
Laksh KV

October 19, 1973

"JOSHILA"

Dear Friends:

It was today i.e. October 19 1973 – 50 years ago this, very hyped movie called "JOSHILA" released – it had all the required ingredients to be a money-spinner – great banner, heavy star-cast – great director plus good music – still the movie had to be dragged for 100 days and on the very 2nd day one song/ghazal had to be edited. I recall seeing this movie on the very first day 6 PM show at Rupam Cinema – Sion. The movie was publicized well and most of us expected another "Johny Mera Naam" with the same lead pair and wrt entertainment this was nowhere close to the earlier hit of Trimurti films. I also recall the stylish Dev Anand singing inside the jail and the Heroine Hema Malini coming to spend her vacation with her Jailor Uncle and gets to read the files of all the convicts and she gets fascinated by the Hero, who is a qualified guy but accused of murder. The other point I recall is Padma Khanna, the cabaret queen plays Dev Anand's sister and master Satyajeet kid brother of Dev Anand (50 year old man) and their dad played by AK Hangal who gives them a very luxurious life as long as he is alive, and all of them get to know the real thing once Hangal kicks the bucket. I also loved the name "Madanlal Dogra" played by Madan Puri and later Dev Anand takes that name and becomes the estate Manager of Pran whose daughter happens to be Hema Malini. It was good to see Mahendra Sandhu playing Rakhee's hubby (Rakhee happens to be Dev Anand's Girl Friend earlier). Well, the movie was running to packed house on day 1 when I saw the movie and was quite disappointed at the final product and was keen to see how it was doing on the following day 6 PM show. I realized that it was not going to be a hit as the black marketers were selling tickets on par once the show started and I visited the hall during the interval and found that people were coming out for a smoke with gate pass and one of the guys who looked frustrated threw the gate pass and his counterfoil and left the hall. Shamelessly I picked both the documents and entered the hall and saw the 2nd half of the movie and that is when I realized that the ghazal/song by Hema Malini was chopped. Well, here is the cast for you:

- Dev Anand
- Hema Malini
- Rakhee
- Bindu
- Mahendra Sandhu
- Pran
- Madan Puri
- Sudhir
- Sulochana
- Padma Khanna
- AK Hangal
- Master Satyajeet
- Manmohan Krishna
- Iftikar
- Jagdish Raj
- Roopesh Kumar &
- IS Johar

The plot is pretty complicated one – in sum, Dev Anand is in jail for a murder he did not commit and once he comes out of the jail, he realizes that his dad is no more and left behind huge debts and his sister who lived a pampered life works as a dancer in a night club. He befriends Madan Puri and a dying Madan Puri tells him to go and do his task which was to be part of Pran's estate as a Manager and slowly edge him out and hand over the property to Sudhir and Bindu (Bindu plays Pran's young wife and seduces Dev Anand) – all their plans get foiled as Dev Anand at every possible opportunity saves Pran from getting killed. Then one can see the usual climax and after a short artificial death of Pran – things fall in place. Overall the movie follows the expected pattern and hence not very interesting. I must hasten to add that music of the movie by RD Burman saved it to an extent and here are the songs for you.

- https://www.youtube.com/watch?v=fICiVfSe-mk... ;

Cheers
Laksh KV

October 11, 1968

"JUARI"

Dear Friends:

It was today 55 years ago on October 11 1968, this flop movie called "JUARI" released. I was still in school – class IX and hence with no money this movie was not in my radar wrt seeing but I do recall well that in an era where there were mostly coloured movies, this one was a Black & White movie. Regarding the movie I have very few recalls and the top one being it was a failure, then it had some real good music by Kalyanji Anandji and finally one song by the heroine where she curses the Hero and prays that he does not get sleep. The movie was directed by one Suraj Prakash and the star cast included:

- Shashi Kapoor
- Nanda
- Tanuja
- Naaz
- Madhavi
- Rehaman
- Madan Puri
- David
- Achla Sachdev &
- Agha

Not much is known about the plot and here I would like my friends to contribute and educate all – all that I could get to know is that a young man falls into the path of gambling (title of the movie) and fraud after experiencing betrayal in love from one woman after another. Eventually realizes that honesty is the best policy. Here are the songs for you:

1. https://www.youtube.com/watch?v=hEKUL60kWcY ;
2. https://www.youtube.com/watch?v=fNQ5MGomiYY ;
3. https://www.youtube.com/watch?v=o5IbLwxPNuk ;
4. https://www.youtube.com/watch?v=oIGof-oym-w ;
5. https://www.youtube.com/watch?v=QQcukHyD-yg ;

Cheers
Laksh KV

October 10, 1970

"UMANG"

Dear Friends:

"YOUTH TO THE FORE" said the news paper ads and Ameen Sayani was in his elements on Radio Ceylon in the morning publicising the movie made under the banner of "Guru Dutt Films Combine" and directed by Atma Ram. This movie was called "UMANG" released today i.e. October 9th 1970 – 53 years ago that had a host of newcomers getting introduced in the movie. The cast included:

- Archana
- Satish Kumar
- Paintal
- Asrani
- Suresh Chatwal
- Subhash Ghai (who later changed from an actor to Director successfully)
- Baldev Khosa
- Yogesh Chandra
- Rehaman
- Jayanta Mukherjee

This was during my class XI and all I can recall is going to Rupam and seeing the posters and as a desperate fan of Shankar Jaikishan, I wanted the movie to do well. But it was a disaster though the music had its position. Much later in the mid 90s, I saw the movie on TV and was more keen to look at Subhash Ghai though he was not in the lead – Archana too made a very ordinary career – more remembered for "Budha Mil Gaya" that released in the following year. Baldev Khosa was a bit popular playing alongside Navin Nischal in "Sansaar" and his main hit movie if one can call it was "Daraar" but he decided to join politics while Subhash Ghai made block-busters like "Karz", "Karma" etc. All I can recall of what I saw was a group of youngsters, form a Musical group and that is not well received by people in the society where they live. I felt that the idea behind the movie was good but somehow it did not appeal to people in general. But the title song by Kishore Kumar and Asha Bhonsle "सच्चा प्यार तो चुप नहीं सख्ता दिल की उमंग ये कहती है" & Mohd Rafi number "बाबुल कौन घडी यह आयी" really caught the imagination of the people.

I really do not have the script to write about even from the internet and hence would request anyone who has a reach or a recall to share the same. I can only recall that a young bunch of boys and girls make a musical club that irritates the people living in that complex and there are some good songs to boast. Here are the songs for you:

1. https://www.youtube.com/watch?v=5tzUuIjbMkc ;
2. https://www.youtube.com/watch?v=SOXNY20LjEw ;
3. https://www.youtube.com/watch?v=ic4M1JvLYT8 ;
4. https://www.youtube.com/watch?v=7pNxz1-YVdc ;
5. https://www.youtube.com/watch?v=E_TDjwdoYHg ;
6. https://www.youtube.com/watch?v=Z1U7PhKyRdY ;

Cheers
Laksh KV

September 07, 1973

"PHAGUN"

Dear Friends:

It was today – i.e. September 7 1973, 50 years ago, this off-beat movie called "PHAGUN" released. Written, Produced and Directed by Rajendra Singh Bedi – the movie was acclaimed by the critics but could not do much at the Box Office and in my parlance it was a flop for it managed to run for only 10 weeks. Though, as a die-hard fan of Dharam Paji, I was happy to talk about how off-beat the movie was and how after playing Guddi's heart-throb, here he played her dad etc. All said and done, I saw the movie on the very first day but the night show. The movie I felt was slow but could not say so to all and as luck would have it the reviews were good but heart of heart I was not too happy for Dharam Paji as I felt he was as good as a guest artist and then it was Waheeda Rehman, Jaya Bhaduri and Vijay Arora all over. I have some memories that I can share here and they are as under:

- Waheeda Rehman was not convincing as a Maharashtrian to me – just coz saying Aaaye or Baba.
- I loved the gossip mongers walk in the seashore headed by Om Prakash who gives advice to people – needless to say unsolicited!!!
- Jaya Bhaduri asking Vijay Arora "घर में माँ बहन नहीं है क्या?" and Vijay Arora responding by saying "नहीं"
- Dharam Paji splashing color on his wife Waheeda Rehaman's expensive Saree & gets humiliated in public & is forced to stage a walk-out.
- An old Dharm Paji with a "पोटली" that he would not part with.

The movie had some good songs composed by Mastero SD Burman da and the title song was outstanding.

The plot revolved around a poor writer (Dharmendra) who falls in love with a rich Maharashtrain Girl (Waheeda Rehman) and they get married much against the wishes of the heroine's rich parents. To top it, Dharam Paji starts staying in his wife's house and gets humiliated by the rich couple and he takes it all for his lady love. On "Phagun" comes "Holi" and an excited Dharam Paji sprays color on his wife's expensive saree and she fires him in public and that does not go down well and Dharam Paji, who walks out never to return. As expected Waheeda was pregnant at that time and she brings up her daughter Jaya Bhaduri who falls in love with Vijay Arora and they get married and now Waheeda – the MIL moves with her daughter and son-in-law. But then there is too much of interference and towards the end, the elderly lady looks for her hubby and they do meet and under what circumstances – it is a good short story material in my view. Good songs also help the movie but still it was not a money spinner. Here are the songs for you.

- https://www.youtube.com/watch?v=TzFIbPkoBKo ;
- https://www.youtube.com/watch?v=K2if11FdqIc ;
- https://www.youtube.com/watch?v=opjbg1o0_Fo ;
- https://www.youtube.com/watch?v=FtNs37_bwhY ;
- https://www.youtube.com/watch?v=dBloGJSPmKE

Cheers

Laksh KV

October 04, 1968

"DIWANA"

Dear Friends:

It was today 55 years ago on October 04, 1968, this popular movie called "DIWANA" released – popular not from the stand-point of doing great box office business,-in fact it was more known for the music of Shankar Jaikishan and songs sung by Mukeshji – however, it ran for just 7 weeks in Mumbai. I would like to add that it was from this movie, my memory database commenced and all movies after this by and large I recall till 1973. About "DIWANA", I recall the advertisement on Radio Ceylon of this movie and was waiting for the release of the movie – knowing fully I will not be allowed to see the movie – even if I get a chance to see the posters I would be very happy. Those days in the weekly film magazine called "SCREEN" I recall seeing an announcement about 4 new RK films that were going to be made & the names were as under:

1. AJANTA
2. SATYAM SHIVAM SUNDARAM
3. MAIN AUR MERA DOST &
4. MERA NAAM JOKER

Only 2 of them were made under the RK Banner – Dilip Apte Saheb, Ambarish, Amitabh Nigamji or any other knowledgeable people – can any of you enlighten me about the above announcement? Well, the movie was directed by Mahesh Kaul & produced by Mukhram Sharma and NC Sippy. The main cast of the movie below:

- Raj Kapoor
- Saira Banu
- Lalita Pawar &
- Kamal Kapoor

Not having seen the movie, I have only option of looking at the plot from various sources and having done that, I was reminded of the movie "Anari" where Raj & Lalita Pawar shared a fabulous relationship of Raju and Mrs. D'sa. Here too it appears to me as something similar and again I would request people who know more of this movie to enlighten the others who do not know much.

Raj Kapoor plays a simple orphan and stays with Lalita Pawar who treats him like her son – very similar to Anari. RK meets a rich girl Saira Banu and they fall in love as expected. Then there is Kamal Kapoor who has brought up Saira Banu but his real child is Raj Kapoor. Then there is a murder and RK is arrested but the profile of the person makes it very tough to accept that he can't even harm an insect but he admits his guilt and wants capital punishment. Then the entire reality comes in the open.

All I can add is about the music of SJ – that was outstanding and shall list the songs for you below with the links:

1. Title song - https://www.youtube.com/watch?v=qbcbaTD-L2k
2. Pate Ki Baat Kahega - https://www.youtube.com/watch?v=7Uriy4t9QOo;
3. Ai Sanam Jisne Tujhe - https://www.youtube.com/watch?v=4ezDmTTkuN8 ;
4. Hum Toh Jate Apne Gaon - https://www.youtube.com/watch?v=qXd13TO6fZo ;
5. Tumhari Bhi Jai Jai - https://www.youtube.com/watch?v=r2TzFR5Glk4 ;
6. Taaron Se Pyare - https://www.youtube.com/watch?v=h_iSCWxmIzk;
7. Tumko Sanam Pukar Ke - https://www.youtube.com/watch?v=r5PFRuAimrA ;

Cheers

Laksh KV

October 02, 1970

"SAMAJ KO BADAL DALO"

Dear Friends:

Gemini Films "SAMAJ KO BADAL DALO" was released 53 years ago today i.e. October 2nd 1970. I recall the radio ads where Ameen Sayani used to announce loudly pointing at many issues and that things have to change "उस समाज को बदल डालो" – Though in class XI, here thanx to the fact that it was a remake of a hit Malayalam movie "TULABHARAM", there was an approval for me to see the movie at Rupam along with my late bro. So, very happily one of the evening shows on a weekday we went to see the 6 PM show and were very impressed with the start of the movie. Before we saw the movie, my next door neighbour, friend and classmate Viswanathan Krishnan had already seen and told me that character actor "Shammi" made a definite impact in her cameo role as the mother of Ajay Sahani (Parikishit Sahani later). While we knew that it was a hard-core tragedy movie I was getting ready to whistle when Ajay Sahani was attacked and did not expect him to get killed. The movie took a different turn after this event. Besides the Gemini Banner, there are some other things I recall of this movie and they are:

- Mehmood being questioned by a Police as to what he was doing outside of Police Station – the cop feels that he is urinating facing the wall with 2 hands in the right position!!! But in reality, he was counting money for he felt that was the safest place.
- Prem Chopra wooing Sharda and taking help of his friend played by Kanchana and singing the song "तुम अपनी सहेली को इतना बता दो"
- Sharda being given a tough time by everyone after she loses her hubby and towards the end she surprises the police department as she speaks in fluent English!!!
- Ultimate thing – mother mixing poison in the food and making the kids eat and she too consumes and dies in the end.
- The popular song "अम्मा एक रोटी दे बाबा एक रोटी दे"

However, despite a good start, the movie ran only for 10 weeks in Mumbai and hence I do not consider it as a Hit though not a miserable flop either – its production cost and other things were low and hence would have generated a surplus for the makers. The main actors of the movie were:

- Ajay Sahani (Pareekshit Sahani)
- Sharada
- Pran
- Mehmood
- Aruna Irani
- Kanhiyalal
- Kanchana
- Prem Chopra
- Dhumal &
- Mukri

The plot revolved around Rich Mill owners versus Poor labourers – and unlike most movies where labourers win, in this movie it was not so – probably the reason for its failure, while it did well in Malayalam for it was in line with the tastes of that segment. The main role or the protagonist is the widow of Ajay Sahani played by Sharada who struggles to get justice from the society and it continues to be a relentless fight till she gives up and kills her 3 kids and herself in the end. Very sad and depressing feeling – the movie had some good songs composed by music director Ravi. Here are the songs for you.

https://www.youtube.com/watch?v=fDY384CeAyU ;

https://www.youtube.com/watch?v=pvmtyM-mix4 ;

https://www.youtube.com/watch?v=fx5DCxUM3ZI ;

https://www.youtube.com/watch?v=3h0dyz-65dA ;

https://www.youtube.com/watch?v=T3hXox8Dh74 ;

https://www.youtube.com/watch?v=QoaiNElEL3Y ;

https://www.youtube.com/watch?v=kDpGs7MU5XE ;

Cheers

Laksh KV

October 01, 1971

"HULCHAL"

Dear Friends:

It was today, on October 01 1971 (52 years ago), OP Ralhan's "HULCHAL" released. In my view this was a unique or a different kind of movie from the earlier movies he had made like "Talash", "Phool Aur Pathar" & "Gehara Daag" – the earlier movies had Big Heroes like Rajendra Kumar, Dharminder etc but this one was different – and OP Ralhan himself played the main role in the movie. There were also others who supported him but the star value was not so high but OP had a decent enough pull to have a good initial for a movie that had Zeenat Amaan and Kabir Bedi making debut. The other stars included:

- Prem Chopra
- Madan Puri
- Gajanan Jagirdar
- Ramesh Deo
- Helan
- Sonia Sahani
- Amrish Puri &
- Tuntun

The "House Full" Board was constant for the first 3 days at Rupam Cinema Sion, and we brothers and our cousin from Armed Forces decided to try our luck on Saturday night but all of us were clear, given that there was hardly any big name, it will not be worth buying ticket paying a premium. So around 845 PM we reached there and were greeted by the "House Full" board and the Shinde brothers (Rupam Black Marketing guys) were busy selling at 100% premium – the slogan was "दो का चार बोलो दो का चार" and we waited and hoped that the price would come down once the crowd goes in and more hopes once the ads and INR starts – but, nothing like that happened – there were some rich folks who somehow wanted to see the movie on the same night and all tickets got sold out.

Having waited till 930 PM, we decided to have "पाँव भाजी मस्का" and nice tea and were home by 1030 – then were keen to see the review in TOI on Sunday morning. We had heard the radio program with the title song in the background and the name "Madan Jaitley" that had got stuck in our heads. Very quickly after reading the review my brother revealed to me that it all was a result of a play on the radio that created enough confusion. It can be considered as a song less movie though with the titles the Asha Bhonsle RDB song was played.

The plot revolved around OP Ralhan and Helan who are in love and want to get married but our man is very poor and chances of marriage are very tough. Once these 2 overhear a conversation and gather that One Mahesh Jaitley is going to kill his wife. Now, this couple intend to save the lady from getting killed. They feel odd to take it up to police and hence they both get into an investigative mode but to their misfortune there are 3 people with the same name and all of them have some issue in their respective marriages but in trying to expose the men, they just about manage to escape police every time and also realize that the men are after all not bad characters. Now, these 3 couples want to find who is trying to screw up their marriage and OP is in the court of law trying to save himself – when he tells the truth the public prosecutor has some inkling about the reality and after taking short break at the court, he comes with a tape with another witness and when they listen to the tape, it is the same conversation that OP and Helan heard. It happens to be a radio play which was misunderstood and the whole confusion took place. All is well that ends well. Here is the link of the song from the movie:

https://www.youtube.com/watch?v=gKG1hYeJnV4 ;

Cheers
Laksh KV

September 29, 1972

"MERE JEEVAN SAATHI"

Dear Friends:

51 years ago it was today – i.e. on September 29 1972, this movie "MERE JEEVAN SAATHI" released. Very well publicized and branded with brilliant music, it was expected to be a hit and the title too was similar from the Hero's earlier hit movie "Haathi Mere Saathi". However, from 1972 after "Apna Desh", Kaka's decline slowly started and this movie did not do as well as it was expected to do. I have excellent memories of seeing this movie on the very first day 11.30 am show at Neptune Cinema located at Bandra along with my great friend Balakrishnan Narayan aka Bedi. In fact, by then I had started becoming a bit sympathetic towards my friend and cleared all the prejudice and agreed to see the movie and was confident that the movie might not do too well. There was mad rush for FDFS (First Day First Show) and another good friend from Matunga – Manikkyam by name was also trying to enter the cinema hall and what was unique was this guy's fountain pen top had fallen off and to prevent the ink from spreading and spoiling his white shirt, he was holding the pen on top of his raised right hand – he was not worried if it was impacting someone else – it was a funny sight indeed. The movie started and we were fully focused but it was not gripping and there were songs at the drop of a hat – though they sounded good, we did feel it was a bit too much!!! Just before the intermission, we had the song with maximum yodelling by KK "चला जाता हूँ किसी की धुन में" and during the break I did mention to Bedi "it was a bit of an overdose" who reluctantly agreed as he was a fan of both Kaka and KK. Well, we did feel bad that Kaka goes blind and gets hit also by Sujit Kumar etc. Still we loved the names of the 2 main charcters – "Prakash & Jyoti". -Bedi was also a fan of Rajendranath who too had a small role in the movie. The movie had the following actors:

- Rajesh Khanna
- Tanuja
- Helan
- Bindu

- Sujit Kumar
- Sulochana
- Nazir Hussain
- KN Singh
- Utpal Dutt &
- Rajendranath

Now coming to the plot – Kaka who is a good painter and Tanuja who is a London returned Doctor Get attracted to each other after some initial misunderstandings. But there is a rich and cruel princess played by Helan who wants to possess Kaka but fate has other ideas as Kaka while driving happily meets with an accident and loses his eye sight. The Princess takes control of him and wants to tame him completely and wants him to love her forcibly. Kaka detests that but tells the Princess to take him to some hilly region and after that he would be her slave. Unfortunately for the Princess, she falls of a cliff and dies while she tries to locate a hidden Kaka. Then it gets triangular between Kaka, Tanuja and Sujit Kumar and after a lot of fights, things end well. Overall the movie was average but RD Burman's music was there to lift it up a bit. It ran for 12 weeks in Mumbai and hence cannot be considered a HIT. Here are the songs for you – this one link has all the songs.

https://www.youtube.com/watch?v=2JJ4q6PSWnc ;

Cheers

Laksh KV

Sept 21ˢᵗ, 1973

"RICKSHAWALA"

Sept 28ᵗʰ 1973

"ZINDAGI ZINDAGI"

Dear Friends:

It was 50 years ago – September 21 1973 & September 28ᵗʰ 1973, two flop movies released and I had the privilege of seeing "Rickshawala" when released but had no inclination to see "ZINDAGI ZINDAGI" though much later in life I did see it on DD and frankly I felt it deserved to do better business than what it did.

So let me first talk about "Rickshawala". 1973 was a comfortable period for we 3 brothers as we were earning and we 3 decided to see the movie – more so because it was a remake of a Tamil hit movie called "RICKSHAWKARAN" *ing MGR & Manjula. Here Randhir Kapoor was essaying the role of MGR and is the guy who makes a living by riding a cycle rickshaw and has Neetu Singh as his girl and there is a sympathetic mother figure in Mala Sinha but there is an Anwar Hussain who is the villain. Now, we 3 had fun seeing this movie and it was on Anwar Hussain as we saw him address his henchmen seated in a revolving bed and he struggled to face the inefficient people working for him. We concluded that Anwar Hussain was one villain, who had over-dependence on his inefficient assistants and all that he could do was to yell at them "Oh You!!!!" We loved Randhir Kapoor and all of us became his fans and the way he did stunt while riding his rickshaw and beating up all the gundas was funny to watch. He and Neetu Singh made a good pair and created good comic effect. However, the songs were average in the movie. I am not getting into the plot of the movie as it is very predictable – rich v/s poor and who wins in the end. Here are some songs for you.

https://www.youtube.com/watch?v=zqQ0AlO3FXA ;
https://www.youtube.com/watch?v=VBVZvHS3u_w ;

Now coming to the 2nd movie "ZINDAGI ZINDAGI" it had an impressive star cast of Ashok Kumar, Sunil Dutt, Waheeda Rehman, Iftikar, Jalal Agha, Farida Jalal and Deb Mukherjee. My vague recall is that of Sunil Dutt is a revolutionary in a college. It had music by the senior Maestero SD Burman and he himself sang the title song of the movie. Since, I do not have more information about this movie, I would request my knowledgeable friends to contribute here. Here are the songs for you.

https://www.youtube.com/watch?v=oe041m1mn4Y;
https://www.youtube.com/watch?v=7y8vQFcMK5c;

Cheers
Laksh KV

September 26, 1969

"WARIS"

Dear Friends:

54 years ago today i.e. Sept 26 1969 was the day this movie called "WARIS" released. It was made by Vasu Menon and was a remake of a big Tamil hit "NAAN". Though, the movie started as a favourite but it did not do expected business. It was still an out and out entertainer & it was also the 2nd movie of Hema Malini who was launched in Feb.1969 in the movie "Sapnon Ka Saudagar". The movie had the following stars:

- Jeetendra
- Hema Malini
- Prem Chopra
- Mehmood in a dual role
- Sudesh Kumar
- David
- Ashokan (Tamil actor playing the chief villain)
- Chaman Puri
- Manorama
- Kamini Kaushal
- Nazima
- Aruna Irani &
- Baby Sonia (later Neetu Singh)

I have memories of this movie in 2 distinct phases – the first one was the week it was released – none of us hoped we would ever go to see this movie – so reconciled to look at the review in TOI and be happy. But on Sunday morning we were in for a huge surprise when my 2 friends Balakrishnan Narayan aka Bedi and Arun Balakrishnan aka Naseeba came towards our balcony and asked if we 3 brothers could join them for the movie at Rupam on the same day – 230 PM show. Unfortunately, their mom took ill and their parents and sister decided not to go for the movie and they gave us the choice to join and as luck was on our side, our Amma said OK – She was in good mood!!! I was so thrilled and I went to Bedi's house on the first floor and wished his Mummy a speedy recovery (heart of heart felt good we got a chance to see the movie) and we 5 boys went to see the movie. I must say we thoroughly enjoyed the movie and even now when it comes on Zee Classic, I try not to miss it. Good entertainer it was.

Now coming to the 2nd phase of memory – this was in September 1971 when I was in First Year College – I used to go to Bandra – opted to be away from Poddar College for I could see more actors and more comfortable to bunk college. So, on one such day when the lecturers took time off, one of my class-mates "Abdul Chunawala" who used to commute from Jogeshwari to Bandra to attend college, asked me if I could join him to see 'Waris' – I could not resist and looked at my wallet and had some Rs. 3/- and felt rich. We took a bus from SV Road Bandra going towards Goregaon – and the journey was never ending I felt and finally we reached the Cinema Hall called "Topiwala" which boasted of "Mirror Screen" – which meant wherever one sat, the image would be clean unlike a flat head when we sit in front row corner seat etc... but here the hall was hardly occupied and we both enjoyed the movie and when it got over, we 2 went to Goregaon station and I stood in the "Q" to buy ticket for I had pass only from Bandra to King's Circle. Now, when my turn came at the counter, I gave Re.1/- and told him one Bandra – which cost 30 paise and the counter guy asked for change and I said I didnt' have. So he said do anything – I can't give you the ticket unless you give me change. I decided, he said do anything and I will travel without ticket. So both me and Chunawala boarded a train going towards Bandra and it was my bad luck, a TC landed and the smart guy Chunawala realized and jumped out of the door and got into the next compartment as the train was moving slowly – in no time I was nabbed by the TC. He cornered me and I told him I have only Re1/- and cannot pay fine. So he made me alight at Jogeshwari and I saw Chunawala moving confidently for he had the pass from that station. I was made to sit on a bench and the TC was trying to get more candidates like me but was a bit unlucky that way – so he kept interrogating me – asked for my identity card which I showed. He asked what my dad did and I said he worked for a company called INCAB. So he said, can I call him and tell him that your son has skipped college and is caught at Jogeshwari and I pleaded to him not to. Here time was running out and I was more worried about what I would explain to Amma regarding delay on reaching home. I kept apologizing but the TC would not release me and now another train came going towards Borivli. He took me into that train and I was heading towards Goregaon again and my worry was the time being lost... We got off at Goregaon and after a lot of pleading the TC told me "Boy, you are from a good family, go buy your ticket and go home". I heaved a sigh of relief as I joined the Q again to buy ticket and this time round, the counter guy returned 70 paise – which he could have done earlier. Then, got into a train and reached Bandra around 4 PM and as I took the harbour train to reach King's Circle, I kept thinking of reasons to give Amma about my delay. As I reached King's Circle station and commenced my walk towards home, I suddenty remembered that Amma had plans of seeing the hit Marathi movie "सौंगड्या" at Rupam – 3PM show. I felt so relieved when I saw the lock at home and picked up the key from my neighbour's house and plonked myself on the chair. I made tea for myself and the door bell rang. I was pleasantly surprised to see my cousin who used to work for Indian Air Force, who had earlier taken us in the mid 60s to see "Do Badan" and "Dil Diya Dard Liya" – and I welcomed him and offered tea and biscuits and we enjoyed the same with our chats. Soon my late brother Raj too came in and it was 445 PM and then came another surprise – my cousin suggested that we go to Rivoli to see a Tamil movie called "KADALIKKYA NERAM ILLAI" – the original of "PYAR KIYE JAA" – so before Amma could come home, we wrote a note for her and left by 515 PM and were at Rivoli before 6 PM for the show. 2 movies in a day for the first time for me and thus I escaped Amma's wrath.... Wow – too much personal memory more than the movie "Waris" – but loved the following things in the movie:

- One after the other claimants for the position of heir – Prem Chopra, Jeetendra & Mehmood land up
- Hema Malini in swimming costume
- Mehmood in his elements as Mom and Son
- Ashokan talking Hindi in Madrasi ishtyle
- Metal glouse worn by Ashokan creating sparks
- Gas Chamber
- Mixture song ending with "An Evening in Bandra"

The plot revolved around a young Prince who leaves his palatial house on his birthday and lives a humble life. After some 20 years, the old King is on his death bed and wants to ensure that the young – grown up Prince is located and given the responsibility to handle the kingdom. Now, 3 imposters land up claiming to be the lost Prince. All of them pass the tests and now the panel is confused as to who is the right one!!! Well, none of them and Mehmood out of them is a cop and has a mother (again Mehmood) who keeps saying "तांगड़ी तोड़ दूँगी" at the drop of a hat. Finally, the real Prince Sudesh Kumar gets it and things are sorted out. Good time pass movie for me. Songs by RD Burman were also well received. Here are the songs for you.

https://www.youtube.com/watch?v=8gzvmeWcJoY ;
https://www.youtube.com/watch?v=is43fptMTMg;
https://www.youtube.com/watch?v=m6U_D9AbAQY ;
https://www.youtube.com/watch?v=s7r7BjUaXmQ ;
https://www.youtube.com/watch?v=waMdcTOHAGs ;
https://www.youtube.com/watch?v=vlqlFbSf71E ;

Cheers
Laksh KV

September 25, 1970

"PAVITRA PAAPI & PUSHPANJALI"

Dear Friends:

53 years ago today i.e. September 25 1970 two movies were slated to be released while one did see the light of the day – there was controversy on the other. Let me take it up one by one.

The first one is "PAVITRA PAAPI" produced and directed by Rajendra Bhatia and lyrics and music by Prem Dhawan. The movie had the following star-cast:

- Balraj Sahani
- Achla Sachdev
- Ajay Sahani (Initial screen name of Parikshit Sahani S/o Balraj Sahani)
- Tanuja
- Baby Sonia (became Neetu Singh later)
- Abhi Bhattacharya
- IS Johar
- Manorama
- Jayashree T &
- Gulshan Bawra

My memories of this movie: My SSC days and this was not going to be released in Rupam but later I had a surprise. The best memory for me is that my neighbour, friend and classmate Viswanathan Krishnan aka JKB managed to see this movie – thanx to his elder brother Bala who was earning well those days – he was going gaga over the young Neetu Singh and the best memory for me is that of the radio ad in which Amin Sayani said "पापी मगर पवित्र" – recall includes Ajay Sahani replaces his real-life dad in a watch repair shop run by IS Johar and here starts problem for the senior pro and the replacement happened for no fault of the youngster but that is it. Some good songs in the movie were being constantly played on the radio. The release date was certainly not a happy one for me, as the

First Terminal results and papers were being distributed and of all papers, I had failed in Hindi for the first time in my school life!!!

Now coming to the plot, Balraj Sahani leads a quiet peaceful life with his family consisting of wife Achla Sachdev, daughters Tanuja and Neetu Singh - working in a watch repair shop till Ajay Sahani replaces him at the job, given that the youngster too wanted too persue the line that he inherited from his family. Now the senior Sahani curses the youngster for bringing his family to streets and walks out of the house and this also makes the youngster very guilty and he does everything possible to help and rehabilitate the family in trouble. He even rents a room and stays to help the family and also teaches the elder daughter and in the bargain falls in love with her. To make them feel good he writes letters as though written by the senior Sahani. However, Tanuja's wedding is fixed with someone else and the Hero realizing that there is no money with the family steals from his office and helps the family. After this he vanishes from the scene and Tanuja ends up in a forgettable marriage into a very bad family and is constantly troubled. Now the senior Sahani returns and finds his daughter in trouble and brings her back. Here too the Jr. Sahani plays a role in turning around the son-in-law and unites them – all behind the scene. A different type of movie and no wonder it was not a big hit... did just about OK business. Here are the songs for you:

https://www.youtube.com/watch?v=ebDNaL14s1E ;

https://www.youtube.com/watch?v=G1oSSNAnJlU '

https://www.youtube.com/watch?v=vPCh-mH8dIE ;

https://www.youtube.com/watch?v=vPCh-mH8dIE ;

The Second movie is "PUSHPANJALI" – now here is the controversy – all I know is that it was publicized enough and on the day of release it was withdrawn and till date I do not know what was the issue. It was supposed to be released in Rupam and I got excited seeing Om Prakash with a hot Babe in the banners. I would await comments from my friends regarding the release of this move and as far as my memory goes, this movie did not release in Mumbai. This movie was made by Kishore Sahu and his daughter Naina Sahu played the main role and the hero's role was essayed by Sanjay. The movie had music by Laxmikant Pyarelal and the Manna Dey number "श्याम ढले जमुना किनारे अजा राधे अजा" was a huge hit.

However, since I also run a quiz column on Facebook, I decided to see this movie on YouTube and had some findings – the topmost was Fariyal played Sanjay's wife and they have a terminally ill son and Fariyal also dies in the movie. It was a tough watch but did go thru the motions and here I would invite comments from others who might have seen the movie in the hall.

The plot is as under:

Sanjay Khan & Faryal discover that their son has brain cancer and will not last very long. This shocks the mother who dies and Sanjay takes his son and his cook played by Manmohan Krishan to an island where they meet many people who are after Lalita Pawar's diamond jewellery. Sanjay meets Naina Sahu in the island and sees that she cares for the young boy. When the boy gets an attack, they get a Doctor of high calibre who recommends surgery for the boy. But Sanjay does not accept the same and takes the boy to a temple and then miracle happens and the boy survives as he offers flowers to God. Sanjay, the child and Naina Sahu leave the island relieved. Well, here are the songs for you:

https://www.youtube.com/watch?v=0hweAcc1IJE ;

https://www.youtube.com/watch?v=ZkIXEbjnVD4 ;

https://www.youtube.com/watch?v=QHz7cK5l_ms ;

https://www.youtube.com/watch?v=WosuMR9GGic ;

Cheers
Laksh KV

September 24, 1971

"GUDDI"

Dear Friends:

"GUDDI" was released today 53 years ago – i.e. on September 24 1971 – when Kaka was at his peak, this was something really off-beat where it is shown that Jaya Bhaduri as a "die-hard" fan of Dharam Paji and the best part was that within the movie Dharam himself says "आजकल मैं राजेश खन्ना का नाम सुन रहा हूँ ..." – I simply loved this aspect of the movie. It was not given enough publicity for movies of Hrishida would not really spend big monies on advertisements but they automatically had a "Pull-Factor" and Guddi was no exception and with so many stars thrown in it as guest artists, it really made an interesting movie. As a First Year College Student and with a megere Rs. 2/- as pocket money, it had to be a carefully thought out decision what to see and what to miss – not to forget that just the previous week saw the release of another Dharam Paji movie called "Rakhwala" and I had to see both – but that is when my late bro helped me big time – working for Asian Paints at Bhandup, he used to earn handsomely, a princely amount of close to R.s 500/- - he was kind to give Rs. 10/- each to both me and my elder brother. But the money had to be managed for we also had a Sarvajanik Ganesha in our building and money had to be reserved for that too – luckily Ganesha happened during end August and September was another month – so no sweat - could afford to see both Dharam Paji movies. Some of the top most thoughts of Guddi for me are as under:

- Spontaneous Jaya Bhaduri in the role of Kusum – very convincing way of telling her teachers why she came late into school. Lolita Kumari, her class teacher buys it.
- Teacher says "Poor Girl" & immediately someone says "गरीब लड़की" & the agitated teacher says "गरीब लड़की नहीं बेचारी लड़की"
- Songs from "Asli Naqli" & "Madhumati" re-filmed on the characters of the movie.

- Jaya's obsession with Dharam Paji and how she goes to see "Anupama" and very diplomatically says how Dillip Kumar movies are a bit dragging.
- Asrani's impact role "पढ़ाई लिखाई तेरे बेटेकी काम नहीं आएगी माँ, तूने बेटा नहीं अल्लहदीन का चिराग पैदा किया है"
- Having seen a lot of shootings, Jaya realizes that it is all show and gets fed up of shoots and vehemently says no to shooting and her uncle Utpal Dutt exclaims "भूत के मुँह से राम राम"
- Utpal Dutt contacts someone from the industry who could help in having Jaya attend some shoots and the gentleman on phone tells how the original stories get changed!!!
- Keshto in the role of a conman traps Asrani in a big way and keeps getting money from him & all he says is "मेंबर बनना पड़ता है"
- Not to forget the closing scene by Utpal Dutt where he says "जय धर्मेंदर" and Paji's last scene after everything is sorted out, he just finishes of a cigarette and is done with his role to ensure that Baby Guddi is back on earth.

Indeed a lot of memories and a great movie to boot - *ing the following:

- Dharmendra
- Jaya Bhaduri
- Utpal Dutt
- Sumita Sanyal
- Samit Bhanja
- AK Hangal
- Asrani
- Keshto Mukherjee
- Vijay Sharma & a host of guest artists like
- Pran
- Dilip Kumar
- Mala Sinha
- Rajesh Khanna
- Vinod Khanna
- Navin Nischal
- Biswajit
- Om Prakash

- Shatrughan Sinha &
- Deven Verama

The movie did good business and was termed a big hit of 1971 with some other movies like Andaz, Haathi Mere Sathi etc. Though 2 songs were reused, the song "बोले रे पपीहरा" was very well received by people. Another invocation song that gained popularity after this movie is "हमको मन की शक्ति देना". Overall a great experience of seeing so many actors in one movie and a totally different subject.

Now coming to the plot, a film crazy girl, Jaya Bhaduri is obsessed with the make believe world and drives everyone crazy at home and also her husband to be played by Sameer. It takes some effort for her to change and this is done very smartly with the help of her uncle Utpal Dutt who lives in Mumbai and arranges for her to see a lot of shootings during her vacation trip to Mumbai. As days progress, she realizes that it is all too much of artificial life and it is better to get back to regular routine life. To make this happen, Utpal Dutt requests Dharampaji (who plays himself) to cooperate and help and very sportingly, he plays the guy who loses in real life at the hands of her hubby to be of Jaya Bhaduri. Eventually all is well that ends well. Here are some of the songs for you from the movie.

https://www.youtube.com/watch?v=6pmKEvD351Q ;

Cheers
Laksh KV

September 22, 1972

"SHOR"

Dear Friends:

51 years ago today i.e. Sept 22 1972, saw the release of Manoj Kumar's "SHOR" – written, edited, produced and directed by the Hero – Manoj Kumar. This one for a change did not have the expected Mr. Bharat, but it was a mill worker Shankar Sharma. This movie did fairly good business and depicted "IRONY OF LIFE" exceptionally well. My late brother, a great Manoj Kumar fan had seen this movie and was going gaga over it and I too decided to see it though not immediately on release but waited for it to settle down and read reviews, heard views of others and given that MK had moved from Kalyanji Anandji to LP, I was not too happy either but the songs were making "NOISE" but sweetly... I recall the frustration shown by Manoj Kumar about noise – given that he was a mill worker – he said "२४ घंटे मशीनों का शोर, कोई पैदा हो तो शोर, कोई मर जाये तो शोर, चरों तरफ शोर ही शोर" with both his hands covering his ears... fed up of noise. Finally, I saw the movie at Broadway when it was in its 4th week on a Sunday afternoon and in all fairness liked the movie for the beautiful treatment given to it to show the "Irony". The main stars of the movie are:

- Manoj Kumar
- Nanda (Special Appearance)
- Jaya Bhaduri
- Premnath
- Master Satyajeet
- Kamini Kaushal
- Meena T
- Asrani
- Manorama
- Manmohan
- Raj Mehra

- Nana Palsheekar &
- Krishan Dhavan

While I felt there were too many flash-backs and flash-back within flash-back – but some of them were needed but some comedy relief that was tried were not really needed in an otherwise serious movie. Now, when I think of this 51 year old movie, the value of Rs.1,000/- today is nothing but that was a lot then... Manoj Kumar is short of funds and he decides to enter into creating a cycling record of non-stop cycling for 7 to 8 days to get that money needed for his son's surgery. It is a bit over done as the deadline gets closer – but it was certainly not funny to see there was a guy running along to shave the growing beard – it would have looked better had he allowed the full growth. Jaya Bhaduri in her fancy dress looked out of place till she went back to her comfort zone of draping simple sarees.

The plot revolved around Manoj Kumar and his son (Master Satyajeet) who saw his Mom (Nanda) dying in an accident and loses his voice and now his dad somehow wants to get his son's surgery done and is keen to listen to his son's lost voice. For this he does everything possible including the cycling for 8 days as mentioned above – all this after he tries to get money from his parents to whom he has been sending money. But as expected he draws a blank and then manages to collect the same on his own. Then comes the happy moment and the surgery is successful and the dad is keen to meet the son but the Dr suggests that he wait for a day. Now, to kill time he goes to the factory and as he is over-excited and ends up injuring himself whereby he loses his hearing capabilities. Now, is this not an irony? The man, who was fed up of noise, is desperate to listen to his son's voice and loses his hearing power when his son regains his voice!!! This has been depicted very well. Over all a good movie, though a bit long but those days it was that way. The songs too helped the movie to do well and here are the songs for you in one link.

https://www.youtube.com/watch?v=iTXk7Qs1keM...

Cheers
Laksh KV

September 28, 1973

"BOBBY"

Dear Friends:

50 years ago it was today – Sep 28 1973, that this milestone movie called "BOBBY" produced by the Big Banner RK Films released. Raj Kapoor launched his younger son Rishi Kapoor in a full-fledged Hero's role and also introduced Dimple Kapadia as a fresh face who had an uncanny resemblance to Nargis – which triggered a lot of discussion and speculation – me not getting there – but have lot of memories of this movie. Recently Rishi Kapoor has told the world that, this movie was not launched for him but to clear off the debt incurred by the earlier disaster called "Mera Naam Joker" from the same banner and that sounds logical too. This was a relatively low cost movie and ran for 55 weeks in Mumbai and brought up a lot of freshness with the tag line "TEEN AGERS LOVE STORY FILMED BY RAJ KAPOOR". There was a lot of publicity for this movie – I guess RK did not mind spending to get the returns – it was a great gamble – the posters were very interesting with Dimple in 2 piece swim suit and imagine the plight of an eighteen year old – this movie had to be seen ASAP – so what did I do, I took some time off from my work and went to Badal Cinema and booked tickets standing in the Q in advance but could get the tickets only for Saturday 29th September 1030 am show. I booked 2 tickets and was waiting for Saturday to come. I wanted to offer my second ticket to my good friend Balakrishnan Narayan but unfortunately he could not make it and I ended up selling that for a premium of 50 paisa… Rs. 2.50 I got – thought bus fare recovered – Jain Society to Dadar. The movie was really exciting – the scenes that come to me – top of the mind are:

1. Little Rishi biting Piloo Wadia on her cheeks
2. Dimple saying "नहीं पहले चने खाएंगे"
3. Rishi saying "गर्मी में गरम चाय ठंडक पहुँचती है"
4. Dimple touching her heart & saying "ये दिल है ना"
5. Rishi reflecting the glass from outside to draw attention of Dimple
6. The annoyance of one of the members in the library

7. Sonia Sahani's Pallu falls off
8. Premnath asking "How is your Munshipalty?" to Rishi
9. Prem Chopra saying "Prem Naam Hi Mera"
10. Above all some of those songs.

It was very disappointing for me to see Shankar Jaikishan knocked out by RK for this movie and the banner music did not sound like it did when SJ duo did it for RK movies. The movie was certainly quite bold and people lapped it up and it is no wonder that it was the top grosser and revived the banner in a big way after the debacles of MNJ and KAK. New faces, new singers added to the success of the movie. Let's look at the cast:

- Rishi Kapoor
- Dimple Kapadia
- Pran
- Premnath
- Durga Khote
- Sonia Sahani
- Aruna Irani
- Shashi Kiran
- Pinchoo Kapoor
- Farida Jalal
- Piloo Wadia

New Singers – Shailendra Singh & Narendra Chanchal

The story was a pure love story between a rich neglected boy Rishi Kapoor and a poor girl Dimple Kapadia brought up by a down to earth fisherman Premnath along with his mother Durga Khote. Durga Khote once was the governess of Rishi Kapoor till he was 6 and had a certain bonding with him which the boy reciprocated too as his parents Pran and Sonia Sahani were very busy people with virtually no time for their only son. The boy sees a great future with the poor girl and they fall in love – needless to say while Premnath has a broad mind and is open to do anything for his darling daughter's happiness but is big time insulted by Pran playing Rishi's dad. Now, the young lovers are in major trouble and decide to elope and there is a chase and police stop them at a toll naka and ask the name – Rishi aka Raja says "Vishnu Prasad Rastogi" & they ask Dimple aka Bobby and she says "Vimla Prasad Rastogi" & they escape only to get trapped by Prem Chopra who acts like helping them by offering his tempo to help them elope but soon the young couple realize and try to escape and finally decide to die together if the world does not allow them to live together... That is when Pran and Premnath end up saving each other's child and accept that True Love wins and not necessarily a tragedy like "Lala Majnu". There are a lot of songs in the movie and here is the link with all the songs for you:

https://www.youtube.com/watch?v=AdRPZ4DYy-I ;

Cheers
Laksh KV

September 20, 1969

"AANKHEN"

Dear Friends:

It was today i.e. September 20 1968 (55 years ago) this hit movie and a spy thriller called "AANKHEN" released. Two brothers out of three in our house were Dharmendra fans and were keen to see this movie but the eldest one was a Manoj Kumar fan. But when we 2 brothers said we wanted to see this movie, he tried to come in the way but my Amma took the call and said all 3 must go to see this movie – and we saw it in the first week after it released on Friday but we had to wait for Monday as the advance booking ensured all 9 shows House full on plans open day i.e. on Monday 16th Sep 1968. We had pataaved our Amma and I recall that she went to do the advance booking after sending me to music class on Saturday Sept 21 1968. She got 3 tickets and managed to get "F" row tickets – thanx to a separate Ladies "Q". Before we saw the movie our dear friend Arun Balakrishan aka Naseeba had already seen the movie and declared to all of us that he wanted to marry Mala Sinha – real ambitious guy – Naseeba – this is what I love about you – you just can't restrain when it comes to such matters!!! Bedi, I am sure you recall this. What was exciting – shot abroad, Mehmood's comedy and post Farz, this spy thriller was in general creating waves – the radio program and the advertisements on the radio had the impactful opening "उस मुल्क की सरहद को कोई छू नहीं सख्त, जिस मुल्क की सरहद की निगाबान हैं आँखें" We 2 brothers were very happy that we were going to see a great movie but not the eldest one who reluctantly came to see the movie and had full of criticism for Dharam Paji – sorry bro – we cannot verify this with you anymore but I am not lying!!! Memories also include Mehmood having his screen name as Mehmood. Dharam Paji's fight with a Tiger and he then inserts a transmitter on his shoulder and how Mala Sinha, Mehmood and Dhumal go in search of him in Beirut singing "तुझको रखे राम तुझको अल्लाह रखे"... Another unique thing in my view – the hero did not lip sync any song!!! The movie was made by Ramanand Sagar under the banner of Sagar Arts International – who had made Arzoo which was a big hit though it resembled Sangam to a certain extent – and this was a drastic change from the love triangle. The star cast for you:

- Dharmendra
- Mala Sinha
- Kum Kum
- Sujit Kumar
- Nazir Hussain (80% sound so familiar with Geet cast)
- Mehmood
- Dhumal
- Jeevan
- Lalita Pawar &
- Madan Puri

Music Director Ravi's songs were quite hummable and here is the plot for you in a summarized fashion.

Some terrorist attacks post-independence in Assam area & that is very concerning for citizens who see deaths from close quarters. They are on the job to kill this and our Hero goes to Beirut and is helped by Mala Sinha who is half Indian and half Japanese. It is Jeevan, Madan Puri and gang making things difficult along with Lalita Pawar. Lot of emotional blackmailing back home to fail the mission and how successfully Dharam Paji with the help of Mala Sinha, Mehmood, Dhumal etc become victorious is the main plot – there is a duplicate Sujit Kumar who has captured the original one and tries to trouble Dharam paji but how can our Hero fail!!! – Overall a hit movie with good collections and the movie did celebrate 25 weeks run in Mumbai. Here are some songs from the movie:

https://www.youtube.com/watch?v=3YZmK9zj3TQ ;
https://www.youtube.com/watch?v=f_SJ2MPDAZI ;
https://www.youtube.com/watch?v=b9m-TMNbRCs ;
https://www.youtube.com/watch?v=QySYa46jhGk ;
https://www.youtube.com/watch?v=oqg6OT9AsYM ;

Cheers
Laksh KV

September 17, 1971

"RAKHWALA"

Dear Friends:

It was today – September 17, 1971 (52 years ago) the average grosser movie "RAKHWALA" released. It was a remake of Tamil hit movie "Kavalkkaran" produced by T Govindarajan and S Krishnamoorthy and directed by A Subba Rao. The movie had good star cast comprising of:

- Dharmendra
- Leena Chandavarkar
- Vinod Khanna
- Madan Puri
- Keshav Rana
- Jageep
- Rakesh Pandey &
- Baby Gayathri

I was a converted MGR fan and since the Tamil movie was a big hit, I wanted this one too to do well but this was an average grosser. It had a good start but from Monday the collection dipped as I could not see the "House Full" board from Monday onwards. However, the suspense part of it was evident to me that the Hero actually is a cop – thanx to the cover of Picturepost magazine where Dharam holds "Hathkadi" and it cannot be with a Driver of a car. What I liked most in the movie was the stunt scenes with parallel bars and some major "Kalabaazi" – lovely looking Leena Chandavarkar and with Dharam this Jodi too looked cute. What was painful in the movie was Jagdeep's imagination as a Dr. Compounder and what not... My good friend Balakrishnan Narayan was much broad minded than me – while I used to refuse seeing Kaka movies, he came with me to see this movie (me seeing for a second time) at Paradise Cinema – Mahim – remember Bedi???

The plot – was recently covered by me in my quiz column – here it is for you again with a little more insight - Dharmendra plays Deepak, an honest, hardworking son.

His family consists of his widowed mother (Pandar Bai) and younger brother Suresh (Rakesh Pandey). By luck, he stumbles on a good job of a driver, but with the wrong man, Mr. Jwalaprasad (Madan Puri). His mother takes his oath to protect his younger brother when on her death bed. She also reveals a family secret about his brother's real identity and missing fortune that is overheard by the dangerous Shyam (Vinod Khanna). Shyam has been plotting against Deepak with Mr. Jawalaprasad since he lost his love, Chandni Jwalaprasad (Leena Chandavarkar), to him. Through a series of bad events, Suresh is murdered, and Deepak is imprisoned. The film also has a light-hearted side story of a love struck pharmacist (Jagdeep) and his boss's daughter (Sanjana). There is good music, plenty of one-on-ten hero fights, and the mandatory twist at the end of the story – that the driver is a cop. Finally it's all happy ending. Here are the songs for you and it was a relief to see and hear Mohd Rafi songs when KK was more popular.

https://www.youtube.com/watch?v=FF3YcDRdgKs ;

https://www.youtube.com/watch?v=gQJxGgM62Nk ;

https://www.youtube.com/watch?v=Q4--2_VFdsU ;

https://www.youtube.com/watch?v=YqgEefB_d3s ;

https://www.youtube.com/watch?v=N03BR-0UacU

Cheers
Laksh KV

September 18, 1970

"GEET"

Dear Friends:

It was today – September 18th 1970 – 53 years ago Ramanand Sagar's much hyped movie "GEET" released and he somehow managed to show to the world that the movie was a hit and sought after. The biggest hype he created was by putting an ad in the paper saying "Beware of Duplicate Tickets" – uff – great marketing gimmick – the movie in my view was just an average grosser and did not run the mandatory 25 weeks to be called a hit. It was 2 years ago in 1968 the same Friday which happened to be September 20th, Ramanand Sagar's hit movie "Aankhen" was released and perhaps, he thought that 3rd Friday of September to be lucky for him but not so this time round. The movie boasted of good star cast as under:

- Rajendra Kumar
- Mala Sinha
- Sujit Kumar
- Kumkum
- Nazir Hussain
- Manmohan Krishna
- Keshto Mukherjee
- Bhagwan
- Daisy Irani
- Brahmma Bharadwaj &
- TunTun

My memories for you – I was in class XI and our First Term exams got over on the 17th of September 1970 and in those days we had exams every alternate days – luckily for us our exams were over but class X exams lasted till the 18th of Sept 1970 and we had a holiday, where we had nothing to study, no home work to do and could step out of the house totally bindaaz – only dampener was weather besides no-money... Many of my classmates decided to see the Tamil movie 'ADEY KANGAL' at Aurora where the movie was running in matinee and my good friend, class-mate and neighbour

Viswanathan Krishnan was lucky to get money from his Amma to see the movie while I reconciled myself by walking up to Rupam Cinema to see the black ticketers having a great time selling "Do Ka Teen" – clear 50% premium and walk back home after seeing the "House Full" board. The star cast looked pretty standard for a Sagar movie – KumKum, Sujit Kumar, Nazir Hussain – heroes would be alternating between Rajendra Kumar and Dharminder and the mounting would remind you of the previous movie of the maker. Despite all the hype and pomp the movie could only do that much though it had some good songs composed by Kalyanji Ananji – I kept wondering as to why he moved from Music Director Ravi in Ankhen to Kalyanji Anandji for Geet. But in all fairness, pretty decent songs were composed by the duo. Ameen Sayani did his bit in the radio programs about the movie and we all listened to it and tried to comprehend the story and once the Sunday TOI review came we could easily figure out the plot which is coming below:

Plot is a triangular one – Mala Sinha is a stage artist working for Sujit Kumar who holds shows and is also fond of her and wants to marry her but still hesitant to take the first step. Our Heroine goes on a vacation to Kulu and sees a Dehati Rajendra Kumar and is floored by his ability to sing and play flute and slowly gets fascinated and our hero too gets attracted to her and our man propses to her which she accepts. Now on return she informs Sujit Kumar who is unhappy and then tries to separate them by trying to kill the Hero who in one of the accidents loses his biggest asset "VOICE". Still the Heroine wants to be with the Hero and this time round Sujit Kumar manages to kill Mala Sinha's dad and you guessed it right, the prime suspect is our Hero. Eventually how our Hero gets back his voice and his ability to play flute when he cauldn't speak helps him to get a break to perform on radio. Eventually Sujit Kumar is exposed and all is well. Decent songs and here are the same for you.

https://www.youtube.com/watch?v=D1KeDDv3hUI ;
https://www.youtube.com/watch?v=7zVGbHW3eM4 ;
https://www.youtube.com/watch?v=KyZit6cxfBw ;
https://www.youtube.com/watch?v=R_amForkvmQ ;
https://www.youtube.com/watch?v=ZLFyp_Z97oA ;
https://www.youtube.com/watch?v=VBDiTaMHvTM ;

Cheers
Laksh KV

September 19, 1975

"PRATIGGYA"

Dear Friends:

It was today i.e. on September 19th 1975, (48 years ago) the movie called "PRATIGGYA" released which was a runaway hit and continued the dominance of the number one pair of Dharam-Hema. The timing for me was perfect as I had come out with flying colours in my Graduation exams – the results were out the very same week and I must say that I exceeded my own expectations and was eligible to do CA Articleship without an entrance test – well, where it mattered most, I was lucky to have done well – but was a working student since the age of 17 – so at 20 armed with 3 years of solid experience in writing and managing books of accounts right from maintaining registers, cash book, petty cash book, ledgers, bank reconciliation, income and expenditure account, trial balance and balance sheet – chasing customers for money, denying suppliers their dues and dealing with Govt authorities like Sales Tax and Income Tax – delivery – getting the tempo and reaching the goods & also monthly statutory reports to govt bodies – above all using the only calculator in the office at breakneck speed without looking at the keys... uff!! Some achievement I felt. As I was earning Rs. 440/- per month, I declined the offer of doing CA that would have brought my stipend to a mere Rs. 60/- a dip of Rs. 380/-... For a middle class guy, who was used to independence and seeing movies this dip was ill-affordable – so what to do – see movies and enrol for something that will keep me a student and look for a bigger brand company to join. Now, I had the option of doing Law and M.com – I opted for the latter for the fees was Rs. 50/- lesser – so M.Com with Costing & side by side do ACS, ICWA – all this in mind and commenced but seeing movies continued regardless and also revive vocal singing. Good bzee life the Post Graduation classes were in the evening from 630 PM to 830 PM at Poddar College. So the schedule was early morning music class, then office at Sion, Evening College – rush home around 845 – grab dinner and see 930 movies at Rupam... Wah kya life thi. Pratigya time the PG College was yet to start and that was the time my elder brother, who had been selected by the Department of

Telecom and was undergoing training at Nashik as an "Engineer Supervisor" later called as "Junior Engineer" – training of some 9 months. Every 2nd Saturday he used to come to Mumbai and return on Sunday night – so I decided one week end I will go to Nashik and I did after seeing the movie Pratigya and both of us hard-core fans of Dharam Paji and me completely besotted with Hema Malini – described the movie to my brother who was all ears. The Dehati Dharam – Truck driver and the stunts were typical dehati style like wrestling somewhere and the song 'MY JHAT YAMLA PAGALA DIWANA" standing out and also the "MIRZA SAHIBAAN" song...took me to a different world.

This movie was made under Paji's home production called "Bikramjeet Productions" – his brother Kanwar Ajit Singh too had a stake in the making of the movie – this is my assessment and I am open for correction. The movie had the following stars:

- Dharmendra
- Hema Malini
- Ajit
- Jagdeep
- Urmila Bhat
- Saten Kappu
- Johny Walker
- Abhi Bhattacharya
- Keshto Mukherjee
- Ram Mohan
- Sundar
- Brahmcahri
- Birbal
- Imtiaz Khan
- Pradeep Kumar &
- Bhushan Tiwari

The music was by Laxmikant Pyarelal and the movie grossed substantially to be part of the top 3 hits of 1975. The plot was very similar to some of the earlier hits but with different treatment – the theme being "Revenge" & the oath

"PRATIGYA" he takes to avenge the guy who killed his entire family. The difference is in the treatment from a Zanjheer and Yaadon Ki Baraat – with a lot of comedy included in this movie – Ajit, by then had specialized in the role of the guy who destroys families and misses out on one or few behind who grow up and finish him off. Over all a great entertainer and here are the songs for you.

https://www.youtube.com/watch?v=JpH2A7jMfjY ;

https://www.youtube.com/watch?v=Ya2Usoov4i0 ;

https://www.youtube.com/watch?v=hi-sdfuv7G4 ;

https://www.youtube.com/watch?v=Urp_eRuiUpo ;

Cheers

Laksh KV

September 15, 1972

"JOROO KA GHULAM"

Dear Friends:

It was today 51 years ago i.e. on September 15, 1972, this movie "JOROO KA GHULAM" released – directed by A. Bhim Singh – this movie had the following stars, playing key roles:

- Rajesh Khanna
- Nanda
- Om Prakash
- Achla Sachdev
- Ramesh Deo
- Sharad Kumar
- Jayashree T
- Manmohan Krishna
- Nana Palsheekar &
- Iftikhar

This movie was one of those early ones where Kaka's decline commenced and I was observing very keenly the proceedings. The fact that Friday 6 PM show was not House Full, at Rupam, I felt nice – in my view the debacle started with "Dil Daulat Duniya" which ran for 7 weeks and this one was dragged for 12 weeks. Around this time, I was in Inter Commerce and my good friend Bedi aka Balakrishnan Narayan was in First Year – I recall he went to see "Dil Daulat Duniya" after checking with me if I would join and being a Dharam fan, I declined then and hence this time he decided not to check with me. There was nothing much to rave about though some songs composed by Kalyanji Anandji were pretty decent and hummable.

The plot revolved around a rich girl falling for a middle class man and much against the wishes of her parents, these 2 tie the knot and in one year have a son too. This was despite her dad, selecting a rich boy for her and now dad and daughter were not on talking terms. But the Heroine stays in touch with her mom and boasts about the riches of her hubby like bungalow, car and all luxuries. Now, the senior couple want to come and meet up the grandson and in a hurry the heroine rents a bungalow, car and everything including a temporary hubby. Now the Hero becomes the servant of the house during the visit of his in-laws. This is the right time for a lot of hilarious situations and the visitors decide to extend their stay by a few more days after the promised 2 days. Now the extension of things is not easy and some of the vendors come to take things back and the truth is out. Then eventually things are sorted out. It makes an interesting plot and I feel it could have been treated better. Well, still the songs were OK and here are the songs for you:

https://www.youtube.com/watch?v=8P-tckjfm10 ;

https://www.youtube.com/watch?v=v7RghFdvT14 ;

https://www.youtube.com/watch?v=hpVsympl1SM ;

https://www.youtube.com/watch?v=friEe-d_2WI ;

https://www.youtube.com/watch?v=YPC9doVL3_M ;

Cheers

Laksh KV

September 14, 1973

"NAINA"

Dear Friends:

50 years ago today i.e. September 14 1973, this almost shelved movie called "NAINA" saw the light of the day. Produced by Babulal Shah and directed by Kanak Mishra, commenced the movie with Shashi Kapoor as the Hero and Rajashtree (of Brahmachari fame) as the Heroine. After shooting the movie for some time, the Heroine got married and vanished and settled in England – leaving the makers in lurch. Probably this was in the late 60s but I gathered that it was revisited and the script underwent major changes and the canned shots were very profitably used in flashback to depict the Hero's earlier life. This flashback really looked very authentic with the hero sporting short hair. I have some more personal memories of this date and then the movie.

My friend Easwar invited me to the wedding of his cousin sister who also happened to be my classmate – I am talking about Lakshmi Nathan– the Muhurtham was in the morning and the reception in the evening at Bharatiya Hall close to Punjab Association and Matunga Atheletic Club (MAC). Now, I was wondering, barely 18 and marriage!!! – Nevertheless, was keen to attend the wedding so that I could meet some more girls from our batch. I was telling Easwar that the whole school was after two girls that included the one tying the knot on this day – how come so early!!! I also knew that she was a big Shashi Kapoor fan as a school girl –and observed that this movie "Naina" was releasing on her wedding day – so as a part-time employed student I thought I will gift the couple the tickets in an envelope – I was clear that it could not be Lower, Upper Stalls or Balcony, it had to be BOX – but as luck would have it, the tickets were sold out for Saturday night show i.e. 15th Sept 1973 and personally was disappointed – the equivalent amount of Rs.5/-, I slipped into an envelope and handed over to my classmate during the reception and to my bad luck she has no recall of me making it to the wedding – and why would she – when Prince Charming was standing next to her!!! Well, today after so many years, we do share a great relationship at the family levels.

Now coming back to the movie "Naina", I recall that music was a strong point of this movie and my favourites Shankar Jaikishan had done a great job – besides the heroine leaving half way, I recall David sporting a very odd looking wig – never seen something like that on him. Both heroines Rajashree and Moshumi Chatterjee could speak with their eyes and no wonder the title of the movie was "NAINA". Besides these 3, we had David, Rehaman & Padma Khanna too in this movie as supporting actors. The movie was shot extensively in Europe before the heroine fled but all said and done – the movie could not succeed at the Box office despite good songs.

The plot revolved around a poet played by Shashi Kapoor who runs away with a Nauch girl played by Rajashree much against the wishes of his family members. That was a bold move by the hero but unfortunately, Rajashree dies (revised script – since she left the movie half way) and our hero is crestfallen. He takes to drinking and loves to wallow in self-pity and at some stage comes across Moushumi Chatterjee whose eyes strikes him and gives him the memory of his wife who is no more. However, he does suffer of some sickness as when it looks as though things are looking up, he slips back to the thoughts of his first wife – and makes him a very complex character. Though I had seen the movie – I do not have a very clear memory of how it ends – I guess it was a happy ending. The songs were great and here are songs for you:

https://www.youtube.com/watch?v=_g4A_Bj-SRI ;
https://www.youtube.com/watch?v=fuI1NNd0qfs ;
https://www.youtube.com/watch?v=asOMMqTEezA ;
https://www.youtube.com/watch?v=rg15kbWG1YE ;
https://www.youtube.com/watch?v=jsa-ft-l_B0 ;
https://www.youtube.com/watch?v=UmOqR49IYvw ;

Cheers
Laksh KV

September 12, 1969

"AANSOO BAN GAYE PHOOL"

Dear Friends:

It was today i.e. September 12 1969, (54 years ago) this movie called "AANSOO BAN GAYE PHOOL" released and it did negligible business at the Box Office. The movie was produced by Anoop Kumar and & SM Sagar and directed by Satyen Bose of Dosti fame. The movie was a remake from a Marathi play called "अश्रूंची झाली फुले". The star-cast of the movie here:
- Ashok Kumar
- Deb Mukherjee
- Alka
- Pran
- Raj Mehra
- Nirupa Roy
- Anup Kumar
- Helan
- Rakesh Pandey &
- Janki Das

While I knew of the Marathi play during my school days (Class X) but I clearly recall the radio advertisement that spoke about a Guajarati version – though I could not exactly catch the words from the radio (normally heard outside the barber shop) it sounded something like "Aatal Mein Hoton Ma Raata Ma" – I will request my good friend Dilip Apte to help with the exact name of the Guajarati version. Besides this, the things I recall are the couple of songs that were well received by the people – the first one being "जाने कैसा है मेरा दीवाना" followed by "इलेक्शन में मालिक के लड़के भी है खड़े".

The plot revolved around Ashok Kumar an honest man teaching kids in a college and helping them and is known for his integrity. He ensures that those going out of track are brought back in good time. But there is a politician played by Raj Mehra, who hatches a plot and traps the honest man who is convicted and is behind the bars. Now, during his tenure in the jail, there is a total transformation for the wronged man who only wants to come out of jail and then take revenge on the politician. On his return to the normal world how he does that and loses his basic values in the system forms the crux of the movie. Laxmikant Pyarelal's music did help the movie a bit but still could not salvage the movie from being a failure. Here are some songs for you.

https://www.youtube.com/watch?v=-oUlcx4LJG8 ;
https://www.youtube.com/watch?v=5-Mn5IQrUOs ;
https://www.youtube.com/watch?v=PCM6vF8cvCQ ;
https://www.youtube.com/watch?v=djTsGkNwm6A ;
https://www.youtube.com/watch?v=avljr1YX9Do ;

Cheers
Laksh KV

September 11, 1970

"BHAI BHAI"

Dear Friends:

It was today 53 years ago on September 11 1970, this average grosser made by Ratan Mohan under the banner of RM Art Production and directed by Raja Nawathe released. The music was composed by Shankar Jaikishan and the movie had:

- Sunil Dutt in a dual role
- Asha Parekh
- Mumtaz
- Pran
- Jeevan
- Mehmood
- Aruna Irani
- Jeevan
- Raj Mehra
- Mohan Choti
- Mukri
- Iftekar etc.

My Memories of this movie – it ran for 15 weeks and I had the privilege of seeing the trailer when I had gone to see "Yaadgar" during the previous week and cursed myself for choosing to see "Yaadgar" and missing out on "Bhai Bhai" – for there was money only for one movie and not to forget I was in class XI. The trailer, as expected looked very interesting – songs like:

- सपेरा बीन बजा बीन बजा नाचूंगी
- ओह दिलवालों थामो दिल मैं तो
- एक तेरा सुन्दर मुखड़ा एक तेरा प्यार से भरा दिल मिलना मुश्किल
- मेरे मेहबूब तेरे दम से
- आज रात है जवान दिल मेरा न तोड़िये

I remember well that Arun Balakrishnan saw this movie later and told all of us that during the climax Sunil Dutt was reading the long dialogue probably written on a black board that was kept behind the camera. In other words the lines were really very long.

Well, now coming to the plot – it revolves around a poor man who lives a poor life but moves out to have a better life. He writes poetries to start with but things do not work and when he is told to write about an imaginary character Sangram Singh, he does so well that he becomes so well known & he wins the heart of his Father in Law (FIL) to be. As luck would have it, his FIL to be gets killed and the blame comes on the poor hero and in the meantime the imaginary character Sangram Singh (Sunil Dutt again) has been creating enough havoc and is a look-alike of the hero. Finally all things fall in place and while the good Sunil Dutt is saved by his injured twin in the court and who breathes his last in the court, the writer Hero gets his reward in the form of Asha Parekh – no show of Mumtaz though... Here are the songs for you:

https://www.youtube.com/watch?v=a3X20XYnkKY ;
https://www.youtube.com/watch?v=5NiijgaqXKc ;
https://www.youtube.com/watch?v=fLqK1YEFY0s ;
https://www.youtube.com/watch?v=igSvOVuhlus ;
https://www.youtube.com/watch?v=_Dpa-LLlwLc ;

Cheers

Laksh KV

September 10, 1971

"KATHPUTLI"

Folks:

September 10 1971 i.e. 52 years ago, this movie 'KATHPUTLI' was released and it ran for 10 weeks in Mumbai and hence cannot be considered a hit movie. The movie was produced and directed by BRIJ under the banner called Dynamo International – the same banner that had made the movie "Do Bhai" earlier which too did not do well. The film cast includes:

- Jeetendra
- Mumtaz
- Helan
- Agha
- Jalal Agha
- Manmohan
- Mallika
- Bhagwan etc.

My memories about this film are as a First Year College student, due to financial constraints could not think of going for the movie. At this point, my cousin from Indian Air Force landed up and asked about what movies were running and quickly I said at Rupam it is Jeetendra Mumtaz starrer "Kathputli" and he asked would tickets be available – I just said we can check – he said we can try the night show at Rupam. I was thrilled to bits and this was the same cousin who had taken us to see "Do Badan" & "Dil Diya Dard Liya" a couple of years earlier – so we all were used to his "Dariya-Dil". So that was it and post dinner my cousin and my late brother Vaidya V Raj went to Rupam cinema and the black rate running during a "House Full" show was – 'दो का तीन' and we felt bad to push him hard to buy in black as he too was not too inclined. Finally, he looked at our eyes and decided to buy it at a premium of Re.1/- per ticket and we entered the hall. Sometime in the 90s we got to know that our cousin left his house and is not traceable – hope he is OK and praying for him. The other memories for me are that – it had Jeetendra renting an apartment that was only meant for married people and declares that Mallika (real life sister of Mumtaz) as his wife and to gain sympathy from people around gets loud firing from her and gains sympathy of Mumtaz whom he meets at the "Q" for filling water and sympathises with him and allows him to jump the "Q". I also vaguely recall that Jeetendra, to manage his fees for education sells tea in the evenings in a tea stall. He looked very sincere in his role and Mumtaz acted brilliantly I felt. Manmohan was in his familiar role of a rapist who does damage to Mumtaz and as expected she conceives and marries Jeetendra who has no idea of her past. Honestly, I liked the movie and wanted it to succeed but it did not. There was one song that came as part of the radio advertisement "रहूंगी रहूंगी तेरे संघ सजना" but did not find it in the movie. Jalal Agha plays Jeetu's friend and tries to manage the child of Mumtaz. Here I end my memories and I guess there is no need for me to move to the plot which is partially covered above.

Still – it is the story of Jeetendra and Mumtaz who get married and meet with an accident while driving and while Mumtaz has minor injuries our hero is in a bad shape and the heroine goes around trying to raise money to get her hubby up and running. Mumtaz is exploited by Manmohan and distances the couple more and more, as days progress they live under one roof without much communication. Jeetendra gets a kid home which his friend was thinking of admitting to an orphanage and its no surprise that it happens to be Mumtaz's kid. After a lot of issues and ego hassles things fall in place in the end. Songs by Kalyanji Anandji were just about OK – the one standing out is the Kishore Kumar number "जो तुम हसोगे तो दुनिया हसेगी " and the other duet with Mohd Rafi & Lata Mangeshkar "एक बात पूछूं दिल की बात पूछूं". Rest of the songs had Mahendra Kapoor and Mangeshkar sisters. Here are the songs for you.

https://www.youtube.com/watch?v=mbeiJUF8eP4 ;
https://www.youtube.com/watch?v=Ncd1_ChbMYY ;
https://www.youtube.com/watch?v=JDYDy0leaKs ;
https://www.youtube.com/watch?v=Obgt7OaG5AE ;
https://www.youtube.com/watch?v=NySlPj7k9qw ;

Cheers
Laksh KV

September 07, 1973

"JHEEL KE US PAAR"

Folks:

50 years ago today i.e. September 07 1973, "JHEEL KE US PAAR" was released which was considered a decent hit though not a jubilee movie. It was produced and directed by Bhappi Sonie. It had enough publicity and started off with good collections in the first week itself but for me unfortunately it was not released in Rupam while it did good business at Aurora – King's Circle. The movie had big star cast as under:

- Dharmendra
- Mumtaz
- Shatrughan Sinha
- Yogita Bali
- Pran
- Anwar Hussain
- Prem Chopra
- Ranjeet
- Veena
- Iftikar
- Urmila Bhat &
- Jr. Mehmood

My recall is that since I was employed on a part time basis where my office timing was from 4 PM, I had done my tickets at Badal Cinema for 1115 am show on the very first day – the craze of 1st day matinee show (ahead of 1st day first show) and was thrilled that my favourite Dharam Paji was very good in the stunt scenes – loved the way he jumped the stairs to beat up the wrong doers. However, I felt Pran overacted a lot in the movie and I felt relieved when he died with Mumtaz singing "सो जाना मूत खो जाना" & he kicks the bucket ... uff relieved!!! The other thing I recall is Dharam Paji is a painter and meets Shatrughan Sinha who is an eye Doctor who could make out from the painting of our Hero that the lady in the picture was blind... When Shatrughan arrived on screen, he got maximum applause – more than our Dharam Paji. The climax fight with Ranjeet at the runway of airport was awesome and needless to say Ranjeet dies. Songs were pretty good in the movie composed by RD Burman.

The plot was that of a small girl child who meets with an accident and loses her eye-sight and grows into Mumtaz with Pran as her dad. They are very poor people and the one who caused the accident is none other than Hero Dharmendra's dad and as expected the Hero falls in love with the blind girl and meets Dr. Shatrughan who is capable of getting her vision back. Hero's mom is not happy with Hero going gaga over a blind girl as she has Yogita Bali in her mind as Bahu, who happens to be the daughter of Iftikar who is her Diwan. Then there is enough effort on the part of Yogita Bali to filter out Mumtaz – but eventually good prevails. Storyline is quite predictable but overall the production values, good picturesque locations add to the beauty of the movie. Some lilting music really helps the movie in a big way. The movie did not meet the expectations that it promised but still the star value ensured decent collections. Here are the songs for you

https://www.youtube.com/watch?v=GcGBa-QPZZE... ;

Cheers
Laksh KV

September 05, 1969

"KISMAT"

Dear Friends:

54 years ago today i.e. September 5 1969 released a movie called 'KISMAT" produced by Kamal Mehara and directed by Manmohan Desai (later specialized in the movies of Lost and Found). The movie's main stars were:

1. Biswajeet
2. Babita
3. Helan
4. Murad
5. Hari Shivdasani (played Babita's dad – came naturally as he is her real life dad)
6. Hiralal
7. Jagdish Raj
8. Polson
9. Paul Sharma
10. Tun Tun
11. Shetty

My memories are only of looking at the posters at Rupam Cinema and imagining things that a 14 year old would do – my friend Mohan (Latha Easwar please tell him) was very excited seeing Helan in those seductive dress that was very evident in the banners. The other thing is the hit songs in the movie and top of the mind is "कजरा मोहब्बतवाला अखियों में ऐसा डाला "and in this song we had Biswajeet looking very cute as a female and the genuine female looked ordinary – all this only when I saw the song on YouTube for I am yet to see the movie. The other song that had a great impact was, "आओ हुज़ूर तुमको सितारों में ले चलूँ" – simply outstanding song and even the other songs were great – kudos to late OP Nayyar Saab. I am sure the lucky people like Dilip Apte would have seen it on release.

The plot was a thriller that had a Hero (Biswajeet) who is a Guitar Player and a Singer in a Night Club. The anti-social elements hide something inside the guitar of the Hero & with multiple girls including the vamp after the Hero & the ultimate success of Hero and the Police to bring the wrong-doers behind the bars marks the main plot of the movie. This movie had some wonderful songs.

Here are the songs for you.

https://www.youtube.com/watch?v=jucXcnZDquI... ;

Cheers

Laksh KV

September 04, 1970

"SAWAN BHADON"

Dear Friends:

53 years ago today i.e. on September 4 1970, 2 debutants made entry into Bollywood and they became instant hits with this movie called "SAWAN BHADON" produced and directed by Mohan Sehgal – the debutants:

- Rekha
- Navin Nischal & supported by
- Iftikar
- Shyama
- Jayashree T
- Agha
- Iftekar
- Narendranath
- Ranjeet
- Madan Puri

My recall is that this movie was not released in Rupam as "Yaadgaar" continued for a second week. Ganesh Chaturthi was still on and our terminal exams were round the corner and escaping from home on holiday between exams was a task by itself and I remember managing that outing in our area near hotel Vasant Bhavan – where the guys playing the songs in the Ganesha Pandal were alternating between Sawan Bhadon songs and Mera Naam Joker that was still a few months away. My friendly neighbour and classmate Viswanathan Krishnan managed to see this movie at Rivoli cinema and was going gaga over the song "मेरा मन घबराये ... तू सोजा तू सोजा". It turned out to be an entertaining movie and a new leading pair arrived in the form of Navin Nischal and Rekha, who is the daughter of a Big Tamil Hero Gemini Ganeshan. Sonik Omi provided some freshness to the music in this movie.

The plot revolved around the Hero who belongs to a wealthy family but he has been living in Europe and decides to return for good and that foils the plans of his Step-mother, step-sister and the Manager who want to cheat the Hero and take over the property. When he returns he is attacked by goondas deployed by his step-mother's brother but is saved by a village girl to whom our Hero gets attracted to and they fall in love. There is objection and the family manages to have the Hero killed thru an accident that they plan for his car. They celebrate his death little realizing that Heroes don't die in Hindi movies, but they are surprised when he returns who actually is a look-alike and a Cop. The family somehow want to prove that he is an imposter and in doing so confess that they indeed killed the original man – that was enough but the original Hero survives with some injuries and all is well in the end. Songs were good and here are the songs for you.

https://www.youtube.com/watch?v=jmxAeVb75Ww ;

https://www.youtube.com/watch?v=T2l7mItTsbQ ;

https://www.youtube.com/watch?v=LLUoc3UIWgk ;

https://www.youtube.com/watch?v=7V_ZH_VdVd4 ;

https://www.youtube.com/watch?v=Iz2nhPWKUSc ;

Cheers
Laksh KV

September 03, 1971

"CHOTI BAHU"

Dear Friends:

52 years ago today i.e. on September 3, 1971 released this movie called "CHOTI BAHU" *ing Rajesh Khanna, Sharmila Tagore, Shashikala, IS Johar, Nirupa Roy, Tarun Bose, Jr, Mehmood, Jairaj, Master Sooraj etc. Among many Kaka hits this was a relatively average grosser but in his successful wave this too is kind of considered a hit though nothing compared to some other movies like Andaz, Anand, Hathi Mere Sathi, Aan Milo Sajna and Kati Patang that released in 1971. My focus in the movie was for the Mohd Rafi song 'YEH RAAT HAI PYASI' and those days it was Kishore Kumar days and it was not so common for Mohd Rafi to sing and that too coming from Kalyanji Anandji who had shifted his loyalties to KK in a big way. The other song that caught my attention was "HAY RE KANHAIYYA KISKO KAHEGA TU MAIYYA". Somehow, from my building group also no one went to see this movie – correct me if I am wrong friends viz. Balakrishnan Narayan & Viswanathan Krishnan.

The plot revolved around an epileptic patient played by Sharmila Tagore who gets married to Rajesh Khanna who is not aware of her illness before marriage. But when they come to know, the entire family accepts her, the way she is and tries to help her come out of it. Kaka's brother's (Tarun Bose) son gets very close to the choti bahu and thinks her to be his mother and she is on the road to recovery thanx to the support of all the family members especially Nirupa Roy who plays her sister-in-law. Soon comes the Hero's sister Shashikala with her husband IS Johar and son Jr. Mahmood and disrupts the peace and succeeds in making the child move away from Sharmila Tagore and she again becomes sick. It is finally the young Jr. Mehmood who helps in understanding the reason behind the boy being away from Sharmila Tagore and in the end all is well that ends well. Some decent songs by Kalyanji Anandji helped the movie in its own humble way in the average success the movie. Here are the songs for you.

https://www.youtube.com/watch?v=vYH-PCSk-Oc ;
https://www.youtube.com/watch?v=tHCBH4CXohE ;
https://www.youtube.com/watch?v=7-mFA-THVBo ;
https://www.youtube.com/watch?v=HIVlpmypPeg ;
Cheers
Laksh KV

September 01, 1972

"RIVAAJ"

Folks:

It was today 51 years ago on September 01 1972, this flop movie "RIVAAJ" released. It hardly did any business despite having decent cast of Sanjeev Kumar, Mala Sinha, Shatrughan Sinha, Nasir Hussain, Farida Jalal, Pandhari Bai, Zeb Rehaman & Mukri. To top it had the music of Shankar Jaikishan and though a great fan of this duo, the music was far from good in this movie. I guess the death of Jaikishan was taking its toll on the quality of music. If I recall right, the child star was Baby Gowri who played Shammi Kapoor's daughter in Andaaz. There is not much memory for me regarding this movie except that it bombed.

Regarding plot, this was a story of a young widow played by Mala Sinha, daughter of a priest played by Nasir Hussain. Sanjeev Kumar falls in love with her and wants to marry her but his mom is against marrying a child widow and arranges his marriage with Zeb Rehaman who then bears a baby played by Baby Gouri. Later Zeb Rehaman dies of cancer and the little girl sees her dad lighting the pyre to cremate her mother and starts hating her dad. However, she gets to know from her grandmother that her mother would come back in the form of a plant and the young girl goes to the cremation ground and sees a plant and starts talking to the plant. In the meantime Mala Sinha listens to the girl and then responds as though the plant is talking to her and this goes on repeating daily and the child feels good. Then comes the villain Shatrughan Sinha where Sanjeev Kumar works as Estate Manager and in trying to do good for the owner Sulochana, he ends up antagonizing her son Shatrughan Sinha who later kidnaps the young baby and eventually things fall in place and all is well that ends well. The average music only ensured movie could not rise up, Here are some links for you:

https://www.youtube.com/watch?v=PgIiNw6wF-c ;
https://www.youtube.com/watch?v=Sdne4qEJOH0 ;
https://www.youtube.com/watch?v=W5gaPMYvbE8 ;
https://www.youtube.com/watch?v=RY1xofddliA ;
https://www.youtube.com/watch?v=A2G59Sa7bE4 ;
Cheers
Laksh KV

August 31, 1973

"JAISE KO TAISA"

Folks:

50 years ago on August 31 1973, this movie 'JAISAY KO TAISA' was released today. The movie did average business that was made by a well-known South banner called AVM. It had Jeetendra in a dual role with Reena Roy and Srividya as the leading ladies with support from Anwar Hussain, Ramesh Deo, Kamin Kaushal, Aruna Irani, Mohan Choti & Baby Roja. My memories of this movie and related events are:

- It was Ganesh Chaturthi day and my parents were busy with Pooja that commenced very early in the day and were done with preparation of lunch by 930 am. They had to go for a condolence as one of my Amma's very close mother-like figure had passed away and as my parents left told us to have Prasadam and lunch as they were not sure when they would return. I had half a mind to tell them about my plan to go for the movie but restrained myself though Amma was aware that I had done the booking in advance.

- An early lunch at 10 and left home saying bye to both my elder brothers and took a bus (385) from Jain Society and my destination was Amar Mahal and then walk for a few minutes to reach Sahakar Cinema. I had absolutely no idea about Jeetu playing a dual role in the movie. The show started at 11.15 am and I had gone to see it alone as all my friends were unavailable due to Ganesh Chaturthi

- I was shocked to see a 2nd Jeetendra in the movie and the movie was quite similar to Ram Aur Shyam with Jeetu playing the Bhola and Chatur characters and Ramesh Deo dominating over Jeetu initially and once the exchange happens and then Ramesh Deo is at the receiving end. The movie did not meet my expectations and even the songs were just about passable.

    I had to struggle to get a bus from Amar Mahal after the movie got over and rain was not helping the matter either.

I don't think it is required for me to talk about the plot as it is very standard and predictable. The performances were also just about OK and nothing worth a big mention – the movie managed to run for 15 weeks and hence not considered a flop. Here the song links for you:

https://www.youtube.com/watch?v=FbDd0rFQU7U ;

https://www.youtube.com/watch?v=gY4VacJ3ayc ;

https://www.youtube.com/watch?v=yUkdgDMddrs ;

https://www.youtube.com/watch?v=ebU9JZDgRJs ;

https://www.youtube.com/watch?v=mNt2806agFA ;

https://www.youtube.com/watch?v=18Mw3HrjQTo ;

Cheers

Laksh KV

August 29, 1969

"PYAR KA SAPNA &
October 17 1969 ANMOL MOTI"

Dear Friends:

It was today 54 years ago on August 29th 1969 a flop movie released called 'PYAR KA SAPNA" (PKS) & on October 17 1969 released another flop movie"ANMOL MOTI" (AM). Both the movies just managed to run for 10 weeks – PKS had the same lead as "Tamanna" that was released and flopped exactly a week ago. AM was positioned as India's "FIRST UNDER WATER FILM" but that could not salvage the movie from being a disaster. My memories are only to the extent that I had no money and only had the abilities to look at posters and read the review in the newspapers on Sunday. However, I got to know later that the character actor "Rajan Haksar" in PKS, was the associate producer of the movie. The movie had good music by Chitragupt and a great director in Hrishikesh Mukherjee at the helm – still the movie could not do much. The star cast of PKS included:

- Ashok Kumar
- Biswajit
- Mala Sinha
- Helan
- Johny Walker
- Durga Khote
- Rajan Haksar

The plot involved around Biswajit who gets married to Mala Sinha without looking at her and if he had declined the wedding, he would not have got the funding for his trip to London. He is least interested in a typical Indian Mala Sinha. Then the chase commences by Mala Sinha who trains herself and projects herself as a modern lady with a different name and as expected our man falls for her and eventually it is how the wayward man is tamed and brought on track by the heroine forms the main part of the story and all this happens in London enhancing the production values. Unfortunately this did not appeal to the people at large. Some songs were decent and the advertisement on the radio was by "Ehasan Rizwi" who had a very unique style of talking. Here are some songs for you.

https://www.youtube.com/watch?v=u-t6Abr_fUM ;
https://www.youtube.com/watch?v=WFC7UNrAW6g ;
https://www.youtube.com/watch?v=uaHpouUftmo ;
https://www.youtube.com/watch?v=LX0g57lY7Nw ;

Now coming to the second movie "Anmol Moti" (AM) it was publicized as "India's First Under Water Film" made by SD Narang as both Producer & Director – the banner was Narang Films. The cast of the movie:

- Jeetendra
- Babita
- Jagdeep
- Shabnam
- Jayant
- Rajendranath
- Tuntun
- Sapru &
- Aruna Irani

It had some good songs composed by Ravi and sung by Mahendra Kapoor, who was in his elements. Since I have not seen the movie, I am unable to add much in the form of plot of the movie. All I can say that this movie too failed to hit the bull's eye. Decent music helped a little and here are some songs for you here.

https://www.youtube.com/watch?v=zAzYOSsFHCI ;
https://www.youtube.com/watch?v=meAbhJPhQRk ;
https://www.youtube.com/watch?v=5nZlDH7Jpy4 ;
https://www.youtube.com/watch?v=KdOJZysonvE ;
https://www.youtube.com/watch?v=ofmOeARl0PM ;

Cheers
Laksh KV

August 28, 1970

"YAADGAR"

Folks:

Today i.e. August 28 1970 – 53 years ago saw the release of an average grosser "YAADGAR" written by Manoj Kumar himself and the main stars being:

- Manoj Kumar
- Nutan
- Pran
- Prem Chopra
- Tiwari
- Kamini Kaushal
- Laxmi Chaya
- Kuljeet
- Tiwari (Senior)
- Shammi
- Ashit Sen
- Mohan Choti
- Polson
- Birbal
- Jr. Mehmood

The movie did average business and my memories are that I did see this movie in its 2nd week run in Rupam Cinema with my late brother Vaidya V Raj who was a big Manoj Kumar fan and with him was his B.Sc classmate Moorthy aka John. We saw the 6 PM show on Sunday September 6th and felt nice to see the trailer of Bhai Bhai that was to release on the 11th Sept 1970. The cost of the ticket was Rs. 2/- and my brother had invested on behalf of his friend and was quite keen to get the money from him and it took a long time for John to hand over the Rs. 2/- and post movie close to the Hanuman Temple, we 3 kept talking as we had to take a left turn while John had to walk ahead and finally he did remove his wallet and paid the money and I could see relief on my brother's face.

The other thing standing out was the song "EK TARA BOLAY" that comes multiple times in the movie and Mahendra Kapoor has done a great job in this song and also a couple of other songs like "Woh Khet Mein Milega, Kaliyaan Mein Milega". Decent acting by all made the movie watchable. The movie ran for 15 weeks and hence considered to be average or can be termed a border line hit movie. Well, the other things were Nutan singing in her own voice in one of the songs and finally we were pretty excited to see Nutan of all the Heroines in SWIM SUIT.... Certainly exciting for a 15 year old!!! Not to forget Prem Chopra chasing a lady thinking it is Nutan but later realises it is his sister.

Plot revolved around Poor idealist vs. Rich Zamindars – the poor working class idealist and honest Hero Manoj Kumar has a group called "POL KHOL" group – who expose a lot of people who are corrupt and not doing their jobs and the righteous man wants to contest election against the rich and powerful. The struggle involved in the whole thing was well depicted and eventually one gets to know that after all he did not belong to the poor category with the flash back in the movie that tells us about the Hero. As always finally right prevails – pretty decent songs and the links are below.

> https://www.youtube.com/watch?v=XtaQ2aSwPRQ ;
> https://www.youtube.com/watch?v=EksD8lCb5eQ ;
> https://www.youtube.com/watch?v=YXLakFgg5OY ;
> https://www.youtube.com/watch?v=MOIP640i-gA ;
> https://www.youtube.com/watch?v=1cVE-_0SiLE ;
> Cheers
> Laksh KV

August 27, 1971

"NADAAN"

Dear Friends:

52 years ago i.e. on 27th August 1971 Deven Varma's movie "NADAAN" was released and it did not do well – it was a below average grosser. This was the 3rd movie of Navin Nischal who made an impact with "Sawan Bhadon" released in 1970 and the next one was "Parwana" in July 1971 and one month later it was "Nadaan" and had a big heroine alongside in Asha Parekh and other stars of the movie were – Madan Puri, Sulochna, Nirupa Roy, Helan, AK Hangal, Deven Verma, Asit Sen and Bela Bose. This movie was produced and directed by Deven Varma. My early memories of this movie are as under:

- Those were rainy days and my late brother Vaidya V Raj had just joined Asian Paints and since he used to leave early to take a bus (302) from Sion to Bhandup, I used to accompany him with umbrella till he boarded the bus and would walk back home and then go to college. All this due to the princely sum or Rs. 10/- he used to give me as pocket money – the seva was to the extent of even removing his shoe lace!!! He loved all this – very nice soul, left me very early – let me move on.

- Though I have not seen the movie till date, I recall the radio program and my recall says that Asha Parekh acts like a Boy or Tomboy and keeps saying 'HEY GOCHU". Before this movie released, we had a senior friend in our neighbourhood by name GOVIND and we used to call him "GOCHU", Mohan as "MOCHU" etc. and when this movie released another friend from our next building Arun Khanna aka Annu loved the term "GOCHU" and acknowledged our (my friend Bedi & mine) creation and held us in high esteem.

- Being Shankar Jaikishan fan, I was trying to make the music sound like big hit though it was just about OK and was a bit surprised why SJ opted for Mukesh so much in this movie – but stand out songs were 'AI BADAL JHOOM KE CHAL, ZAMEEN KO CHOOM KE CHAL" &

"MEHNAT HUMARA JEEVAN, MEHANAT HUMARA NAARA".

The plot revolved around one Ranee Maa who had a bad past and had some major prejudice/rivalry against a specific community. The next in line heir wants to bring about peace but the senior lady is unhappy and reprimands her. The younger one meets the Hero and they fall in love and again the Ranee Maa is unhappy at her choice and does her best to stop but the Heroine is clear that she wants to only get married to her Hero. Ranee Maa eventually succumbs but then there is Madan Puri who has the background of Ranee Maa and does his act of blackmailing but finally all is well. Nothing much to talk about performances too. So here are some songs from the movie:

https://www.youtube.com/watch?v=wKs2VgBJ_1U ;
https://www.youtube.com/watch?v=ZXzVdmwX5EE ;
https://www.youtube.com/watch?v=cN6HxSClJMs ;
https://www.youtube.com/watch?v=rMBNuxY-o9w ;
https://www.youtube.com/watch?v=CNg9YgrFU0A ;

Cheers
Laksh KV

August 25, 1972

"ZAMEEN AASMAN"

Dear Friends:

51 years ago today i.e. on August 25 1972 this flop movie called "ZAMEEN AASMAN" was released. Produced by the banner AV Films and was directed by A Veerappan and the movie had the following actors:

- Ashok Kumar
- Sunil Dutt
- Rekha
- Indrani Mukherjee (dual role)
- Yogita Bali
- Sharad Kumar
- Ramesh Deo
- Achla Sachdev
- Dulhari

My memories about this movie are as under:

1. My good friend Balakrishnan Narayan aka Bedi and I skipped college and landed at Bijli Cinema to see this movie – hoping to see some steamy scenes of Rekha and Yogita Bali but were very disappointed.
2. Ashok Kumar's screen name was "Shanti Swaroop" and he turns blind in the movie.
3. The Kishore Kumar number "आँखें तुम्हारी दो जहां" filmed on Sunil Dutt and Rekha & "हम तुम चले तुम चले हम चले" filmed on Yogita Bali and Sharad Kumar stood out.

The plot revolved around mainly Ashok Kumar who is a strict disciplinarian alienates himself from his wife Indrani Mukherji and son and daughter played by Sunil Dutt and Yogita Bali. When his wife dies, he gets married again to another lady who is a look alike of his dead wife. But this new wife has an affair with

Ramesh Deo and is only interested in the property. Ashok Kumar has a fall and loses his eyesight and then becomes dependant on his wife and a nurse Rekha. His daughter is in love with a poor guy Sharad Kumar and that does not go well with Ashok Kumar and there is total disintegration as Sunil Dutt leaves the house and the house is open for the wrong doers but eventually things fall in place. Overall, it was a boring movie. Very average music too to top it and here are some songs from the movie for you.

https://www.youtube.com/watch?v=gOmeDGV21CM ;
https://www.youtube.com/watch?v=BHndcB7ZD5o ;
https://www.youtube.com/watch?v=8Iin0i6Ce7Y ;
https://www.youtube.com/watch?v=7ESd5f_qf2I ;
https://www.youtube.com/watch?v=0QnM7oxsW_k ;

Cheers
Laksh KV

September 14, 1973

"AAJ KI TAAZA KHABAR"

Folks:

It was today 50 years ago on September 14, 1973 a very interesting movie by Rajendra Bhatia called "AAJ KI TAZA KHABAR" released and while it cannot be termed as a super-duper hit but given the budget, it did well and it did tickle the audience. The movie did not boast of a big star cast but they were very effective and each one did justice and the master of remakes Rohit Shetty did some work to modify this script and created "Golmaal" not so long ago. The movie had Kiran Kumar (Character actor Jeevan's son) playing the lead with Radha Saluja of "Do Raha" fame as the heroine. The other key contributors were Asrani, IS Johar and Paintal while Narendranath and Manju Asrani too had some exposure in the movie. My memories of the movie are as under:

- My late brother Vaidya V Raj and myself went to see this movie and when the song "मुझे मेरी बीवी से बचाओ "came on screen it was hilarious to see Kiran Kumar with his face and body covered with soap and at that point he looked so much like his dad "Jeevan" that we could not control our laughter.
  - Paintal in the role of "Champak Bhoomiya" was outstanding and brought the house down.
  - Music by Shankar Jaikishan certainly did not meet the high expectations set by the duo but this was post Jaikishan's demise and the days when it was more Kishore Kumar than Mohd Rafi.

The plot of the movie revolved around a couple Kiran Kumar and Radha Saluja but the lady is ever suspicious about her miya and it so happens that on one night he does not return home as he genuinely gets stuck in a giant wheel with an unknown lady (Manju Asrani) due to the mal-functioning of the equipment. As a result of this, they are forced to spend the full night at an altitude and obviously they cannot just keep quiet – so they engage in some small conversation and it is in the early hours of the next day that they both reach their respective homes. Now the hero is clear that his wife is not going to buy his story of getting stuck on a giant wheel – so he fabricates a story that he was with his old friend called "Champak Bhoomiya" about whom the heroine has never heard and hence asks about the address and gets some weird address from her hubby. Just to double check the wife sends a telegram to Champak Bhoomiya and invites him home. To make things authentic the hero plans to invite his friend Asrani to save him and act as Champak Bhoomiya and things go very smooth till the real Chamapk Bhoomiya in the form of Paintal lands up with the telegram. Then there is enough chaos and confusion that creates a lot of funny situations. It was a very enjoyable fare and no wonder Rohit Shetty recreated it recently. Here are the songs for you.

https://www.youtube.com/watch?v=T9s8Xxe89KU ;

https://www.youtube.com/watch?v=_naCbqvGb_M ;

https://www.youtube.com/watch?v=cFxdViuW8nY ;

https://www.youtube.com/watch?v=ACtBxNcr8qU ;

https://www.youtube.com/watch?v=Qn0sPzN8-nE ;

Cheers
Laksh KV

August 22, 1969

"TAMANNA"

Dear Friends:

It was today exactly 54 years ago on August 22 1969, the flop movie "TAMANNA" released – directed by KP Atma and *ing Biswajeet, Mala Sinha, Shashikala, Nazir Hussain, Deven Verma, Nazima, Sulochana, Ashit Sen and Agha. The lead pair was quite well accepted in general and has some good hits to its credit though this one was a disaster. I have only two memory points to share and they are as under:

1. Back to back movies of this lead pair released – 22nd Aug 1969 – TAMANNA & on 29th Aug 1969 – PYAR KA SAPNA & both failed.

2. The only hit song from the movie "Tamanna" was sung by Mukesh and filmed on Ashit Sen and the song was "ताश के बावन पत्ते, पंजे छक्के सत्ते"

I had no other way but to check all sources and gathered the following:

Rich Hero and a Poor Heroine fall in love and as classmates they decide to tie the knot. But the Hero's dad is against the match as he plans to have his son married into a wealthy family. This is a decision point and the Hero leaves home and becomes a cop while the Heroine is a practicing physician. Our Hero has a step sister and with her brother having staged a walkout, she eyes the property and then, as it happens in normal Hindi movies – things fall in place.

Songs for you:

https://www.youtube.com/watch?v=FcKBTwDbXvA ;
https://www.youtube.com/watch?v=RnPSNjaBPz0 ;
https://www.youtube.com/watch?v=AZp7o0WHMuE ;

Cheers
Laksh KV

August 21, 1970

"TUM HASEEN MAIN JAWAN"

Dear Friends:

It was today August 21 1970 – 53 years ago the out and out entertainer called "TUM HASEEN MAIN JAWAN" released. Produced & Directed by Bhappi Sonie and the stars who contributed are:

- Dharmendra
- Hema Malini
- Pran
- Helan
- Rajendranath
- Anwar Hussain
- Sulochna
- Dhumal
- Mohan Choti
- Anjali Kadam
- CS Dubey
- Shabnam
- Iftikar ...... etc.

My memories are as under:

- The movie was a hit and ran for 20 weeks
- As a class XI student who was allowed movies only during vacations – this was a no no but was keen listener of radio program
- Radio Ceylon used to play the Kishore Kumar hit song 'मुन्ने की अम्मा ये तो बता तेरे बेटे के अप्पा का नाम क्या है?'
- Regular visit to Rupam Cinema to see if I could see the familiar wooden "House Full" Board and was very happy to see that constantly displayed.
- Soft corner for SJ music and trying to make the songs hit by constantly singing

I could manage to see the movie only as a college student during its matinee run at Rupam and as a big fan of the lead couple, loved the movie. Also loved the style of Pran, who had something different – some style in every movie he acted in and here he used to say "Uff.... ufffff.. Ufff". The other memory I have is that of an absent minded boss in Anwar Hussain who was easily fooled by all his subordinates in the ship. The small kid inside the ship was a total entertainment and the song dedicated to the child with Dharam Paji and Rajendranath in their elements was par excellance.

Coming to the plot, it starts with the reading of a will where in the property of a rich man is supposed to go to his son or if he is no more, to his grandson & if they too are not traceable to Pran – the villain of the piece. So the soul objective of Pran is to ensure that the kid is finished off & his scheme is known to the lawyer and the well-wisher doctor. They manage to hoodwink Pran by declaring that the lady delivered a dead child and have the kid smuggled in a fruit basket which lands in a ship with the naval officers where our Hero Dharam Paji is the live-wire. Hema Malini is supposed to be the custodian of the kid but now is in hunt of the ship that would reach Mumbai in a couple days' time. Then it is a struggle for her to locate the child and then become a governess to protect the little one from Pran. The remaining part of the movie is to ensure that things fall in place after a lot of confusion and Pran who is already married to Helan and has a baby learns the lesson the hard way of not to be avaricious.

Good acting by all the key players and foot tapping music helped the movie to be one of the early hits of the real life couple Dharam Paji and Hemaji. Here are the songs for you

https://www.youtube.com/watch?v=TAjNIMBFhHI ;
https://www.youtube.com/watch?v=r-lqR0zWwZ8 '
https://www.youtube.com/watch?v=8MWL9ICohMw ;
https://www.youtube.com/watch?v=JzZ3d1S8PKw ;
https://www.youtube.com/watch?v=AiglwdF50gQ ;
https://www.youtube.com/watch?v=VO0oW7wBMnc ;

Cheers
Laksh KV

August 20, 1971

"AAP AAYE BAHAAR AAYEE"

Folks:

It was today exactly 52 years ago ie Aug 20 1971, this disaster called "AAP AAYE BAHAAR AYEE" released. This came from the banner of EMKAY films that had earlier given a decent hit called 'ANJANA" – having seen that one which was again an average entertainer, I thought this one would be somewhat similar – but though the heroines are related to each other the senior one dished out a flop movie. The cast included – Rajendra Kumar, Sadhna, Prem Chopra, Rajendranath and child artist Bobby who was introduced as a wonder child in "Ek Phool Do Mali". The others were Raj Mehra, Meena T etc. My memories are as under:

- There was enough hype during the pre-release of this movie. We were in the first year of our college days and my class mate from school KR Easwar (Lakshmi Nathan please inform him as he is not in FB) was a big LP fan and wanted to see the movie. I was a SJ fanatic and was not keen to see this movie but he insisted and I relented. We saw the movie at Bandra Talkies during the first week of the movie – not the first day. Now Bandra Talkies is a shopping complex. We stood in a very small "Q" and got the best seats in the lower stall – cost of the ticket being Re. 1/- each.

- The movie started with Rajendra Kumar and Sadhna coming close and it becomes a still and the title rolled and my friend was excited at the concept.

- During the movie, we both remembered the child star from Ek Phool Do Mali, Mastana and Aansoo Aur Muskaan and I just told Easwar that Bobby was a girl and he said NO. I said "Bet" – he said yes and we decided that next movie has to be funded by the loser and he was the loser and believe you me, he insisted we see the movie once more and we did. I still cannot forget his comment "What a waste of good music in a bad movie!!!" – I felt he was right heart of heart but did not acknowledge LP's good music for the next week SJ movie "Naadan" was to be released *ing Navin Nischal & Asha Parekh.

The plot was pretty triangular in nature but not done purposely. Rajendra Kumar (RK) falls in love with Sadhna and meets her dad and she too falls for him. With no background Prem Chopra (PC) too applies as a prospective groom for Sadhna's hand and she rejects him which he does not take very kindly since he was made to look as a laughing stock. Now it is the turn of PC to act and act he does by raping Sadhna before the marriage and this makes the once good friends RK and PC to become bitter enemies. More problems as the rape results in pregnancy and now the hero wants to help her and give his name for the child. PC gathers that the child is not RK's and starts black-mailing him for money and then the movie follows the expected path and good prevails in the end.

An immensely forgettable experience, but for some good music, and here are the songs from the movie that ran for 5 weeks in Mumbai and considered a miserable FLOP.

https://www.youtube.com/watch?v=nxPAthBV00E ;

Cheers
Laksh KV

August 18, 1972

"BAWARCHI"

Folks:

51 years ago it was today – Aug 18 1972 – the very tasty movie "BAWARCHI" released and captured the hearts of the audience in a jiffy. While the claim from wiki is that it was a very Big Hit, my memory says that while it was very well accepted and liked by all, the number of weeks it ran did not justify to me that it was a run-away hit – 12 weeks is average and I guess "Hrishikesh Mukherjee" was not from the school of thought to show the world that his movies are big time hits – he made wholesome movies with excellent messages. My memories are from what I saw at Rupam cinema in Sion – after seeing the mad rush for "Be-imaan" that ran for 2 weeks from August 4th, the crowd for this movie was there but not overwhelming. I did not see the movie on release due to my prejudice towards Kaka, but was definitely monitoring its progress and when I saw that on 1st day 245 pm show the "House Full" board took a while to come out, that was an indicator to me that it is not going to be a big hit. 6 PM show had some empty seats as the wooden board indicating HOUSE FULL was inside the hall and the tall security man at Rupam was waiting for indication to move the board – I was working close to Rupam Cinema in a company called "Pentagon" and my office timing was from 3 PM to 630 PM and had finished early by 6 and was lurking around Rupam to see what was going on and heart of heart was feeling good that this Kaka movie is not doing well. But, I did see it much later on Door Darshan and loved the movie and felt it should have done more business than what it did. By then my prejudice had vanished, for Kaka himself slumped.

Some observations from my side are:

- Jaya Bhaduri is a great actor but not a great dancer – proven earlier in Ek Nazar too
- Asrani was really creating a special place for himself in Hrishikesh movies – right from Satyakam

- Having seen Hero No 1 many times, I tend to compare the 2 movies and found Govinda too doing justice to the role of a Bawarchi...
- Chatopadhyaji had some style
- Excellent commentary by AB

The plot revolved around a joint family with the head of the family being an old man with his own idiosyncrasies and others had to put up with him – ironically their bungalow was called "Shanti Niwas" which had absolutely no peace – there were squabbles galore within the household and the old man was a pain to all and in fact each inhabitant pained the other – They were constantly on the look out for a cook as no one lasted in this madhouse. So our man "Raghu" arrives with a magic wand and wins over each member of the family and brings them together – a very noble work indeed – there is the old man's grand-daughter played by Jaya Bhaduri who unfortunately has lost her parents and is subjected to a lot of taunts by the others. Our "Go to man" or "Man Friday" helps her too and the climax is when he unites her with her boy friend by himself becoming a bad man and the house returns to its normalcy. Finally, it is shown that this man is on the lookout for next "Shanti Niwas" to bring some Shanti in the new house. Music of Madan Mohan had his stamp and here are the songs for you

https://www.youtube.com/watch?v=g9uY_-9EBCU

Cheers
Laksh KV

August 17, 1973

"CHALAK"

Folks:

It was today 50 years ago on 17th Aug 1973 the movie "CHALAK" released. *ing Kiran Kumar, Radha Saluja, Alka, Jayashri T, Brahmchari, Keshto Mukherji, Jagdish Raj, Brahmma Bharadwaj, Maruti & Lalita Kumari.

The movie was a big disaster and it was not expected to do well either – all that I can recall are the 2 songs that have remained in my mind – one filmed on Alka – "MAN GAAYE WOH TARANA" and the other a duet filmed on Kiran Kumar & Radha Saluja "DIL KA NAZRAANA LAY". Unfortunately, nothing beyond this I can recall. This one is just for records that 50 years ago a movie called Chalak was released – period... I shall provide the links of these 2 songs and may be there are other songs from the movie too. But I would request my friends who might have seen it or have more information about it to share. – So here are the songs for you.

https://www.youtube.com/watch?v=GRo-B9STgSE ';
https://www.youtube.com/watch?v=M-_S4GBf-Go ;
Cheers
Laksh KV

August 15, 1969

"BADI DIDI" & "CHANDA AUR BIJLI"

Dear Friends:

54 years ago, it was today 2 movies released – going alphabetically – first "BADI DIDI" *ing Jeetendra, Nanda, Om Prakash, Raj Mehra, Mehmood, Aruna Irani, Dilip Raj etc. and as luck would have it, it was being shown on one of the channels on TV on August 14 2017. The print was bad and it was very tough to comprehend the movie – and the movie did not do too well either – Nanda had the distinction of playing "Choti Behan" earlier and later "Badi Didi" - even songs were just about OK – the one which became a hit was the one filmed on Mehmood – "CHAT MANGNI PAT SHAADI" – there is very little I can share about this movie and would request those who have seen this movie to throw more light on this movie. Here are the songs of the movie for you.

    https://www.youtube.com/watch?v=YAYdxr_RRqU ;
    https://www.youtube.com/watch?v=2Lbw33DSM88 ;
    https://www.youtube.com/watch?v=HNmAbS_4_qo ;
    https://www.youtube.com/watch?v=B6V6uQ3zE38 ;
    https://www.youtube.com/watch?v=LUsDdFqysVo ;
    https://www.youtube.com/watch?v=WAr9A42lp_E ;

Second movie released on the same day was "CHANDA AUR BIJLI" *ing Padmini, Sanjeev Kumar, Master Sachin, Jeevan, Mohan Choti, Jr. Mehmood, Keshto Mukherji etc. This movie got its publicity as the 100th movie of Music Directors – Shankar Jaikishan and one week before this was the release of yet another SJ movie "Prince" that had outstanding songs & during the premier when asked about the music, Shankar mentioned that "Yeh Bhi Hit Jo Jayegi". There was some portion of the shooting that was done at Sion Fort where Padmini danced and sang "Dekh Tamasha Dekh" and the radio ad on radio Ceylon was people shouting/chasing 'CHOR CHOR CHOR CHOR' & the person who is chased is a young boy and he responds saying "NAHI NAHI, MAIN CHOR NAHI MAIN CHANDA HOON". Some catchy songs and at times Padmini gets a bit inviting with the song 'AAJ KOYI AAYEGA" & the duet with Mohd Rafi 'KHUD TOH BADNAAM HUVE, HUMKO BADNAAM KIYA" had intoxication all over while the most popular song was "KAAL KA PAIYYA GHOOMAY BHAYYA...RAM KRISHNA HARI" - my other memory here is that of Ganesh Chaturthi of 1969 and around that time I was down with fever and had to miss the terminal exams – though outwardly I showed as though I was upset, I was very happy actually lying down at home, not studying and listening to Vividh Bharati and focusing more on SJ songs like from Yakeen and appreciating "BACHKE KAHAN JAAOGAY" along with songs of PRINCE and CHANDA AUR BIJLI. This movie came from the Guru Dutt banner and was directed by Atma Ram.

The plot revolved around Padmini who danced on the streets representing a gang of thieves. Master Sachin, though from an affluent background, due to turn of events he lands in an orphanage. He has his royal blood that comes to his rescue when he fights with the manager of the orphanage and once the Manager gets to know about the real background of Sachin, he wants to eliminate him and Sachin escapes and joins hand with the thief gang but cannot blend there and fate takes him to his original house and eventually meets his grandparents after a lot of confusion. Nothing much to talk about – the movie ran for 10 weeks and not considered a hit and not a big flop either. – Songs were still good and do listen to them from the link below:

https://www.youtube.com/watch?v=NJjwJZqxbKo ;

Cheers
Laksh KV

August 15, 1975

"SHOLAY"

Folks:

48 years ago it was today the MILESTONE movie "SHOLAY" released – coming from the famous Sippy Banner. Almost everyone of that era would have some experience to share about how they ended up seeing this great movie. The movie had exceptional characterisations and though a bit long, people lapped it up after the initial negative feedback that it started with. The advance booking counter opened on Monday August 11 1975 and my dear friend Balakrishnan Narayan had decided to get the tickets in advance. The saying that morning was "All Roads lead to Basant Cinema" which claimed to be on 70 mm besides Minerva – the pride of Maharashtra – but my dear friend found that it was all incorrect and the crowd was massive and it was only the normal 35mm – so the smart guy that he is, he decided to go to Sahakar and managed to book some five tickets for 530 PM show as first show was impossible for him to get. We were all excited and were waiting for the day and as we waited impatiently, we were generally speculating about how the movie could be etc. Etc.

Come 15th August 1975, the first thing I did was to participate in Leo Club's Blood Donation Drive. I was the first one to donate blood and in turn had a lot of things to eat including Rasgullas – as a 20 year old was very enthused to donate blood, for already I had done it during my college days and by this time, I was awaiting our Graduation results and thanx to my job, I was earning a princely amount of Rs. 355/- pm gross but used to feel bad to give away Rs. 1.25 per Saturday towards ESI contribution – so it could be either Rs. 5/- per month or 6.25 depending on number of Saturdays – used to feel bad if there were 5 Saturdays and if it happened to be in Feb with a max of 29 days, it was killing!!! Well, post tea on Aug 15 1975, we as a group of 5 that included our building boys – Balakrishnan Narayan – aka Bedi, Arun Balakrishnan aka Naseeba, Viswanathan Krishnan aka JKB and my brother Radhakrishnan and yours truly and we all got a train from Koliwada (now called GTBN) station to go to Chembur and from the station we walked to Sahakar Cinema. While we waited for our train anxiously, we could only see 2 trains towards VT coming with all efficiency and I am sure Bedi will remember how a stray dog that got disturbed in its post tea nap and the way he/she gave a dirty look at the train going to VT and then resumed its sleep. We reached the cinema hall well before 5 PM for a 5.30 PM show but we gathered that the 1st show was running behind schedule and that the show might start later – how long no one knew – the wait was very painful and slowly some information was trickling in that there were not enough prints and 4 halls were sharing one print and hence it was taking time – eventually our show started at 7 PM and there was one short 5 min break for the print to arrive once during the show. We were very impressed by the production values, stunts and the mounting in general – western style fight scenes etc and yet a new comer Amjad Khan pitted against seasoned campaigners like Dharam Paji, Sanjeev Kumar and Amitabh Bachhan and he held his ground in a brilliant way. Media said Amjad Khan – "Giant, Jayant's son" – I guess everything about this movie was just right including the publicity, marketing and if at all there was something that could have been a bit better it was the songs which were a bit on the average side while the background music was very well received including the Tabla when the dacoits chase Basanti and her Dhanno. There was a lot of violence and the censors made the Sippys reshoot the climax wherein, Amjad instead of getting killed by Sanjeev Kumar gets handed over to police which was not a great idea – since we have seen the original end on YouTube, I feel that was more in line with the expectations. Here is the link of the original –

https://www.youtube.com/watch?v=W0rGcuKGU0k ;

The movie made money even from sale of 56 minute summary audio cassette of the movie that included the original dialogues and songs and that had also caught on in a big way those days. It was something different though it did remind us of Mera Gaon Mera Desh and Khote Sikkay, here the uniform of Gabbar Singh was unique and not the usual dhoti we are used to seeing a dacoit. Not just that, Amjad had a unique way of having tobacco that he removes from a small cotton bag and for everything he checks with his trusted go to man "Sambha" and the way he said "ARRE OH SAMBHA – KITNA INAAM RAKHAY HAIN SARKAAR HUMPAR?" or the more famous 'KITNAY AADMI THAY?" – People fell in love with Gabbar and mind you that was not easy with so many others around. Great job indeed overall. For us the movie got over at 11 PM and the night show was to start after that – just imagine when it would have ended. Well, it was also some kind of a task for us to get back home and all the parents were worried as to why we had not returned yet, for dinner was planned to be had at home and it was well past 12 when we reached home and had to explain things to them. This is one movie where I am not going to write about the plot but only talk of other things – like how Danny was approached for the role of Gabbar but he had committed his dates for DHARMATMA and could not go ahead – so it was a matter of luck for Amjad Khan and not so long ago we also gathered that there was a Qawali that was recorded for the movie but was not included, for the movie was already over 200 minutes.

Here is the link of the song that did not find a place in the movie –

https://www.youtube.com/watch?v=KOXkCBKbwKs ;

On way to Mysore in the hilly area Mr. Sippy had created Ramgarh Village and it was a tourist attraction for many years and the movie took over 2 years to complete. Dharmender was keen to play the role of Thakur Baldev Singh – Sanjeev Kumar's role but that was also the time Dharampaji was wooing Hemaji and Sanjeev Kumar too had interest in Hemaji. On the other hand Jaya Bhaduri went thru 2 pregnancies and a delivery during the making of the movie. The role played by Jagdeep was inspired by one of his acquaintances and there were people who started asking him if he was a dealer in Jungle wood and he wanted to file a case too. The movie had high production values and stereophonic sound system had its impact that we could feel as if the coin fell next to us when Dharam Paji throws the faulty coin that always ensured AB won with both sides "Head". The ticket prices were hiked – the normal Rs.2/- tickets were now available at Rs. 5/- officially and to get tickets in the only cinema hall in 70 mm at Minerva was impossible – so we kept seeing the 35mm version at Sahakar, Aurora, Sharada as and when we felt like. Even now, it is able to hold our interest and I must have seen the movie over 50 times by now – & when it was released in 3D in Jan 2014, we saw twice again here in Blore and more than the movie we enjoyed how people enjoyed the movie with so much of knowledge of the lines that were being mouthed by the actors and when Sanjeev Kumar would call "Ram Lal" the whole crowd would laugh thinking about all those tasks that he would have performed for the handless Thakur. AK Hangal too had a role that had so much of an impact and when he loses his grandson Sachin – the entire village is in favour of getting rid of the 2 guys Jai and Veeru who had come to save them but Imaam saab – AK Hangal said that "DUNIYA MEIN SUBSE BADA BHOJ TOH WOH HI

– BAAP KE KHANDON PAR BETAY KA JANAZA" – While Hema Malini played the chatterbox, Jaya Bhaduri played the subdued young widow but showed her true colors in the Holi flash back where she too talked no end. There was comedy too in the scenes of Asrani as a jailor and Keshto Mukherjee as his informer – Hari Ram. Well, perhaps it will be easy to write a book on this movie but will stop here and talk of commercials and song links.

The movie ran for 3 years 3 shows at Minerva and till now, SHOLAY is considered as the BIGGEST hit though many new movies have come and collected 500 crores but I am sure Amitabh Nigham would be able to throw more light wrt the numbers after adjusting the inflation.

Here are some songs for you from the movie which I still feel did not do justice to the stature of the movie.

https://www.youtube.com/watch?v=sOl7kVq6cPk ;

Cheers
Laksh KV

August 14, 1970

"MAHAL"

Dear Friends:

53 years ago it was today, the Dev Anand-Asha Parekh starrer "MAHAL" released which did not do well at the Box Office. The supporting cast included Farida Jalal, Abhi Bhattacharya, David, Sundar and Sapru plus others. My memory as a class XI student was one that of envy of those friends like Chintya Arun who was a college student and on Sunday evening walk after the movie was released, he said on the following day he was going to bunk college and go and see "Mahal" – My good friend Balakrishnan Narayan aka Bedi and myself just looked at him with total envy and felt "Bhy HUM KAB SCHOOL SE BAHAR NIKLENGAY AND ENJOY LIFE!!!". Whether he saw the movie or was it a repeat of "Gambler" bluff, we did not go to find. The other memory for me is that those days, my second brother and I were big fans of Prem Chopra and would imitate him – almost every talk we had with our dad would be in his style. We started calling our APPA as Daddy thanx to Prem Chopra. Imagine the song of the movie 'OH TU KYA JAANAY DIN RAAT HUM JEETAY HAIN, TERA NAAM LEKAR, OH TERA NAAM LEKAR' we would speak like Prem Chopra with an additional term "Daddy" added in between like "OH TU KYA JAANAY DIN RAAT HUM JEETAY HAIN – DADDY!!!" – The sporting man that He was, He would laugh it off.

My friend Bedi and myself saw this at Rupam in its reduced rates run in 1973 and still felt the movie was not so bad to be such a big flop – may be we were happy with the songs and felt there was sincerity in the acting of all the actors.

The plot revolved around a poor man driver "Dev Anand" who is keen to make big money so that he could marry off his sister – so the struggle is on and in comes a total stranger who promises him good money if he plays an imposter to be the Brother-in-law of an old man in his death bed – who has a lot of property and riches. Dev Anand also falls in love with a rich Asha Parekh and thinks playing an imposter till the old man dies would only help him little realizing that he was getting into a trap of the murder of the real owner of the huge mansion. All complications later things fall in place. Decent songs and seductive number filmed on Farida Jalal made a lot of impact. Here is a link for you with all the songs of the movie-:

https://www.youtube.com/watch?v=ETXljK9DHa4... ;

Cheers
Laksh KV

August 13, 1971

"MERA GAON MERA DESH"

Folks:

Exactly one week after Naya Zamana released, it was today ie. August 13 1971 – 52 years ago yet another hit movie "MERA GAON MERA DESH" released. It came from the Khosla banner with Director Raj Khosla at the helm with Bolu and Lekhraj Khoslas producing this Dacoit movie. This movie too was a big hit like Naya Zamana and clearly the 1975 hit from the Sippy household called "SHOLAY", had inspirations from this movie.

This movie had Dharminder playing a jail bird and, when he comes out, he is helped by an ex-army now crippled guy played by Jayant. Jayant sees some promise in this guy and being childless thinks of taking help from him to take care of his agricultural land and help a small time thief lead a good life in the village. There is also an old lady who is termed mad in the village, who assumes Dharam Paji to be her lost son and to keep her happy he plays along. Dharam also falls in love with Asha Parekh and gets her reciprocation after some initial hesitation. This village is constantly in fear and has the threat of a Dacoit called "Jabbar Singh" very effectively portrayed by Vinod Khanna & Amjad Khan's role of "Gabbar Singh" was kind of inspired by this for sure. The Dacoit group also has an attractive girl played by Laxmi Chayya and she flips for Dharam Paji (Who will not!!!) and while being the trusted person of the dacoit, she actually betrays him. Lot of fights and violence is part of the movie and the best part of it is that there is a quote of Mahatma Gandhi right in the beginning of the movie and it goes like this... "If there is a choice between Cowardice and Violence, I will choose Violence" – Mahatma Gandhi – this coming from someone who was known for getting independence with total "Non-Violence" is tough to accept but I believe it is very profound. The biggest enemy for this village is not Jabbar Singh but the "FEAR" and it takes a lot of effort on the part of Dharampaji to get to the people and make them understand the reality of Unity and that is what comes in the climax when the entire village gangs up to give the same kind of fear to "Jabbar Singh". The entire movie has been mounted well and 95% of the movie is shot outdoors and looks very authentic. Great movie, good acting, lovely foot-tapping music ensured a 100% Box Office Hit.

Now, coming to my memories:

- During this phase my monthly pocket money was Rs.2/- and it was thanx to my late elder brother Vaidya V Raj who had joined Asian Paints as a Chemist who used to give me a princely sum of Rs. 10/- as pocket money that stood me in good stead.

- This movie, we saw in the rainy season of Mumbai and at Nandi cinema and my classmate and neighbour Viswanathan Krishnan was with me and I recall how he had to make some monitory adjustments with one Shetty who was his classmate.

- Subsequently, we had a second visit when Balakrishnan Narayan joined me and we both saw the movie at Citilight and were thrilled – for our return, we managed to get bus number 314 which unfortunately stopped near Wadala and we waited for another bus endlessly and there was a cabbie who was enjoying our plight – there was also a good looking lady with a kid in hand waiting for bus and we thought of hiring a Kaali Peeli and offering her lift. As we were deciding who would sit with her behind, the smart lady said that she would sit in front and the beneficiary was the driver!!! And Bedi and me haath malte reh gaye... Remember Bedi?

- Some of the lines delivered ensured applause and whistle regardless of who said e.g. Vinod Khanna trying to find as to who leaks the information about the gang "SAATH SAAL MEIN PEHLI BAAR ANDHAR KI KHABAR BAAHAR GAYI HAI... KAUN HAI WOH VISHWASGHAATI, APNE AAP BAAHAR AAYGA, TOH CHAIN KI MAUT MAREGA – SIRF EK GOLI, DHOONDKAR NIKALA GAYA, TOH KUTTAY KI MAUT MAREGA"... Dharam Paji promising the village 'AAJ SE YEH GAON MERA BHI HI".... whisile.

- During the song 'SONA LAI JAA RAY" – Dharampaji is clad as a Sanyasi or Jogi... but when some of the genuine Sanyaasis paas thru, the effect is exactly opposite with Asha Parekh sitting on top blessing the saffron clad Dharampaji who sits below.

- While Asha Parekh had a couple of lilting numbers including a duet 'KUCH KEHTA HAI YEH SAAWAN", the songs filmed on Laxmi Chaaya had greater impact like 'HAAYE SHARMAOON KIS KIS KO BATAAOON" or "AAYA AAYA ATARIYA PAY KOYI CHOR" where she identifies to Dharampaji and Police, Jabbar in disguise and of course the climax song 'MAAR DIYA JAAY KE CHOD DIYA JAAY – BOL TERE SAATH KYA SULOOP KIYA JAAY" – All these songs were picturized very well and extremely good characterization.

- The village men folk indulging in drinking and making sounds of "GUGGI" – whatever that meant – it was hilarious with Bhagwan & Birbal enjoying themselves – What I could relate best as a 16 year old was Dharam Paji taking some deep breath when he sees a bevy of girls taking bath in a pond and then is in for trouble looking at them from Asha Parekh.

- The depiction of coward villagers was exceptional and in the climax when each one thinks, what can I do all alone, the lady of the house tells her hubby – wear these bangles and let me step out – that was awakening.

Well over all fantastic movie, well made and here are the songs for you

https://www.youtube.com/watch?v=a6-cmKcj994 ;

Cheers
Laksh KV

August 11, 1972

"RAMPUR KA LAKSHMAN"

Folks:

It was exactly today 51 years ago one of the major hits of Randhir Kapoor's career released – i.e. On August 11 1972. It was dished out by the Nadiadwala banner with the lost and found specialist Manmohan Desai as the director. It had good mass appeal and went on to become a Silver Jubilee hit in Mumbai. While Randhir Kapoor played the title role of a "Dhoti Clad" guy coming from a village to the city, his lost brother is played by none other than the happening guy from Bihar – Shatrughan Sinha. Timing of release of this movie was just right as it was our 25th Independence Day round the corner & here I have to go back in time as flash back.

- We friends – Balakrishnan Narayanan, Arun Balakrishnan, Viswanathan Krishnan, my brother Radhakrishnan and yours truly suddenly decided on 15th August to see this movie. I had started my employment as a 17 year old from June 1972 and had got 2 salaries of Rs. 75/- each by the time we decided to go for the movie... So funding was a non-issue. Now, the issue was which cinema hall to go to – Rupam had Be-imaan running for a 2nd week and we all decided to go to Kalpana Kurla and we reached in good time for the 3PM show. All that we could see was a "House Full" board and there were very few and far between black-marketers and in general, we wanted to see giving fair price not really go the black way. So we all were at the steps of the entrance hoping to meet someone who had extra tickets to sell and we did not mind sitting separately inside and all 5 were attempting to get extra tickets and extra tickets we did get in instalments – 2, 1,1 & 1 and all 5 were scattered and anyone who entered made a noise on entry that indicated that "yes he has come in" and all of us were in and we had missed some part of the start – but one can easily guess how the kids got separated.

- During the interval we exchanged notes and understood how much was missed and were confident of catching up later during our 2nd visit as we had all liked the movie and all of us were mighty impressed by Shatrughan

Sinha's dialogue delivery e.g. "JOOTA KITNA BHI KEEMTI HO, USAY PAIRONPAR HI PEHANA JATA HI, NAKI SARPAR" & another one "RAAVAN NAY BHI HANUMAAN KO EK MAMOOLI BANDHAR SAMAJH LIYA THA, LEKIN USNE SAARI LANKA KO.....AAG LAGA DI"..... Indicated that by lighting a cigarette with his LIGHTER... what style – total paisa vasool for all of us.

- Randhir Kapoor made us feel good especially in the title song and we all could relate to the 25th Independence Day when he sang "IS LAATHI SE ANGREZ DARKE BHAAGA HI". It also had a song where all 3 main characters Randhir, Rekha and Shatru participated and we could get to hear Kishore Kumar and Mohd Rafi together in the song "PYAR KA SAMAY KUM HAI YAHAN". Good hit songs made the movie watchable though RK changing his look from Lakshman to Lewis was not very credible.

The plot revolved around a family of parents and 2 boys who get separated in a train while the younger son continues with his dad, the elder son is brought up by a gangster and the mother works as a maid in the heroine's house. By turn of events where an elderly man tries to save a young Randhir Kapoor and in the bargain gets run over by a vehicle and gets crippled. Then the crippled man with his son lives with young Randhir Kapoor and his dad. When the kids grow up the crippled man's son Ramesh Deo leaves for Mumbai for employment and after a few months there is no news about him and so our villager hero comes to city in search of Ramesh Deo and finds that he is jailed and is accused of murder that he did not commit. He then decides to get into the root of the issue and changes his get up and as Lewis he finds out about the real culprit that happens to be Shatrughan Sinha who is his long lost brother – now the major issue for our hero whom to save but you guessed it right – Shatrughan dies like a hero after recognizing his "MAA". The cast includes:

1. Randhir Kapoor
2. Rekha
3. Shatrughan Sinha
4. Ramesh Deo
5. Roopesh Kumar

6. Tiwari (Senior)
7. Ranjeet
8. Faryal
9. Sulochana
10. Padma Khanna
11. Manmohan Krishna
12. Randhir (Character actor)
13. Raj Mehara
14. Bhushan Tiwari

Here is a link with all the songs for you:

https://www.youtube.com/watch?v=Tf0nVyDehz4 ;

Cheers
Laksh KV

August 10, 1973

"KUCHHE DHAAGE"

Folks:

50 years ago it was today (Aug-10-1973) – Raj Khosla's movie "KUCHHE DHAAGE" released in Mumbai. The same banner had made a hit dacoit movie in 1971 called "Mera Gaon Mera Desh" and looks like the banner wanted to continue in the same fashion. This movie had the Villain turned Hero Vinod Khanna playing Lakhan and pitted against Kabir Bedi who played Roopa. In fact Kabir Bedi also played Roopa's dad Tulsiram who gets sentenced by virtue of Lakhan's dad and Lakhan's mom pregnant at that time wants revenge and hence brings up her son to finish off Roopa's dad which he does efficiently. Now, Roopa who is part of armed forces gets to know about his dad's demise and he resigns and his only mission in life is to finish off Lakhan. So both these are just living to kill each other. Needless to say, both of them fall for the same girl Sona – Moushumi Chatterjee who is slated to get married to her real life Hubby Ritesh (son of Music Director Hemant Kumar). The two at some point go out of the way to help Sona more so there is no one to do "Kanyaadaan" for the wedding and having been very rough in their lives, they do not understand what "Kanyaadaann" is and mistake it for "Kanyadas" and even think of kidnapping "Kanyadas" and getting the marriage done. During one of their encounters earlier, both Lakhan and Roopa escape from each other as coincidentally both of them run out of bullets and then both of them decide to keep one bullet reserved to kill the other – while one of them adores his wrist band with a bullet, the other one has it on his armband. Police is after these two for all the not so good things they did and having successfully marrying off Sona as brothers, they find police confronting them and they are clear that their demise is inevitable and so what do they do – they both pull out the bullet kept in reserve from the wrist and armband to kill each other and finish off the job in style.

What a plot and what a story-line!!! All said and done, I did like the movie though it was very much an average grosser at the Box Office. The other memory I have is that of it came in and around Raksha Bandhan and jelled well with the theme and some decent songs too - Pretty decent performances though Kabir Bedi as an old man looked very artificial when the young Vinod Khanna kills him. Here are the song links for you:

https://www.youtube.com/watch?v=6x2cva8By3Y ;

https://www.youtube.com/watch?v=D5G-BSPzYjY ;

https://www.youtube.com/watch?v=g2RTnnJj_dM ;

https://www.youtube.com/watch?v=aqbVd5bZVac ;

The link below is the last 5 mins of the movie where the 2 guys marry off the Heroine and how they finish off each other:

https://www.youtube.com/watch?v=KVJjQcRyp98 ;

Cheers
Laksh KV

August 09, 1968

"GAURI"

Dear Friends:

55 years ago, it was today this movie called "Gauri" saw the light of the day. It was a remake of a hit Tamil movie called "Shanti" and the Hero of the Tamil movie Shivaji Ganeshan made this movie in Hindi and made a quick appearance on screen with folded hands saying "Namaste" and opening the banner of the movie by moving the flowers from the board. Just to verify this, I went to Youtube and checked and yes, I was right and saw Shivaji do this in about 1 minute and 5 seconds. Well, the movie was directed by Bhim Singh and had Sunil Dutt playing the lead with Nutan in the title role of Gauri and Sanjeev Kumar as the close friend of Sunil Dutt and Mumtaz as Sunil Dutt's girlfriend. All these form part of my memories of this movie which did not do too well at the Box Office. But the most talked about thing in the movie was the "Eye Surgery" of the heroine Nutan who is blind and if I recall right, the operation procedure on screen lasted very long as the maker alternated between the operation and the hunting adventure of the Heroes - and it was talked about a lot those days. But as a teenager my strong memory is the first song of the movie "DIL MERA TUMHARI ADAAYE LAY GAYEE" filmed on Sunil Dutt and Mumtaz and both of them in a swimming pool really made our bachpan kay din. Needless to say, we saw this movie at Rupam Cinema Sion and the only reason we were allowed by Amma to see the movie out of turn was that it was the remake of her favourite hero Sivaji Ganeshan's hit Tamil movie Shanti. Well, it was a week day and 6 pm show with not much crowd and that indicated that the movie was not going to be a hit. The other memory is a song sung by the Music Director Ravi "LOG TOH MARKAR JALTAY HONGAY, MEIN JEETAY JEETAY JALTA HOON" – I always knew Music Directors could sing but very seldom saw them doing play back and here was one. Later it was recorded again with Mohd Rafi and used in the movie. One more thing was that the names of the Sunil Dutt and Sanjeev Kumar in the movie were Sunil and Sanjeev respectively.

Now, coming to the plot – Sunil Dutt and Mumtaz are in love and Sanjeev Kumar is his good friend whose uncle Om Prakash is very greedy and for the sake of money he tricks Sanjeev Kumar into marrying a blind girl Nutan. Sanjeev Kumar realizes after the "Saath Phere" that his legally wedded wife is blind and walks out. Om Prakash requests Sunil Dutt to help and get Sanjeev back on track and he does succeed in convincing that it could have happened to him after marriage too – so would his wife desert him etc. Well, then Sanjeev thinks of how he would help his wife and still find happiness but all this is short lived as during an adventure of hunting, Sanjeev Kumar is deemed dead and now Om Prakash pushes Sunil Dutt to double up as Sanjeev since the blind heroine has not seen nor heard him. While they were hunting a surgery on Nutan's eye is done successfully and she gets her vision. Now, Mumtaz is in a bad shape and so is Sunil Dutt who is playing the role of Nutan's husband – eventually, Nutan gets to know about this and the dead man too returns after walking thru music director Ravi's song. Nutan, when she gets to know of it, decides to give herself to river Ganges as she is very clear that she cannot have 2 husbands. When we saw the movie, the movie ends as a tragedy with Nutan drowing while later the end was changed and it was shown that the river rejects her and throws her back at the feet of her real husband Sanjeev Kumar and she accepts this and life goes on - The change of end did not help the movie to be a success at the Box Office.

Music too was average and here are some of the songs for you.
https://www.youtube.com/watch?v=5HZklDq1c4I ;
Cheers
Laksh KV

August 08, 1969 (54 years ago)

"PRINCE"

Folks:

It was exactly today 54 years ago on August 8th 1969, this movie called "Prince" released that was hyped big time. This movie came from the banner called "Eagle Films" and was made by FC Mehara and directed by Lekh Tandon. The music was given by the hit duo Shankar Jaikishan. I have some recalls about this movie and that is what I would like to share in this column.

1. My classmate K. Suryanarayanan aka Chury (not on FB) was a very big fan of Shammi Kapoor (SK) and I too had a bit of a conflict between Dharam Paji and SK and when the choice was given to me between Yakeen (2 weeks earlier) & Prince, I opted for Prince. Chury went gaga over the movie having seen it before me – he said the moment the movie started, an eagle came and sat on a globe – "useemay paisa vasool" he said.

2. Prior to that we used to listen to Vividh Bharati where there was this advertisement that said "FC Mehara Ka" and the name of the movie – somehow, since our PYE radio had very poor reception, I could not figure out the name of the movie. Next at school, I checked with Chury and he had also heard it and felt the title of the movie was "BLIMSE" and till now, I keep referring to "Prince" as "Blimse".

3. Now, my maasi Kamala Narayan also wanted to see the movie and on the following Monday – August 11 1969 6 PM show we had the tickets booked at Rupam Cinema where the cost of the ticket was Rs.2/- and we were all excited and reached home rushing from school before 415 PM. We had our usual tea and tiffin (most Madrasis had it – something like Idli, Dosa, Upma etc.)

4. Finally, after the advertisements and INR, the movie started and it was welcomed by the whistles of the crowd. As my friend Chury had said, I was waiting for the Eagle to come and see the banner and it did come and frankly I was not impressed by the animation, though I had given a lot of

hype to folks at home. So my Maasi immediately asked me – "you happy now?" - then it started with SK who is unable to get sleep but there are people at his beck and call – there is a person to hold his cigarette – truly he was living like a "Prince". Needless to say, this Prince was a spoilt brat and was full of arrogance and attitude and no one dared to raise his/her voice against him. But there was one priest, who did not bow down to the Prince and his expectations, instead suggests to the arrogant man to go and be with the ordinary people and experience the life they lead. Strange enough, the Prince engineers a situation by which he is assumed to be dead by all in the palace and our man mingles with the poor and also becomes a son to an old lady. There are some hilarious scenes too – where SK with his big built and height covers himself in a Saree and joins the ladies just to hide from those who would recognize him. Our Hero also gets to know as to all the close people to him are after all fighting over the property that belongs to him.

5. Excellent songs helped the film though in all fairness, it was not very entertaining and in fact it was a bit boring too. Music was outstanding for sure and the top of my mind songs are

"BADAN PAY SITARAY LAPETE HUVE",

"MUQABLA HUM SAY NA KARO"

"MADHOSH HAVA MATVAALI FIZA",

"NAZAR MEIN BIJLI ADAA MEIN SHOLAY" &

"BACHKE JAANE NA DOONGI DILDAAR".

6. This was the last movie released in the old "Minerva" Cinema and then it was demolished and it was later reopened and was known as "Minerva – Pride of Maharashtra" and if my memory serves me right the first movie to release in the renovated hall was "Lal Pathar" on March 31 1972.

From the point # 4, the plot is quite clear as to how a spoilt Prince understands human values entirely thru his experience.

Well, these are all my memories and here are the song links for you.

https://www.youtube.com/watch?v=kKttNFQAW3s ;
https://www.youtube.com/watch?v=tUOGSByRSEc ;

https://www.youtube.com/watch?v=nEyO4AVl2eg ;
https://www.youtube.com/watch?v=O0Gmz7nFIQQ ;
https://www.youtube.com/watch?v=sb4ONNxdI0g ;
https://www.youtube.com/watch?v=_urdOEWttN8 ;

Hoping to get comments from my friends

Cheers
Laksh KV

Aug 07 1970 (53 Years Ago)

"SAFAR"

Dear Friends:

It was today 53 years ago MR FIlms "Safar" hit the Cinemas in Mumbai. Made by Mushir & Riaz - the film did very well and was one of those 17 successful movies that Kaka had from 1969 onwards. The movie had Rajesh Khanna as the Hero, Sharmila Tagore as the Heroine, & Feroz Khan, Ashok Kumar, IS Johar & Nadira as supporting characters. My memories are as follows:

1. Monsoon on one side and my dental treatment was still on with Dr. Arora in Sion.
2. I could see my friends Balakrishnan Narayan aka Bedi and Viswanathan Krishnan aka JKB feeling very happy at Kaka's success at the box office and JKB was constantly singing "Jeevan Se Bhari, Teri Aankhen". I was praying for Jeevan Mritue to do better than Safar but luckily both did well.
3. Our another neighbour Mochu (Latha Easwaran - please remind your BIL) was the lucky guy to see the movie in the very first week and being a good Sharmila fan, kept explaining to us how FK flips for her and sings for her "JO TUM KO HO PASAND WAHI BAAT KARENGAY" - he got very excited and cursed FK for lifting Sharmila in his arms...!!!
4. The movie had good music too by Kalyanji Anandji and that really enhanced the movie further - Asit Sen who besides writing the screen play also directed the movie with a lot of sensitivity.

The plot is as under:

Movie commences with a valient attempt of surgeon Sharmila Tagore to save a patient, who she knew was going to die. Dr. Chandra (Ashok Kumar) is her Mentor who tells her that Doctor has to do his or her best. Flashback starts at this juncture. Sharmila meets Rajesh Khanna at medical college and as always it happens, after an initial misunderstanding, they come close. Our Hero is a poor guy who works in parallel to attending medical college. He paints very well and Sharmila discovers herself in most of his paintings. Though he loves Sharmila very much, he never brings the topic of love or marriage. Everyone attributes it to his poor financial status, but it is later unearthed that he is a victim of terminal illness.

Sharmila, due to financial challenges, starts working as a tutor where she ends up meeting her student's elder brother, businessman Feroz Khan. Feroz instantly falls for her and later meets her elder brother IS Johar to ask her hand in marriage. IS Johar tells him to meet up with Rajesh Khanna saying that Sharmila would understand things well if explained by Rajesh Khanna. Since Rajesh Khanna is not keen to get married, Sharmila agrees to tie the knot with Feroz Khan. Somehow Feroz feels low intensity of love from his wife while he is besotted. Soon his business goes down and losses accrue but his wife is unable to empathise with him and that upsets him no end and with his wife visiting Rajesh Khanna frequently, Feroz starts suspecting that the those two are in a relationship and puts his younger brother on the job of a detective to see what is going between the two. Some wrong evidence results in suspicion becoming confirmation and Feroz commits suicide and the police suspect the leading couple and Sharmila faces the trial as Rajesh Khanna is not traceable. Sharmila, however, gets acquitted due to her mother-in-law's statement. All along Rajesh Khanna was not aware of Feroz's suicide as he moves away so that the relationship of the married couple could get better and comes back to the hospital towards the end and breathes his last which upsets Sharmila further and is on the verge of giving up medical practice but with Ashok Kumar's convincing abilities, she relents and makes it a point to send her young brother in law abroad for higher studies and dedicates herself to the noble profession of serving the ailing. The movie had good music to boast.

Here is the link for all the songs if you want to listen to the songs:

https://www.youtube.com/watch?v=IUC0sfA4hoM

Cheers
Laksh KV

August 06 1971 (52 years ago)

"NAYA ZAMANA" (NZ)

Folks:

The radio ad started saying right from the beginning of the year 1971 - "1971 means Naya Zamana" ... I was wondering from the first quarter as to when would this movie release and finally it did today 52 years ago on August 6th 1971.

This movie came from the banner of Pramod Chakravarty who always made good entertainers - and this one was a Big Hit - grossing Rs. 7,02,000/- in the first week - the only movie to collect more in 1971-72 financial year was Hare Rama Hare Krishna that did Rs. 7,43,000/- in the first week as it was hyped and with Dev Anand. Coming back to NZ, this had Dharam Paji playing the central character and his lady love Hema Malini and supported by Aruna Irani, Pran, Manmohan, and with a Special appearance by Ashok Kumar and Chakkida's lucky mascot Mehmood. My memories are as under:

1. Monsoon and my early college days and we had decided to see the movie ASAP and being in the first year of college was a bit worried too - but I had the support of Easwar who too was my classmate from school and both going to Bandra College (MMK) went to Nandi Cinema to see this movie first time round - so you can imagine we must have seen it multiple times.

2. Second time round, I saw with my late bro Vaidya V Raj at Neptune Cinema Bandra and though he was a big fan of Manoj Kumar , he agreed to join me on a Sunday 3 PM show and he too liked the movie.

3. When the advance booking started on August 2nd, there was a very huge crowd at Rupam Cinema and very soon the board started showing Sunday 2nd show, Saturday Night show and Friday all 3 shows as full - in about 2 hrs time all the 9 shows for the first 3 days showed RED LIGHT indicating "Sold Out". It was Kaka wave then and I was pleasantly surprised that Dharampaji had his own following.

4. For a change this movie did not have Dharam Paji and his fight scenes - just one imaginary scene when he beats up Pran - that is it.

5. Some good lines for Dharam Paji like his sister Aruna Irani asking when she finds her brother writing a speech for Pran "BHAYYA TUM LIKHKAR BHASAHN DENA KAB SAY SHURU KIYA HI?" & Dharam Paji responds "ARRE PAGLI MY LIKHKAR BHAASHAN NAHI, BHAASHAN LIKHKAR DE RAHA HOON" - the other powerful line was when confronted by the rich Dharam Paji says "HUMKO MITHA SAKHAY IS ZAMANE MEIN DUM NAHI, HUMSE ZAMANA KHUD HAI, ZAMANAY SE HUM NAHI" - and the whistles and claps would not stop in the hall. This really made me aware that Dharam Paji indeed had a lot of followers even during Kaka days.

6. Very good music by SD Burman da added a lot of value to the movie. . Lucky Mascot of Chakki da Mehmood too had 2 songs, who starts a mobile restaurant after returning post his higher studies abroad. The Lata solos take the cake like the title song "Kitne Din Aankhe Tarsengay", "Choron Ko Saaray Nazar Aatey Hain Chor" & the rain dance "Rama Rama Ghazab Hoi Gava Re" - simply soulful and not to forget the KK number "Duniya Oh Duniya - Tera Jawab Nahi" and "Dass Gayeeeee Sui...." Jai ho Senior Burman ki!!!

7. Manmohan who had some ulterior motives continued to be exasperated with things and would constantly utter "How Disgusting and Damaging!!!"

Well, coming to the plot - it is straight Rich vs Poor - so our Heroine is Rich and Hero Poor - they fall in love, elder brother does not like this but despite differences of views, he finds utility in a struggling writer played by the Hero. The elder brother Pran employs the poor hero and eventually manages to publish a novel written by the poor as his own. Well, eventually good has to win and it goes thru the motions and Mehmood who is rich but helps the poor as he too falls in love with the poor hero's sister Aruna Irani... Over all good acting and Ashok Kumar in a special appearance as the dad of Pran and Hema Malini makes a great impact in a cameo role. Dharam Paji was outstanding in this movie and all others supported him well. Truly a worth seeing movie of that era. Here are some song links for you.

https://www.youtube.com/watch?v=NqAhnJXQ6G8 ;
https://www.youtube.com/watch?v=ql_EnCTgjdU ;
https://www.youtube.com/watch?v=MQchcMTy7cQ ;
https://www.youtube.com/watch?v=pG6T4J4cR-U ;
https://www.youtube.com/watch?v=RbeiNR1wUYM ;
https://www.youtube.com/watch?v=DyJ84QcYCZM ;
https://www.youtube.com/watch?v=FkBfqnaUmA0

Cheers
Laksh KV

August 04 1972 (51 Years Ago)

"BE-IMAAN"

Folks:

Yes, it was released today 51 years ago the movie "Be-Imaan" produced under the banner of Filmnagar by Producer & Director Sohanlal Kanwar. The movie had Manoj Kumar in the title role along with Rakhee, Pran, Premnath, Prem Chopra, Nazima, Sulochana, Snehalata, & Raj Mehara. This banner earlier gave another big hit in "Pehchaan" and in 1975 another hit "Sanyasi" though it was not a great movie. I would like to share my memories and for the movie details and songs I shall give you the links.

1. Constant "House Full" board at Rupam Cinema made me feel good for it had music by SJ. Due to high collections, this movie continued for 2nd week at Rupam till "Bawarchi" displaced it on August 18th 1972.

2. The movie was a very big hit and merited many Filmfare awards including the controversy of Pran not accepting the award for his supporting role. According to him "Pakeezah" released on February 4th 1972 should have got the award for Best Music.

3. As a working student, I used to see the Rupam Cinema everyday as I had to cross the hall to go to my office where I worked as a part time Accounts Assistant while also going to Morning College. Somehow, I could not see the movie in the first few weeks though my late brother Vaidya V Raj, a big Manoj Kumar fan having seen the movie was going ga-ga over it and was pushing me too. Eventually on a Sunday, we both saw the movie at Neptune Bandra and we both enjoyed the movie - while he enjoyed his hero, I enjoyed the music of SJ and also Prem Chopra's acting and some of his typical lines. As the son of DIG Gopaldas he used to tell his dad, "Daddy THISH ISH Nonsense" when he was confronted for the wrongs he did. To all those gangsters he used to introduce himself as "MAIN, DIG GOPALDAS KA IKLOUTA BETA DEEPAK".

4. The radio advertisement yelled 'BOLO BE-IMAAN KI JAI' and the title song of the movie would be played - mainly on Radio Ceylon in "Aap Hi Kay Geet" & having learnt some figures of speech in class XI school, I would say "Alliteration" when the lines "BE-IMAAN KE HI BANTAY HAIN BANGLAY BAAGH BAGEECHAY" played on radio.

5. If I recall right, Premnath and Pran play honest cops while Premnath's son Prem Chopra is a negative character who gets killed or who tries to kill his dad. The Hero himself has a shaded character but like all Heroes, there is a reason for him to do what he does!!! Method to Madness I guess!!!

6. There was one song "Hum Do Mast Maang Pilaye" - that had one full antara that talked about film stars.

Well, not many felt that SJ deserved the Filmfare award for their score but I was very happy and liked the songs. So here are the songs for you.

https://www.youtube.com/watch?v=0Kv62TDaukI ;

https://www.youtube.com/watch?v=bBfJGdyRwe8 ;

https://www.youtube.com/watch?v=3UtEtcw7NI8 ;

https://www.youtube.com/watch?v=LGtc5k920QA ;

https://www.youtube.com/watch?v=3UtEtcw7NI8 ;

https://www.youtube.com/watch?v=i5TK-Ij24Qs ;

Cheers

Laksh KV

August 03 1973 - (50 Years ago)

"JUGNU"

Folks:

It was today 50 years ago this movie "JUGNU" a Big Box Office hit saw the light of the day and I was personally happy to see a Dharampaji movie do well as a big fan of his. My memories of this movie:

1. Indeed I was waiting for this day to come and had done my tickets in advance - money issues were not there as I was an employed college student. Since my dearest friend Balakrishnan Narayan was a big Kaka fan, he did not join me to Badal Cinema where I enjoyed the movie all by myself.

2. The claps and whistles were very heavy when a young Satyajeet grows into Dharampaji who played some kind of a Robinhood who robs from the rich people and helps the poor.

3. Jr. B.Com is a relatively easy year the way it is class XI now and was very easy to go for movies. Luckily the classes on Fridays were too easy and made things convenient for bunking.

4. Some of the scenes that are embedded in my small brain are: The way Dharampaji shoots Hema Malini's cap in the air to impress her. The other one is "बाप के नाम का का सहारा सिरफ कमजोर लॉग लाते हैं" both Pran and Dharampaji use this, Pran had a get up of Sheikh Mujib Rehman of Bangladesh & of course the robbery of a Golden fish that has all the protection in an exhibition was well executed. It was very well received.

5. The other important personal recall which my Maasi Kamala Narayan will be able to relate to is that in those days my maasi and maasa late S Narayan sir (A noble soul) used to visit us in the evenings and he used to be a big critic of Hindi movies and my elder brother would always get into arguments with him and would support Hindi movies. The senior pro would just say that things will improve for Hindi movies only when they move away from triangular plots of 2 men, one woman or the other way. According to him all fight scenes are reused and that only camera positions

change. The climax was when my brother told him that you should be in the auditorium watching Jugnu and the moment a suspended Dharampaji who comes down like an acrobat and lifts the golden fish from its protected area - the crowd goes ballistic with claps and whistles galore. On this he would laugh away and brand us as mads. -All said and done, he used to love reading the magazines like Filmfare, Stardust & other filmy magazines that used to come from my dad's office. Our grievance was that he was reading Hindi film mags and not allowing us to read ahead of him and to top it criticise... Yet a very lovable character - we miss you Chittappa!!!

6. Times of India review heading was "JUGNU - Slick despite Flaws"

7. Finally, I was a regular at the movie halls to see this movie and saw it several times-sometimes alone, sometimes with cousins and brothers.

Now, coming to the plot it was very simple and straight forward as mentioned somewhere above, -Dharampaji robbed the rich to help the poor, took care of orphaned kids. He had a tough childhood and hence does what he does. Well, rest is for all to see. Here is the songs link for you

https://www.youtube.com/watch?v=P6BzuVVofKU

Cheers
Laksh KV

August 01 1969 (54 years ago)

"SAJAN"

Folks:

It was 1st of August 1969 and those days our school used to have a holiday on every 1st August, not sure if it is being continued now as it was for "Tilak Punyatithi". As long as chutti, its great news. On this very day the movie "Sajan" produced and directed by Mohan Segal *ing Manoj Kumar, Asha Parekh, Om Prakash, Madan Puri, Sulochana & a young Shatrughan Sinha was released. It was an average grosser and my memories having seen the movie much later on TV are as under:

1. Though it was a school holiday, I had to go for my Maths classes that started at 7 am - so no late waking up as I used to go to Sudarshan Classes opposite to Premier High School in Sunil Building ground floor.
2. It was drizzling and still left home by 645 am and saw 2 senior guys from our neighbouring buildings - Arun Khanna aka ANNU and Govind who were going to the milk center to fetch milk. We greeted and Annu said "Kyon Paapa aaj chutti ke din bhi padhayee? Hum toh aaj dekhengay Sajan Rupam Mein". I felt how lucky these seniors are and they have the money too to enjoy.
3. On the way I used to cross one tree that would have a slate hanging with a number written with chalk & it said "Final 3". Those days Ratan Khatri used to run something called "MUTKA" where people would put money with a hope to multiply as-this gambling thing was very popular then.

Well, I guess that is all from my recall and the movie revolved around a well to do man who is surprised to see a news item that announced his marriage to a dancer. He is annoyed and goes to meet her and ends up falling in love with her. He keeps his identity a secret for some time and eventually they decide to tie the knot. Then they get trapped in a murder case and there are 3 people who claim to have committed the murder. Well, all is well that ends well -- the movie had some very good songs including the title song sung by both Hero and Heroine as solos. Here are the links for you

https://www.youtube.com/watch?v=ACftsHMgbsM ;

https://www.youtube.com/watch?v=ROuZcbCNrnI ;

https://www.youtube.com/watch?v=4K0Fm9FjQ_Q ;

https://www.youtube.com/watch?v=Jr41s2CfQKE ;

https://www.youtube.com/watch?v=3UqQaejIFUs ;

Cheers
Laksh KV

July 31 1970 (53 Years ago)

"JEEVAN MRITUE"

Folks:

It was today 53 years ago this all-time big hit movie "JEEVAN MRITUE" released, made under the banner of Rajashree Productions that is well known for making clean and good family entertainers. The movie had Dharmendra doing a dual act that of a banker and later as a business tycoon and Rakhee was introduced in this movie. Others who played key roles in the movie are:

Rajendranath

Ajeet

Ramesh Deo

Kanhaiyalal

Bipin Gupta

Jayaraj

Kishan Dhawan

Gajanan Jagirdar

Shabnam

Roopesh Kumar &

Zeb Rehaman

This movie does its round on Zee Classic at a good frequency and is always a pleasure to see the movie again and again. My memories are as under:

1. This was the time I was getting a root canal treatment being done for my tooth as I broke my front teeth during the previous summer vacation besides fracturing my wrist.

2. The makers of this movie experimented with a new concept of releasing it in Alankar Cinema (the main theatre) where it was screened only at 11 am, Matinee shows in other words.

3. I was quite keen to see the movie but for obvious reasons it was a NO NO... Class XI - only during vacations we could see. So it was an inordinate delay for me

4. The movie had only 2 songs - one was repeated twice and one was a ghazal.

5. During monsoon it was a regular practice for me and friends to take a walk to Rupam Cinema and look at the posters and assess if the movie was doing well. When I saw the wooden "House Full" board, I used to feel good for my favorite Hero Dharam Paji.

6. My elder brother who was in college managed to see the movie and kept talking about the movie and to top it, it had the music of LP, his favourite.

7. Eventually, saw the movie on Deepawali day at Alankar Cinema with my elder brother and Balakrishnan Narayan aka Bedi and all of us liked the movie.

8. The movie ran in Alankar Cinema for over 100 weeks and also in other halls for a long time. It must have made good money and would await my friend Amitabh Nigam to let us know what it would be in terms of current movies.

Well, coming to the plot it deals with an honest Banker, who gets cheated by his jealous colleagues who want to make quick money. The Banker gets jailed for no fault of his but for being so gullible. His aged mother dies on finding her son guilty and his "wife-to-be" is unable to take care of the old lady and avoids seeing him in the jail. After a 7 year term in jail, he wants to start afresh and gets an opportunity when the person who robbed him off dies in a train accident and the news comes that "Ashok Tandon" is dead - so here he gets a chance to avenge all the wrong doers thanx to a good Samaritan who gives him a new identity of "Sardar Bikram Singh" - Rest of the movie is how he finishes off the guys who trapped him and also win back his girl who was leading a life of a widow as she too got to know about her boyfriend's death. Director Satyen Bose has kept the movie quite interesting as I still can sit thru it when it comes on Zee Classic - over all a nice experience. Here are the song links for you

https://www.youtube.com/watch?v=uex2GnRrqFU ;

https://www.youtube.com/watch?v=xKNZ-DBNPaQ ;

https://www.youtube.com/watch?v=ofBxcU-Jr04 ;

Cheers
Laksh KV

July 28 1972 (51 Years Ago)

'EK NAZAR'

Dear Friends:

I wrote about Abhimaan and Gehri Chaal yesterday and today is the turn of "EK NAZAR" which released today 51 years ago. AB had seen success in Anand and Bombay to Goa, got appreciated in Parwana and here was a solo hero movie for him with his the then "Wife to be" Jaya Bhaduri as his co-star. This movie was a big FLOP coming from the shop of BR Ishara who had become famous post Chetana for the bold themes that he could deal with.

My memories are:

No pull factor for me to see this movie for both me and my partner in crime Balakrishnan Narayan aka Bedi - we both used to take a train from Kings Circle to Bandra to go to our college then and in the 2nd half of the day I used to work for a company called Pentagon located in Sion and I had to cross thru Rupam Cinema to reach my office. I could see at Rupam Cinema that there were hardly any takers for this movie, so 1st day 3 PM show was not HouseFull. We were not very fond of Jaya Bhaduri and found it tough to accept that she was playing a Nauch girl - knowing fully well that she had limited dancing talent. While my friend Bedi was fond of the Kishore Kumar's title song, I was the Rafi Bhakt humming "Patta Patta". We both managed not to see the movie but my elder brother did see and expressed his regret but was keen to see as a big Laxmikant Pyarelal fan and liked the music.

The plot revolved around a poet AB who did not get into his dad's line of being an advocate but gets impressed by the Nautch Girl who sings the song written by him and soon falls for her. Much against the wishes of his elders, he wants to get married to her. He goes out of the way to get her released from the clutches of the Madam who runs the brothel but she has other ideas and soon she is killed and as expected the Heroine is the prime suspect. Then the court scenes where Raza Murad gets a chance to show that he is a promising youngster with a solid voice like his dad. Eventually the Heroine is cleared and all is well. Very predictable and did very limited business in the 6 weeks it ran. Songs were reasonably hummable. Here are the links for you:

https://www.youtube.com/watch?v=YR1TofZXiJE ;

https://www.youtube.com/watch?v=DAOcEChNp-A ;

(The 2nd link has 4 songs)

Cheers

Laksh KV

July 27 1973 (50 years ago)
TWIN - release of Big B.....

"ABHIMAAN' & "GEHARI CHAAL"

Friends:

It was today 50 years ago 2 movies of Amitabh Bachhan released - "Abhimaan" & "Gehri Chaal". While "Abhiman" won the hearts of both critics and masses resulting it to be a decent Box Office hit, the 2nd one Gehri Chaal "GC" despite 2 Heroes could not hold the interest of the audience. Maestro Dada Burman had dished out some real beautiful songs in "Abhimaan" while the LP duo came with a sub-standard score in "GC" - worst song being "AE BAAI TU KAHANSE AAI AUR KAUNSI NAGAR TUJHE JAANA".

My memories are that of monsoon time and better days for me financially as an 18 year old I was in funds thanx to my job with a Private company called "Pentagon" located in Sion. My good friend Balakrishnan Narayan was thru out with me to see both these movies at Badal and Bijli on 2 consecutive days (bunking college). Due to better star-cast, we saw Gehari Chall first and though I used to be fond of Jeetu, I found him to have bloated & felt that he looked like one of our neighbours from the next building called Sudhir Saxena (Yaad hai na Bedi?) - We both concluded that it was a terrible movie though the heroine was my heartthrob... We were definitely enjoying Prem Chopra who switched off the lights to have fun with Bindu and she said "Andhere Say Mujhe Darr Lagta Hai" & PC said "Haa Mujhe Andhere Mein Lipat Lo" in his typical style with a bit of tongue in cheek pronunciation. The song "Jaipur Ki Choli Mangwa De Re Saiyyan" was equally painful and we were relieved to come out of the hall & another thing we both could relate to was the term "Final Audit" both being Accounts students and me writing books of accounts for Pentagon,- in this movie it had a major role to play as AB's dad plays a banker who allegedly swindles INR 20,00,000/-.

We were having 2nd thoughts if we should bunk the next day to see "Abhimaan" but we could not afford to bunk a Cinema to attend the college and better sense prevailed and we decided to go for "Abhimaan" on the very next day.

Both movies were being screened in the twin cinemas Badal and Bijlee and we were very much there to see it then.

We went with minimal expectations to see "Abhimaan" and started enjoying it straight away with the first stage song by AB "Meet Na Mila Re Man Ka" and Asrani who played AB's Manager spoke in Sindhi on phone and that looked terrific. Zanzheer's success was reflecting very well on the confidence of AB in the role of a play back singer cum stage performer who goes to his village to spend a few days with his Maasi Durga Khote. I simply loved when he took a puff from a cigarette and as the smoke came out his Maasi landed and very quickly AB tries to fan away the smoke with his hands!!! Very natural indeed!! Both of us were taken aback to see a completely different Bindu here from what we saw the previous day in GC. (Bedi remember Deep Trick?)... Well, multiple voices for AB that included Kishore Kumar, Mohd Rafi and Manhar Udhaas and then some master singing by our very own Nightingale Lata Didi who sang some lilting melodies for Jaya Bhaduri to lip-sync. No wonder AB fell for her as she swept him off his feet. Very quick marriage and a decision by AB to always sing with her was indeed a decision for him to regret later and what was coming was very evident to David, a well-wisher of AB. The first time AB gets hurt when a fan takes away the autograph book from AB to get Jaya's autograph - ufff!! then it takes a turn and results in a separation for the singing couple...The entire saga is handled with a lot of sensitivity as there were complications in the form of a miscarriage for Jaya and going into a shell and how eventually she is brought out of that with a stage show forms the climax of the beautiful movie. Excellent acting by all the characters and the brilliant music makes this Hrishikesh movie an immensely watchable experience.

Here are some of the songs for you from both these contrasting movies:

https://www.youtube.com/watch?v=92wQAtX1ZQw...;

(All songs of Abhiman in the link above)

https://www.youtube.com/watch?v=7l9yXufqh90 ;

(All songs of Gehari Chall)

Cheers & awaiting feedback from my friends

Laksh KV

July 25 1969 (54 years ago) - Twin Release - synonymous Titles:

'YAKEEN' & 'VISHWAS'

Dear Friends:

For the past few months, I have been on the move and have not been doing justice to this column that I commenced. But I was pleasantly surprised when my dear friend and classmate Sekhar Krishnan asked me as to why I stopped doing this column... I was happy to know that he missed it and not just him and even his brother too... So, I said now that I am likely to be a bit more stable - will continue from where I left and also cover in a summarised fashion rest of the movies that I missed in July so far.

As you can see, that it was a twin release - Yakeen and Vishwas both released today 54 years ago today (July 25, 1969), while Yakeen did average business with a 15 week run (105 days), Vishwas ran for 49 days and was termed a flop. Yakeen was made by the character artist Deven Varma where Dharampaji played dual role with Sharmila Tagore as his Heroine and Vishwas was made by Kewal P Kashyap and here Jeetendra played the poor lover to Aparna Sen. Yakeen had good songs and music by SJ while Vishwas too had some hummable numbers by KA duo. My memories are below:

It was a rainy Friday that morning before I headed to school - I recall my dad sitting on the chair and reading the newspaper that was folded for his comfort. Luckily the backside of the paper was visible and I could sit on the floor and read the various movies released - it said "Gala Opening Today" for both these movies while "Balak" had entered 2nd week - but the 2 new movies were right up there with big coverage and the radio ads came to my head and the songs too. All this around 730 am in the morning without brushing and bath and was quickly admonished by my strict Amma to get ready to go to school and I kept saying due to rains school may be closed. She said nothing doing - get ready and that was the end of my HOPE - well, I promised to study well etc and that I am willing to sacrifice both these movies but allow me to see PRINCE *ing Shammi Kapoor (my fav) due for release in 2 weeks' time!!! I got the nod from Amma and my day was made. Now about the movies:

"Yakeen" was a thriller slickly made - story revolving the Hero playing a Scientist and some rival group who want to replace the Hero with a look-alike.

Some bit of suspense, good songs makes the movie watchable. Music by SJ had its impact and besides all Rafi numbers, the Asha number by Helan stood out "Bachke Kahan Jaaogay" - Radio Ceylon too had an ad which had a bit of an echo when the name of the movie was pronounced "YAAKEEEEEEN" - wish I could post the audio file. The movie was a decent money-spinner.

"Vishwas" had a scheming mother played by Kamini Kaushal and her innocent son Jeetendra with poor background and an alliance has to be with a rich girl in Aparna Sen... Very predictable and hence the movie could not do well that lasted just 7 weeks and termed a flop. The 3 songs of the movie did very well one a solo by Mukesh "Chandi Ki Deewar Na Todi" - this song comes to my mind when I think of the movie "Vishwas" - second was a duet by an upcoming singer Manhar Udhas and Suman Kalyanpur..."Aap Se Humko Bhichde Huve, Ek Zamana Beeth Gaya" - did well and 3rd one was a duet by Mukesh & Hemlata "Le Chal, Le Chal Mere Jeevan Saathi".

Yet another memory of Manhar Udhaas for me was when I joined Richardson Hindusthan Limited in Nov 1976, the Annual Day at Shanmukhananda had live performance of this singer. One of the senior employees Kantilal G Parekh was telling the staff, Manhar was a great singer and sang in the movie Vishwas and pointed out a wrong number by saying "Chandi Ki Deewar Na Todi" - I was very new - just 2 weeks old but without making it sound like an argument I told him that not the right song - the right one was "Aap Se Humko Bhichde Huve" and he retorted as a senior "You don't know anything" and I smiled at him knowing fully well that the senior guy was wrong - later after the event in December, he did agree that he was wrong - but he did that one to one... I wish he recovers fast as I gathered not so long ago that he was not keeping well. Kantibhai - get well soon.

Here are some songs for you from both movies
https://www.youtube.com/watch?v=XisEURcXB-0 ;
https://www.youtube.com/watch?v=oM91K55qwYY ;
https://www.youtube.com/watch?v=vVxEl0CHDCg;
https://www.youtube.com/watch?v=QMVUihfr4TM ;
https://www.youtube.com/watch?v=Kh8YMzjW240 ;
https://www.youtube.com/watch?v=3wjLM3alZUg ;
https://www.youtube.com/watch?v=tqKv7Z9S2mY ;
Cheers
Laksh KV

July 2nd 1971 (52 years)

"PARWANA"

Folks:

52 years ago released a movie with relative new-comers who were yet to make it big - Navin Nischal - one movie old (Sawan Bhadon), Yogita Bali, again one movie old (Pardey Ke Peechay), Amitabh Bachhan few movies old and just was recognized in Anand for his role, Shatrughan Sinha the bad man those days had a guest appearance and who was seen earlier in Sajan, Prem Pujari, Ek Nanhi Munni Ladki Thi, Khiona etc... Yes, I am talking about the movie "PARWANA". This movie got a good opening and it was all it could manage. At a personal level, I can say that having just seen college for a few weeks, with just Rs. 2/- as monthly pocket money, I had to really decide as to which movie to see & which to avoid. But luckily from the month of August, I became a bit richer with an additional pocket money that I got from my late bro Vaidya V Raj who had landed a job in Asian Paints then. But what is fresh in my mind are as under:

1. On Sunday afternoon post lunch (4th July 1971), we boys were sitting on the compound wall, below the shade of a tree with some clouds hovering up threatening to drizzle and we were discussing the TOI review of the movie. All wanted to see the movie but the pull factor was missing. We felt might as well wait for a better movie to go as a gang.

2. Radio advertisement yelled "KHOON BAMBAI MEIN HUA PAR KHOON KE WAQT QATIL BAMBAI MEIN NAHI THA" - amazing concept we felt.

3. Kishore Kumar days and we all had made both Kishore and Rafi rivals - but they sang together "YOON NA SHARMA" & Rafi had another duet "JIS DIN SAY MAINAY TUMKO DEKHA HAI".

Well, eventually saw the movie at Broadway in matinee at reduced rates with my good friend Balakrishan Narayan and did not like the movie one bit. We felt though the concept of murder was interesting, they could have given some more slickness and made it entertaining.... well great critics at 17.

All said and done, not so long ago Johny Gaddar was inspired by the Murder plot and reused where Neil Nitin Mukesh having seen the movie kills Dharmendra the way AB did to Om Prakash in Parwana. I guess now no need to go thru the plot except a bit of elaboration required to explain the murder:

AB plans to kill Om Prakash who refused to give Yogita Bali's hands to him as she was in love with Navin Nischal. How he goes about the whole thing is:

1. He buys a train ticket to Calcutta and boards at VT
2. He hands over his ticket to his co-passenger saying to show his ticket when the TC comes as he would be back in a while.
3. AB alights at Dadar and goes and kills Om Prakash
4. AB then takes a flight to Nagpur from Bombay airport
5. He then resumes his journey from Nagpur station with his co-passenger.
6. The chief suspect is Navin Nischal as AB frames him.

So for all practical purposes, he was travelling when the murder happened. Shatrughan Sinha plays the lawyer and is unable to save the Hero - when Yogita Bali eventually tells AB that she would marry him but help NN out - he realizes she could never be his and confesses and ends his life.

Here are some songs from the movie composed by Madan Mohan :
https://www.youtube.com/watch?v=rA1T012Bhwc ;
https://www.youtube.com/watch?v=WXxBDFxxm_Y ;
https://www.youtube.com/watch?v=Z9sPt1g-eZk ;
Cheers and await comments and inputs from friends
Laksh KV

July 3 1970 (53 years ago)

"DARPAN"

Well, 53 years ago today (July 3 1970) was the day of release of this Sunil Dutt, Waheeda Rehman, Rehaman, Sonia Sahani, Sulochana, Ramesh Deo starrer called "DARPAN" under the banner of Babu Movies Combines with Direction by Subba Rao. My memories are not as interesting as it was just the 3rd week after our school reopened and there was no hope of seeing this movie as the earliest for me to see any movie was after the 1st Term exams that would normally end in the 3rd week of Sept. I was confident that this movie would not last that long for me to see at Rupam if I miss, it directly goes to Diwali vacation - so most movies released would not come in our "See" list - only see poster, read reviews and live life feeling jealous of those rich Gujju boys in our area who had money to see all the movies. The movie did not do too well and I would term it as a FLOP as I recall reading 7th & Last week in the newspapers.

The plot revolved around Sunil Dutt who played a professor in Sidharth College and fell for Waheeda Rehman who had left behind the oldest profession which was the dark side of her past to a decent present. But Sunil Dutt's Shaukeen elder brother Rehaman has visited Waheeda Rehman in the past and so did Ramesh Deo who happens to be Sunil Dutt's friend. Despite opposition, the couple get married and the past troubles them and very well proven by the title song "Darpan Jhoot Na Bolay" - But I guess things would have ended well in the movie though for the movie it would have barely broken-even. Songs were decent that were composed by LP and here is the link with all the songs for you:

https://www.youtube.com/watch?v=67NEoynAznA ;

Cheers

Laksh KV

June 26 1964 (59 years ago)

"SANGAM"

Folks:

Well, folks here I am talking about RK Films one of the Biggest and Landmark movies "SANGAM" released on June 26th 1964, 59 years ago *ing Raj Kapoor, Vyjantimala and Rajendra Kumar forming the triangle and supported by Iftikar, Hari Shivdasani, Lalita Pawar, Raj Mehra, Nana Palshikar & Achla Sachdev. Let me share my memories of this movie and the time and environment that prevailed then:

1. I was just 9 and had entered class V - school just reopened on 9th as the school had one extra day chutti as Monday 8th June, as it was the 13th day after Pandit Jawaharlal Nehru's demise.
2. Ameen Sayani was the radio announcer yelling the names of the actors on radio Ceylon as Vividh Bharti had not yet gone commercial.
3. The big posters were on every lamp-post that we crossed on our way to SIES School thru floods at King's Circle.
4. Exceptional Music (sad that it lost out to Dosti in Filmfare awards)
5. Released in a brand new main Cinema Hall Apsara along with Lotus, Plaza and JaiHind. Apsara had a lot of reputation and all of us in school were only discussing how beautiful the cinema hall was - though most of us did not go to see the movie at Apsara. One of our classmates Prithviraj told about the water fountain and the height of imagination was that there was a "Hand" instead of tap in the loo of the cinema hall... what level of exaggeration!!!
6. We, all growing up kids, knew that there was something in the movie that was not for us though the movie was not certified "For Adults" - when we suggested that we wanted to see the movie, the strong persona of our AMMA came forward and just snubbed us by simply dismissing the idea.
7. But our neighbor Mohan aka Mochu (Latha Easwaran fyi & Khan's) had managed to see the movie at Plaza and kept singing Bol Radha Bol Sangam and later when the entire family went to see the night show at Apsara, they did not allow Mohan to see the movie again - instead of leaving him alone at

home, they dragged him along and deposited him at nearby hall called Novelty to see KHANDAAN *ing Sunil Dutt, Nutan.

8. Without seeing the movie we were speculating about the love scenes - when Rajendra Kumar came close to Vyjantimala and the reflection was shown in water and as they came closer the still water is deliberately shaken!!!
9. The rumours of Krishna Kapoor walking out and staying at Natraj hotel & Dr Bali helping the Heroine and eventually winning her.
10. In no time, we also saw the banners saying Sangam in 10th week - wow time flew & every week the banner would get an increment as 11th 12th week etc. It got a big face lift when it entered 25th week and in Hindi it said "RAJAT JAYANTHI"
11. Major point of discussion was length of the movie with 2 intervals - never ending singing sessions - one and only one Mohd Rafi song - all others were Mukesh numbers
12. Eventually, I could see the movie when I was in class IX when it came for a re-run at Rupam Cinema and surprisingly the movie was so much edited that we had only 1 interval!!!

Well, after all this, do I write about the plot that all are aware - will give it a skip - just point out that 2 men after 1 lady and the good friend kills himself. I did observe some flaws like Raj Kapoor who is not capable of reading having someone else reading for him manages to read the love letter written by Rajendra Kumar to Vyjantimala - not just reading, he puts together the torn papers and solves the jigsaw and finds out about the love between his wife and his friend!!! Then to make things worse as he sings the sad version of 'DOST DOST NA RAHA" & Vyjantimala tries to cover things up by singing 'OH MERE SANAM DO JISM MAGAR EK JAAN' but will her hubby be convinced!!! No way – What follows is a long drawn discussion by the 3 main characters standing in a room & Rajendra Kumar kills himself. The highlight those days - Technicolor movie and shot ABROAD partially. Big luxury...

Overall a great movie and have seen it multiple times later - the outstanding music played a major role in making the movie a hit that did run for 65 weeks at Apsara. Songs link below:

https://www.youtube.com/watch?v=MISzXVVVFUo ;

Will request Amitabh Nigam to let us know how much money the movie made - 59 years is a long time!!!

Cheers

Laksh KV

Jun 02 1972 (51 years ago)

"TANGEWALA"

Folks:

It was today 51 years ago on June 2nd 1972, the average grosser "Tangewala" released in Mumbai. By then we had started disliking Rajendra Kumar and avoided seeing his movies - another thing that dampened our spirits was the song "DO DEEWANAY AAYE, KHEL TAMASHA LAAYE" - more coz of the way Asha Bhonsle yelled 'AAO AAO" - not a very strong reason to dislike but I could not take it coming from such a great singer. The banner of the movie was Dimple Films and was directed by Naresh Kumar (Dilip Apte Saheb, can you confirm if he was the Hero's bro?) *ing Rajendra Kumar in a dual role, Mumtaz, Kumud Chugani, Sujit Kumar, Kamini Kaushal, IS Johar, Jr. Mehmood, Mohan Choti, Leela Mishra and Jagdish Raj. No more memories except that I did not see but the plot I just picked up from various sources and sharing with you.

Sujit Kumar plays a rich zamindar who has vices like Wine, Women & Wild attitude. His right hand man Kanhayyalal fetches women for him and once he sources the Hero Rajendrakumar's sister Kumud Chhugani. He wins the confidence of Kumud Chhugani and secretly marries her in Mandir and Kanhayyalal plays the priest who gets the two married. Logically soon Kumud Chhugani is in the family way and at this point our Hero and his sister go to Sujit Kumar to get the marriage to be formally done. But Sujit Kumar does not recognise her and the family of our hero is in total depression and the hero moves out of the village. A boy is born to the unwed mother and the hero tries to get her to remarry but on the D day she vanishes. All along our Hero Rajendra Kumar's love affair with Mumtaz is on the back-burner and our Hero's mom waits for her hubby's return. All this results in one more round of relocation and then our Hero goes to Sujit Kumar to take revenge and how things come back to normal is the crux of the story.

Naushad's music was not up to his standards still pretty decent and here are some links for you:

https://www.youtube.com/watch?v=kZ8lSz-1itw ;
https://www.youtube.com/watch?v=Q5EYrFwDJ-M ;
https://www.youtube.com/watch?v=BeAq6zbtnXQ ;
https://www.youtube.com/watch?v=8ovjV9gtwRM ;

Cheers - anyone having more info please share

Laksh KV

June 15 1973 - (50 Years ago)

"SAMJHAUTA"

Folks:

50 Years ago the movie "Samjhauta" was released which was an average grosser. Somehow from 1970 onwards Anil Dhawan despite his limitations could make his presence felt though more often he got overshadowed by Shatrughan Sinha most of the times. The starcast was Anil Dhawan, Yogita Bali, Shatrughan Sinha, Pradeep Kumar, Jagdish Raj and Brahmma Bharadwaj. Movie was not a hit and given the low cost of production, it would have made some money.

My memories of this movie - yes, I was earning and I saw this movie on the Saturday of its release and was impressed by the acting of Shatrughan Sinha and the sincere attempt by Anil Dhawan but the real contribution came from the Music Director Duo of Kalyanji Anandji. The outstanding song was "SAB KE REHETAY LAGTA HAI JAISAY KOI NAHI HI MERA" sung by Mohd Rafi soulfully that brings about a change in the life of a Blind Anil Dhawan. The movie was not running to full houses but still there was something that gave a feeling that this movie should do well and in my view it did reasonable business.

The plot revolves around Anil Dhawan who is a gifted singer and who wants to make it big and migrates to Mumbai where he befriends Shatrughan Sinha who sympathises with him and helps him - essentially, it is a big struggle for the singer and at some point he loses his vision. Then given his talent, there is someone who wants to leverage his blindness and make money out of it and also give the singer a platform to perform. Shatrugan Sinha is jailed (someone can confirm, is the movie where he gets caught not when stealing, but returning the excess from the stolen amount?). Eventually things end well for the "Do-gooders". Here are some of the songs composed by Kalyanji Anandji:

https://www.youtube.com/watch?v=91mA7GA6mIk ;
https://www.youtube.com/watch?v=-sQmU8CDiHc ;
https://www.youtube.com/watch?v=SNn3jpR2Ns0 ;
https://www.youtube.com/watch?v=OXjxckQHrUg ;

https://www.youtube.com/watch?v=m04Wjj69huU ;

https://www.youtube.com/watch?v=xHzqgpmqnZ8 ;

Cheers & awaiting comments from the group

Laksh KV

May 26 1972 (51 years ago)

"DHADKAN"

Folks:

Devendra Goel's "Dhadkan" was released 51 years ago in Mumbai *ing Mumtaz, Sanjay, Rupesh Kumar, Rajendranath, David, Bindu, Helan and Murad - above all Master Alankar. The movie was a reasonable hit and had the flavor of Goel movies - that normally caters to family audience. The movie did decent business and the music was quite foot-tapping provided by Ravi.

My memories of seeing this movie - saw it 1.5 times in the first week - once on the day of release evening show and on another occasion next week post interval when I found an abandoned gate pass outside the Cinema during interval. I loved the creative ad song in the movie "TITLI CHAAP CHAMELI AGARBATTI, POOJA KE LIYE AADARSH" and also had "Elpar Suitings and Sarees" "Piyo Limca" etc. This was something different when Sanjay waits for his sweetheart Mumtaz and dozes off with his transistor and dreams of all the ads where he has a role to play with his darling. Murad with his deep voice declares 'YEH CASE REBIRTH KA HI' - Master Alankar, who plays Mumtaz's younger brother is reincarnation of someone who was killed by Roopesh Kumar and the little boy makes life difficult for the villain.

The plot is of a rich boy who shoots his friend by mistake and assumes him to be dead and flees from home. But the reality is his friend Sanjay grows up and on the other side the rich boy too grows up and finds that his friend actually is alive. He shares his happiness with Roopesh Kumar who travels with him in a train and also shares information about himself - now having captured the data, Roopesh Kumar kills him and lands up as the grown up rich boy - makes things difficult for Sanjay. Roopesh Kumar then gets married to Mumtaz and makes her life miserable - but he has the baggage of Master Alankar to carry as his wife's younger brother who is just 5. Now this boy has the soul of the person who was killed by Roopesh Kumar and then how Sanjay, Mumtaz, Rajendranath and Alankar scare Roopesh Kumar and get him to confess is the crux of the story. Over all a decent entertainer I thought. Here are some songs for you:

https://www.youtube.com/watch?v=rJzR-Y7ffr4 ;
https://www.youtube.com/watch?v=7Ta2t9O_JBc ;
https://www.youtube.com/watch?v=T4lxly370sc ;
https://www.youtube.com/watch?v=ne1BWaf936Y ;

Cheers

Laksh KV

May 27 1977 (46 years ago)

"AMAR AKBAR ANTHONY"

Dear Friends:

46 years ago on May 27 1977 saw the release of one of the biggest blockbusters of 1977 called **Amar Akbar Anthony**. This movie possibly had all the ingredients required for a hit movie - Big star cast consisting of:

Amitabh Bachhan - Parveen Babi

Vinod Khanna - Shabana Azmi

Rishi Kapoor - Neetu Singh

Pran - Nirupa Roy

Jeevan & Jeevan (dual role of Robert and Albert)

Mukri, Yousuf Khan, Nazir Hussain, Ranjeet & Helan

It had good music of LP and was some kind of a revival for Mohd Rafi with hit songs sung for Rishi Kapoor - the Quwali "PARDA HI PARDA" & "SHIRDIVALE SAIBABA" touched the right pulse of the audience.

It had a familiar story line of lost and found and Manmohan Desai could handle this theme very well and kept everyone occupied well. There was enough comedy thrown in with both AB and Mukri playing their bit with aplomb. The emotional angle was not missed when the 3 brothers got separated, the poor dad escapes from police but the mom goes blind and the kids raised by different religions and fate keeps them bringing together. Overall this was a great Masala movie that did fabulous business. –Hope to have Amitabh Nigam give the numbers in terms of current worth.

My memories, yes saw the movie several times as I was employed in a multi-national company and money was no more an issue - not just seeing but also taking a group of people to the hall and must have contributed sizably for the revenue of the movie. One of the occasions I bumped into my school class mate KR Easwar (Lakshmi Nathan) please remind your brother of this - and the 2 of us walked back from Badal cinema together and the way he was going gaga over AB is still fresh in my mind. It looks very stupid to see on TV now as to how Dr. Neetu Singh holds Parveen Babi's wrist and declares her pregnant. AB and his drunkard scene which was very similar to the Dilip Kumar scene in Kohinoor triggered a lot of laughter. Not to forget the climax title song when the 3 brothers come together to fight their adversary - Jeevan in a dual role of Robert and Albert. Overall only good memories of this movie and exactly one week later my late brother Vaidya V Raj tied the knot - the day "BUNDALBAAZ" released (Jun 3 1977) directed by Shammi Kapoor... a big flop.

Here are some song links for you:

https://www.youtube.com/watch?v=XjRgw1naMsc ;
https://www.youtube.com/watch?v=aPwS1UOSSM4 ;
https://www.youtube.com/watch?v=LqauPpCbQ7Q ;
https://www.youtube.com/watch?v=QrCnhwtVujQ ;
https://www.youtube.com/watch?v=MzUgAL_sX2E ;
https://www.youtube.com/watch?v=3GhGq7db9v0 ;

Cheers
Laksh KV

May 28 1971 (52 years ago)

"JAWAN MOHABBAT"

Dear Friends:

It was on May 28 1971 i.e. 52 years ago the Shammi Kapoor, Asha Parekh, Balraj Sahani, Shashikala, Nirupa Roy Rajendranath, & Pran starrer "Jawan Mohabbat" released and it marked the decline of the Great Hero from the Kapoor Khandan. - The movie flopped big time and ran for 6 weeks. But as a big SK fan, myself and my friend Shankar aka Aadya from Sion West, went to see the movie on the first day first show (230PM) at Rupam. Despite the ageing star, we both loved the movie for the songs and the energy of the Hero but the audience could not accept the movie. My memory also tells me a very familiar sequence that kept coming in the hospital scenes of the movie wherein Rajendranath aka Popatlal every time hurts the foot of a person who has a fractured leg and stamps his foot and that did tickle the funny bones a bit. We both have been SJ fans and we loved the music big time and we were all along praying for the movie to do well... but alas... Still loved the twin song of 'MERE SAPNON KI RANI TUM NAHI HO & MIL GAYI MIL GAYI MERE SAPNON KI RANI MUJHKO MIL GAYI'

The plot revolved around the family of Balraj Sahani (BS), his wife Nirupa Roy and the younger brother Shammi Kapoor (SK) of BS. As expected SK is an eligible bachelor and falls for Asha Parekh and they both enjoy singing songs. Soon some history takes over in the form of BS's past when he had an affair with Shashikala (Vamp) and she in a well-planned way entices him and soon the senior bro is completely besotted and under the control of the vamp. During one of the sing song sessions at the end of it, SK sees his elder bro BS with the vamp. Now he takes up on himself to sort things out and eventually things fall in place with enough action. The redeeming feature of the movie was the songs - here are some of them:

> https://www.youtube.com/watch?v=uPZ3zY5_q6Y ;
>
> https://www.youtube.com/watch?v=4Nvz0c9EofI ;

https://www.youtube.com/watch?v=OnelXl0k75c ;
https://www.youtube.com/watch?v=QhHbj-Ic3HI ;
https://www.youtube.com/watch?v=JdlBbdt50UU ;
https://www.youtube.com/watch?v=tEYzPsxsdvo ;
https://www.youtube.com/watch?v=bxvaYij2z9g ;

Cheers & awaiting comments from my friends

Laksh KV

May 29 1970 (53 years ago)

"SHARAFAT"

Dear Friends:

53 years ago we saw the release of the hit movie "Sharafat" - made by Madan Mohla & directed by Asit Sen. This movie boasted of a good star cast in Ashok Kumar, Dharmendra & Hema Malini supported by Sonia Sahani, Jagdeep, Abhi Bhattacharya & Kanhayalal, Mohan Choti, Birbal etc... The movie was a runaway hit and in my view should have made a lot of money that enabled the banner to make "Raja Jani" with the same lead pair which too was a money spinner in 1972.

My memories - having been to Hyderabad and spending a fair amount of money, did not have the guts to ask Amma for money to see this movie. All I did was to go to Rupam and see the posters and prayed that the movie should be a hit as it had my favorite pair & God did answer my call and the movie really went on to make a whole lot of money. I eventually saw the movie at Rupam in matinee show while in college few years later. Hema Malini was still getting established into the industry and Dharam paji was managing his own space in competition with Kaka and Jeetendra. LP's music was a rage and songs were dominated by Lataji.

The plot revolved around Ashok Kumar who looks after Dharamendra when he loses his dad and also finds a job of a lecturer in a college for him. He feels happy that he has found a good "Son-in-law" in our Hero for his only daughter Sonia Sahani. The lecturer finds that the students were cutting classes and were visiting a "Nautch Girl" Hema Malini. So Dharampaji wants to bring the boys on track and personally visits the place to meet the owner and Hema Malini to discourage the boys and not allow them. Needless to say, the teacher in him decides to teach the dancer but the dancer is interested in the teacher and they fall in love. Now that makes Ashok Kumar livid and eventually things get sorted out and Ashok Kumar's dark past too comes to the fore. Here are some songs for you:

https://www.youtube.com/watch?v=vo1t7z1lVCM ;

https://www.youtube.com/watch?v=uO8Q41DHHQc ;

https://www.youtube.com/watch?v=Qjqo0G14I_c ;

https://www.youtube.com/watch?v=ez05QppcP3w ;

I will call for comments from my friends now

Cheers

Laksh KV

May 30 1969 (54 Years ago)

"MADHAVI"

May 30 1975 (48 Years ago)

"JAI SANTOSHI MAA"

Folks:

We have 2 movies to talk about for May 30th 1969 and 1975 - one a disaster (Madhavi) and one a low budget unexpected Box Office Hit (Jai Santoshi Maa)

My memories of Madhavi are very limited except that it came in and around the rainy days and there was big poster near the King's Circle railway station. It had music of LP and some hummable songs that is it and the movie vanished from the halls in no time. It looked like some piece of history or Raja Rani Story which hardly appealed to me and did not have a big star cast - Sanjay, Padmini, Aruna Irani Mehmood, Mukri and Pran. On top of my mind is the song by Lataji "SAANJ SAVERE" & the other one is "PARDA HATA DAY MUKHDA DIKHA DAY" - Not much to write about, let me give you the song links:

https://www.youtube.com/watch?v=ncWQ4e1jZOs ;

http://www.dailymotion.com/.../x2ebyp7_saamne-mere-paani-bhar... ;

https://www.youtube.com/watch?v=PzcjPyhQyjo ;

https://www.youtube.com/watch?v=W_2F4TkExt8 ;

Now, I would like some Gyaanis to add value to this post as I have only data from external sources that I do not intend to cut and paste.

The second movie was- the surprise packet 'JAI SANTOSHI MAA' - *ing Kannan Kaushal, Anita Guha, Bharat Bhushan & Ashish Kumar. My memory was that it was released on the day my Final Exams of B.Com started in 1975. I was happy that it did not take away my attention as I had no inclination towards this release. I was just not interested as to how it was doing and on the last day when 4 of us (none on FB) were walking back from Bhurani College to Sion (some long distance) with a break at Parel for some snacks, we heard a couple of people in the restaurant talking about how good a movie is JSM and we laughed at it. But soon we realized that it was indeed drawing a lot of crowd though it did not change my stand as the first movie I saw after my last exam was "Do Jasoos" which was released on June 6th 1975.

The information I gathered said that it collected Rs. 5 crores those days and I guess it should have grossed over 200 crores with current Time Value of Money. I have only seen the movie on and off thanx to DD in the 80s but no going to hall. This movie created the awareness about Santoshi Maa to a lot of us and some other movie makers tried to make similar movies but could not repeat the success of JSM. Here are some songs for you from the hit movie:

https://www.youtube.com/watch?v=tZ8VKSh3rL0 ;

https://www.youtube.com/watch?v=er2ggmmQS3o ;

https://www.youtube.com/watch?v=MkaPXgFAn-c ;

Inviting more comments from my good friends

Cheers

Laksh KV

April 13 1973 (50 Years ago)

'SHAREEF BUDMASH"

Dear Friends:

One of the Dev Anand disasters called "Shareef Budmash" saw the light of the day 50 years ago today. It had all big values - like produced by Dev Anand and Kalpana Kartik, Director Raj Khosla and *ing Dev Anand, Hema Malini, Ajit, Jeevan, Helan, Trilok Kapoor, Sudhir and Janki Das. I had avoided this movie as I could not accept Hema Malini with anyone other than Dharmendra even from those days!!!

But my late brother Vaidya V Raj and Radhakrishnan went and saw the movie at Rupam and towards the end they felt that Hero should lose to Ajit the villain and - they both came back saying the movie was terrible except for some songs that captured the imagination. E.g. the Asha Bhonsle Aalaap in the song "Neend Churakay Raaton Mein" & the other one they were happy about "Rocky Hai Naam Mera, Subko Salaam Mera" - they told me that a short guest appearance by Shatrughan Sinha as Rocky lifted the movie a bit. Beyond this, I have no idea as till date I have not seen the movie.

About the plot:

Its regarding an Aircraft the Indian Government has plans of launching but the anti-social elements manage to get the plan from some corrupt Military folks and which in turn gets stolen from them. Then it is a wild chase with some imposters thrown around with the name of Rocky. The standard things like arresting of suspect, Rocky managing to get into the jail to save the suspect and finally the real Rocky shows up – a real hotchpotch kind of an offering. No wonder, the movie didn't do well

Here are the song links for you:
https://www.youtube.com/watch?v=lKkOuEXFVEU ;
https://www.youtube.com/watch?v=mDNNNI9ykdM ;
https://www.youtube.com/watch?v=jfHpC6yixxA ;
https://www.youtube.com/watch?v=YyVBhjJW8QM ;
https://www.youtube.com/watch?v=f3gc7yaQmkc ;
Cheers
Laksh KV

May 23 1969 (54 Years Ago)

"HASEENA MAAN JAYEGI"

Folks:

54 years ago, today was the release date of "Haseena Maan Jayegi" *ing Shashi Kapoor in a dual role with Babita as his Dream Girl with others like Manmohan Krishna, Johny Walker, Ameeta & Younes Parvez etc. I have put the star cast upfront lest you mix it up with the Govinda Sanjay Dutt flick which too did well. Well the movie in question released towards the end of our summer vacation and ran for 15 weeks in Mumbai and so considered a hit.

I was quite keen to see this movie but with my hand in cast post a wrist fracture and loss of front teeth had to sit tight and was painful to others at the cinema hall as I used to defend myself by hurting people with my cast. Hence had to wait till 1970 September, when the movie was shown at Rupam in matinee at reduced rates and for me it was the first change of thread post "Naarli Pournima" - there is one day for "Gayathri Japam" when we have to chant the Gayathri Mantra 1008 times and do havan. I ensured that I did not go to school that day by prolonging the event and once done at 10 am and when I was sure school was not happening that day, managed to cajole my Amma for Rs 1.25 and went to see the movie at Rupam and simply loved the environment - I was all alone as it was a regular school day. Even in the hall it was filled up only to the tune 0f 30% and particularly enjoyed the 3 tests given by Babita to Shashi Kapoor to prove him to be the right person and he fails in all the 3 despite being the right person. There is one scene where Babita winks and the guy's spectacles break!!! Wow what an impact I felt then!!! Well, it was a decent entertainer with good songs by Kalyanji Anandji and 3 songs stood out for me and they are "BEKHUDI MEIN SANAM UTH GAYE JO KADAM", "CHALE THAY SAATH MILKAR" & "OH DIL BHAR JAANIYE" - the title song was enacted with a lot of zest and energy by Shashi Kapoor. Also do not miss the first song of the movie "Suno Suno" - not so popular but you can see Shashi Kapoor dressed like a lady!!!

The plot revolves around 2 look-alikes who are not brothers and studying in the same college (though SK looks 30+ still in college gives a true feel of a failing student - but one of them is a good boy and good student). They both fall in love with Babita and the Heroine wants to get married to the good boy and though the bad boy tries to spoil the case but gets trapped in his own net and allows the right one to get married. Both of them are in the armed forces and then there is a call for national duty and out there a fight ensues and one of them is missing and assumed to be dead and the rest you can assume as to who is the right one and the wrong!!! Eventually the wrong one comes to the rescue of the right one after reading in the paper about a court trial on the right one for no wrong done by him. Highlight for me was the good music and here are some songs for you:

https://www.youtube.com/watch?v=W8TZktcXMnk ;
https://www.youtube.com/watch?v=L8NJD0NLudo ;
https://www.youtube.com/watch?v=LC9m9uWR0g4 ;
https://www.youtube.com/watch?v=nyr1VSl62Hg ;
https://www.youtube.com/watch?v=35LoFtsfcdo ;
https://www.youtube.com/watch?v=_fuOegCyYGU;

Cheers

Laksh KV

May 22 1970 (53 Years ago)

"ABINETRI" "ROOTHA NA KARO"

Dear Friends:

Today 53 years ago 2 movies of Shashi Kapoor released - one was an average grosser and the other a flop. I felt the flop movie had better songs than the better one... Very limited memories for me as all I recall is our return from Hyderabad after attending the wedding of K S Lakshminarayan (my cousin) and getting initiated as Brahmins following the wedding and enjoying stay at Hyderabad. Those days a maximum of 5 movies during annual vacation, 3 during Diwali and 1 during Xmas vacation was the norm. So we had to be very choosy and these 2 movies did not fall in the category of "Must See".

Let me talk about Abhinetri first... *ing Hema Malini and Shashi Kapoor (Nice looking couple) and Deb Mukherji who got a chance to be close to Hemaji as a stage artist did not go well with me!!! Standard artists like Nasir Hussain, Nirupa Roy filled the bill. Story revolved around a stage artist and the hero who played a scientist. They fall in love and get married but as the hero gets busy with his profession, the heroine who had given up her dancing and stage wants to revive and this creates the rift among the 2 leading to separation till the mother lands up and these 2 have to show that all is well. Rest you can imagine what happens. Decent songs but not outstanding 'SA RE GA MA PA" did make an impact and as a true Mohd Rafi fan, felt bad KK singing for SK... Here are some links for you:

https://www.youtube.com/watch?v=T7mG3g4l29Y ;
https://www.youtube.com/watch?v=pPI6fdt2Dv0 ;
https://www.youtube.com/watch?v=Hz2pdFDS6Zo ;
https://www.youtube.com/watch?v=tF9noDZKDFk

The second movie is Rootha Na Karo *ing Nanda & Shashi Kapoor in the lead. This couple had a quite a few films together though nothing matched the success of Jab Jab Phool Khilen. Rootha Na karo was a disaster at the box office but somehow I loved its music of C Ramchandra. Having not seen the movie, I had to gather from multiple sources:

The Heroine Nanda lives with her mom Sulochana and Naaz who is her cousin. Shashi Kapoor is Nanda's friend and they both have intentions of tying the knot. While the couple and the mother are OK with the alliance, Naaz starts poisoning the mind of Nanda saying that the Hero is only interested in her property and not her. This is actually her own insecurity for Shashi Kapoor as he does not respond to her advances. Naaz then finds that some documentation is being worked on by Shashi Kapoor with a lawyer and this is projected as a ploy to convert the property ownership moving towards him and this creates a big crack in the relationship between the loving couple. Much later it gets clarified that Shashi Kapoor was doing the transfer of property in the name of Nanda's cousin Anil. A triangular plot that ends with Naaz confessing her acts and consumes poison and dies at the hands of Nanda and tells her that Shashi Kapoor is a good person and finally they both join hands and all is well. So, it was very predictable indeed.

Here are some good songs from the movie for you and to me 2 songs one with Arabic background "Mere Saakiya, Mere Dilrubah" & "Aap Ka Chehara Mashal-Allah" stands out:

https://www.youtube.com/watch?v=g1BSzkiTLCQ ;

https://www.youtube.com/watch?v=i9f_glLTl4c ;

https://www.youtube.com/watch?v=Ruy1FDkOCf4 ;

https://www.youtube.com/watch?v=5TazZGuoJ5o ;

Inviting more inputs from my friends

Cheers

Laksh

May 21 1971 (52 Years ago)

"HAATHI MERE SAATHI"

Folks:

Today 52 years ago one of the Biggest hits of Rajesh Khanna was released - yes, I am talking about "Haathi Mere Saathi" *ing Kaka, Tanuja, Madan Puri, KN Singh, Jr. Mehmood, Sujit Kumar and whole lot of animals. It was made by Sandow MMA Chinappa Devar whose brother MA Thiurmugam was the Director under the banner of Devar Films. This was one of the 17 consecutive hits given by Kaka between 1969 and 1972 & I gathered that he was not very keen to act in it and had no clue about the affordability of Sandow. So to get away from it, he apparently quoted an astronomical figure and the gyaanis of those days from Tamil Industry said that Devar always had money inside his "Komanam" ie "Langot" & gave the amount to Kaka who was shocked. Well, that is the story bit and I have my own memories.

Given that it was a Kaka movie and my prejudice, I did not want to see and in fact I was saving the money for my favourite hero Shammi Kapoor's movie Jawan Mohabbat due to release the following week. But was hoping it will not run to full houses but those were the days when anything Kaka touched would turn into gold. So it was a hit and in early June before my SSC results were out without telling my good friend Balakrishnan Narayan, I went one day and saw the movie quietly at Broadway and really liked it. The concept of Pyar Ki Duniya created for all the animals to stay in harmony was indeed so cute. On his wedding day, all animals sit together and eat kheer and that too looked very nice. Another important memory - Anuradha S Iyer to note - you and Your Amma ie my Maami were to join along with Anjali Iyer and Akhila Iyer your late dad at Singapore in June 1971. Anu, you were barely 6 months old and in June & you were all getting geared to leave and this was the last movie before your departure. There are a lot of such pleasant memories for me. Well, now coming to the plot:

As a child Rajesh Khanna is orphaned and finds himself in a jungle where he is saved by some elephants and they become his SAATHI. He grows up with these 4 elephants and does road shows for his livelihood and slowly and steadily he becomes big with bigger and better shows and creates a personal zoo. In between he also falls in love with Tanuja who enjoys the company of animals and she too blends well with the animals. But once the kid comes, she gets scared that the animals around could end up killing the little one. Then it is a choice situation for Kaka either to live with Tanuja or animals and he chooses animals. Then it takes a sacrifice on the part of Ramoo Haathi to bring the disrupted peace back in the house-hold. The movie ends with the demise of the elephant with the song 'NAFRAT KI DUNIYA KO CHOD KE PYAR KI DUNIYA MEIN, KHUSH REHANA MERE YAAR" - the only Rafi song that drew me to the movie. Good songs by LP were another highlight of the hit movie. Here are some links:

https://www.youtube.com/watch?v=NzUGxYbAv4w ;

https://www.youtube.com/watch?v=7rzWRxTFcuA ;

https://www.youtube.com/watch?v=6ip2F8FUwco ;

https://www.youtube.com/watch?v=5Dgz6e57pjU ;

https://www.youtube.com/watch?v=W54zZMJ4qcg ;

Cheers
Laksh KV

May 19 1972 (51 years ago)

'BHAI HO TO AISA' & 'BANDAGI'

Dear Friends:

Today in the year 1972, 2 movies released while one did well at the Box Office - the other one did not make any impact whatsoever. Let me quickly cover the successful one first.

1. Bhai Ho To Aisa

This movie was made by the famous Nadiadwala banner and directed by Manmohan Desai. It had good starcast in Jeetendra, Hema Malini, Shatrughan Sinha, Indrani Mukherjee, Jeevan, Bipin Gupta, Jagdeep, Bela Bose & Viju Khote besides the SNAKES... I did get a chance to see the movie when released and in fact so impressed I was with Jeetu Hema jodi that I saw it once at Rupam and again at Bharat Kurla - but second time was not as enjoyable. My memories are as under:

1. The song 'AI PHULJHADI' sung by Mohd Rafi in the days when KK dominated picturized on the Hero and Heroine named "ROOPA", sounded great when Mohd Rafi sings "ROOOOOOPAAAAAA". Another one is the puppet show song "BOL MERI GUDIYA GUDDAY SANGH JAAYEGI" and how slowly the puppets become Jeetu Hema and towards the end of the song it gets faster like a 33 RPM record running at 78 RPM. Finally, the last song of the movie dedicated to the snake "Nagaraja" by Hema Malini had the desired effect.

Story revolves around 2 brothers - Shatrugan the elder one and Jeetendra the younger one. While the elder one is married but has his weakness with other girls while the younger one is a good boy variety. When their dad Thakur suddenly dies, the responsibility of managing things falls on the responsible younger son who is not liked by the elder one and in the company of their Mamaji these 2 want to get the property to themselves. When it was not coming their way, they decide to get rid of the younger one & having overheard the conversation, the younger one plays along and dies for them only to return as a DAKU and set things right. It was quite an enjoyable movie and SONIK OMI gave some decent songs - here are some links for you:

https://www.youtube.com/watch?v=Swqmw3wRHzc ;

https://www.youtube.com/watch?v=14L2evoWizM ;

https://www.youtube.com/watch?v=4dvr9emMGro ;

https://www.youtube.com/watch?v=qDdsXlLv840 ;

2. Now coming to the 2nd movie for which I have virtually no data - it was called "BANDAGI". My limited memory says that it was made by the same banner of Em Ce R films that made earlier movies like "Parde Ke Peechay" and "Sachaai" and Shankar Jaikishan was the common factor. I do not recall the name of the Heroine of this movie but the Hero was late Vinod Mehra. In all fairness the music of SJ was truly sub-standard - and here I request anyone who has more information about the movie kindly share. My memory is that those days (Summer vacation after FY Commerce), I used to go to my dad's offices (INCAB) to learn some of the office work like Telex Operations and also help a bit in typing of memos for the big Bosses - thanx to my dad's induction to the corporate life at a young age that stood me in good stead in the later years. At the end of one month they gave me a nice pen set as they were impressed the way I picked up telex operations.

About the movie just recall one song "PHOOLON KI TAAZGI HO TUM KALIYON KI NAAZNI HO TUM " - nothing beyond that - let me give you some links and will request those who know about this movie, kindly share

https://www.youtube.com/watch?v=IayvjvxW5Ig ;

https://www.youtube.com/watch?v=oMMTq-4QSeE ;

https://www.youtube.com/watch?v=RpHJnp06N1c ;

https://www.youtube.com/watch?v=xRNwkihIpSk ;

Cheers
Laksh KV

May 18 1973 (50 years ago)

"CHUPA RUSHTAM"

Folks:

50 years ago today was the release of an average grosser from Vijay Anand & Dev Anand combo called "Chupa Rushtam" under the banner of Navketan Films - in my view it was a flop movie that was dragged on for over 100 days. It boasted of a big star cast like Dev Anand, Hema Malini, Ajit, Premnath, Prem Chopra, Bindu, Vijay Anand himself with AK Hangal, Sajjan and Sudhir.

I recall seeing this movie alone at Gaiety Cinema when it was well into its 4th week and hardly anyone in the hall. I was mainly interested in the title song "पूछो तो यारों हम कौन हैं?" that Manna De had rendered so beautifully besides the SD Burman special reused tune of "धीरे से जाना खत्तियाँन में खटमल " - it was nice to see Dev Anand having a handful of "खटमलs"!!! And he wanted to protect his "Rajkumari". Another recall for me is the constant introduction by Vijay Anand by saying "बंधा आपका गुलाम है जिमी फ़र्नांडेज़ नाम है" and above all the song "लकड़ी जले, कोयला बने"

Now, I do not have very good memory of the plot and hence sharing what I gathered from multiple sources:

The plot hovers around Mountains that is between Tibet and India where in there is a hidden golden temple and the Government of India has granted a big sum for this project called Nangla project. Then there are people who want to take advantage of this project to get hold of gold – so there are abductions and killing galore besides blackmail. Some smart cookies enter and salvage things and bring all the wrong-doers as victims of law. The saving grace for the movie was some good songs composed by the Senior Burman.

Here are some song links for you:
https://www.youtube.com/watch?v=NhfQ7o8NacQ ;
https://www.youtube.com/watch?v=P59N8JY5eQU ;
https://www.youtube.com/watch?v=5Wrr6c6VNzw ;
https://www.youtube.com/watch?v=BVTEBx1coMw ;
Cheers
Laksh KV

May 17 1968 (55 years ago)

'SHIKAR"

Dear Friends:

55 years ago was the release date of the Golden Jubilee Hit movie "SHIKAAR" - under the banner of Guru Dutt films made by Atma Ram, younger brother of late Guru Dutt. The movie had Asha Parekh, Dharmendra, Sanjeev Kumar, Rehman, Johny Walker, Helan, Bela Bose, Ramesh Deo & Manmohan etc. All that I can recall about the movie is the ad on Radio Ceylon where Ameen Sayani used to scream "SHIKAAAAAAR" & this was followed by the title song by Mohd Rafi - only till 'SHIKAR HO KAY CHALAY'. Needless to say, I could not see the movie then or later as it hardly came for matinee shows. I feel those days the makers felt to move a movie to a Matinee show at reduced rate to be a prestige issue and when we suddenly saw some movie move from regular to reduced rates, we would feel "Oh God!!! So quick for matinee" & in the recent past used to feel the same way when the movie moved over to TV from the Hall which is very quick these days.

I have tried to see the movie on TV but could never see from the beginning nor could I complete the movie - it was always in bits and pieces and I always wondered on the basis of what little I saw, how could this movie do 50 weeks run though it had my favourite hero and if I see dispassionately, it was not a movie worth golden jubilee - but the reality is that it was and won several Filmfare awards including Sanjeev Kumar getting it for the best side actor. It had some good songs but again I will never say that they were among SJ's top ones but certainly hummable and the one that takes the cake is by Asha Bhonsle with Arabic flavour 'PARDE MEIN REHNAY DO PARDA NA UTHAO'. Here are some songs for you and I will hope to read comments from those people who have seen the movie and Amitabh Nigam ji any data on its collection please do share.

 https://www.youtube.com/watch?v=Vi_uN9BntoE ;
 https://www.youtube.com/watch?v=37G0GDAMxfA ;
 https://www.youtube.com/watch?v=rd-9tLE2RZU ;
 https://www.youtube.com/watch?v=Nd3HHm1gCnY ;
 https://www.youtube.com/watch?v=v2O6LLyYLBc ;
 Cheers
 Laksh KV

May 16 1969 (54 years ago)

"CHIRAG"

Folks:

The Director Raj Khosla, who was known for making suspense thrillers those days, decided to direct a different kind of movie and the movie I am talking about is "CHIRAG" released today 54 years ago. The movie had Sunil Dutt and Asha Parekh at the helm with support from Om Prakash, Kanhaiyalal, Sulochana, Mukri, Dulari and Lalita Pawar.

My memories again - nothing new - fractured wrist, no money and hence no ability to see the movie but never gave up listening to the radio programs on Vividh Bharati at night. The movie did not do well at the Box Office as it ran only for 7 weeks those days and hence in my view it was a flop. The highlight of the movie of course was the music of Madan Mohan ji.

Another gyaan I gathered 10 years after the movie released was that this was the first movie that was beamed when a new B&W Telerad TV was acquired at Lalita Laxminarayan's house in Pune some time in 1978 - well before we tied the knot. She says that there was a crowd to see the movie from her neighbourhood (I can agree as post marriage the scenario continued when the movie School Master was beamed on a Sunday evening and I could see kids crying - all from the neighbourhood). She adds further that the whole crowd waited for the famous song "CHIRAG DIL KA JALAO BAHUT ANDHERA HI" which never came in the show - may be DD deleted it. She consoled herself saying that it may be a song from some other movie. All these discussions happened post our wedding!!!

Well, the plot revolved around a well to do Hero, who falls for a simple Heroine and she reciprocates and they have the seniors' "Go ahead" for the big event. She gets a good welcome and good treatment in the new house but unfortunately, she does not conceive though the small plant she plants on her coming to the house has now grown into a 7 year old tree. Now the concerned MIL decides to bring in a second wife to ensure there is continuity of the Vamsh and things go from bad to worse as Asha Parekh loses her eyesight. But you can trust that all ends well - Decent songs I guess must have kept the audience glued to the movie.

I will wait for comments from those who have seen the movie and here are some links for you.

https://www.youtube.com/watch?v=4tadKQhLcoE ;

https://www.youtube.com/watch?v=kRDyiGZy_o4 ;

https://www.youtube.com/watch?v=8_HydJDcv3c ;

https://www.youtube.com/watch?v=WFcj64F2X4o ;

https://www.youtube.com/watch?v=VsodEd8l2fg ;

https://www.youtube.com/watch?v=1ElXyN1T7tw ;

Cheers
Laksh KV

May 15 1970 (53 Years ago)

"PEHCHAAN"

Folks:

It was today 53 years ago Sohanlal Kanwar's movie "Pehcaahn" hit the cinema halls. It was a big hit and had some fantastic music by Maestro Shankar Jaikishan, while as against the normal trend, it was Neeraj, Indivar and Varma Malik penning most of the songs and just one left for Hasratji. The movie had an unlikely pair of Manoj Kumar and Babita at the top with supporting stars like Balraj Sahani, Shailesh Kumar, Chand Usmani, Tuntun and CS Dubey. My memories are:

My late brother Vaidya V Raj, who was a big Manoj Kumar fan went ahead and saw the movie and was completely fida over it and recommended us to see it.

This movie ran for 2 weeks at Rupam before "Sharafat" took over and my second brother Radhakrishan (not on FB) and I went to see at Rupam - we too liked the movie though my brother accepted the good music a bit reluctantly for he is a big LP fan even today. We have had unending fights on who is better LP or SJ or RDB etc.

Story revolved around a Bhola Bhala village guy, who comes to Mumbai City to get married - a very clear objective of Mr. Gangaram - A simpleton a good human goes around the village playing the violin sold on the roadside and sings "BUS YAHI APRAADH MAIN HAR BAAR KARTA HOON, AADMI HOON AADMI SAY PYAR KARTA HOON". Heroine and her friends make fun of him when they get to know the purpose of his visit by singing "WOH PARI KAHAN SE LAAON, TERI DULHAN KISAY BANAOON" & the poor guy kept saying 'YEH GANGARAM KI SAMAJH MEIN NA AAYE". As expected the rich heroine falls for him and they decide to tie the knot but her brother and mom are not thrilled and then there is an angle of Chand Usmani who is in a kotha and is into the oldest business. This is where the character of CS Dubey is terrific as a pimp. There is one theory of "Money" being the most important thing with the sole song of Mohd Rafi in the background 'PAISAY KI PEHCHAAN YAHAN INSAAR KI KEEMAT KOI NAHI", filmed on the lyricist Neeraj. While all other male songs were sung by late Mukesh, this was an exception. Excellent songs helped the movie in its goal of making money. The 8th song in the movie was chopped off 'KAR LE DIL KI BAAT" - may be they might have found the length of the movie too much. Here are some songs for you from the movie:

https://www.youtube.com/watch?v=E00ZwKHi0Cg ;
https://www.youtube.com/watch?v=d4R1Z_BpPqI ;
https://www.youtube.com/watch?v=N7-vqyme-sA ;
https://www.youtube.com/watch?v=XA-BriSVvuY ;
https://www.youtube.com/watch?v=jDhmWbraGpA ;
https://www.youtube.com/watch?v=cfF8dFz6AkY ;
https://www.youtube.com/watch?v=tT5ixm0S21o ;
https://www.youtube.com/watch?v=x5YJhW-du94 ;

Cheers
Laksh

May 14 1971 (52 years ago)

"PARAS" "PYAR KI KAHANI"

Folks:

52 Years ago 2 movies released and both did slightly below average business. The movies are "PARAS" & "PYAR KI KAHANI"

1. PARAS

This movie had Sanjeev Kumar, Rakhee, Shatrughan Sinha, Farida Jalal and Mehmood who played the key roles. I did not see this movie during my summer vacation but once I started going to college from June 20th 1971, I had to pass thru Bandra Talkies where this movie ran for 8 weeks. So, on one of the college days, we, i.e. Viswanathan Krishnan along with some other class fellows on a very rainy day went to see the movie at Bandra Talkies 11.15 AM show. We were all very wet and had to rush to the loo time to time. We enjoyed the movie and the scene stealer was Mehomood who played "Munna Sarkaar" who had the unique habit of hallucinating and thinks of unreal disasters and would commence crying. All others around him, would cry too as the Munna Sarakar was crying. Shatrughan too made a great impact with his unique style.

Plot revolved around a true farmer - a true Gandhian who sings 'SUNO SAATHIYON SACHAYI SE BADKE DHARAM NAHI DOOJA', who moves to a city and one lie gives him all the comforts in the world and falls in love with Rakhee but the one lie haunts him on an on-going basis but since he is impersonating the Prince, it suits the real Prince who enjoys his life as a common man and falls for the Hero's sister Farida Jalal. Well, the director CP Dixit did a neat job in the movie and the songs were hummable composed by Kalyanji Anandji. Here are some of the links:

https://www.youtube.com/watch?v=f9-ZrxUtJpI ;

https://www.youtube.com/watch?v=tbNv2GXepIo ;

https://www.youtube.com/watch?v=xsWUC9HHrKI ;

https://www.youtube.com/watch?v=JP1w4poDeF8 ;

https://www.youtube.com/watch?v=8vcyP2cS51A ;

https://www.youtube.com/watch?v=SXzjFD6lxIo ;

2. PYAR KI KAHANI

The second movie was a remake of a hit Tamil movie "Kai Kudutta Daivam" - but let me confess that I have not seen both the Tamil and Hindi versions. All I know is the movie did not do well. Amitabh was still establishing post Anand and till Zanzheer happened he was not a pull factor - Anil Dhawan was far from interesting - so gave a skip but do recall some songs from the movie though not a big hit - "Ek Patay Ki Baat Suna Doon".

The plot revolved around 2 friends Amitabh and Anil who work in the same organization by some strange situation one is a peon while the other is a Manager. Anil falls in love with Farida Jalal a colleague and they tie the knot while Amitabh finds his match in Tanuja which his friend does not approve of and then comes some skeletons from the cupboard. This is what I gathered from various sources as I have not seen the movie. Well, there is not much to add from my side except some links of the songs. I would request my good friends to fill in the plot and the conclusion of the movie.

https://www.youtube.com/watch?v=-HzR2CNRNqc ;

https://www.youtube.com/watch?v=1PYQpm_PXFo ;

https://www.youtube.com/watch?v=mGOaiip72Y8 ;

https://www.youtube.com/watch?v=q4PUXxhvtP4 ;

Cheers

Laksh KV

May 12 1972 (51 years ago)

"PIYA KA GHAR"

Folks:

Today, 51 years ago was the release of "PIYA KA GHAR" by Tarachand Barjatya & Basu Chatterjee combo under the banner of Rajshri Films. The movie had Anil Dhawan, Jaya Bhaduri, Sulochana, Suresh Chatwal, Agha, Asrani, Keshto Mukherjee, Mukri, Sundar, C S Dubey & Paintal with special appearances by Amitabh Bachan and Dharmendra.

I have not seen this movie as I was not impressed by the Hero who was lucky to get some good movies under good banners. This one was a clean movie that depicted life in a chawl of Mumbai which did average business. How much liberty the neighbours can take with each other is beautifully depicted - given all the space constraints, water problems and a toilet/bathroom shared by multiple families besides large families of brothers and wives with parents staying in real small rooms. The camaraderie between the neighbours is absolutely fascinating and having lived in similar houses, I can relate to the life in chawls very well.

The plot revolves around Jaya Bhaduri who has grown in a village where she had enough space for herself and when her marriage is fixed to a boy in Mumbai the impression she gets is that the boy stays near the sea-shore of Mumbai in a big building called "Bharat Mahal" only to be disappointed to see that while the building is big but what her hubby and family have is a very small house with too many people staying virtually giving them zero privacy. This experience is depicted in a brilliant fashion and also how the neighbours stay back in their house for too long and not allowing the Hero's family to hit the bed. There were some good songs composed by LP duo for this movie. The song that makes maximum impact is 'YEH JEEVAN HAI, IS JEEVAN KA YAHI HAI RANG ROOP". Here are some of the links for you.

https://www.youtube.com/watch?v=VnaLbRHE1PM ;
https://www.youtube.com/watch?v=vUHCo-FMZAs ;
https://www.youtube.com/watch?v=ekKboaSX8tE ;
https://www.youtube.com/watch?v=5ywpma1h3GM ;
Cheers
Laksh KV

May 11th 1973 - (50 years ago)

"ZANJEER"

Hi Folks:

THIS DAY THAT YEAR – **ZANJEER** – May 11 1973

Let us go back 50 years – May 11th 1973 – a star was born though he had made his presence felt in 1971 and 1972 – OOPS!!! Why am I building up this like a QUIZ – well, let me be open about this – Yes this is none other than BIG B & "ZANJEER" that was released on May 11th 1973 wherein Amitabh was positioned as an "Angry Young Man" and after this movie, there was no looking back. Before this movie, he had made an impact in both Anand and Bombay to Goa & I am not talking about 'SAATH HINDUSTANI" & "RESHMA AUR SHERA" – where he was almost unknown. "PARWANA" also was released in 1972 wherein he played a negative role while Naveen Nischal took away the Heroine. Well, when I write, I happen to digress a lot and hence now coming back to ZANJEER, Produced under the banner of Prakash Mehra Productions (PMP) – written by the famous duo of Salim-Javed where almost all characters played their roles to perfection. Amitabh played the wronged Vijay, Jaya played Mala the CHAKOO CHOORIWALI, Pran played Sher Khan, Ajit was at his menacing best as Dharam Dayal Teja with Bindu as his Mona Darling. Om Prakash played the role of a police informer (De'Silva) who had lost 3 grown up sons & had almost given up with the prevailing system till he found a fighter in AB. Keshto Mukherjee as Gangu very innocently trapped AB into a corruption case to see him behind bars. The movie opened to a very Luke-warm response till the review on Sunday TOI which hailed AB as the new Superstar – then there was no looking back so much so that the leading couple decided to tie the knot at the success of the movie. Well the media then said "THE SURPRISE WAS NOT UNEXPECTED".

Very powerful dialogues & good characterization marked this movie – e.g. the first meeting of AB and Pran at the Police station when AB pushes the Chair to deprive Pran from taking the seat and says "JAB TAK BAITHNE KE LIYE NAHI KAHA JAAI SHARAFAT SE KHADE RAHO, YEH POLICE

STATION HAI TUMHARE BAAP KA GHAR NAHI" & then Pran retorting saying "YEH TUM NAHI, TUMHARI KURSI, TUMHARI WARDI BOL RAHI HAI SAHEB". Then follows the fight scene between the two – in the night in Pran's ILAKA and AB says "AB NA MERI WARDI HAI, NA KURSI, ILAKA TUMHARA HAI AUR MAIN AKELA HOON" & comes the Drop Kick – at the end of the fight both become friends with a clear understanding that Sher Khan will stop all the illegal activities. It is noteworthy that Sher Khan calls Vijay Khanna as Vijay Khan. The highlight is the song on friendship between the two sung by Sher Khan 'YAARI HAI IMAAN". The meeting between Ajit and AB after AB comes out of jail is very interesting – AB says "TEJA – MAIN AA GAYA" & Teja says 'KAHO TO PHIR ANDAR KAR DOON?". Slick editing & good music by Kalyanji Ananji gives the movie the required pace and a very chirpy Jaya is too good in the movie. From Sunday May 13th 1973, the Black marketers had a great time and made a lot of money. The movie celebrated Golden Jubilee at Imperial Cinema – Grant road & I also gathered that it raked up over Rs 6 crores those days.

For this landmark movie, Salim Javed duo won Filmfare awards for best Story and Screenplay while Gulshan Bawra who had a cameo (he sang the song Deewane Hai Deewanon Ko on screen) won the award for best lyrics. Over all a great movie and if I recall I must have seen it for at least 15 times with 2 consecutive shows at Aurora Cinema from 6 Pm to 12 midnight. People have stopped making such lovely movies is my regret. But the Golden era still continues with some channels showing the movies of 60s and 70s. Long live Bollywood.

Cheers & Happy Reading & here are the links for some of the songs:

http://www.youtube.com/watch?v=7KIcWTV3MME

http://www.youtube.com/watch?v=Bghg1DNrR3M

http://www.youtube.com/watch?v=flmj_t5fgGM

http://www.youtube.com/watch?v=JC1BcaCg7xs

http://www.youtube.com/watch?v=CflTK4Q8dy4

Laksh KV

May 10 1968 (55 Years ago)

"BRAHMACHARI"

Folks:

It was today 55 years ago the banner of Sippy Films gave us a big hit in "Brahmachari" - a very well made movie and lapped up by audience and critics too. It ran for 25 weeks in multiple cinema halls - though released during summer vacation, I got a chance to see during Diwali vacation at Plaza for the 11 am show with my Amma who was in the ladies "Q" and got 2 tickets for both of us. That was some advantage of being the youngest and laadla of Amma. The movie had Shammi Kapoor playing the title role at his best that earned him "Filmfare" award for the category of Best Actor. Rajashree was the Heroine and there was Mumtaz, Pran, Dhumal, Jagdeep, Mohan Choti, Manmohan and a whole lot of kids that included Baby Farida, Master Sachin & Jr. Mehmood.

My top memories of this movie are -

The radio ad that said "BARA BACHON KA BAAP AUR BRAHMAHARI!!! - HAHAHAHAHAHAH - RUKO YEH HASNE KI CHEEZ NAHI HAI, DEKHNE KI CHEEZ HAI".

Junior Mehmood got noticed in this movie and was a big hit with the unique way of dialogue delivery with gaps or can we say start and pause and restart??? Not to forget the song "Hum Kale Hain Toh Kya Hua" In the end when Brahmachari marries Sheetal (Rajashree), the smart kid had the presence of mind to remove the title "Brahma" and leave only Chari on the board of the Aashram they were living in.

The standard comedian jokes between Jagdeep and Dhumal where Jagdeep almost every time gets trapped but somehow escapes.

Manmohan as a blackmailer uses the term like "Fatafat" constantly.

Pran giving the same lines to every girl he meets and succeeds till he cheats on Mumtaz for Rajashree and Shammi Kapoor takes over.

The standard issue of "No Money" for running the Aashram and some sauda by Pran with Brahmachari

Shammi Kapoor looking Jet Black with White uniform of a hotel waiter called "Hatari" breaking crockeries and troubling Pran.

How the chinky child moves away when both SK and R try to give the child a peck on the cheeks so that it could be a lip to lip for the main players

Beautiful songs to make the kids sleep and then the nice manner of waking them up - adoption by a rich couple and how the other kids resist parting with "Suraj" - Master Sachin and how Brahmachari goes at night and gets him back.

Over all a very well made movie - no need to talk of the plot which has somewhat come out above. The movie with hit music of SJ had a lot of chart busters and still, am at a loss to understand as to why one song was chopped of "Tu Bemisaal Hai" - I am sure some knowledgeable people can throw more light here. Here are some song links for you

https://www.youtube.com/watch?v=KIvLi9JT8tE ;
https://www.youtube.com/watch?v=9eeIYoAAxgg ;
https://www.youtube.com/watch?v=Re_Goo0KHZ4 ;
https://www.youtube.com/watch?v=no6psn4h0wo ;
https://www.youtube.com/watch?v=34xSqvzWvXk ;
https://www.youtube.com/watch?v=1pMrwHB2kpc ;

Cheers

Laksh KV

May 08 1970 (53 Years ago)

"HUMJOLI"

Dear Friends:

Yes, it was today 53 years ago the Hit movie "HUMJOLI" released - regardless of the Kaka wave, Jeetu continued to give hits like Himmat & Humjoli plus a key guest appearance in Khilona though Maa Aur Mamta was a failure. Here was a real Masala entertainer from the home banner Tirupati films of Jeetu with Prasanna Kapoor producing and directed by Ramanna. This was a remake from the Tamil hit "Panakkara Kudumbam" - meaning "Rich Family" that had MGR & Saroja Devi while Humjoli had - Jeetendra, Leena Chandavarkar, Mehmood, Aruna Irani, Pran, Manmohan, Shashikala & Nasir Hussain & above all MUMTAZ in a special appearance. It was a Silver Jubilee hit and was an out and out entertainer. My memories are as under:

1. The day it was released, all 5 of us had to go to Hyderabad to attend the wedding of our cousin Lakshminarayan - the wedding was on 10th May 1970 and we were enjoying the heat of Hyderabad not worried about the fate of the movie Humjoli.

2. Post wedding, since all the relatives were under one roof, my parents decided to complete the "Thread Ceremony" of my elder brother and myself at Kacheguda Hyderabad and we all left Hyderabad on Friday 15h May 1970 when the movie "Pehchaan" released.

3. By the time we returned, the movie had moved from Rupam and I recall seeing the posters and banners with 3 Mehmoods overshadowing the Hero and Heroine. However, we saw "Pehchaan" but Humjoli slipped but not for too long.

4. Four months later during Diwali Vacation, the movie had a re-run at Vijay Chembur & it was nearing 20 weeks and at that time, we decided to see the movie. The best way to convince Amma was to tag along our Maasi Kamala Narayan with whom we ie my elder brother, self and Maasi's sons Arun Iyer and Ravi Narayan joined too went to see the movie & that is

when I realized that the Balcony was just a wall away from the stalls at Vijay Cinema - just about 4 feet wall and was easily jumpable for any active guy. The hall is next to Fire station of Chembur and we enjoyed the movie and especially Mehmood's antics right from sharing the news paper with Jeetendra, to giving laxative to folks waiting for interview or getting trapped for giving lift to a female with his wife Aruna Irani escalating to her FIL and Grand FIL. The 3 Mehmoods were modelled as Prithviraj Kapoor, Raj Kapoor and normal Mehmood for we had not seen Randhir yet as Kal Aaj Aur Kal was still 18 months away. But strictly it was not 3 but 4 Mehmoods as the movie ends with the 4th generation of look alike as yet another baby Mehmood is shown with some terrible camera work - nevertheless, it is still funny. The senior most Mehmood speaks like Prithviraj Kapoor ("BUTTAMEEZON, ISKA FAISLA ADALAT MEIN HOGAAAAAAAAAAAAAAA").

The movie revolves around Pran who wants to make money and gets married to a rich lady in the city but is also in love with a village girl Shashikala - he plans to kill his wife and inherit the property which he does, though his wife escapes and now Shashikala and Pran live in a big mansion with their daughter Leena Chandavarkar. Jeetendra and Aruna Irani are kids of Sapru & the dad of Jeetendra decides to marry again despite marriageable children - so these 2 run away to city and befriend Mehmood - another unemployed guy staying with his dad and granddad. Shashikala's nephew has an eye on the property and the Heroine and does everything possible to grab things but fails eventually as Good prevails. Good songs by LP and unique dance steps - give any location and Jeetu can dance be it a Tabela or a Tennis Court. Here are some songs for you:

https://www.youtube.com/watch?v=zYAoigvm38U ;
https://www.youtube.com/watch?v=9UoLrhbVtQA ;
https://www.youtube.com/watch?v=mLEDHANpzRc ;
https://www.youtube.com/watch?v=IsJ5MaAcHMI ;
https://www.youtube.com/watch?v=IWNxCWVsPaQ ;

Cheers & over to Amitabh Nigam for collection data and others for their views and comments

Laksh

May 07 1971 (52 years ago)

"ELAAN"

Folks:

It was today in 1971 FC Mehara's "ELAAN" saw the light of the day *ing Vinod Mehra, Rekha, Vinod Khanna, Helan, Madan Puri, Iftikar, Jagdish Raj and Rajendranath. This was the second movie of Vinod Mehra after his debut in "Parde Ke Peechay" - for him it was a family production and this one had Vinod Khanna in a negative role and above all the Big Boss Madan Puri who obviously has a weakness for girls was the Bad Man.

My memories of this movie:

1. I saw this movie on the first day 11 am show at Sahakar Cinema in Chembur. Though the hall was full, the movie would not start probably the print had not arrived and finally when there was too much noise from the crowd, they started with the "No Smoking" slide and INR to keep the crowd quiet.
2. This movie has a scene where Madan Puri touches Rekha very suggestively & I felt "Kya aadmi Hi!!!"
3. The movie looked interesting to me with the story of an invisible man.
4. Wanted the movie to do well for the music directors Shankar Jaikishan - but was very average grosser.
5. Vinod Mehra taking advantage of being invisible gets into the bathroom to see Rekha in the shower. The song "Ang Se Ang Laga Le" was a rage those days.
6. Vinod Mehra proudly says that he is a "Journalist Cum Photographer" & Vinod Khanna to look menacing, is shown as plucking and eating grass and spitting. I don't recall the character that plays Scientist (probably Jankidas) who gives the Hero a ring that would make him invisible if he puts in his mouth and strips himself.

7. Finally, to save some money, I did not eat anything during the interval and at the end of the movie walked all the way from Sahakar to Sion in about 75 minutes.

By now, you would have understood the plot from the above 7 points. Vinod Mehra who is a Photo-Journalist is on the job to expose some gangsters and lands in a cell where he finds Vinod Khanna and an old scientist who gives him the magic ring. Then it is all a matter of getting invisible and fight the battle. Hilarious scenes with bike going without the rider but the pilion Rajendranath still holds the hero in the air. SJ's music was not what was expected from them but still some hummable songs are there. Here are the links for you.

https://www.youtube.com/watch?v=6s7SiofRCuQ ;

https://www.youtube.com/watch?v=6i12BFoFukA ;

https://www.youtube.com/watch?v=cW_1EZQozMU ;

Cheers
Laksh KV

May 09 1969 (54 years ago)

"EK PHOOL DO MALI"

Folks:

On May 09 1969 the movie "Ek Phool Do Mali" released, that was made by Goel films produced and directed by Devendra Goel who was known for making movies with some message. The previous movie by the banner was "Dus Lakh" which too was a silver jubilee hit. This one too was a big hit with stars like - Balraj Sahani, Sanjay (Khan), Sadhna, Durga Khote, David, Brahmchari and Wonderchild Bobby. This movie was followed by "Dhadkan" by the same banner and again had Sanjay at the helm.

My recall about this movie:

1. I had a fractured hand in cast from April 19th so was still in that state
2. I used to go on vacation to my uncle's place in Thane - Anuradha S Iyer - please note, I had seen this movie at Prabhat Cinema Thane and during interval one of the boys got hurt with my plastered hand
3. This movie had Brahmachari trying to romance his girlfriend Shabnam but the MIL Manorama makes things tough for him.
4. There is a parody song with David's bald pate shown on full screen when he says "Mere Tarah Ganja"
5. The movie ran for 25 weeks and was considered a hit those days.
6. Ravi's music had its distinct stamp of his own.
7. Sanjay's younger brother Sameer played his friend

Story revolved around the hilly region where Sanjay and Sadhna fall in love & sing some good songs composed by Music Director Ravi. Inside the cave after getting wet, the inevitable happens and the Heroine is pregnant and as luck would have it in some expedition, a land slide occurs and some guys who are in this adventure are declared dead - so Sanjay goes leaving Sadhna in the family way & in comes the gentleman Balraj Sahani who gets married to Sadhna and does this selfless act with his eyes and ears open. He is happy to father the wonder child

Bobby. All is well but some years later, Sanjay returns and things get tough as the child develops a fondness with his biological dad. Balraj Sahani is worried that the child would be taken away...more so when on the child's birthday Sanjay sings "Oh Nanhesay Farishtay, Tujhse Yeh Kaisa Naata" - eventually after some action and some smart act by the wonder child, Balraj Sahani dies and hands over his wife to Sanjay to take care of things. All in the predicible fashion but still the overall impact is good - nice locale and decent acting plus good music helped the movie a lot. Here are some songs for you

https://www.youtube.com/watch?v=1rQZgeaoNf0 ;
https://www.youtube.com/watch?v=fxBKJ2p3bM8 ;
https://www.youtube.com/watch?v=aqkqofQWfd8 ;
https://www.youtube.com/watch?v=4t5b-OaSrRo ;
https://www.youtube.com/watch?v=2jfMFyhbjBA ;
https://www.youtube.com/watch?v=jVYgHOPFOo8 ;
https://www.youtube.com/watch?v=bUcvFmecZsI ;

Cheers

Laksh KV

May 04 1973 (50 Years ago)

"ANHONEE"

Folks:

It was on May 04 1973 the movie "ANHONEE" *ing Sanjeev Kumar, Leena Chandavarkar & Bindu released in Mumbai. It was an average grosser and had a fair amount of suspense built in. But the real USP of the movie was the song "HUNGAMA HO GAYA" which was a rage those days.

I had not seen the movie but my elder brother saw it and very quickly opened up the suspense to me saying that Sanjeev Kumar is a Police Officer who acts like a Mad-man - now I am sure you thought of the movie "KHILONA"... But this was 3 years later and Sanjeev Kumar was doing solo hero movies too and I am told that this movie was quite gripping. Since I have very limited gyaan about the movie, am sharing herewith what some sources had to say about the story line

There is one Dr. Rekha who runs a Mental Hospital. While travelling she encounters one Sunil who has a knife and is on the verge of attacking – but she manages to counsel him and take him to her hospital for treatment and Sunil shows good improvement where he is being treated by Dr. Mathur. On another occasion when some goons try to molest Dr Rekha, Sunil saves her and that makes them fall in love. They are ready to get engaged and during the party, reality dawns on Dr Rekha that Sunil is not a patient at all and Sunil too unearths some skeletons from Dr Rekha's cupboard and all that she was doing due to the blackmailing done by one Tiger and then everything gets cleared.

Here are some of the songs for you:

https://www.youtube.com/watch?v=H6_cykai2yE ;
https://www.youtube.com/watch?v=Wjvcjotk2EE ;
https://www.youtube.com/watch?v=BI-VbflxyUw ;

Cheers

Laksh

May-05-1972 – (51 years ago)

"APNA DESH"

Folks:

Going back 51 years – May-05-1972 saw the release of one of the big hits of that year called "APNA DESH" *ing Rajesh Khanna (AKA KAKA) & Mumtaz playing the lead roles with some major support coming from Manmohan Krishna, Om Prakash, Kanhaialal, Madan Puri & Jagdeep. Kaka was called Superstar then and the movie was released at Liberty as the main theatre and this hall had the reputation of not having too many Hindi movies doing well and some of us who were Dharam Paji fans wanted this movie to fail – but those were Kaka's days and anything that he touched turned gold. The posters had Mumtaz and Kaka in some western outfit with Mumu revealing a lot and at that impressionable age were amazed at the TINOPAL white complexion of Mumu revealing her legs and other vitals. I felt that I should make a negative contribution to the success of the movie by ignoring and did it for close to 3 weeks. But my dear friend Balakrishnan Narayan (BEDI) who was a big Khanna fan recommended that I see the movie and I did eventually at Broadway Cinema – Dadar and while I liked the movie, I still tried to find faults like "Too Long", "Editing could have been better", "Credibility" – how can the trio Om Prakash, Madan Puri & Kanhaiyalal (representing the Evil) not recognize the leading couple when they come as Phirangs & sing DUNIYA MEIN LOGON KO DHOKA KABHI HO JATA HAI sung by Asha Bhonsle & RDB himself. To start with the hero and heroine are poor people – hero a clerk in a Govt organization and the heroine sells tender coconut water – I have always wondered as to when I will be able to see a Mumtaz like Narial Pani wali but no luck whatsoever all over India (My bad luck)

The movie itself was good against evil theme based and after a lot of struggle how good prevails and has a lot of good music by RD Burman that helped the movie to do well. Yes, the status of the Superstar ensured heavy initials and the female crowd into the hall. The movie ran for over 25 weeks and janata lapped it up – the movie was directed by Jambu. Some of the songs are here:

http://www.youtube.com/watch?v=NiO4YIIUF7g&feature=fvst
http://www.youtube.com/watch?v=Bw4-8SmRXow
http://www.youtube.com/watch?v=ew_E5vaAOKo
http://www.youtube.com/watch?v=WWfG0_gUILg
http://www.youtube.com/watch?v=WkSByJCL6P4

Well friends, I recall those days with a lot of fondness

Cheers & Happy Reading

Laksh KV

May 01 1970 (53 Years ago)

"SACHHA JHOOTA"

Dear Friends:

This time I am writing about Manmohan Desai, Kaka combo movie "Sachha Jhoota" released today in the year 1970 when I had given the Class X exam and moving to SSC class XI in another month plus. This movie was a runaway hit and for all Kaka fans it was double maja... in all 3 Khannas - 2 Kaakas and a Vinod Khanna. I was hoping that this movie would fail but the superstar's stars were such that anything he touched would turn Gold. I ensured that I did not see this movie when it released but managed to see it in bits and pieces on TV and was very impressed by the acting of the DOG Moti... In the court scene it was astonishing to see that both Kakas could play the same tune using the Baaja.

My memory also says that the movie shifted from its main theatre clearing space for "Sharafat" on May 29th and moved to MOTI Cinema where it ran till it did 25 weeks. However, in my arguments with my friend Balakrishnan Narayan aka Bedi would be "See Kaka had to vacate the hall for Dharam Paji". The biggest point of debate however was, how come Kaka got Filmfare award for this "Smashing" performance and Sanjeev Kumar was ignored for his **"Super"** performance in "Khilona"!!! This is something that we could never answer. These are some memories for me.

Well, story revolved around a Village grown Kaka who is Mr. Good and his look alike in the City who is the extra smart guy who does all kinds of robbery of diamonds and other precious stones. The village guy has a sister and for her sake, he decides to earn money in the city and reaches the city to find his look-alike who makes him to play his character. Vinod Khanna is a police man and is after the Bad Kaka but now since the replacement has happened, it gets tough. There is Mumtaz who adds to the glamour. Music of Kalyanji Anandji was a big hit those days and the signature song was "Meri Pyar Behaniya Banegi Dulhaniya". Here are some links for you.

https://www.youtube.com/watch?v=9G6gBFrrpDQ ;
https://www.youtube.com/watch?v=CoN9LbZS27E ;
https://www.youtube.com/watch?v=U-YQkFTi1Zk ;
https://www.youtube.com/watch?v=FnBWeO0UcUM ;

Cheers - hoping Amitabh Nigam can enlighten us with the collection data

Laksh KV

April 30 1971 (52 years ago)

"ANDAZ"

Dear Friends:

It was today 52 years ago we saw the release of one of the Hit movies of the year 1971 called "Andaz" that came from the Sippy Banner - also was the launch of Ramesh Sippy as the young Director. The movie had good starcast with Shammi Kapoor, Hema Malini, Aruna Irani, Sonia Sahani, Randhava, Roopesh Kumar and Special Appearances of Rajesh Khanna, Simmi Garewal & Ajit plus above all the adorable kids Baby Gowri and Master Alankar.

My Memories are as under:

Being a big Shammi Kapoor & SJ fan, I wanted to see the movie - but I had thought of seeing this movie on our parent's 25th wedding anniversary that was on May 6th 1971. In general, the special appearance bit was kept quite confidential and was not known to ones like me - only recall is reading in the Filmfare that some guest artists are there in the movie. When I learnt that it had Kaka having an impactful role, I had my doubts of seeing the movie. My dear friend Balakrishnan Narayan aka Bedi had gone to native place during the vacation. There was a cobbler (Mochi) outside the building called Ram Nivas diagonally opposite to our building, who was also a good friend and he had already seen the movie and came home to deliver some of our footwear and announced loud and clear "Andaz, Ekdum 'HOPELESS' picture Hi" - so Amma decided no need to see the movie on 6th May. So I ended up seeing the movie at RIVOLI Matunga with my classmate Suryanarayanan (not on FB). Frankly, we liked the movie for Hema Malini first & SK next...Kaka, we thought was lucky to get good roles like Anand and Andaz - koi talent nahi (all prejudice mind you). We two walked back home via the S bridge and via Dharavi talking of SJ's great music and Hema and SK but nothing about Kaka.

Well, the storyline was quite progressive that supported widow remarriage - both SK and HM have lost their respective spouses and are saddled with a kid each and both kids are part of the same school and they bring their Dad and Mom together to form an awesome foursome. Life cannot be all that easy and smooth as there is a Roopesh Kumar, a Sonia Sahani & to create more misunderstanding Randhava and Aruna Irani too add their bit. Eventually, things fall in place. The highlight of the movie was music by Shankar Jaikishan and was the last hit movie of a fading Shammi Kapoor - though after this he had 3 movies Jawan Mohabbat, Janay Anjanay & Preetam that were total washouts. The signature song of the movie "Zindagi Ek Safar Hi Suhana" comes in the movie thrice with 3 different singers and characters - no wonder it was an award winning song. The movie ran for 25 weeks in Mumbai though it was dragged in the later part of its tenure. But music has been ever-green and here is the link with all the songs for you:

https://www.youtube.com/results...;

Cheers and will await inputs from my knowledgeable friends
Laksh KV

April 28 1972 - 51 years ago

"Mom Ki Gudiya" "Mangetar" & "Shararat"

Folks

On this fateful day (April 28 1972) 3 immensely forgettable movies released and I saw 2 of the 3 and ended up missing the better one among the 3. Yes, I missed "Mom Ki Gudiya". Let me share my memories.

1. Mom Ki Gudiya

When I had gone to see "Apradh" I happened to see the trailer of "Mom Ki Gudiya" and it did not appeal to me. What I found unique was Tanuja paired with a new comer Ratan Chopra & Anand Bhakshi making his debut as a singer with LP giving the music. Thought the song "Ladki Punjab Di.... Reshma Jawan Ho Gayee" had the rustic flavour, but it could not help the movie and ended up as a big disaster.

Story line was something like the Hero expires on the wedding day and I have honestly not gone to find what it entails but just not worth it - here are some songs for you and would request knowledgeable people to share their gyaan. Here are some songs for you:

https://www.youtube.com/watch?v=VgMFBF9mJPQ ;

https://www.youtube.com/watch?v=mkuL1zDlC3U ;

https://www.youtube.com/watch?v=jH0NKssxySI ;

https://www.youtube.com/watch?v=W7iZSRUXmpU ;

2. Mangetar

The most forgettable movie is Mangetar which I and my good friend Balakrishnan Narayan aka Bedi went and saw at Paradise Mahim and were so disappointed. It had Deb Mukherjee playing some scientist who does some major research and finds the image of the killer in the retina of the eyes of the dead. Some vague concept - we had some disinformation about the movie where we were told Nutan was doing some cabaret numbers and it was unbelievable. Sudhir Sen played her hubby and there were no sizzling numbers and the whole movie was a terrible disappointment. Since, we failed; we wanted some of our friends to fail too. We both decided to hype about the movie to all our building boys and only one succumbed ie Ramani Kanaka's (kanaka please tag your brother) Venkatramani Krishnamoorthy. We told him he must see and by the time he decided it was running in matinee only at Maratha Mandir - we had told that Nutan had 6 cabaret numbers after interval - idea was to ensure he does not walk out of the movie during the break. He had a mouthful to give once he was back... to recover the shock, he walked all the way from Bombay Central to Sion!!... I searched for data on this movie and with great difficulty found one song and here I share that. Anyone has more data please do share

https://www.youtube.com/watch?v=LSaJ_hOR9wQ ;

3. Shararat

This was a movie we all saw at Rupam and were thrilled to see the Villain Shatrughan getting a rousing welcome who was still making his mark in the industry and Biswajeet was playing the lead with Mumtaz. Shatrughan was not interested in Mumtaz but his elders wanted him to marry Mumtaz for property that belonged to some rich guy where she had gone as their lost bahu or daughter - Jr. Mehmood played dual role of a boy and a girl. It had some good music by Music Director Ganesh and was exceptionally lip synced by Biswajeet. Here are some songs for you:

https://www.youtube.com/watch?v=in0iFaPJy9Y ;

https://www.youtube.com/watch?v=M0g8l55RgEk ;

https://www.youtube.com/watch?v=P1szh3BW6aI ;

https://www.youtube.com/watch?v=o4pzrAeEQQE ;

https://www.youtube.com/watch?v=b4iSiQ89qzw ;

So friends - this was the worst week as far as releases were concerned. Will await more details from others

Cheers
Laksh KV

April 27 1973 (50 Years ago)

"DAAG" - a Poem of Love

Dear Friends:

50 years ago was the date of release for YashRaj films "Daag" - a Poem of Love. This movie helped Kaka to rebuild after a host of flops in 1972 starting with Dil Daulat Duniya, Jhoroon Ka Gulam, Bawarchi (average at BO) Mere Jeevan Saathi, Shehazada etc. It was the first independent venture of Yash Chopra and Kaka and Yashji joined hands and Daag was born. A very sensitive love story and well-made that also did well at the Box Office.

My memories - I was just finishing my Inter Commerce exams and was treated for food poisoning (recall Neera episode during the release of Gaai Aur Gori?). My friends Balakrishnan Narayan and Viswanathan Krishnan were of great moral support and both were Kaka fans and I decided I will not carry my prejudice and decided to see the movie but still did not want to make it known to them and went to see it secretly and enjoyed it. I then confessed to them that I saw the movie and liked the acting of Kaka too. The other thing that remains at the top of my mind is the alleged hot bedroom scene between Sharmila and Kaka when they meet again though Kaka is married to Rakhee. Those scenes generated a lot of interest for folks my age - just 18 you see...

The movie gave a feel of some English movies too with excellent photography and late night scenes. Story revolved around Kaka and Sharmila who fall in love and get married and his boss's son Prem Chopra has evil eyes and tries to rape Sharmila but the timely return of Kaka ensures she is saved and Prem Chopra is killed. Now police case, jail and escape resulting in a new identity for Kaka in a different location and as a good Samaritan helps Rakhee who is pregnant and has been ditched by her boyfriend. Now the inevitable happens and the trio meet and this part has been dealt with a lot of sensitivity and beauty - good to see the co-existence of all 3 in the end. Good music by LP too helped the movie which was a money spinner. Here are some songs for you:

https://www.youtube.com/watch?v=OYjjlIq7nRQ... ;

Cheers - Amitabh Nigam – I gathered that the movie collected 6.5 crores in 1973... So this must be a bumper hit in the current era.

Laksh KV

April 25 1969 (54 years ago)

"JEENE KI RAAH"

Folks:

Yes, it was today 54 years ago the lovely family drama from the farm of Prasad Production was dished out to us *ing Jeetendra, Anjali Kadam, Tanuja, Sanjeev Kumar, Durga Khote, Manmohan Krishna, Jagdeep, Bela Bose, Viju Khote etc. includes some child artists who are all the responsibility of our Hero Jeetendra.

My memories - with a fractured right hand during the summer vacation one day before the annual results this movie was released when I passed out from class IX and moved to class X. Since my rank was a big number, parents were not happy and to top it with a hand in cast, it did invoke some sympathy & some allowance to see extra movies. So we 3 brothers went to see the movie and all were excited - the movie starts with a train chugging along and coming and halting at a station and the Hero comes out and when the TC demands for the ticket, he does not take it out from his pocket but has it stuck between his teeth and tells the TC to take it from there as his hands are full with luggage. We 3 brothers simply loved the movie and despite the heat in the cinema hall we did not get headache and we gave credit to the movie but my middle brother gave the whole credit to the music of LP (He is a big fan of LP while I was a big fan of SJ) and we have had enough fights and arguments on who was better. Here I was still in school but again in 1972 while in college I and my dear Balakrishnan Narayan saw this movie again at Paradise Cinema Mahim and we not only enjoyed the movie but also started calling Viju Khote as Raghunandan (screen name in the movie). This was the time, we 2 as friends had only one major difference of opinion and I refused seeing Kaka movies and automatically he would avoid Dharam Paji movies. So the neutral hero won - who Jeetendra, Shashi Kapoor & co...

The posters read as view-points of various stake-holders:

'BETA HO TOH AISA'

'PATI HO TOH AISA'

'BHAI HO TOH AISA'

'DOST HO TOH AISA'

Story revolved around Jeetendra who had a huge family to support and moves to Bombay for a job and tells a lie to the Boss - Manmohankrishna, that he is "Unmarried" so that he clinches the job. But the boss's daughter - Tanuja, is on a wheel chair with no hope in life and as a Good Samaritan, the hero tries to help her come out of that life of a handicapped person. Needless to say she falls for him as from her viewpoint he is an eligible bachelor but in fact he is married to Anjali Kadam, The stress and pressure he has to go thru and back home there are issues, as his mother, wife and the kids of the house move out and start looking for him in Mumbai singing "Chanda Ko Dhoondne Sabhi Taare Nikal Paday"... Enough drama and confusion later all ends well and Sanjeev Kumar comes in handy to handle Tanuja and they get married while Jeetu is loyal to Anjali Kadam. Decent music contributed to the family drama from the popular banner. Here are some links for you

https://www.youtube.com/watch?v=X4rwcNuTShA ;

Cheers - waiting for collection data from Amitabh Nigam and special tippaniya from Dilip Apte Saheb

Laksh KV

April 24 1970 (53 years ago)

"BANDHAN" & "MAA AUR MAMTA"

Folks:. Golden Jubilee

Today 53 years ago 2 movies released with a common Heroine Mumtaz... Now, here is some data for you regarding Mumtaz who had 6 movies released in 5 weeks in 1970 - started with

Khilona - April 10 1970

Himmat - April 17 1970

Bandhan & Maa Aur Mamta - April 24 1970

Sachha Jhoota - May 01 1970

Humjoli (Guest Artist) - May 08 1970

Of the 6 movies 5 were Silver Jubilee hits...

Well, let me write about Bandhan first (alphabetic order) - my recall is the radio program on Vividh Bharti where the top line was "DHARMA GAURI SAY PYAAR KARTA THA" & then hear Mahendra Kapoor's voice "AAJAAO AABHI JAAO" - then again "JAANA HAI TO JAAO MANAYENGAY NAHI" or Mukesh number "BINA BADRA KI BIJURIYA". I have mentioned earlier that while my best friend Balakrishnan Narayan was a great Kaka fan, I did not want to go and see this movie and instead preferred to see the other release of the day. The movie did good business as it was a silver jubilee hit and came from the Sippy Banner with Rajesh Khanna, Mumtaz, Jeevan, Achla Sachdev, Kanhaiyalal, Anju Mahendru and Sanjeev Kumar making good contribution.

Story revolved around the life of a farmer family that had a sincere son, a bechari mom and an irresponsible dad who is also jailed due to some theft. His son who takes care of farming falls in love with a Gaon ki Gori - Gowri... who is a firebrand but golden hearted. The situation demands that the Hero move to City to make money and finds a lady who is sympathetic to him and so is an advocate in a guest appearance ie Sanjeev Kumar. He comes back to his village only to fight with his dad who gets killed and our Hero is the accused and has a very strong reason to take the blame on himself. Well made movie with good songs helped the movie do good business. Here are some songs for you:

https://www.youtube.com/watch?v=3eAkbPO_bLA ;

https://www.youtube.com/watch?v=I4kIWQlLgtw ;

https://www.youtube.com/watch?v=Q7HbBs29-f0 ;

https://www.youtube.com/watch?v=yLNMGKyLMjI ;

The second movie was Maa Aur Mamta *ing Ashok Kumar, Nutan, Nirupa Roy, Jeetendra, Mumtaz, Roopesh Kumar, Jayant, Sujit Kumar and Rehaman. This movie did not do well - my memory is strong about the character of Taxi Driver played by Jayant who has total sympathy towards Nutan who has been wronged in general. The other memory is that there is a Hockey match in which Jeetendra and Roopesh Kumar play and Roopesh Kumar purposely hits Jeetendra with the hockey stick and injures him and needless to say that both men have the common objective of being on the right side of Mumtaz... Come to think of it Mumtaz and Roopesh Kumar are real life cousins but not only in this movie but also in Dhadkan they played a couple and that is all acceptable in movies. Overall nothing much to talk about in this move - we were disappointed to see a boring movie but continued to say it was better than Bandhan but the Box Office collections made it very clear as to which one was a better movie. Songs too were average composed by LP and here are some links for you:

https://www.youtube.com/watch?v=NT31su-zPnQ ;

https://www.youtube.com/watch?v=z_Yd3BroChg ;

https://www.youtube.com/watch?v=BxJYn9zbxbg ;

https://www.youtube.com/watch?v=p-BxbTwmWSc ;

https://www.youtube.com/watch?v=FMIrmuhCEfw ;

Cheers - waiting for more inputs from others

Laksh KV

April 23 1971 (52ears ago)

"MAIN SUNDAR HOON" & "PARDESI"

Hello Friends

It is likely that you folks (those who read This Day That Year) must be wondering that Lax writes about taking people back 40 to 45 years – but what to do – the period October 1968 to 1973 is embedded too strongly in my mind while I don't recall much about what is going on in Bollywood now. Be that as it may – you may have to put up with some 4 decades old History.

So let me take you back 52 years i.e. April 23rd 1971 – that saw the release of a Jubilee Hit movie called "MAIN SUNDAR HOON" *ing Mehmood, Leena Chandavarkar, Biswajeet, David, Nazir Hussain, Sulochna, Mukri and some guest artists notably like Waheeda Rehman and the Genius Kishore Kumar recording the Hit song 'NAACH MERI JAAN FATAFAT'.

This movie was not marketed very well but we, who knew about the original Tamil Movie called "Server Sundaram" were sure that a good movie was releasing. It picked up well in the days to come. I had done the booking in advance for the first day first show (FDFS) at Rupam Sion with my friends since Rupam used to have different movie running at reduced rates for the 11am Matinee show – we had to be happy with 1st show. In the movie, Mehmood (with coconut scraping teeth in front) works in a Hotel as a Server and entertains all the people who come to eat. The hotel owner's (David's) daughter is the heroine of the movie Leena & she is fond of Mehmood's pranks and says that she "Likes His Innocence" and the uneducated guy thinks that she loves him. When Mehmood gets to know that Leena's name is Radha – he yells at the chef "Radha – NIKAAL TEEN SADA (DOSAS)". There are many hilarious scenes but he steals the show with his performance when there is a screen test for him to get into movies. His friend Biswajeet who loves Leena helps him to get into movies – Once he becomes a celebrity, he realizes that money is not everything after all and he does keep the uniform of the waiter in a prominent place in his house to stay grounded. Despite all this, there are situations when he missed out on important personal stuff that distances him from his beloved mother played by Sulochna. For some orphaned kidz, he does a show that has a parody song where there is a curse on men to have the ability to become pregnant and the period instead of 9 months would be 18 months and then Mehmood says "YE DARD APPUN KO NAKKO". Outstanding performance by Mehmood marks this movie produced under the banner of AVM Studios and this article will be incomplete if I did not talk about our own Kishore Kumar coming and singing the hit song 'NAACH MERI JAAN FATAFAT" filmed on Mehmood and Jayashree T in the movie. Biswajeet and Leena too have done well and the infectious laughter of Leena is lovable. A Hit movie of the early 70s when many Heroes were afraid to work alongside the talented Mehmood who gave comedians the status of Hero – something similar to what SALIM-JAVED duo did to the status of writers when Deewar got released in 1975.

Some of the Songs are here for you to enjoy

http://www.youtube.com/watch?v=MS9bcXCxBvI

http://www.youtube.com/watch?v=gb339Cw_7ns

http://www.youtube.com/watch?v=B880xf1arAw

http://www.youtube.com/watch?v=k8gVuQNmkPU

http://www.youtube.com/watch?v=2M38CsIAXMI

http://www.youtube.com/watch?v=qSAfVu3wJkw

The second movie released on This Day in 1971 was "Pardesi" *ing Biswajeet, Mumtaz, Manmohan Krishna, Sulochana, Jeevan, Sujit Kumar and the famous rapist Manmohan. This movie was a flop and dealt with the theme of memory loss and revival when the same situation strikes the hero for a 2nd time.

The only personal memory I have besides the flopping of the movie was the senior pro Manmohan Krishna was in our area and I went and spoke to him asking about which movies are round the corner and he mentioned "Paresi Dekhiye" - but I did not see it though, on and off have seen it on TV when one could notice that a rich looking Biswajeet is rescued by tribal people who are basically snake charmers and slowly make him also one. Kundan Kumar made this movie who also made Aulad earlier and later Anokhi Ada - but most of his movies were either flops or average grossers. Well some songs of the movies were OK and not meeting the standards of the famous Chitragupta. Here are the links for you.

https://www.youtube.com/watch?v=yJPK1oDvxOg ;
https://www.youtube.com/watch?v=HO-taou1ntQ ;
https://www.youtube.com/watch?v=a7v8HJ0MK08 ;
https://www.youtube.com/watch?v=O3-a52inmqw ;

Happy Reading – Cheers
Laksh KV

April 21 1972 (51 years ago)

"APRADH" "SHADI KE BAAD"

Folks:

51 years ago today 2 movies released - first one was from a new banner FK Internationals "Apraadh" and the second one was from a seasoned banner of Prasad Productions called "Shadi Ke Baad". My memories are as under:

1. My Final Exams of First Year Commerce got over on April 22nd and the first thing I did was to reach out to see the well marketed and publicized movie Apraadh...
2. Radio ad said. "International Car Race.... BBRrrrrrr" - Ehasan Rezvi was the guy who was on the radio for this movie.
3. Mumtaz in Swim Suit and all of us were maha fida and FK being the swashbuckling hero had his own suave style – when he gets to know her name as Sunita, he just pulls her and says "Ghaseeta"
4. Prem Chopra playing his elder brother and the way he would address his younger bro as "Raaaaaam"
5. FK had something unique in every movie of his and here it was - the Car Race and it was always India's Ram Khanna in the lead...
6. Mukri had a key role and is fascinated towards Faryal who plays Suzy. But he had his own style of addressing her as "Fify" and when he finds her dead in the bath tub, it is worth seeing his face.
7. How the smugglers use the fishing route to get gold across the border by slitting the fish and inserting gold coins inside is fascinating.
8. How the elder brother does not allow the younger brother to lead an honest life.
9. Well mounted and excellent production values, good photography definitely are an asset as far as this movie is concerned. The movie ran for 15 weeks and is considered a hit - but wrt return on investment - not too sure as it was a lavishly mounted movie - will await Amitabh Nigam to enlighten us.

10. Good songs in the movie where it is very evident that the loyalist Kalyanji Anandji of Mohd Rafi and Mukesh, changed over to Kishore Kumar who was taking the industry by storm. Here are some of the songs for you:

https://www.youtube.com/watch?v=EElyTvutdcU ;

https://www.youtube.com/watch?v=4Sd85eF2rRM ;

https://www.youtube.com/watch?v=3DNHtpaLAkI ;

https://www.youtube.com/watch?v=yuxOJSp_hAw ;

In contrast the 2nd movie "Shadi Ke Baad" was released with minimum publicity and came from a down to earth banner that made good homely family tearjerkers/entertainers. I have relatively less memory of this movie though I and my brother had gone to see the movie at Surya Cinema subsequently called Dharti (not sure if it still exists - Dilip Apte Saheb can perhaps enlighten us). The top memories for me are as under:

1. Shatrughan Sinha plays a senior pro who keeps saying "Insult" - he actually plays Rakhee's Father-in-law... a dramatic difference in the character from Bihari of Khilona of the same banner to Chowdhary Bhisahn Swaroop Singh
2. What happens "After Marriage" is the over all theme and is also shown thru a stage drama song "Brahmma Oh Brahmma"
3. Jeetendra riding a bicycle that has no wheels but only handles, as a mad man
4. Rakhee playing a dumb mad girl
5. Master Satyajeet plays an important role
6. Shekar Purohit has his own style of dialogue delivery with a bit of religious tone.
7. I genuinely enjoyed this movie and felt that if it had been positioned and marketed well, it could have reached the larger audience - the less impact was some what similar to a hilarious comedy movie "Pyar Kiye Jaa" which again in my view, if only had been marketed well - would have been a bigger money spinner.
8. Production values were very average and not comparable to Apradh.
9. Laxmikant Pyarelal had some catchy songs in this movie and here are some links for you:

https://www.youtube.com/watch?v=dKse_jCCvPA ;
https://www.youtube.com/watch?v=V8LEYMJuiYY ;
https://www.youtube.com/watch?v=VjE3BfE8yi8 ;
https://www.youtube.com/watch?v=Z7npjXLw2F0 ;
https://www.youtube.com/watch?v=HIxUiDPTf8Q ;

Cheers
Laksh KV

April 20 1973 (50 Years ago)

'GAAI AUR GORI' 'ANOKHI ADA'

Folks:

2 movies released today in 1973 - not going in alphabetic order... Gaai Aur Gori first and then Anokhi Ada

1. Gaai Aur Gori

Made by Sandow MMA Chinappa Devar of "Haathi Mera Saathi" & "Janwar Aur Insaan" fame gave another chance to Shatrugan Sinha as a Hero - who was trying his best to move from negative to +ve character. More than this movie, I have some very personal memories about this period. I was on study holiday for my Inter Commerce Exams that were starting on the following day and my dad felt sad that his son who was working as a student till April 1st was studying hard for his exams...He told me let us step out and have some Neera from Neera Kendra near Aurora Cinema - King's Circle. I was very happy and joined him and it was around 9ish in the morning and both of us crossed the Cinema hall and I was telling my dad, after the exam I will see this movie - dad agreed. We had Neera and came home and I resumed my studies. Late night my dad took ill and threw up and I rushed to our Doctor's house and got her home who gave some medicines and he became better. So the night went off and my exams were to start in the morning and I started visiting the loo and went 4 times in the morning on Saturday and I felt "Am I nervous due to exams? - not likely" but with that went to SIES College and wrote the first exam and came home for lunch - visited the loo once more and then gave the 2nd exam from 3 to 6 PM and returned home and visited toilet 4 more times post the 2nd exam. In all 9 visits and then went off to sleep - since Sunday was a holiday could sleep a bit early. But when I woke up around 4ish in the morning I was shivering and had running temperature. Now my dad got worried and it was all due to the Neera we had, that was stale. Dad threw it out and he was free and mine was taking the route of Southern Gate - and on that fateful Sunday I went to the loo 39 times and was drained. My dad felt very guilty and got Dr. Sudha G Patel home and when I told her I had 3 more days of exams, she resorted to Opium to stop the motion. Then I managed to give the exams, & I was seated in a separate room closer to the toilet - Organzation of Commerce (OC) was the first paper on that Monday and in between the exams went to the loo 6 times and could attempt only 4 questions which meant had to score 35 out 65 and that was tough but God was with me and I scored 46 in that paper when I saw the results. I took it easy and that is why I am right now writing this column - if I had known that I was close to death, I would have been nervous and would have collapsed after going to the loo for 39 times. My dad never excused himself for pulling me from studies and taking me to Neera Kendra - after that till date I have not touched Neera.

So my memory, a harsh one at it, I will stop and continue with the movie - which was a story about a rich spoilt Hero and a Bholi Heroine who get married and the Heroine has a Cow whom she loves dearly. Needless to say the hero does not like the cow as he eventually pushes her to choose one of them between the cow and himself. Well, we all know all will end well and the same Cow will save the Hero when in trouble and so on and so forth - very predictable stuff. This movie did not do too well at the BO and could not make Shotgun a big hero despite the heroics of the animal as it is always in Devar films. Some hummable songs were there like "Gori Oh Gori" - here are the links for you:

https://www.youtube.com/watch?v=H7npC_4VJC8 ;
https://www.youtube.com/watch?v=qnMl6tOG7D0 ;
https://www.youtube.com/watch?v=UKi7Q5qlFvQ ;

2. Anokhi Ada:

This was yet another flop movie from the house of Kundan Kumar, who had made a better movie in Aulad earlier. This one had Jeetendra, Rekha and Vinod Khanna with Mehmood Manmohan Krishna and Nasir Hussain. Very predictable story line of the Hero playing double act purposely and like a stupid person the villain cannot see thru the game. It had Mehmood playing a research doctor who discovers a medicine to make people young and tries on himself and as expected (for comic effect) becomes older... I recall seeing this movie with my elder brother in the month of May 1973 at Aurora on a Saturday night and all I went for is the Quwali "Haal Kya Hai Dilon Ka Na Poocho Sanam" which was the last song of the movie. After the movie we brothers were walking back home and as we reached Gandhi Market, we saw some drunken people coming from the opposite side. Now in my pocket I had a princely sum of Rs. 40/- (10 *4) and was worried but showed some artificial confidence and crossed over those 2 who actually got scared of the 2 of us. Well, it was a relief once we reached home.

There were some good songs by LP in this movie but that could not salvage the movie. Here are some links:

https://www.youtube.com/watch?v=dQFKVpIiZIg ;
https://www.youtube.com/watch?v=Pa2R1-Cm3AM ;
https://www.youtube.com/watch?v=RsOLDH-3gnI ;
https://www.youtube.com/watch?v=96avGcD6xlI ;
https://www.youtube.com/watch?v=sH2xjTsbDTg ;

Thank you for your patience to go thru this.

Cheers & waiting for more inputs and comments

Laksh KV

April 19th 1974 (49 Years ago)

'HUMSHAKAL'

Folks:

It was today 49 years ago the movie "Humshakal" released *ing Rajesh Khanna in a dual role with Tanuja & Moshumi Chatterjee. Support cast included Asrani, Jagdeep, David, Asit Sen and Ramesh Behl. This movie was an average grosser and I had managed not to see it as I did not want to add to the revenue of a Kaka movie. What I recall mainly are some really hummable songs:

1. Kaheko Bulaya Mujhe Baalma
2. Hum Tum Ghum Sum Raat Milan Ki
3. Main Tumko Doongi Piya Pyar Ki Nishani
4. Rastaa Dekhe Tera Vyakul Man Mera...

In a standard dual role script, one can expect exchange of places between the identical looking people, misunderstandings, some fights with villain & some songs and all this were available in this movie. Unfortunately the decline for Kaka had peaked by this time and he started slowly losing his steam though in 1974 he did see success in the form of Aap Ki Kasam and Prem Nagar - but this one was only an average grosser. I have not yet seen the movie and hence sharing what I gathered from multiple sources - read on...

The plot is about one Ram who is a labourer and a helpful man. He helps an old woman in trouble and while assisting her as a good human gets to know that she has a daughter. When the old lady is about die, she tells Ram to marry the daughter and look after her and soon they are blessed with a son. When the child falls ill, Ram's wife goes to his employer for help and discovers that Ram is Laxman out there with another wife Lalita. Then rest of the movie is clearing the misunderstandings.

Here are some songs for you:
https://www.youtube.com/watch?v=KHuEDy6lYMM ;
https://www.youtube.com/watch?v=ZL4bQN5KCf4 ;
https://www.youtube.com/watch?v=xTTZlMN9vHc ;
https://www.youtube.com/watch?v=Nau8q4nKHeM ;

Cheers - will wait for comments from my friends

Laksh KV

April 18 1969 (53 years ago)

"SAMBANDH"

Folks

53 years ago today was the day when an immensely forgettable movie called "Sambandh" released *ing Deb Mukherjee, Anjana Mumtaz, Pradeep Kumar, Sulochana, Achla Sachdev, Abhi Bhattacharya and Nana Palsheekar. However, what comes to my mind is the outstanding music of OP Nayyar and on top is the Mukesh number "Chal Akela".

The other piece of memory for me is that since Aashirwad was still running at Rupam in its 2nd week, there was no chance of seeing this movie and on the very next day ie Saturday 19th April 1969 disaster struck me - while playing in our building compound, I had a fall and fractured my right wrist and broke my front teeth which now is covered with a crown. Then it was all single handed stuff for me during the entire vacation - the only good thing was that I was allowed to see a few extra movies in that vacation out of sympathy.

I had some soft corner for Deb Mukherji who had made his debut in a movie called "Tu Hi Meri Zindagi" earlier and hence wanted this movie to do well. My late brother Vaidya V Raj used to feel that he resembled our wicket keeper Kundaran - well, all said and done the movie did not pass muster - it was below average at the box office. OP Nayyar apparently had a tiff with Mohd Rafi and had shifted to Mahendra Kapoor (MK) for most songs and this movie had a couple of very nice songs sung by MK. Till date I have not seen this movie and hence for the story-line I am picking up from multiple sources:

Story of one Manav born in a rich family but his dad Umakant is a drunkard and his wife i.e. Manav's mom is unhappy and does her best to clear Umakant from this drinking habit. Eventually, they separate and Manav grows up as a very cynical person. He then lives with his foster parents who are rich and then it's time for him to fall in love and marry Sandhya. But soon things fall apart in his marriage and they get separated. Later Manav finds that Sandhya's dad is contemplating for her 2nd marriage and Manav with a changed identity gets helped by his dad Umakant to salvage the relationship – at least this good deed would make his life a bit fulfilling. – Fairly complex!

Here are some song links for you:

https://www.youtube.com/watch?v=KomIawxml_w ;

https://www.youtube.com/watch?v=BojAVUajGoI ;

https://www.youtube.com/watch?v=fExQ6agCR00 ;

https://www.youtube.com/watch?v=-gWuj-VAHOc ;

Cheers and over to my friends for their comments

Laksh KV

April 16 1971 (52 years ago)

"HEER RANJHA"

Folks:

This Day That Year i.e. on April 16 1971 was the release date of the tragic love story of "Heer Ranjha" produced by Ketan Anand son of Chetan Anand and directed by the legendary dad Chetan Anand. Those days at the age of 16, somehow, it was beyond me to sit thru a movie that was poetry all the way. So skipped it then but my dearest friend Balakrishnan Narayan was an ardent Raj Kumar fan and enjoyed it. He was kind to accompany me when it was on re-run at Nepture Bandra - by then I had commenced accepting this kind of off-beat movies.

But my biggest disappointment was the Heroine... I felt a good role was wasted on Priya who could not really speak her lines well - that continued with her even in Kudrat from the same maker - but finally it is the call of the makers to cast and we are sitting here to air our views. Madan Mohan had given some great music for this movie and here I need not talk about the story line which is again well known and the subsequent movie "Laila Majnu" which was with similar plot *ing Rishi Kapoor also did great business - though Heer Ranjha was an average grosser. They say these are "Epic Love Stories" - not sure whether it is Love or Obsession, be that as it may, here are some songs for you from the movie in caption

https://www.youtube.com/watch...;

Cheers & over to my friends for their views and comments and value added information

Laksh KV

April 17 1970 (53 Years ago)

"HIMMAT"

Folks:

Today 53 years ago the movie "Himmat" released *ing Jeetendra, Mumtaz, Jagdeep, Prem Chopra, KN Singh, Asit Sen & Aruna Irani. Released in competition with some big hits of Kaka, Himmat did well and was a silver jubilee hit. However, I did not see the movie as soon as it released for the most sought after Hall Rupam was still showing "Aashirwaad" and there was no easy money available to go to distant halls.

The main memory for me is my neighbour Viswanathan Krishnan's uncle Chinna Ambi who now lives in Coimbattore had seen the movie and we named him "Himmat Mama" - the other memory is of Jeetendra singing "Ai Shukar Ke Tu Hai Ladka, Tujhe Dekh Mera Dil Dhadka" to Mumtaz who is in a boy's disguise - well, eventually saw the movie at Chitra Dadar in matinee show much later and found that there was enough luck factor with Jeetendra to fight it out with Kaka, though the climax fight on top of a train was too long and dragging.

The story revolved around a criminal who tries his best to turn a new leaf and become good but his past and his bosses coerce him to get back to crime and everything that one can expect this movie had - lot of action, some good songs & item number - quite slick - no wonder it did good business. Songs composed by Laxmikant Pyarelal had become hit those days. Here are some links for you

https://www.youtube.com/watch?v=7174Vf_mGuI ;
https://www.youtube.com/watch?v=dluRn2FfC44 ;
https://www.youtube.com/watch?v=NvxYSB6FVF4 ;
https://www.youtube.com/watch?v=s19CS3txJ68 ;
https://www.youtube.com/watch?v=xNwLaxPE8rM ;
https://www.youtube.com/watch?v=Hlea8teO7R8 ;

Cheers - will await expert comments from my friends with more information and data

Laksh KV

April 14th 1972 (51 years ago)

"HAAR JEET"

Folks,

It was today in the year 1972 the movie "Haar Jeet" released. Main actors were Anil Dhavan, Rehana Sultana, Radha Saluja, Mehmood, Madan Puri and Sarika. NN Sippy and CP Dixit combination made this movie which did not do too much business. I have very limited memories of this movie except that Anil Dhavan was still enjoying his Chetana popularity and for me since the movie was not released in Rupam, not much I could do about seeing the movie by travelling some distance.

I am fairly certain that no one from my gang saw this movie and hence I resorted to other sources for the plot

This is a story of a single woman named Kamal who takes care of one Mr Gupta's 3 children as a governess. Gupta's brother Ashok too stays in the same house and both Kamal and Ashok seem to be in love and Gupta expects them to approach for his approval but then Ashok decides to marry one Radha who happens to be Kamal's friend and now both the friends stay under one roof. Here is when Radha discovers that her friend Kamal is in love with Ashok and was hoping to get married and then things change big time as Radha becomes wheel-chair bound post an accident and becomes dependant on the members of the family including Kamal.

Well, the movie had some decent songs and here are some links and will wait for comments from those who would have seen this movie.

https://www.youtube.com/watch?v=dt8OO5slqJo ;
https://www.youtube.com/watch?v=cm0Z1LNQNRk ;
https://www.youtube.com/watch?v=ql2-DOC3QCM ;
https://www.youtube.com/watch?v=uG5J5s_t58w ;

Cheers

Laksh

April 12 1974 (49 Years ago)

"DOST"

Folks:

49 Years ago today released the movie "DOST" produced by Premji & Directed by Dulhal Guha *ing Dharmendra, Hema Malini, Shatrughan Sinha, Rehaman, Abhi Bhattacharya, Ravindra Kapoor & Kanhaiyalal. This was a very clean movie with a good message and was a big hit. My memories of the movie are as under:

1. I had seen the picture of the Mahurat Shot in a weekly paper called "Film Industry" where the caption read "From Dushman to Dost With Love" - the picture showed the Hero of the banner's earlier movie "Dushman" Kaka giving the clap and must have said "Action"!!!
2. Kaka had a great time from late 1969 and it went on till 1972-73 then the dip started and I was very thrilled to see my favorite hero Dharam Paji chosen ahead of Kaka which my good friend Balakrishnan Narayan was not very happy about.
3. I saw the movie after my Jr. B.Com exams in the month of May 1974 at Sharda Cinema Dadar all by myself on a Saturday evening (not to forget, I was an employed guy then).
4. I thoroughly enjoyed the movie and the message in the movie of "Honesty" appealed to me.
5. While Kaka and Big B, had made a good jodi only to be changed as Shashi Kapoor and AB in the later years, we had endless arguments that Dharam-Shatru was a great jodi despite the not so good business done by "Blackmail" earlier.

The story revolved around an orphan who was brought up by a Father of a church and inculcated excellent values, completes his education and when he returns he is shattered to find that his mentor is no more but continues on the values he has learnt – He meets Shatrugan - a local goonda who has been wronged by the society and is far from the theory of "Honesty" - Somehow, these 2 become friends and Mr. Honesty wants to change the Negative man. The Heroine develops a fondness for Dharampaji and her dad Rehaman is unhappy about it and does everything possible to separate them - but eventually has to accept the reality and gets the punishment he deserves of not recalling the stock of contaminated milk powder manufactured in his factory where Dharampaji used to work. Well all is well that ends well - good performances are the highlights besides some good songs, the top number being "Gaadi Bula Rahi Hai" that comes in the movie on and off. Here are some of the links of the songs.

https://www.youtube.com/watch?v=v2lVtG3LWTk ;

https://www.youtube.com/watch?v=JtZa58nP2Qo ;

https://www.youtube.com/watch?v=n-QDqZdIkF0 ;

Now over to Amitabh Nigam for the collection numbers

Cheers
Laksh KV

April 11 1975 (48 Years ago)

"CHUPKE CHUPKE"

Folks:

48 years ago the ever-green movie "CHUPKE CHUPKE" was released and lo and behold what a comedy riot it was. My recall is that I was an employed guy aged 20 and had done advance booking for 1st day 6 PM show at Rupam - there were 45 days for my final B.Com exams to start so I had not put a curfew nor were my parents too much worried as I had done decently in my college without failing or threatening to fail. My office was also very close to Rupam Cinema & I had the full support of my bosses as they had touched my feet when I saw 5 movies on August 15 1974. So I reached in good time to see the movie and being a big Dharam Paji fan, I desperately wanted the movie to do well. This was made by Hrishikesh Mukherji who always made good and meaningful movies. This was an out and out comedy with some "Sanskritised Hindi" spoken by Dharam Paji. After enjoying the movie, I do not know how many more times I would have seen this movie - both in halls and on TV and I never get tired of seeing this evergreen comedy. Excellent acting by Om Prakash, Dharam Paji, Amitabhji and Asrani are the higlights of the movie and ably supported by Sharmila Tagore, Jaya Bhaduri, Usha Kiran, Keshto Mukherji and David. Some of the scenes I cannot forget:

1. First encounter of Dharam Paji with Om Prakash - the "Shuddha Bhasha" bit irritates the senior guy no end. Dharam Paji says "Bhojan Toh Humne Laupathgaami Agnirath Mein Kar Lee"

2. Keshto informing Om Prakash "Srivasatav Peekay Aaye Hain" Its PK stands for Prashant Kumar

3. Nervous Amitabh gets ready to get off at Dadar station and then yells "Coolie, Coolie" - the background has the poster of the movie "SAGINA".

4. The manner in which Amitabh woos Jaya trying to teach her and the night out by him to study about Corolla and rattles the definition next day and at

every possibility or drop of a hat AB wants to talk about "Shakespeare" - "What a sublime tragedy!!!"

5. Dharampaji going to meet Sharmila (his wife) chupke chupke and encounters a thief and who feels bad that both are thieves but his luck is nowhere close to Dharam paji's

6. Above all the term "JEEJAAJI" used by the heroine to irritate the Hero, triggers this role play in the movie.

The whole movie one can be writeen as bullet points!!!

The movie did run for 25 weeks and I am sure with reasonable production cost, it would have made substantial profits - will wait for Amitabh Nigam to talk about this.

Maestro SD Burmanda was in his elements and we had some real lilting music and also enough to tickle the bones. Here is the link of the songs of the movie:

https://www.youtube.com/watch?v=FpypRAGMrX4 ;

Cheers
Laksh KV

April 11 1969 (54 Years ago)

"INTEQAM"

Folks:

54 years ago was the release of the movie "Intequam" *ing Ashok Kumar, Sadhna, Sanjay Khan, Rajendranath, Helan, Rehman and Jeevan. This movie did decent business and completed 100 days run & was directed by RK Nayyar, the heroine's husband. My memories are very limited as I could not see this movie though my exams got over on the following day of its release - it was not released in Rupam our usual hunting ground as "Ashirwad" released in parallel and continued for 4 long weeks in Rupam. However, my friend Balakrishnan Narayan aka Bedi did see this movie when he went to Indore for his summer vacation and on his return told me the story of the movie.

The movie revolved around Sadhna who plays a poor girl with her izzat intact and her Boss Rehman trying to make use of her and then trap her and send her behind the bars. She wants to avenge (Intequam) and then other characters like Ashok Kumar and Sanjay are thrown in. Ashok Kumar also was cheated by Rehman and both Sadhna and Ashok Kumar have a common objective of revenge and for this they make use of Rehman's son Sanjay. Very predictable but what was new for me was - Lata Mangeshkar's rendition of a cabaret number filmed on Helan "AA JAN-E-JAA" & an intoxicating song "KAISE RAHOON CHUP KE MAINAY PEELI KYA HAI" filmed on Sadhna. These were real out of the way stuff I felt - rest of it were run of the mill. Here is the songs link for you:

https://www.youtube.com/watch?v=qrwMXLKdFqc

Cheers
Laksh KV

April 10th 1970 – (53 years ago)

THE TRAIN & KHILONA

Hello Folks

Today I am taking you back to April 10th 1970 when 2 movies released – while one was a hit, the second one was a bigger hit.

1. The Train: *ing Rajesh Khanna, Nanda, Helan & Aruna Irani /Rajendranath produced under the banner of Rose Movies by Ramesh Behel and Directed by Ravi Nagaich was a hit. It had excellent photography and brilliant music by RD Burman.

There is a lot of nostalgia for me personally – as it released towards the end of our Annual exams that ended on April 11th '70. Every show was going House full with Kaka at his peak & our friend Chintya (Arun) managed tickets in Rivoli Cinema for his family and while Bedi and myself watched, he and his brothers (Prakash with a neck-tie in Mumbai Summer & Satish) went to see the movie. The other bit of nostalgia was when we went to National College Bandra, we saw the place where the movie was partially shot and made us feel good.

The story revolved around Kaka who plays a Police Officer in charge of solving multiple murders that were taking place in a train and is also in love with Nanda who is the heroine. There is Helan to play the seductress and has a key role too. Rajendranath was funny when he told the coolie at the station in the movie to come on the next day to collect his charges of loading the luggage. One thing was not credible where Kaka fights and wins over Shetty - but those were his days as anything he touched turned gold... The movie had some kind of mixed response and was declared hit as it completed 100 days run (15 weeks) for the crisp editing and suspense in the movie but the music was outstanding. Here are some links of the brilliant songs:

http://www.youtube.com/watch?v=ezVzSxthVW0
http://www.youtube.com/watch?v=ExOraPlzDNA
http://www.youtube.com/watch?v=h41W4l21ZOM
http://www.youtube.com/watch?v=nBpU8ysBiug

2. Khilona: *ing Mumtaz, Sanjeev Kumar, Jeetendra in a Special Appearance, Ramesh Deo, Jagdeep, Durga Khote & a young relatively unknown Shatrugan Sinha was released 54 years ago today. This was made under the banner of Prasad Productions & directed by Chander Vohra with lovely music by Laxmikant Pyarelal. All the lead characters performed brilliantly and this movie had several nominations in the most prestigious Filmfare Award & bagged the Best Film and Best Actress awards. Mumtaz was at her brilliant best playing the Nauch girl who tries to help an abnormal Sanjeev Kumar to get him to normalcy. Sanjeev Kumar was outstanding but the popular votes went in favour of Rajesh Khanna for his stylish performance in "Sachha Jhoota" that gave him the Filmfare award ahead of Sanjeev Kumar which was not liked by many.

This movie had a slow start at the Box Office but it picked up when the songs became popular and I recall going to see the movie with my elder brother and a neighbouring young uncle - Varada Maama - my dear friend Viswanathan Krishnan's uncle in a theatre called "Surya" that was renamed later as "Dharti" which is located diagonally opposite to "Hindmata" a bit ahead of "Chitra" Cinema at Dadar. Shatrugan Sinha played "Bihari" (his name in the movie) and introduced the style of flicking cigarette from his finger to lips from a distance and then blowing out "Rings" – commanding voice coupled with flawless dialogue delivery ufff, he arrived with this movie. Rest is history – this movie ran for over 25 weeks in the renovated "Krishna A Dreamland" cinema rechristened as "Dreamland". Lovely movie, Brilliant acting & excellent music ensured a Silver Jubilee Hit. Some of the songs are here for you to enjoy:

http://www.youtube.com/watch?v=1LxeFFJjFYw&feature=fvst

http://www.youtube.com/watch?v=-Ns3oDxxy6c

http://www.youtube.com/watch?v=y17kHsmr7LE&feature=fvwrel

http://www.youtube.com/watch?v=ayGc5A6X9Go&feature=relmfu

http://www.youtube.com/watch?v=58AaVUsPkrU

Cheers & Happy Reading
Laksh KV

April 9th 1971 – (52 years ago)

"LAKHONE MEIN EK"

Folks

It was today in the year 1971 this movie "Lakhon Mein Ek, released, which was made by the Gemini Banner of South which was also a remake of a Tamil movie. This had Mahmood playing the lead role of one "Bhola" who lives free of cost below the space that is available under the staircase of a huge chawl. Folks living in Mumbai can relate to this very well - the role of the Heroine was played by Radha Saluja who is mentally retarded - but she finds that Bhola who is being used by everyone in the chawl is really being exploited and these two fall in love. I was late to see this movie as by the time I returned from Hyderabad after a brief stay the first 3 days of the movie was done - but my good classmate and friend K Surayanaran aka Chury was waiting for my return so that both of us could go and see the movie at Rupam which we did. We saw that tickets had to be booked as the movie was liked by people at large - so current booking was not an option. We loved the movie and some of the points that came to our minds are:

1. The attitude of the people how it changes when they realize that Bhola was actually rich - thanx to a cameo played by Madan Puri... who actually is a worker in a garage.

2. Jalal Agha - the way he boasts about himself and his capabilities - but finally adds that he has only one vice "Main aksar jhoot botla hoon"... which means he bluffs quite frequently.

3. Role of Pran as Sher Khan - he goes around with a begging bowl when Bhola is sick and sounds like Mehmood when he says "Main Bhola Aagaya"

4. When Nasir Hussain (one of the chawl residents), who is always dependant on having his medicines from Bhola but when he is driven away by all the members of the building, Nasir Hussain does not get his medicine on time and the people from the chawl try to call Mehmood back - with so much time already elapsed, Mehmood is just walking outside the complex.

5. How the residents of the chawl take back the gifts given to Bhola once they know that Madan Puri who comes as Mehmood's dad as a rich business man is actually worker in a garage.
6. Some decent songs in the movie and good acting by Mehmood and Pran really lifted the movie which ran for 15 weeks and celebrated 100 days in Mumbai - considered a decent hit. Here are some of the links:

https://www.youtube.com/watch?v=a55oUxRfLQ4 ;

https://www.youtube.com/watch?v=7IGoKxWOsVA ;

https://www.youtube.com/watch?v=NeJsuxI-EJk ;

https://www.youtube.com/watch?v=WGsi-S8H2M8 ;

Cheers
Laksh KV

April 7th 1972 - (51 years ago)

"DASTAAN"

Hello folks:

Now here I would like to take you back by 5 decades to April 7th 1972 - 51 years ago when BR Chopra released his ambitious movie "DASTAAN" that had Thespian Dilip Kumar playing a dual role with Sharmila Tagore, Prem Chopra & Bindu giving adequate support.

It was exam time - during my First Year of college and the exams were to start from April 18th 1972 and the usual dilemma was how to hoodwink the strict Mother and see the movie – but I could not handle her and had to miss out on the movie on release though saw it much later in life. Also what I remember is a connected episode – Filmfare awards those days used to be at Shanmukhananda Hall and as a student of the music school there, I could get an easy entry inside. I also managed to get my close friend Balakrishnan Narayan aka Bedi inside and were at the corridor with the crowd waiting for the big names to arrive and that time we had the privilege of seeing Dilip saab very closely as I walked alongside him and I requested for his autograph but he refused saying that he had a "Sprained Neck". This was the time when the versatile Kishore Kumar was making waves with the superstar Kaka (Rajesh Khanna) but till then he had not lent his voice to Dilip Saab and even in Dastaan he did not. The fights among we friends would be who is better Md Rafi or Kishore and these were never-ending debates – but the feelings with which the song "NA TU ZAMEEN KE LIYE" was rendered by Rafi Saab, is something outstanding indeed.

Unfortunately, the movie, despite all the hype did not do too well as things were very predictable and the exchange of the 2 Dilip Kumars was not credible especially how can one shave off the beard and re-use the same beard on one's own face... Bindu double crossing Dilip Kumar for his best friend Prem Chopra was again a very predictable thing. It was the first time that Sharmila Tagore acted opposite Dilip Saab. Normally, it would have been Naushad Saab giving music for Dilip Saab's movies but it was Laxmikant Pyarelal for the first time doing this for BR Films where normally it would have been Ravi Saab. However, the constant was Mahendra Kapoor singing for the banner. In a nutshell, all aspects of the movie did not meet expectations of the people and hence the movie did not do too well. But, as a loyalist of Hindi movies, I still have a lot of nostalgia, the time – post Bangla Desh war, the struggle for money to see a movie, the pressure of board exams and what not.

Here are a couple of links for the songs:

http://www.youtube.com/watch?v=ltc_ItEGH-M&feature=fvsr

http://www.youtube.com/watch?v=O5PBGp3MY5k

However, you can listen to all the songs in Raaga.com and the link is as under:

http://www.raaga.com/channels/hindi/moviedetail.asp...

Happy Daastan-ing
Cheers
Laksh

April 06 1973 (50 years ago)

"ANURAAG"

Folks:

A clean and wholesome movie called ANURAAG was released today 50 years ago. This came from Shakti Samanta's banner *ing Ashok Kumar, Nutan, Vinod Mehra, introducing Moushumi Chatterji, Master Satyajeet and with a Special Appearance of Kaka Rajesh Khanna. I had gathered those days in the midst of our final exams that were looming large that as there were not many takers to distribute this off-beat movie, Shakti Samanta and Rajesh Khanna joined hands and distributed as "ShaktiRaj" a joint venture by them. The movie did good business and the real stars of the movie were Master Satyajeet and Ashok Kumar who showed a fantastic relationship between a grandpa and grandson.

I recall that afternoon I had a walk towards Rupam Cinema to see what was going on and saw the "House Full' board and on return at Sion Circle met my school classmate Krishna aka Kitchie and both of us concurred that Moshumi can best be described as "CUTE". Nevertheless some self-imposed rules ensured I did not see the movie before the exams got over by end of the month and then saw the movie at Sahakar Chembur and generally liked it though I was a bit unhappy that Kaka was getting yet another good movie and my good friend Balakrishnan Narayan was happy about it.

The story revolved around a grandpa Ashok Kumar, his Daughter in law (widowed) Nutan and her son Satyajeet staying together and the young one is the Cynosure of every eye - a smart child full of energy but cancer strikes him and there is a blind girl Moushumi who is fond of this young boy and they have a very cute relationship going as an elder sister and a kid brother. Vinod Mehra falls for the blind girl and wants her to get her eye-sight. There is a family phoolvala played by Rajesh Khanna who loves all the members in this family. In the end while the young boy dies, his eyes come in as a donation to the blind heroine who can now see the world with her chote bhayya's eyes. Nice concept with some good music SD Burman da. Here are some of the songs for you:

https://www.youtube.com/watch?v=5tep8hVOnws ;
https://www.youtube.com/watch?v=alF3RmIIaPI ;
https://www.youtube.com/watch?v=xGNlOVyahWQ ;
https://www.youtube.com/watch?v=HtqjzIaA8HM ;
https://www.youtube.com/watch?v=Ig3HlFMkI_k ;
Cheers
Laksh KV

April 05 1974 (49 years ago)

"MANORANJAN"

Folks:

Shammi Kapoor made a debut as a Director with the movie "MANORANJAN" today in the year 1974. It was inspired by the English movie Irma La Douce. In this Sanjeev Kumar played Jack Lemmon while other English names I do not know. This movie was quite different than the other Hindi movies of that era. Zeenat Aman played a Business woman!!! And Shammi Kapoor himself played the owner of Restaurant where a lot of action happens!!! This was one movie where the Heroine playing a fallen woman or a prostitute had no regret playing her part - not really worried about moral values etc. The term "Fallen Woman" reminds me of the radio ad "AAP GIRE HUVE KO UTHAYA NAHI KARENGAY?" - Sanjiv Kumar (SK) throws a banana skin on which Zee falls and when SK tries to move ahead she asks him the above question. Radio ad also said "Entertainment...Haaaa" - "Manoranjan Hi Manoranjan" - In the English movie the guy who played Shammi Kapoor equivalent used to talk of something and left it saying "That's another story" and in Hindi Shammi would say "Woh Kissa Phir Kabhi" - The movie was bold and the prostitute would say "HUM PYAAR BAAT TAY HAIN" - meaning they share love & see nothing wrong in it. It looked like a movie ahead of its time and and hence did not create the expected wave or tehalka.

The story revolves around a Hawaldar who has been assigned the task to look at the happenings in a red light area and the honest policeman arrests all the girls but realizes that his Boss is also a visitor in that area and before he knows he is out of job - Boss is after all Boss. Zee feels sorry for the jobless youngster and having built some rapport earlier, invites him to stay with her - but our man does not like Zee sleeping with others so visits her in disguise as a Nawab. This dual role takes a toll and in the end he decides to kill the Nawab but police believes that He has killed the old man and then it is commotion all thru. Sanjeev Kumar does justice to his role, Zeenat too is good and very comfortable in the role of a fallen woman - Shammi Kapoor makes faces and in general has overacted in my view. Others like

Dev Kumar, Madan Puri, Faryal, Paintal, Asit Sen and Agha fill the bill. RD Burman has given some foot tapping numbers and here are some links for you:

https://www.youtube.com/watch?v=d74UnkQlgjU ;

https://www.youtube.com/watch?v=Y19LRZDlmY8 ;

https://www.youtube.com/watch?v=UHb6UR-dDu0 ;

https://www.youtube.com/watch?v=gteDROkgVwA ;

https://www.youtube.com/watch?v=fFL1U8OmjRI ;

Cheers & waiting for more inputs from my good friends

Cheers
Laksh KV

April 11 1969 (54 years ago)

"ASHIRWAD"

Folks:

Yes RAP music in Hindi movies was born on this day with Ashok Kumar doing a brilliant job of "RAIL GAADI, RAIL GAADI, CHUKCHUKCHUKCHUK" - what a brilliant way to introduce RAP!!! - Yes friends, the outstanding movie "ASHIRWAD" was released today in 1969 - the combination of NC Sippy and Hrishkiesh Mukherjee brought this hit movie into this world. The main actors Ashok Kumar, Sanjiv Kumar, Sumita Sanyal, Harindernath Chatopadhyay & Abhi Bhattacharya - some of my recalls of this movie are:

This movie ran for 4 weeks in Rupam which was so unusual - normally this hall has weekly change - very rarely movies did 2 weeks run but somehow, with not a big star value, I did not want to put money on this movie and avoided it. My neighbor Jyothi Shankar saw this movie at Rupam in one of the noon shows and when we all boys were in the building compound under our favorite tree in the evening that consisted of Balakrishnan Narayan Arun Balakrishnan Viswanathan Krishnan Raman Kp (younger brother of Jyothi Shankar) she told her brother "Miss Pannaday" meaning "Don't Miss" - probably her idea was for all of us to know that she had seen the movie which we all had not!!! My inference - will await clarification provided all my friends remember this.

Now coming to the story line since I did see the movie on Door Darshan sometime in the 80s though not fully in one go as our dear daughter Sanjivani Iyer was very young and needed attention!!! Well, here is the story line from sources I connected to - but would add that music composed by late Vasant Desai too played a key role in the movie.

This is the story of one Jogi Thakur a very principled man and by some fraud and turn of events has to break his marriage & moves out of his house leaving his daughter behind and moves to Bombay and keeps kids engaged and entertained with his Rap number "Rail Gadi Chuk Chuk". He encounters a kid who has his daughter's name and develops fondness towards her but unfortunately the girl dies. He then decides to go back to his village and in trying to help his friend's daughter he ends up killing the wrongdoer. Villagers knowing the goodness of the man, try to make a story but Jogi being truthful decides to tell the truth and is jailed. He takes care of plants and trees as his job in the jail and Dr who attends to the prisoners develops a fondness towards Jogi. By the way Jogi comes to know that his daughter is soon going to get married to the Doctor and feels good about the alliance but also comes to know that his daughter hates criminals and hence he avoids or covers his face while coming face to face with his daughter. In a while he takes ill and due to his good conduct, he is released from jail. The Doctor is happy as he had told Jogi that he will tie the knot the day he is freed. Jogi is keen to attend the wedding but to avoid getting recognized, he joins the group of beggars who too are invited for food. The young couple serve all the people and Jogi blesses the newlyweds and moves out of the scene in a hurry but on the way, he succumbs and is identified as Jogi – on hearing the news of her dad's demise, the newly wed bride rushes to meet her dad at the last minute.

The movie had excellent songs composed by Vasant Desai with lovely ones like Rail Gaadi Rail Gaadi Chhuk Chhuk Chhuk Chhuk Chhuk Chhuk, Beechwale Station Bole Ruk Ruk Ruk Ruk Ruk Ruk Ruk Ruk, that was rendered by Ashok Kumar aka Dadamoni himself,

Ek Tha Bachpan by Lata Mangeshkar

Jeevan Se Lambe Hai Bandhu Yeh Jeevan Ke Raste by Manna Dey The movie is a journey that is charged with emotions through a man's life who is principled but the love of daughter has its own position in the story

Some song links for you here:

https://www.youtube.com/watch?v=nUWLmC1r6aQ ;

https://www.youtube.com/watch?v=rqGZDkAO_8M ;

https://www.youtube.com/watch?v=jK_xfJ8OEk4 ;

https://www.youtube.com/watch?v=b6oqDVWRB4Q ;

Cheers
Laksh KV

April 03 1970 (53 Years Ago)

"DEVI"

Folks:

Today 53 years ago we saw the release of the movie "DEVI" - when I think of this movie 2 things come to my mind - first is the song 'SHADI KE LIYE RAZAMAND KARLI, MAINE EK LADKI PASAND KARLI"... sounds so much like the song from "SAPNON KA SAUDAGAR - SIKHANA YE SABAK TUNAY PYAAR KA"... & then the "SLAP" by Nutan on Sanjeev Kumar's cheek made the headlines....

Well other than that my standard recall as a class X student with no money and only hopes of getting the ability to see movies at will when I commence earning - that is it... The movie was an average grosser with a couple of good songs - the 2nd one being "TERI HASEEN NIGAAHA KA EHSAANMANDH HOON, MAIN KHUSHNASEEB HOON KE MAIN TUJHKO PASAND HOON"

A few years ago I had done a quiz on this movie on this very day and that came in my FB memories to refresh the story of the movie - though till date I have not seen it!!! Very standard story of a well to do Doctor - Sanjeev Kumar falling in love with a poor village girl Nutan and the Dr. has the right ideas to serve the less fortunate people in the villages and so on - very idealistic views. These 2 get married but the new Bahu is not accepted by the elder brother Rehaman and mother - but on some persuasion they accept her who in quick time is in the family way. Then comes a mandatory foreign trip for the Dr. and he is away for some time in a conference and when he returns he finds his wife missing and gathers that she has gone to the oldest profession!!! They have a son (Sarika as a boy) and then rest of the movie is all how things come back to normal and how evil loses the ground.

Well, more than the movie the "Nutan Slaps Sanjeev Kumar" got a lot of publicity and here are 2 links for you to see what happened then - how much truth is anyone's guess - but I do believe that there cannot be smoke without fire and unfortunately both are not around to clarify things!!!

https://www.youtube.com/watch?v=fEv6E51HpgY ;

http://ww.itimes.com/.../slap-controversies-nutan-and... ;

Some of the songs from the movie are here:

https://www.youtube.com/watch?v=TZ5OG16QxVc ;

https://www.youtube.com/watch?v=iXYzkQFNQas ;

I will await comments from seniors in the group to throw more light on the movie and the gossip aspect as well

Cheers
Laksh KV

This Day That Year
March 26 1971 and April 02 1971 52 years

"UPAASNA" "MELA"

Folks:

I missed doing Upaasna on March 26th while I wrote about Lagan *ing Ajay Sahani - and I realized it a bit late but then felt it was ideal to do 2 movies with identical 3 main actors released back to back in 1971. Yes the 2 movies "Upaasna" released on March 26 1971 and "Mela" released on April 02 1971 had Sanjay Khan, Mumtaz & Feroz Khan playing the main roles in both the movies. The ads said "Brothers in Real Life fight on the screen".

Unfortunately I could not see both movies despite being free of SSC exams as I ended up seeing Lagan over Upaasna and on the following day ie on the 27th March 1971 went off to Hyderabad with my late dad for over a fortnight. I kept thinking of these 2 movies there for they had not yet released in that zone - out there Kati Patang had just released while it released on Jan 29 1971 in Mumbai. So ended up seeing that and also very thrilled to see "Mehboob Ki Mehandi" in April 1971 while it saw the light of the day only in May 1974 in Mumbai....So coming back to the 2 movies:

1. Upaasna

This is a story of 2 brothers who are lawyers and fight a court case for and against Mumtaz regarding a murder. The senior Khan (FK) made a better impact than SK - over all a flop movie in Mumbai for by the time I returned from Hyderabad, both movies were only running in the main theaters and I did not have the money and bandwidth to go all the way as "Lakhon Mein Ek" was waiting for me... There were some catchy numbers in this movie and the Mukesh song "Darpan Ko Dekha" filmed on FK was the pick of the lot. Here are some links for you:

https://www.youtube.com/watch?v=hxozHNknYxY ;

https://www.youtube.com/watch?v=VwBF09xo9TY ;

https://www.youtube.com/watch?v=RaUQUP65N5k ;

2. Mela

As mentioned earlier, the same star cast but the difference is the setting - from luxury of city to rustic village of rural India was some change. Here the 2 brothers get separated in the childhood in a Mela (Kumbh Mela!!!) and one becomes a dacoit Shakti Singh and the other one is brought up by a Muslim lady but is called Kanhayya. There is Panchayat, lot of injustice, rape and what not - then confrontation between the 2 main actors and all this laced with some good songs. Still this could not salvage the movie from biting the dust and in a matter of weeks the movie was gone. The songs that had some good effect were "Rut Hai Milan Ki Saathi Mere" & "Gori Ke Haath Mein" - Here is the link for all the 6 songs of the movie.

https://www.youtube.com/watch?v=PikKK_xxTmg

I will wait for more comments from those who have more insight about these 2 movies.

Cheers
Laksh KV

March 31 1967 – (56 Years Ago)

"ANITA"

Friends:

I want to take you back 56 years - i.e. on March 31 1967 - the year when my late eldest bro Vaidya V Raj wrote his SSC exams and was free at this point of time to freak out.

Let me take you to Rupam Cinema in Sion - yes the inauguration of the theatre was done today 56 years back with the 1st movie that released in Rupam - Manoj Kumar & Sadhna starrer "ANITA". The movie did not hit the jackpot but still had the impact that a suspense thriller could create produced and directed by Raj Khosla who had earlier made 2 suspense movies like WOH KAUN THI and MERA SAAYA. Probably this was the last suspense movie made by Khosla banner as he soon moved to family dramas like Do Raste and action movie like Mera Gaon Mera Desh towards late 60s and early 70s.

I will remember ANITA for the simple reason that as class VII boy, we finished the Annual Day in our dear SIES School and rushed towards the theatre on 30th March to see how ready the hall was and my class mate KR Easwar, Kirshnadas, Jairaj & self evaluated Rupam and felt the AC to be very effective. Not waiting for the entire function in the school and running away (bunking) was some experience for all of us and we enjoyed the experience big time.

The movie however, I could not see immediately and felt very "J" about my late bro who could see the movie without any problems but we could not, given that our exams got over only by April 12th and the movie moved out of Rupam by the time our exams were over made it that much more difficult for me.

Well coming back to the movie, the suspense element was interesting with Sadhna vanishing (declared dead) but appearing again and again much to the exasperation of the Hero Manoj Kumar and all of it being the ploy of an upcoming villain Kishan Mehta (who also was the villain in Jeetendra Asha Parekh starrer Caravan of 1971) who made an impact. However, the highlight of the movie was music of LP not Long Play but Laxmikant Pyarelal and all of us enjoyed the songs then. The movie ran for 15 weeks and was there by declared a decent hit.

The songs are here for you:

http://www.youtube.com/watch?v=8xtb_KPNP4o

http://www.youtube.com/watch?v=1oiFSmt3xkQ

http://www.youtube.com/watch?v=SXHlbu5OAM4

http://www.youtube.com/watch?v=GqxVC2ocYfo

Enjoy
Cheers
Laksh KV

March 31 1972 (51 Years Ago)

"Lal Pathar", "Annadaata" & "Wafaa"

Wow!!! Friends

3 movies released on the same day ie. On March 31 1972. I am sure I will not do justice in recalling all but still will do my bit.

1. Lal Pathar

My memories of this movie is only my friend Balakrishnan Narayan who had completed his SSC Exams and a big Raj Kumar fan went and saw this movie and was going ga ga over it. After this movie released, we stopped referring to Jaani as Raj Kumar but we started calling him "Gyan" for his name in the movie was "Gyan Shankar". This was an off-beat movie with a triangular plot with lot of history to go by. Some of the dialogues were just extraordinary and created the necessary impact. While Raj Kumar aka Gyan played the role with his characteristic brilliance, the surprise packet was Hema Malini, who was considered mostly a show piece in movies prior to this. But in LP she had a meaty role and did justice. Rakhee and Vinod Mehra too played their parts well. The highlight of the movie was music by SJ and that gave me a lot of happiness being a big SJ Fan - the stand out songs being "UNKE KHAYAAL" by Mohd Rafi Saab & the next one "RE MAN SUR" by Manna Dey and Asha Bhosaleji. Filmfare used to do review of the films and most films would get one STAR but this one got 3 stars and that made my friend very thrilled. The newly renovated Minerva Cinema commenced its 2nd innings with the release of this movie in Mumbai. Here are some songs for you and hoping for your comments.

https://www.youtube.com/watch?v=OTHxpe4fwoI ;
https://www.youtube.com/watch?v=hjr8Q_i-Kc0 ;
https://www.youtube.com/watch?v=RKQXlsl4tXI;

2. Annadata

A very clean family entertainer or a wholesome movie where Om Prakash had a lovely role along with Jaya Bhaduri and Anil Dhawan who played the Hero and

Heroine. There was also a DOG that was important for the movie. I have not seen this movie and have very limited memories of this movie which did average business - but given its low production cost, it must have made money is my view. However, I must add that the songs were brilliant in the movie. The story outline as under

Om Prakash a well to do man is supposed be dead in an accident and all his relatives assemble at his house with an idea to know what they can inherit and the extent to which one can fall is evident when one of them claims that she is carrying his baby in her womb. The lawyers open the eyes of Om Prakash and in a fit of disgust and anger; he leaves the house along with his dog. He lands up in a village where he meets an artist played by Anil Dhawan who makes a portrait of Om Prakash sleeping under a tree with the dog as the one watching him. Assuming Om Prakash is a poor man, Anil Dhawan offers him money. In a while Om Prakash faints due to fatigue and the faithful dog gets Jaya Bhaduri to help with medicines. There is some automatic bond that ensures that Om Prakash moves to Jaya Bhaduri's family wherein he also finds that she has a disabled younger brother too. Jaya Bhaduri helps the village people with her medicines and charges nothing for the services – but she earns by doing some tailoring work for people. Anil Dhawan and Jaya B are in love and make a nice couple but seeing that money will not be coming in constantly from Anil D, he thinks in terms of finding a more suitable hubby for Jaya B, but his proposal is rejected. In the end both of them realize that Om Prakash is rich but these two noble souls are not bothered about his riches and at this juncture Om Prakash too decides to stay with the young couple till he dies. This was a very clean family movie indeed.

Song links are here:

https://www.youtube.com/watch?v=bblHYBckf8g ;
https://www.youtube.com/watch?v=Dx-VusrvucU ;
https://www.youtube.com/watch?v=aJz2mCcXe7E ;
https://www.youtube.com/watch?v=IsLK8T_G17w
https://www.youtube.com/watch?v=lOL2K5iACm4 ;

3. Wafaa

Again I will only think of my dear friend Balakrishnan Narayan who went and saw this movie after his SSC exams and used to talk about Jagdeep playing a Hippie and cockroach coming out his long hair that never ever saw water and the song "Azaadi, Hum Sub Mastane Hippie" - the other song he talked about was a comical one "Aloo Ki Bhaji Baingan Ka Barta" where the Hero Sanjay tries to cook for his wife Rakhee. I have seen this movie on TV not so long ago and sat thru only for the nostalgia element. We used to discuss about Ramanna coming up with a release every year around exams - the earlier one being JAWAB!!!

Movie revolved around a well to do hero Sanjay who cheats on Heena Kausar after quietly marrying her, disowns her. He gets married to Rakhee and is happy at home. Heena Kausar who was jailed for some wrong allegations comes in search of her hubby and eventually goes to meet a lady lawyer and who is the lady lawyer - no prizes for guessing it has to be Rakhee and Rakhee only. Now rest of the movie is how this conflict is handled by the lawyer and how the Hero is cornered. Again not a very successful movie - did below par business. Music was definitely the strength for this movie too. Here are some songs for you:

https://www.youtube.com/watch?v=afpnjtuDmr0 ;

https://www.youtube.com/watch?v=S-e_6IUr518 ;

https://www.youtube.com/watch?v=uXmlGEL_20Y ;

Awaiting comments from my knowledgeable friends on these 3 movies besides ANITA that got an independent write up.

Cheers
Laksh

March 30 1973 (50 years ago)

"BANARASI BABU"

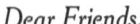

Dear Friends:

It was today the movie "Banarasi Babu" released 50 years ago. It was an average grosser and my usual exam time and not seeing movies for some time was a pledge to self and had to wait for the exams to get over and saw this at Rivoli - Matunga - ticket cost Re.1.25 along with my dear friend Balakrishnan Narayan and loved the movie not so much for the Hero but loved Jeevan in the role of the Manager and the way he would address Manorama as Monica Darling!!! Well my memories are as under:

Since it was well into its 4th week when we saw the movie on a Monday morning 11 am show, there were only about 25 people in the hall. We felt that Dev Anand looked too sophisticated to play the role of a Dehati Pocket Maar - Banarasi Babu. The typical dialogue delivery by Dev Saab to his ailing mother "POORI KI POORI UMAR DE DOONGA, MARNAY NAHI DOONGA" & the way he said "DHANDE KI KASAM" to Yogita Bali and when Yogita Bali tells the wrong Dev Saab "KHAA NAA!!!" and our man says in stylish manner "KASAM DHANDE KI!!!". All those lines above were not going well with a Dehati Dev Anand. Good songs by Kalyanji Anandji helped the movie to be interesting.

The story revolves around a rich Dev Anand who is happily married to Rakhee but his Manager Jeevan wants to swindle his property of Rs. 70 lakhs (it was a lot those days) and sends him off to London for an extended period. The crook Manager comes across a look alike of his Boss who is an expert pocket maar and lock breaking Champion and this simple looking man has an ailing mom and needs money - so gets ready to become an Imposter - creates a lot of confusion and eventually all is well. Here are some song links of the movie

https://www.youtube.com/watch?v=_WedMrdzhrs ;
https://www.youtube.com/watch?v=6WcDWnjq2xY ;
https://www.youtube.com/watch?v=A7_tpu0WefA ;
https://www.youtube.com/watch?v=I01JfAgD0oA ;
Cheers
Laksh KV

March 29 1974 (49 Years ago)

"KHOTE SIKKAY"

Folks:

On March 29 1974 the movie Khote Sikkay was released and did average business. All movies released around annual exams have some limitations for students like me and this one was no exception - but still managed average business. Though money was no more an issue for me, but some personal determination saw thru to it that I did not see the movie before my exams got over on April 30 1974. My memories are:

1. Post our exams when the movie had done over 5 weeks run, it came for a re-run at Aurora Cinema and we six friends went to see the movie - night show - Balakrishnan Narayan, Arun Balakrishnan Iyer Viswanathan Krishnan, Kannu, Radhakrishnan and myself - we really enjoyed this movie and were amazed at the action or non-action of Kanwar Ajit Singh (Dharam Paji's bro) who in one go ate some dozens of boiled eggs and well-focussed on that - someone attacks him and breaks a chair on him but our man continues to hog and then punishes the one who disturbed his eating.
2. Sudhir in the movie had a very happy go lucky image and was an expert at wooing girls and could do that with effortless ease and we were 19 and wanted to emulate him but we were far from successful!!!
3. Overacting of Paintal when he invites these 5 gunda like people to his village to protect them from the fury of one Daku.
4. Danny, Narendranath and Ranjeet were excellent too - Ranjeet especially was lovable when the other 4 agree to go to the village and he is left out as he was not keen but very sheepishly says "Koi Mujhe Bhi Roko Yaar!!!"
5. Feroz Khan says "Raahi Pyasa Hai" - can't he just say, "Main Pyasaa Hoon"... (I am a bit worried if i am mixing this line with Kala Sona - hope someone can correct me!!)

Well, the story line of 5 good for nothing guys go to a village as "False Coins" and turn things around by managing to stop the Dacoit Ajit from finishing them off. Feroz Khan is also on the lookout for the Dacoit to avenge his dad's murder by Ajit but joins hands with these 5 with a common goal and objective of finishing off Ajit though FK wants to do it alone. Overall an interesting movie – it's a bit like some English western on one hand and clearly Sholay was inspired by this movie and Mera Gaon Mera Desh. Average music and here are some links:

https://www.youtube.com/watch?v=zyQnl86Kpa8 ;

https://www.youtube.com/watch?v=Sl-jJbDTRG4 ;

https://www.youtube.com/watch?v=iZWiNCHgKHU ;

Cheers and awaiting expert comments
Laksh KV

March 28 1969 (54 years ago)

'SUHAAG RAAT"

Folks:

It was today, March 28th 1969 the movie Suhaag Raat *ing Rajshree, Jeetendra, Mehmood, Sulochna, Jr. Mehmood & Dhumal...etc released. My memories are:

Nothing new - exam times and me in class IX one week for annual exams - just about managed to see the posters at Rupam with my ever-reliable good friend Balakrishnan Narayan aka Bedi and kept regretting that we had not grown up to earn and see movies. Another weird memory for me is that we had a batchmate called "MAYYAZHAGAN" and was called "Maiyya" and I would call him by the title song of this movie "Maiyya, Oh Ganga Maiyya". The movie did not do well and hardly ran for some 5 to 6 weeks. I have not yet seen the movie but gathered the story which is as under:

The heroine Rajshree loves Jeetendra, the Airforce guy. They are about to get married but the National duty pulls him away and leaves his wife to be. In an encounter with the enemies, Jeetendra is injured and hence hospitalized. During the war there is bombing and the village where Rajashree lives is destroyed and when a crippled Jeetu comes to the village is shocked to find that the village does not exist and all are killed. He is unable to take it and wanders around and while seated outside a temple a motherly lady Sulochana takes sympathy towards him and offers work to him makes him the Manager in their business. Unfortunately, she has a son who is a drunkard and womanizer and she wants Jeetendra to help him and Jeetendra suggests marriage. It is some providence that the marriage is fixed with Rajashree who had survived the bombarding but both Jeetu and Rajshree keep mum. True to his style the newly wed groom goes to the brothel and gets into a fight and ends up killing his adversary. He runs away and takes shelter with Rajashree and dies only to leave behind a pregnant Rajashree that raises a lot of questions.

There were some songs that left behind some mark - here are the links:

https://www.youtube.com/watch?v=dpT0JtpwDXU ;

https://www.youtube.com/watch?v=Xwf2rowiYco ;

https://www.youtube.com/watch?v=KlCgs1FllPQ ;

https://www.youtube.com/watch?v=4U-OYNoF9QE ;

Cheers
Laksh KV

March 26 1971 (52 Years ago)

"LAGAN"

Folks:

On March 26 1971, the movie LAGAN was released - do not mistake this with Amir Khan's LAGAAN - this is minus one "A". I was a free bird having given my SSC exams that ended on March 20 1971 and opened the account of seeing movies with Parde Ke Peechay and myself and my classmate and good friend Chury aka Suryanarayan saw Aan Milo Sajna at Vijya Chembur and then saw Lagan at Rupam - first day first show. Lovely memory of seeing a good movie and we both enjoyed the movie - I guess more than the movie, it was the feeling of liberation and life away from studies and books that triggered a "Feel Good" factor. We had booked the ticket in advance and were very impressed by the performance of Ajay Sahani and the way he dealt with Prem Chopra. But somehow people did not like the movie and it hardly did justice at the box office. Faridal Jalal was the heroine for Ajay Sahani, and Prem Chopra had Nutan as his wife, and there was Bindu too, to make things spicy.

The story revolved around 2 brothers Prem Chopra and Ajay Sahani, who get married to 2 sisters Nutan and Farida Jalal and live in bliss but the elder brother PC abuses Nutan and the younger couple want to get him back on track as Bindu disrupts things for them. This is the gist and nothing spectacular. Average music did not do much for the betterment of the movie. Here are some links of the same:

https://www.youtube.com/watch?v=eSZvgd-Jcw4 ;
https://www.youtube.com/watch?v=4oQsZU9BLB8 ;
https://www.youtube.com/watch?v=n16Y9QEDD5o ;

Cheers
Laksh KV

March 23 1973 (50 years ago)

"HANSTE ZAKHAM"

Folks:

Today 50 years ago the Chetan Anand movie "Hanste Zakham" was released - main actors were - Navin Nischal, Priya Rajvansh, Balraj Sahani, Jeevan, Nadira, Mac Mohan, Achla Sachdev and Sateyn Kappu. The movie did reasonable business and had some great songs composed by Madan Mohan. Till date I have not seen the movie - just in bits and pieces in some channel on TV that is it. But the taxi song, I have seen many times. Lataji and Madan Mohan combo just amazes me both "Betaab Dilki Tamanna" & "Aaj Socha Toh Aansoo Bhar Aaye". - Just enjoy the depth when she sings "Muddaten Ho Gayi Musukuraakay"... very touching indeed.

Now coming to my memories - nothing much of the movie but this day was a very key day for our IYER family - my Amma's parents i.e. Grand Parents, fiercely independent were living by themselves in a place called Tirutanni in South India and health had started failing my grandpa as he got paralyzed on one side. With one son away in Singapore, the 5 sisters living in Mumbai wanted to put pressure on the other brother who was living in Ghatkopar to bring the seniors to Mumbai and take care. For this all the people were to assemble in our humble hut of 350 sq feet 1 room kitchen flat – so, in those telephone-less days we had to reach out to people. I was on study leave for the impending Inter Commerce exams. Amma and myself stepped out and called out men on their office numbers and informed and in the evening we had all of them around 630 at our home - great reunion and the best thing was my Uncle Ram Maama never objected to anything - before others could put pressure on him, he said he is going and getting their parents and will keep them in his Ghatkopar house - great soul who left us in 1993 when he was barely in his early 60s. So both Maama and Maami and their eldest sister decided to go and get the seniors. They had to leave ASAP and to sort minimum things they needed at least a day and on Sunday they were to take a train and go. Here too I enjoyed playing the role of seeing them off - they were going by unreserved compartment with open ticket but with my initiative, I managed to get them berths and my other relatives started feeling that I was very resourceful - ha I enjoyed this state and in the bargain made friends with a guy at VT station who could give us berth at the last minute.

Well, folks - the above is far from relevant to the movie but just shared it. The other part I would like to mention is that I am made fun of at home as I have some fondness for these big built heroines like Zaheeda & Priya Rajvansh (very poor at dialogue delivery) Now will share some good song links from this movie for all to enjoy and would hope to get comments from some of my friends with data on its performance, collections and other stuff.

https://www.youtube.com/watch?v=Sxgq4K4xwuU ;

https://www.youtube.com/watch?v=h8-8UyHQOTw ;

https://www.youtube.com/watch?v=h8-8UyHQOTw ;

https://www.youtube.com/watch?v=tIWvKw7hzms ;

Cheers
Laksh KV

March 22 1974 (49 years ago)

"CHOR MACHAYE SHOR"

Friends

49 years ago it was today the movie Chor Machaye Shor released - this turned out to be a big hit and good songs by Ravindra Jain added to the pleasure of seeing the movie. This movie had Shashi Kapoor, Mumtaz, Danny, Asrani, Tarun Ghosh, Madan Puri and Kamal Kapoor. Narrative was interesting - my memories for you.

No more moneyless days as I was earning though still in college and ability to fund was there too. But I was determined to see the movie only after my exams were over which was still over a month away.

Another important event I can recall is that 3 days after the release of the movie my cousin Vishwanath KR tied the knot to Vijaya Bhabhi (Mar-25-1974) and quite likely that it would have been their first movie after their wedding!!! Please enlighten us Vichu...

Finally I saw the movie in May 1974 after the exams got over during all India Railway strike - the movie being a hit and a money spinner, it kept on running and eventually completed silver jubilee and that enabled me to see the movie at Badal in the month of May.

Though the story was familiar - hindsight I feel there have been many similar movies where the Hero spends time in jail and with the help of the jail-birds comes out and does justice to his unjust happenings. Here too, Shashi Kapoor, not so wealthy person falls in love with a rich Mumtaz and her dad does not approve of it as he wants her to get married to a Politican's son. Then very smartly the seniors trap the Hero and with the Heroine as a witness, the Hero is thrown behind the bars so that he could sing "GHUNGURU KI TARAH BAJTAA HI RAHA HOON MAIN" and befriends Danny who keeps saying 'TERI MA KO APNI MA KAHOON!!!' On hearing his story where he has been wronged, they escape from jail and then the saga of vengeance starts - I am sure someone would have recalled GHAYAL of 1990 too!!! Well, all said and done this movie did entertain and people lapped up what was dished out!!!

Here are some links to the songs from the movie

https://www.youtube.com/watch?v=K0_jpigjv1c ;
https://www.youtube.com/watch?v=u8rxOUz-bPA ;
https://www.youtube.com/watch?v=S9ticLRysrk ;
https://www.youtube.com/watch?v=IX_hxJa243Q ;
https://www.youtube.com/watch?v=r1MljwiHe0s ;

Now over to my friends for giving some added gyaan

Cheers
Laksh KV

March 20 1970 (53 Years ago)

"DHARTI"

Friends

53 years ago today was the day the movie "DHARTI" released. Produced by Chitralaya Banner and directed by CV Sridhar who had directed successful movie like Dil Ek Mandir earlier - the movie was a remake of a hit Tamil Movie called "Shivanda Mann" - meaning red coloured mud. This movie was an average grosser despite high production values - may be again the timing of release could be the reason but those who appeared for SSC board exams were lucky to see this movie after their exams. My top most memory is:

My dear friend Arun Balakrishnan aka Naseeba who had given his final exams of class XI, was privileged to see this movie at Rupam. I still recall the trio - Balakrishnan Narayan, Viswanathan Krishnan and myself walked with Naseeba to Rupam Cinema and saw him off - He went those 5 steps to the entry door - handed over half of the ticket and was looking at the counterfoil with smile which told him the Row and Seat number. He saw the movie and was happier to have seen it ahead of all of us and not so much for the movie though. The Hero of the Tamil version Sivaji Ganesan (SG) had a role of a "Fighter" and did make an impact for the happiness of all the Madrasi fans of SG. But my other 2 friends Ramanathan Krishnan aka Mani and TS Balasubramanim aka Rajaram had seen the Tamil version and were very strong in their views of how the original version was better than Dharti. Again in this movie SJ's music was quite average as we had expected the duo to do better than what was churned out.

Well, to talk about the movie - it had a good star cast of Rajendra Kumar, Waheeda Rehman, Balraj Sahani, Ajit, Kamni Kaushal & Rajendranath. Hero's name is Bharat and is a patriot & his dad Balraj Sahani is serving as the Inspector General who has his duties that includes bringing his son back on track who wants to end the tyranny of the Diwan played by Ajit. The most impacted is Kamini Kaushal who has a dutiful hubby and a patriot son and the dad is after the son!!! Is it not very predictable? Waheeda Rehman plays a Princess whose dad played by Pahari Sanyal is imprisoned by the Dushth Diwan... Well, eventually good prevails. Here are some musical links for you.

https://www.youtube.com/watch?v=EaUIC-OpWVA ;

https://www.youtube.com/watch?v=rzwYM3JJ1Qg ;

https://www.youtube.com/watch?v=huzIk509TjY ;

I will now invite comments from those who have any more inputs.
Cheers
Laksh KV

March 19 1971 (52 Years ago)

"PARDE KE PEECHAY"

52 years ago it was today Vinod Mehra made his debut as a Hero in a suspense thriller called "Parde Ke Peechay" that released in Bombay on March 19th 1971. This was produced by one MC Ramamurthy who had the unique style of spelling the banner as Em Ce R Films or Productions & directed by K Shankar. Lead actress was Yogita Bali - "Asli Ghee Girl" as known then - my memories are:

1. My exams were to end on the following day & had decided to see this movie first as the banners showed Yogita Bali taking bath - what else can a 16 year old see!!!

2. Waiting to get thru with the exams...

The movie was unique with a haunting song coming on and off "Tere Bin Jiya Na Lage - Aaja Re" - Pran had a unique style of writing in the air the first alpha of the word he utters - e.g. "Maama Pyare, Yeh Kaam Toh Humne Bachpan Mein Hi Chod Diya Tha" - when he says this he would write "M" & "P" in English on an imaginary board with his fingers - as usual he plays a bad man but half way thru the surprise is that he gets murdered and the prime suspect has to be the Hero - Vinod Mehara - Myself and my friend Churi (Suryanaranan not on FB) had gone to see this movie at Rivoli Matunga - it was sweating noon on the Sunday but managed to get tickets in the 2nd row. Both of us were quite crazy about cricket and saw an uncanny resemblance of Vinod Mehra with off spinner EAS Prasanna. The suspense of the movie ... no harm in announcing now... of all people the least suspected character in the movie "Jagdeep" commits the murder.

SJ music was a pull factor for me though I must confess that the music was really below par. Still here are some songs for you and no wonder the movie was a disaster.

  https://www.youtube.com/watch?v=zE1MNrInS8g ;
  https://www.youtube.com/watch?v=OOHFggnKKeg ;

https://www.youtube.com/watch?v=aIzofOaoz38 ;
https://www.youtube.com/watch?v=9KD21zj7LoA ;
https://www.youtube.com/watch?v=VxZQ9J1ntts ;

Will await comments from my learned friends
Cheers
Laksh KV

17th March 1972 (51 Years ago)

"MEMSAAB"

---

51 years ago on this day the movie "Memsaab" *ing Vinod Khanna, Yogita Bali, Asrani, Johny Walker, Bindu, Jayashree T, Abhi Bhattacharya etc was released. Villain turned Hero Vinod Khanna was trying hard to establish himself as a Hero and was finding his feet slowly. This movie did precious little for him to move up the value chain as it was a disaster. I guess many movies suffered those days as they got released during exam time - but need to figure out who were the true audience. I would guess the salaried class would have been the major one - may be something we can discuss. My memories of this movie (having not seen it then & saw in bits and pieces on TV not so long ago)

1. It was the day when my closest friend Balakrishnan Narayan aka Bedi's SSC exams started. The girl from our building Jyothi Shankar also was from the same batch and I have some immensely forgettable things to talk about which we 3 can relate to. Well, I saw Bedi off at the school for the 11 am exam and the center was on the way to Rupam Cinema.
2. My exams for FY Com was to start on April 18th - so good one month plus time and after wishing him luck walked towards Rupam to see the situation of the matinee show which was "Awara" and it had quite a crowd waiting to get the tickets and also long "Q" at the ticket counter for Re.1.25.
3. The movie (Memsaab) flopped but still felt like seeing Bindu and hoped it continues after my exams got over on April 22nd 1972.

My friend Venkataramani Seshadrinathan informed me that Asrani got a lot of applause when he appeared on the screen - he had made an impact in Guddi earlier.

Quite recently the movie was on in one of the TV channels and in fact it was aired multiple times and I invariably switched on the TV almost at the same time. Johny Walker tries to mix up with some local fishermen folks to find out about the culprit. Vinod Khanna apparently belonged to Police dept. There was one haunting song of Lata ji "Mujhe Dhoondlay" and a duet with Mohd Rafi Saab "Suno Suno Ek Baat Kahoon" - these did well. Here are some links of the songs:

https://www.youtube.com/watch?v=u8bTNuJrG20 ;

https://www.youtube.com/watch?v=8mrIz1MJAks ;

https://www.youtube.com/watch?v=DJtnlXS5iHU ;

https://www.youtube.com/watch?v=j1k8TWZFcE0 ;

I will request my friends to add more information about this movie for the benefit of all

Cheers
Laksh

March 16th 1973 (50 Years)

LOAFER

50 years ago Dharam Paji sang 'AAJ MAUSAM BADA BE-IMAAN HAI' to Mumtaz - yes March-16-1973 saw the release of the movie "LOAFER" produced by RC Kumar under the banner "Century Films" and directed by A Bhimsingh. This was a big Box Office grosser those days. This was my Inter Commerce Days and I could not study till I saw the new release and was there at Badal Cinema for the 11 am show and felt great to get a ticket (used to be and still am a big Dharam fan). Money was no more a limitation for I was earning with a part-time job!!!

2 ka 4 bolo 2 ka 4 was the Black Market slogan and I wanted this movie to do well and it did. Probably Dharam Paji played a Chor for the nth time and did well.

Movie starts with 2 boys fighting after the school hours and accidentally one of the boys (Junior Dharam) pushes the other boy from the 3rd floor and the kid dies. This episode stays with the boy despite growing up to be the He-man Dharam and develops a superstition - every time he goes to do a big Chori, he would pick up one apple from a fruit vendor and the task is done well. Needless to say or you guessed it right - the fruit Vendor played by Om Prakash is the father of the boy who was pushed by young Dharam. On knowing the fact, Dharam wants to go out of his way to be of help to Om Prakash - which he does and eventually the old man comes to know as to who killed his son. But the greatness of the old man - he eventually accepts the reality that is more enhancing than the truth.

Host of villains in the movie are present in the movie headed by Premnath with his henchmen like Bhushan Tiwari, Senior Ramayan Tiwari, Anwar Hussain etc. Mumtaz plays a seductress in the song 'MOTIYON KI LADI HOON MAIN' but Dharam does not get impressed. The last song in the movie is really a lilting one "OH KOYI SHEHARI BAABU DIL LEHRI BAABU HI RE'. Overall an entertainer that did well with the makers making money...

Some of the songs and the links are here:

http://www.youtube.com/watch?v=aSJ_jcEPOu0&ob=av3e

http://www.youtube.com/watch?v=evUaRzK-I9c

http://www.youtube.com/watch?v=QPLCVWht68U

http://www.youtube.com/watch?v=0Uikwj2W_aY

Cheers folks - waiting for inputs from my other friends - Laksh KV

March 14th 1969 (54 years)

SHATRANJ

Folks

54 years ago on this day i.e. March 14 1969 saw the release of the movie "SHATRANJ" produced by Gemini Filims - Directed by SS Vasan *ing Rajendra Kumar, Waheeda Rehman, Mehmood, Manmohankrishna, Agha, Madan Puri and above all Shashikala. Good production values and photography by Kapadia took it to a different level as Gemini Productions were known for making low budget movies but this one was well mounted.

My memories:

Needless to say, it was released in and around annual exams and our exams in SIES School would normally end latest by April 13th every year so that on the Tamil New Year Day - kids would have no Home Work and the summer vacation would commence. I recall that on 12th April 69 my 9th standard exams got over and started the vacation earnestly. As luck would have it, one week later on 19th April 69, we had plans of seeing Shatranj in Chitra Cinema at Dadar. On the same day while playing I had a fall and had my right wrist fractured and broke my front teeth. So clinic, plastering & pain killers took over but despite this I did not want to miss the night show & we did see and enjoy the movie. This movie was sponsored by our cousin KS Sivaramakrishnan's & Lakshminarayan's brother KS Vaidyalingyam who took us (we 3 bros) from our home near Koliwada station by "Kali-Peeli" Taxi post dinner and me with my hand in a sling seated with the driver in the cab. When we reached, the previous show was still on & the doorman opened it for a few seconds and I and my late brother Vaidya V Raj saw one helicopter flying & the door was slammed on our faces - immediately my bro said, good production values!!!

Shatranj was a spy thriller with our Hero Jubilee Kumar going to a country that resembled China to rescue our Heroine Waheeda Rehman and her mother Achla Sachdev. Our Hero has a big support in the form of Mehmood and both make a mockery of the armed forces of the country where they go for the rescue act.

They succeed in the end to get the 2 ladies back home. Mehmood really stole the show with the song "BAKKAMMA BAKKAMMA EKKADA PATORA - IKKADA IKKADA RA" and Helan played his perfect partner. One cannot forget the fantastic acting of Shashikala who played the vamp. The music by Shankar Jaikishan was indeed outstanding & here are some of the links:

http://www.youtube.com/watch?v=9_Y5FE2OdPU

http://www.youtube.com/watch?v=tDJQ78Ak_Ls

http://www.youtube.com/watch?v=gBk5A3c8CBc

http://www.youtube.com/watch?v=6f6vAE4p-_A&feature=relmfu

http://www.youtube.com/watch?v=UREHDZfEFbw

The movie in general was a breezy entertainer worth one visit.
Enjoy & wait for the next
Cheers
Laksh KV

March 13 1970 (53 Years ago)

"MAN KI AANKHEN"

Folks:

This Day in 1970 the movie "Man Ki Aankhen" saw the light of the day. Made by I.A. Nadidadwala and directed by Raghunath Jhalani, the movie was an average grosser and managed to run for 10 weeks in Mumbai when released. By now we all know, it has to be something outstanding for a movie to be a commercial success despite releasing during the annual exams of kids - this was proven by the movie "Anand" released on March 12, 1971. But no such luck one year prior for this movie. My memories are not so much connected to the movie for there was no possibility of getting a chance to see it. Well, here they are:

1. On that fateful Friday, I and my late brother Vaidya V Raj went to a furniture shop at Sion Circle around 7 PM. We felt our house needed a small table that we called "Teapoy" and we both entered the shop and the owner was just seated with a total lazy look - probably disappointed to see a customer walk-in!!! My brother told him "Tepoy" LENA HAI" & pat came the reply that showed so much of disinterest "LEV NA!!!" We succeeded in making him get from his cosy chair and identified the piece we wanted and imagine a good wooden piece we got for Rs. 50/- only. We came lifting the piece, taking turns as we also wanted to walk towards Rupam Cinema with our load and then reach home. I felt happy to see the "House Full" board for my Hero Dharam Paji for both evening show and night show.

2. This is a painful memory - we lost one of our senior citizen relatives who had gone to Delhi to spend some time with his daughter and had promised to get me a lot of goodies but he left us on that day. We used to call him "Mac" short form for "MacDonald" the balding cricketer then as this gentleman resembled him.

Well, now coming to the movie, story of a spineless son (Dharampaji) who marries the Heroine (Waheedaji) and is worried about the reaction of his dowry demanding Mom played by Lalita Pawar - I guess the story has the required melodrama - the poor Manmohan Krishna playing the heroine's dad and a scheming brother of the hero played by Sujit Kumar. Some songs were good in the movie composed by LP. Here are some of the links for you:

https://www.youtube.com/watch?v=FXBgNIFBMS8 ;

https://www.youtube.com/watch?v=Ul3wufPJ4UE ;

https://www.youtube.com/watch?v=cNv8xq2cBec ;

I will now request my friends to add value to this post with their know-how of the movie.

Cheers
Laksh

March 12 1971 (52 years ago)

"ANAND"

'ANAND', 'PARAMANANAD', 'SATCHITANAND', 'NIRMALANAND' & DEV ANAND... –

WELL FRIENDS, I WOULD LIKE TO TAKE YOU BACK 52 YEARS - MARCH 12 1971 - THE HIT MOVIE "ANAND' RELEASED *ING RAJESH KHANNA IN THE TITLE ROLE, BIG B (WAS THIN B THEN) PLAYED DR. BHASKAR (I THINK) & JOHNY WALKER BECAME MURARILAL WITH SUPPORT FROM RAMESH DEO, SEEMA DEO & SUMITA SANYAL.

What a movie it was - it had no major hype and none of us knew that Hrishda was making such a movie for there were no advertisements those days. Personally for me it released at a wrong time as I was giving my SSC exams starting on March 15 1971. One day prior to the release, many of us went to School (SIES) to collect the Hall Ticket but were more interested to know about what this movie was all about - but soon we started discussing the first 2 exams - English and General Science... Well, the movie went on to become a big hit by word of mouth - and on the very same evening I heard on Vividh Bharati Aakashwani at 10.30 PM when the announcer said "AB SUNIYE FILM ANAND KA RADIO PROGRAM" - My elder brother heard it and exclaimed - "What movie - Anand - Vithal etc - just shut the radio off and study". Now who is Vithal is the question - we had a family that had many kidz and the second and third brothers were Anand and Vithal of Sameer Building Sion.

Coming back to the movie - this had a lovely message which I try to follow - the essence being "Life is Short, Live it to the fullest, Be Happy and Spread Happiness". The way it was tackled was outstanding with powerful performances by all the actors. Hrishida though felt that his best contribution was "Satyakam" but Anand did very good business with very limited investment. Needless to say that I could see the movie well after my exams got over & I will not hesitate to say that something that one can see multiple times and still feel touched every time. How can we forget the brilliant music of Salil Chowdhary and the song that stands out is Manna Dey's "ZINDAGI KAISI HAI PAHELI" - JUST TOO GOOD FOLKS - we can see the movie again and again.

So let us now take it upon ourselves to "Live well, Love All & Spread Happiness"

Here is some of the songs link

http://www.youtube.com/watch?v=3vgDb4TQneA

http://www.youtube.com/watch?v=Rh9-HvCUd3Q

http://www.youtube.com/watch?v=SC8DuvNCjbY&feature=fvsr

Cheers
Laksh

March 9 1973 (50 years ago)

PANCH DUSHMAN

Dear Friends:

Today 50 years ago with great hype this movie "Panch Dushman" was released with 5 major villains (Pran, Vinod Khanna, Shatrugan, Prem Chopra, Manmohan) in the movie and a completely unknown Manu Narang and Manjushree playing the main lead. I was very keen to see this movie on the very first day being a big fan of Shatrugan Sinha and was at Citylight Cinema but no tickets were available. I was not prepared to pay a premium and returned home without seeing the movie. Soon I learnt that the movie was a big disaster and vanished from all the halls in a matter of weeks.

I also gathered that this was re-released with a new title "Daulat Ke Dushman" in 1981 - but simply no idea as to why, what etc... It did create some wave on day one but that was it and one song by the new lead pair "Jaana Hai, Humay Toh" was a big hit - beyond that nothing to say.

I will request my knowledgeable friends to share more. I had done a quiz on this movie a few years ago and my friend Dilip Apte did talk about Mr. Manu Narang what he did post this movie etc. Well, it is just a memory point lying on my head and I am sharing it hoping to learn more about the movie from others.

Will try to get some song links:

https://www.youtube.com/watch?v=LWks8EDiPak ;

https://www.youtube.com/watch?v=CNmsfSFQ2Pk ;

https://www.youtube.com/watch?v=Cz905NJscb8 ;

Cheers
Laksh KV

March 7th 1969 (54 years ago)

Mere Huzoor

Folks

I want to take you back to March 7th 1969 - flashback 54 years ago. This day saw the release of the Muslim Social "Mere Huzoor" *ing Raj Kumar, Mala Sinha & Jeetendra in key roles. This was produced by the Banner "Movie Moguls".

The radio ad said "MALIKCHAND KOCHAR AUR VINOD KUMAR KA MERE HUZOOR" & this was followed by the title song's MUKHDA - "Rukhse Naqaab". This movie released before our Annual exams and hence there was no scope of going and seeing the movie and the only option was to go and see the posters at Rupam Cinema and act like "Dekha Hai Yeh Film - Kya Dialouge Hai Raj Kumar Ka !!!!". I am sure Balakrishnan Narayan and Arun Balakrishnan will be able to relate to what I am going to say here under:

I recall college students dividing work between them (Interval ke Pehle Ka Dialouge Main Likhoonga aur Tum Baadwale Likho) and the most famous dialogue delivered by Raj Kumar who played Nawab Salim was "LUCKNOW MEIN AISI KOUNSI FIRDAUS HAI JISE HUM NAHI JAANTE?" & my friend Balakrishnan Narayan aka Bedi (lives in Indore now) was a great FAN of Raj Kumar & to please him I had created an ad that said 'DEKHIYE - FILM MERE HUZOOR MEIN RAJ KUMAR GUM UTHATE HUVE AA RAHE HAIN' little realizing that this hit song was picturized on Jeetendra who played Akhtar Hussain & needless to say both men fall for Mala Sinha who plays "Sultanat". These 3 were supported by Johny Walker, Laxmi Chaya & Zeb Rehman.

Eventually I recall that 3 of us Viswanathan Krishnan Balakrishnan Narayan and yours truly saw this movie much later in life when money was no more an issue at Nataraj Chembur on a Saturday matinee show during one of its re-runs. Honestly, we kept paining Bedi asking "Arre Bol Yaar - when will the movie pick up?" - Nevertheless, I love the nostalgia involved with this Urdu social.

Brilliant and highlight of course was the music of Shankar Jaikishan & here are some of the songs for all of you.

http://www.youtube.com/watch?v=RJBqyi-o4qw

http://www.youtube.com/watch?v=0qpIQygF-VQ

http://www.youtube.com/watch?v=MTwtrF243kY

http://www.youtube.com/watch?v=njPugDI-qA0

http://www.youtube.com/watch?v=doNp-mC1ky8

The movie ran for 15 weeks and hence considered a hit. If one sees it now, it may look a slow movie but those who love URDU must see this movie.

Cheers
Laksh KV

March 5 1971 (52 years ago)

JAWAB

Dear Friends:

Today in 1971 saw the release of Producer Director Ramanna's family entertainer "JAWAB" *ing Jeetendra, Meena Kumari, Leena Chandavarkar, Mehmood, Aruna Irani, Prem Chopra etc. My limited memories given that it was my SSC exam days and had to wait for the exams to get over to see the first movie in 1971:

1. The radio ad had Ameey Sayani yelling 'DIRECTOR PRODUCER RAMANNA KA PAARIVAARIK DHAMAKA - JAWAB".
2. It was a flop movie and apparently very predictable.
3. Even Music was very average
4. By the time my exams got over on March 20th, the movie was gone from all the suburban halls and was running only in the main hall where too it lasted just 6 weeks. So till date not seen and no regrets!!!

I picked up the plot from multiple sources and the movie is very predictable..

Our Hero Jeetu lives in a small village with his sister Meena Kumari who is a widow. Unlike his real character, Ashok Kumar plays a very unfair Zamindar and with his son Prem Chopra and daughter Leena Chandavarkar makes Jeetu's life difficult. To top it to rub more salt on the wound, they decide to get Prem Chopra married to Jeetu's sweetheart. Ashok Kumar also plays dirty with Jeetu's sister who ends her life after this kind of humiliation. All this leaves a very bad taste in the mouth of Jeetu and he migrates to a city. In the city, he meets Mehmood who too has been a victim of Ashok Kumar's wrong doings. Then Mehmood and Jeetu join hands and come up with strategy to settle things with Ashok Kumar. This is what the movie is all about.

Some song links for you:
https://www.youtube.com/watch?v=piJaVPb5jZA ;
https://www.youtube.com/watch?v=C6rSRvgL-Ig ;

Anyone who has more recall of this movie kindly share - I am limited here except that I recall that this movie released today in 1971.
Cheers
Laksh KV

March 6 1970 (53 years ago)

SAAS BHI KABHI BAHU THI

Dear Friends:

It was exactly today 53 years ago the captioned movie "SAAS BHI KABHI BAHU THI" released *ing Sanjay Khan, Leena Chandavarkar, Om Prakash, Jagdeep, Shashikala & above all Lalita Pawar etc. The title of the movie clearly indicates what to expect - must be the story of a Mamma's boy, stern Mother-in-law, a henpecked father-in-law and a rebel Bahu!!! I have not seen this movie on release but recall seeing in bits and pieces on DD on one of those Sundays - an absolutely predictable movie. My memories:

1. Movie did not do well - ran for 10 weeks
2. Lalita Pawar was a terror
3. One of our building boys - Mohan (not on FB) [Latha Easwaran to note & convey] saw the movie and reverted with his comment in Tamil "MANDA POGARDU" meaning "HEAD TURNS or SAR PHIR JAATA HI"

Music also was average but this movie did well in Marathi if I recall well and the famous Ravana (Arvind Trivedi) of Ramayan made by Ramanand Sagar played the Son-in-law (Ghar Jamayee) in the movie.

I would request our friends to give more details of the movie if they have seen - I am pretty limited with my dope - all that I can say is this movie released today 53 years ago.

Some songs for you:

https://www.youtube.com/watch?v=1HiRwxvUthQ ;

https://www.youtube.com/watch?v=EiYtZukhVg4 ;

https://www.youtube.com/watch?v=f9hJ5wQU4no ;

https://www.youtube.com/watch?v=t-yBkdBEFt4 ;

Cheers

Laksh KV

March 3rd 1972

BOMBAY TO GOA

51 years ago i.e. on March 3rd 1972 - the Hit Movie "Bombay To Goa" was released. It was presented by the banner Mahmood Productions and produced by NC Sippy and Directed by S Ramanathan. The movie had a very interesting starcast - I have special memories of this movie and where the money for this movie came from for a FY college student. As part of NCC in college, I was entitled for washing allowance (uniform, polishing of belt and shoes) a total amount of Rs. 36/- out of which Rs. 3/- got dedcuted for Bangladesh Relief (felt let down then). Now the balance of Rs. 33/- was available - so we 3 brothers and 2 friends including Balakrishnan Narayan aka Bedi and Arun aka Naseeba saw this movie on the first day 6 PM show - the cost of the tickets being Rs. 2/- each & there was still money left for eating Samosas supplied by Gurukrupa (that was a small shop then). Be that as it may - coming back to the movie -

It was a remake from a Tamil movie called Madras to Pondicherry which was a hit too. It is tough to say who had the main role as all of them had meaty roles. Mehmood played the bus conductor Khanna while his real life brother Anwar Ali played the Driver Rajesh and when they addressed each other in turns it sounded "Rajesh Khanna". Aruna Irani played the Heroine who runs away from home with lots of money and jewellery and enters the bus from Bombay to Goa while Shatrugan (Sharma) and Manmohan (Varma) played negative roles and did the chasing bit to grab the money while Amitabh (Ravi & not Vijay) was there to protect Aruna Irani. There was assorted crowd in the bus including:

An ever-sleeping Keshto, Panditji – Sundar, Boxer - Yusuf Khan, Madrasi Passenger – Mukri, Kashi Bai - Lalita Pawar (with Murgi) Mukri's fat son - Pakoda Kadar, Fat lady passenger - Manorama & above all Kishore Kumar as Kishore Kumar

RD Burman gave some great music & we had Usha Iyer (Usha Uttup now) singing farmaishi songs for AB and AI and then getting confused and leaving the stage in a huff. One song that was deleted from the movie later "TUM MERI

ZINDAGI MEIN KUCH IS TARAH SAY AAYE" was supposedly the first tune composed by RDB.

    http://www.youtube.com/watch?v=PN0rH8dLn28

    http://www.youtube.com/watch?v=fF3q0_1hwLI

    http://www.youtube.com/watch?v=eXJwadeydSI

A movie that can be seen again and again - enjoy folks

Cheers
Laksh K V

March 2 1973 (50 yrs)

HEERA PANNA

Folks:

It is 50 years since the movie Heera Panna released. Made under the banner of Navketan - Written, Produced and Directed by the Ever-green Dev Anand, who also played the main role - though slowly he was moving towards his decline after the big success of Hare Rama Hare Krishna in 1972. It did not do too well despite the presence of big names like Dev Anand, Zeenat Aman & Rakhee. My memories are:

1, Though, I was earning and could have seen the movie, I decided not to see as the posters did not appeal to me despite Zeenet's legs.
2. Being a big Mohd Rafi fan, was feeling bad for him that he was not finding a place in some of the big banners & I said "No, I will not see this movie"
3. I felt happy that the movie did not do too well.

I read the review in TOI which certainly was not kind to the makers - story of a man (Dev Saab - Heera) who passionately loved his wife Rakhee & was equally passionate about photography. Unfortunately for him, his Air-hostess wife dies in an air-crash and he is left with only his 2nd passion of photography. While going thru his photography project with a rich person, he comes to know about the theft of a priceless diamond which is hidden in his car by Panna (Zeenat Aman) and he discovers her to be his deceased wife's sister. Some good songs try to lift up the movie and the intended pun in the song "PANNA KI TAMANNA HI" & "HEERA TOH PELAY HI KISI AUR KA HO CHUKA" was not missed by people at large. Here are some links for you:

https://www.youtube.com/watch?v=ugUaNU2m0oE ;
https://www.youtube.com/watch?v=rCUi-ZaUX-c ;
https://www.youtube.com/watch?v=vND7yb7ZmUw ;
https://www.youtube.com/watch?v=3J78eSZcORA ;

Cheers
Laksh KV

Feb 28 1969 - (54 years ago)

SAPNON KA SAUDAGAR

Dear Friends:

It was today 54 years ago that "Dream Girl" Hema Malini got launched as a Heroine in Hindi movies with a senior pro Hero Raj Kapoor in the movie Sapnon Ka Saudagar - Dream Merchant!! It was produced by B. Ananthaswamy & directed by Mahesh Kaul. I recall the big banner near King's Circle Bridge opposite to Gandhi Market where it showed Hema Malini inside a wooden bath tub and Raj Kapoor around. We, as teenagers would pass thru that and would sing our National Anthem hoping that the banner will get life and the Dream Girl will get up to respect the anthem - but no such luck - no money and had to be only pleased with seeing the posters and banners. This is the top of the head memory about this movie & the second one being seeing the trailer of this movie when we had gone to see Duniya that was released 2 weeks before this movie.

I could not see the movie then & even now seen only in bits and pieces on TV on and off...but wanted the movie to do well as a big SJ and Hema fan - but no such luck - even SJ's music was sub-standard by their standards - the hyped launch of Hema was something but she looked far better in the later movies than the debut movie. Having no idea about the plot and story line, I chatted with 2 of my friends who are repositories ie. Dilip Apte saheb and Amitabh Nigam and both gave me some insight about the movie.

Here is an extract from what Dilip had to say:

"This movie introduced Roopesh Kumar along with Hema Malini. Hema looked a typical South Indian here and not as beautiful as she looked in later years. Raj Kapoor is the son of a Jagirdar, who has donated all his wealth to the poor, including the land and roams about selling dreams to people. Jayant is actually the father of Hema Malini, but his ex-love [a banjaran] exchanges the children in Childhood as Jayant marries an aristocrat lady. She witnesses the exchange of girls and dies of shock. Thus Tanuja the daughter of the Banjaran is raised in his house but is hated by him. Jayant wants to marry off this panauti and get rid of her. Raj

Kapoor comes accidentally to his house to sell a dream. He is mistaken as a match for Tanuja. Ropesh Kumar is a Prince and comes to wed the daughter - but instead Hema Malini is shown to him. She acts funny with a squint in her eyes etc.and Roopesh Kumar runs away. Later Raj Kapoor lands himself in Hema Malini's house and their love blossoms."

Song links for you:

https://www.youtube.com/watch?v=Or-LcjfYpV4 ;

https://www.youtube.com/watch?v=PJrlpkUwywE ;

https://www.youtube.com/watch?v=foZiEOv_QdY ;

https://www.youtube.com/watch?v=XBasVR3OsfQ ;

Cheers
Laksh

February 27th 1970 - 53 years ago

AADMI AUR INSAAN

Folks, I am taking you back to February 27, 1970 (53 years back) - the movie that released was BR Chopra's 'AADMI AUR INSAAN' *ing Dharmendra, Saira Banu, Feroz Khan, Mumtaz, Johny Walker & host of others like Madan Puri, Ajit, Anwar Hussain, Iftekar etc.

The Radio Ad said 'NAU JAWANON, UTHO, JAAGO - BR FILMS KA TEHELKA - AADMI AUR INSAAN' & the song would start 'JAAGEGA INSAAN ZAMANA DEKHEGA, UTHEGA TOOFAN ZAMANA DEKHEGA'. This movie was made by BR Chopra & Directed by Yash Copra with music by Ravi. A lot of hype was created; good production values & the movie did excellent business at the BO. The time of release was not so good due to the final exams for school kids would normally be in March time frame and despite that this movie ran pretty well.

A few things stand out in the movie:

1. Feroz Khan's performance as Dharam Paji's friend JK (Jai Kishen), who turns into his foe.
2. The term "ITTEFAQ" was used so many times by Mumtaz in this movie that the banner was probably influenced by the movie they had churned out while waiting to complete this movie.
3. I recall putting up a quiz on Johny Walker going to buy sweets and how he buys but does not pay any money. Do see the attached clip. I am sure you would enjoy this.
4. Good Music by Ravi with Mumtaz doing the "Zindagi Ittefaq Hai " number a few times in the movie. The other good songs were "Ye Neele Parvaton Ki Dhara", "Watan Ka Kya Hoga Anjam Bata De Ye Moula He Ram" & "O Dil Karta O Yara Dil Dara" etc.
5. I and my elder brother saw this movie at Kohinoor Dadar when it was in its 10th week paying a hefty Rs. 2.50 for stall tickets.

It has very restrained performance by Dharam Paji who continues his friendship with Feroz Khan despite getting humiliated by him. FK also got Filmfare award for this role as the best supporting actor that year. True to the tradition of BR Films, we had songs by Mahendra Kapoor that were generally at high octave and enjoyable. Overall, a good movie with a decent screenplay despite the triangular plot of 2 men and one lady with an additional woman in Mumu thrown in.

Do have a look at the clip:

Johny Walker Comedy movie gulam rasool Aadmi aur insaan in lockdown - YouTube

Enjoy –
Cheers
Laksh

February 26 1971 (52 years)

HASEENON KA DEVTA

Dear Friends:

52 years ago today released a flop movie Haseenon Ka Devta that had Sanjay (Khan), Rekha, Sujit Kumar & Bindu playing the main roles. Exactly today last year I had done a quiz on this movie and the background I gave was as under:

Story of a Raja Saab tricked by the wrongdoers to sign the power of attorney & ends up murdering another character actress erroneously. He fakes to be a gentleman and tells Raja Saab to hide himself from the cops. Raja Saab's daughter returns from abroad and needless to say becomes the sweetheart of Hero, who promises to help her dad's position. The daughter does not know that the Hero too had a key role to play in pushing her dad in this situation. Eventually things end well.

Well, I have only some memories of this movie that I never saw -

1. I was enjoying my study holidays and was feeling corrupted when I saw a picture of Bindu displaying her legs - imagine all before my SSC exams that were to start in < 20 days time.
2. No chance of seeing this movie on release - only posters
3. Determined to see the movie once I start earning - but till date not seen, though I retired in 2011, and no regrets.
4. It failed at the BO and was not there for me to see once my exams got over on March 20 1971 in the close by halls but perhaps continued its run in the main theater for some 6 weeks in total.

Here are some of the songs for you.

https://www.youtube.com/watch?v=wtbzGkb3ilc ;

https://www.youtube.com/watch?v=OrY5FmKhNNI ;

https://www.youtube.com/watch?v=cLww0Fi5btA ;

Cheers

Laksh KV

Feb 25 1972 (51 years)

SANJOG

Dear Friends:

On this day the movie with a triangular plot (1 man and 2 women) SANJOG was released that had Mala Sinha, Amitabh Bachhan and Aruna Irani forming the triangle. There was Madan Puri and Nazir Hussain playing the seniors and Johny Walker too had a role that had an impact - more so as he had a small kid who used to go to his office as a motherless kid.

Story revolved around Hero getting married to the heroine but the marriage is not acceptable to his family and hence they separate. Heroine's dad a watchman thinks of getting the heroine remarried but finds that she is in family way. So a determined dad decides to educate his daughter and she becomes a Collector. The Hero marries a second time and works as a clerk in a government department and also has 3 kids. A new collector comes to the department and no guesses here it's the Heroine as the Big Boss and there are gossips galore in the organization - thanx to Johny Walker - Collector too has a kid and needless to say the kids get connected and creates complications. In such a triangular plot, one of the characters has to die and the main heroine dies but before she goes donates her eyes to the current wife who loses her vision during the climax. As a result, the first heroine continues to see her Hubby thru the eyes of the 2nd heroine!!! Too complex - not really... Movie was a bit slow but could not do well at the Box Office.

My memories are - we all wanted to see this movie as it was a remake of a Tamil movie called "IRU KODUGAL" meaning 2 Lines or 2 parallel lines. I had earlier shared boastfully with my family that post "Mere Apne", I had connections with Ranganathan - the Projector Operator of Rupam Cinema and no more waiting in long "Q" of advance booking. When the movie was House Full we got tickets of "A" row for Mere Apne so here I was too confident of repeating the feat but alas - Ranga gave me 5 tickets that cost Rs. 10/- totally with H 20 to H 24 and my late bro Vaidya V Raj was livid with me at my boastful claim of "A" row tickets. Be that as it may - we all went for the movie and I had promised

Samosas for all during the break - so all 5 including my parents and 2 brothers went to see the night show at Rupam on Saturday night. Some of the scenes that made an impact for me were:

1. When Mala Sinha comes as the Boss and while driving her car her eyes get moist and she starts the wiper of the car.
2. An important File in the office is misplaced and Mala Sinha asks AB about the same & he mistakes it to be a discussion of their past life. At that point she raises her voice and tells "I am talking about the FILE and not LIFE"
3. The song Ek Do Teen Chaar sung by Johny Walker was a good one for the game of Musical Chair.

Overall we, as a family were disappointed that the movie was not as gripping as the Tamil version. Here are some of the song links for you:

https://www.youtube.com/watch?v=E-q0gBRfi4I ;

https://www.youtube.com/watch?v=31TwZtRnTU0 ;

https://www.youtube.com/watch?v=AsT86FNtoT8 ;

Cheers
Laksh KV - waiting for your comments and experiences

Feb 23 1973 (50 Years)

DHUND

Friends:

50 years ago today released BR Films thriller "DHUND" meaning FOG - it had some thrill, good acting and suspense and the movie too did decent business at the Box Office.

My memories - movie released one day before my Birthday and wanted to gift myself this movie on my Birthday and went and saw the movie at Citylight - Dadar Shivaji Park area - all by myself. Money was no more an issue as I had started earning from June 1972 and had the capability to fund my friends too. I did not enjoy the movie as I would have liked to since I was alone in a crowded hall. I loved Danny and his violent attitude in the movie and the pleasure he derived by killing birds - very sadistic indeed. He also gets to know the budding romance between his wife and Sanjay Khan who he refers to as "Leader" if I recall right. I also loved the song Deven Verma got to lip-sync "Nazuk Tann Aur Ushpay Jawani". My friends wanted to know about the suspense and I told them that I would not reveal it and they must see the movie and enjoy it.

On Sunday the TOI gave the review and it talked about the unhappy marriage of Danny and Zeenat - the love angle with a budding politician played by Sanjay who falls in love with Zeenat and then the paper that said there was a Stranger played by Navin Nischal who kills Danny. Uff - suspense gone I told myself. BR Films has been a reputed banner known for making both romantic and thrillers too and this one was purely some kind of a suspense thriller. Ravi's music was hummable though not outstanding as he has given better music in other movies. Here are some links:

https://www.youtube.com/watch?v=Al_C8ZdLpfY ;

https://www.youtube.com/watch?v=8KJ3ApQki_4 ;

https://www.youtube.com/watch?v=Ei7pX6Hd33Y ;

Cheers
Laksh KV

Feb 21 1969 (54 Years)

WAPAS

Dear Friends:

54 years ago the movie Wapas released in Mumbai today. There is hardly any recall about this movie except that there are some good lilting numbers composed by LP. Master Satyajeet had a role to play etc.

Any of our knowledgeable friends can enlighten all of us a little more. So here is a link of all the songs you can see and play with lyrics.

http://www.hindigeetmala.net/movie/wapas.htm

Cheers
Laksh KV

February 20th 1970 – (53 Years)

SACHAAI

53 years is a long time but still fresh in my mind. So here comes February 20th 1970 when I was in class X when the movie "SACHAAI" released. The movie was produced under the banner of Em Ce R Movies by M.C. Ramamoorthy & Directed by K. Shankar. It was like a multi-starrer with Shammi Kapoor, Sanjeev Kumar, Sadhna, Pran, Johny Walker & Helan.

The movie opened with a lot of promise and fan-fare but soon slumped to be an average grosser. By the time it was into its 5th week, we were all in for a big surprise - a pleasant one at it. The movie that was not doing well needed some boost and we got "Free Passes" to see the movie at the main theatre NAAZ at Grant Road. Being a big Shammi Kapoor fan, I kept defending all the negative comments that were coming about his size & not so good acting etc from some of my friends. Well, all said and done Shammi was the winner.

Movie was about 2 friends (SK and SK) who are opposites - one good and one bad. They have arguments & then enter into a "SHART" to meet after a few years - you go your way and I go my way. The irony is that the roles reverse in 3 years as Good becomes bad and Bad becomes good eventually Shammi Kapoor (Policeman) shooting Sanjeev Kumar (Thief).

The highlight of the movie was its music by Shankar Jaikishan duo with wonderful songs - the highlight being "Bottle Dance" by Helan with Shammi Kapoor "KAB SE DHARI HAI SAAMNE BOTTLE SHARAB KI" & the duet by the two SKs 'AE DOST MERE MAINE DUNIYA DEKHI HAI', "SAU BARAS KE ZINDAGI SE ACHHE HAIN PYAR KE DO CHAAR DIN" & "MERE GUNAAH MAAF KAR" - here are the links for some of the songs:

   https://www.youtube.com/watch?v=Vj6A2gAgQLE;
   https://www.youtube.com/watch?v=Z2y7vMn7mkE;
   https://www.youtube.com/watch?v=WDnT4FHHbiY;
   https://www.youtube.com/watch?v=plUaIyagI9k;

Eventually the movie was dragged for 15 weeks as the yardstick for a hit movie was 100 days run and this managed to reach that line. Not sure how many of you would have seen the movie. But I still liked it –

Cheers
Laksh KV

February 19 1971 – 52 Years

GAMBLER

I would like to take you back to February-19-1971 - i.e. 52 years back to the release of Dev Anand movie "GAMBLER". Nostalgia for me is that it was during my study holidays for the Board exam of standard XI from SIES School. I was banned from seeing any movies till the exams got over and those were the days when I found reasons to get out of the house and be away from books and studies - thruout was restless and willingly helped my Amma to check if the milk van had come for the afternoon quota of milk to be procured from the milk center. And that is when I saw one of my friends "Chintya" who was going home around 2 PM on that Friday. I asked Chintya - "Kahan Se Aa Raha Hai?" - He responded "Gambler Dekhke AA Raha Hoon - 1st day Matinee show" - I exclaimed "Great Re - lucky you - Kaisa Tha?" - To this day I cannot forget when he said "Just like JOHNY" - Johny Mera Naam released a few months ago was still going strong - a big hit then. But the reality was "Chintya" was pulling a fast one and I caught him one year later on his bluff. Be that as it may - but I am sure my friends Balakrishnan Narayan Arun Balakrishnan and Viswanathan Krishnan can relate to this and also our next generations!!!

"Gambler" was directed by Amarjeet and the posters read 'DEV ANAND PLAYS GAMBLER" - however, the movie did not do too well at the Box Office despite dashing performance by the ever-green Dev Saab - it was a thriller where the blackmailing Jeevan gets killed in haata-payee between Dev Saab and him and then the long & familiar court scenes. It had good performances by Jeevan, young Sachin & Kishore Sahu and above all in a guest role it was Shatrugan Sinha who stole the show. Zaheeda, who was introduced earlier in Prem Pujari by Dev Saab played the heroine who looked very huge for a slim Dev. The highlight of the movie was the fantastic music by S.D. Burman Saab & here are some of the links of the lovely songs.

http://www.youtube.com/watch?v=pmHgKxuD1uM

http://www.youtube.com/watch?v=Wg3GUZq3jWw&NR=1...

http://www.youtube.com/watch?v=0xzj1lT6jhU

http://www.youtube.com/watch?v=85uJg1HXP28

The songs- Mera Man Tera Pyaasa, Dil Aaj Shayar Hai, Choodi Nahi Mera Dil & Apne Honton Ki Bansi

I still loved the movie which I saw much later in life in matinee (reduced rates) during my college days - just for its music and ofcourse Dev Saab - May He rest in peace

Cheers
Laksh KV

Feb 12 1971 (52 years ago)

EK NANHI MUNNI LADKI THI

Today was the Release of a flop movie "Ek Nanhi Munni Ladki Thi" 52 years ago *ing Prithvijaraj Kapoor, Mumtaz, Jayant, Sajjan, Shyam Kumar & an upcoming Shatrughan Sinha - above all child star Bobby.

When my friend Balakrishnan Narayan and myself saw the posters at Rupam, we felt it was a hot movie with some horror thrown in coming from Ramsay family. We saw scantily clad Mumtaz being raped on sand by Shatrughan Sinha and Jayant dancing to an Iranian tune with Helan. We both were very desperate to see the movie but multiple reasons ensured we missed the movie. But at 16 we had only thoughts of seeing this movie once we have funds but to our bad luck this movie bombed and was not available for us to see even in matinee shows a year later when I was in funds. But before I wrote this column, I thought let me have a look at the movie on You Tube. I have seen 80% of the movie and my observations are as under:

1. During the titles, there is no mention of Shatrughan Sinha though he is there quite prominently in the movie. This was wrong as my friend Amitabh Nigam showed me a screenshot that had Shotgun's name.
2. A very ageing Prithiviraj Kapoor (1906 born in 1971 around 65) has a baby girl in wonderchild Bobby who is around 5 yrs old. Imagine in the same year about 9 months later he played his real life role of Randhir Kapoor's grandpa in Kal Aaj Aur Kal. In other words it looked very unrealistic.
3. The combination of Jayant and Prithviraj - 2 huge guys looked nice but in comparison Jayant looked lean.
4. Low production values in the movie is very evident.
5. Story revolves around Prithviraj trying to protect his family belongings from Phirang smugglers.. Police suspect that he is upto something unlawful and arrest him but he, with the help of Jayant escapes and we soon see that he has been hiding for several years and the baby girl grows into Mumtaz.

6. Then it is all revolving around the property created by Prithviraj that is about to be inherited by his only daughter and the effort of her care-taker played by Nadira to usurp the same though her hubby played by Sajjan, who is not in favour of that. Shatrugan is their son and is not so much interested in the girl but happy to inherit the property by proving Mumtaz to be a mad girl and does his best to put her in an asylum.
7. Very predictable movie - still brings nostalgia to me.
8. Some songs are good to listen, specially the title song. Here are some of the links for you.

https://www.youtube.com/watch?v=vKo22gIAVq4;

https://www.youtube.com/watch?v=NqShYxhupPE;

https://www.youtube.com/watch?v=wYNcKXYH3Lw;

Cheers
Laksh KV

Feb 11 1972 (51 years ago)

MERE APNE

Hi Folks

This Day (11th Feb) That Year (1972) i.e. 51 years ago saw the release of the revolutionary movie "MERE APNE" which happened to be the first effort by Gulzaar as a Director. The term "THE WHOLE THING IS THAT" was created in this movie and was used by late comedian Mehmood who played the role of a politician - this term was then taken into the next movie that Mehmood produced called "SABSE BADA RUPAIYAA".

The radio ad was quite funny with late Mehmood imitating late Prithviraj Kapoor that said "THE WHOLE THING IS THAT - THIS IS THE STORY OF MERE APNE WHICH IS PRESENTATED BY NC SIPPY & DIRECT BY GULJAAAR". Try saying the quote in Prithviraj Kapoor's voice.

The movie depicted the problem of Unemployment, gang fights, selfish people & one selfless lady - played by Late Meena Kumari. Two friends Shyam and Chenu (Vinod Khanna and Shatrugan Sinha) become foes due to a girl played by Yogita Bali & then there are never-ending fights between the two and their groups - the groups included Danny, Asrani, Paintal, Dinesh Thakur etc. Finally the fight ends with the end of Meena Kumari who does a lot to bring these two together.

Salil Chowdhary provided lovely music and the outstanding song was sung by none other than Kishore Kumar - KOYI HOTA JISKO APNA HUM APNA KEHTE YARO & the other one was on the umemployemnt problem HAAL CHAAL THEEK THAAK HAI SUB KUCH THEET THAAK HAI, BA KIYA HAI MA KIYA, KAAM NAHI HAI VARNA YAHAN, APKI DUA SE SUB THEEK THAAK HAI - here are the links for you.

http://www.youtube.com/watch?v=ZkbQ9g9FEx8

http://www.youtube.com/watch?v=uIg8xq5KAOE

My memory of this movie is that of going to see this movie that had "House Full" Board at Rupam Cinema on the very first day 2.30 PM show. With me were 2 of my friends - first one Venkacham aka Kundoti (not in FB) and the other Venkataramani Seshadrinathan who lived in the middle east but left us a few years ago. We 3 were very eager to get tickets without paying any premium and suddenly Kundoti - just said -"One minute" and vanished from the scene. After about 5 minutes he came with 3 tickets - we both asked "How did you manage this?" & he said that he saw a familiar face and he happened to be one Mr. Rangarajan who worked as the projector operator - he got the tickets from inside. Now, this became a regular thing for us - no more standing in "Qs" on Monday for advance booking - go thru Rangarajan and we also got a backup in one Mr. Tripathi - fondly called as Tripa... who used to guide people inside the hall with a torch to their respective seats. Tripa was put up in our next building Kamal Kunj - my friends Balakrishnan Narayan and Arun Balakrishnan will be able to relate to this for sure.

Well, this movie did reasonable business – Rs. 1.7 Crores - Amitabh Nigam can now convert this into Time Value of Money using Gold standards.

Thanx - enjoy reading this

Cheers
Laksh KV

February 18 1972 (51 years)

DO RAHA

Folks:

On this day in 1972, a very desperately awaited movie was released for all of us in our teens. The posters proudly said "Story of Bed Partners" !!! Uffff.... Ram Dayal's "DO RAHA" was released. The movie had promised a lot of erotic scenes and all of us did not want to miss out right Balakrishnan Narayan Balakrishnan Narayan Viswanathan Krishnan!!! Nandi Cinema Bandra - 11 am show on the first day, we landed after getting the tickets. Wow it was some real excitement for all of us and the movie did keep up the promise for us with some steamy scenes and if I recall right the First Night (Suhaag Raat) scene between Anil Dhawan and Radha Saluja just before the interval had everyone run towards the loo and the long "Q" was never-ending and most took a long time to relieve themselves and later again there was a major climax scene for all of us when Rupesh Kumar has a go at Radha Saluja before I think he gets killed. I thought there was nothing much to the story line it was "Paisa Vasool" for our gang. The movie was not a big hit and ran for 10 weeks then and by the time it was July 1972, it had come in the Matinee and reduced rate category. And then we wanted to see it again at a cheaper rate and Balakrishnan Narayan and myself went to see the movie at Broadway by giving a miss to our lectures at college and this time round, we felt the effect not so strong !!! Right Bedi?

Now coming to the story line - it had to do with a writer who was honest and was not getting justice for his efforts and he was coaxed into writing some cheap pot-boiler stuff and he eventually succumbs and hands over the control of his life to his Boss. This Boss has an eye on our Hero's wife, who had just about started feeling neglected by her hubby who is after money. Inevitable happens when the Boss takes advantage of the wife and later gets killed. Nothing much and things are pretty predictable. Sapan Jagmohan's music was OK OK. Here are some links for you:

https://www.youtube.com/watch?v=J1oHcSj56bg;
https://www.youtube.com/watch?v=ku-_KzRavUQ;
Enjoy and add value to this experience
Cheers
Laksh KV

February 16 1973 (50 years ago)

BANDHE HAATH & GORA AUR KAALA

Two movies released one a flop and one did just about reasonable business. The movies are:

1. Bandhe Haath (Flop)
2. Gora Aur Kaala (15 weeks - 100 days run)

My memories - Bandhe Haath did not release in our usual Rupam Cinema but very well remember the radio program and the advertisement - the lady on radio used to shout "Bandhe Haath" - I wish I could record it and post it here - AB plays "Shyamu" a Chor a robber who is being chased by Police and finds another poet who is his look alike and thinks of a plan to finish of the poet and take his place - luckily for him he does not have to kill the poet as he was anyway going to die. Mumtaz plays the female lead and somehow the jodi of AB and Mumu did not click. While studying for Inter Commerce, my priority was clear not to go too far to see movies and hence sacrificed this movie. The movie barely ran for 6 weeks and was done and dusted. Here are a couple of links of the songs from the movie.

https://www.youtube.com/watch?v=psZDsIrvgQM;

https://www.youtube.com/watch?v=IvoIw28WnWM;

https://www.youtube.com/watch?v=Y8nkl7qSjPc;

My memories of Gora Aur Kala - yes this one did release at Rupam and we were hardly interested to see a fading hero's last minute ditch to revive his stardom. Rajendra Kumar was going downhill but got to read in the papers that he had done the role of Kala very sincerely and we 3 brothers thought thru and decided to see the movie on a Wednesday night at Rupam - so we did not see the movie in a hurry. The movie was funny and we enjoyed this part where the Gora would get hit and Kalya will also feel the pain - in all fairness we enjoyed the acting of Kala and in one scene he is shown inside a big cage and some Lilliput trying to cause harm to the Gulliver looking Kala. Hema Malini (my favourite) looks very elegant and the story revolves around an emperor whose wife delivers twins and there are others who are interested in the property who kill him and some loyalists save the kids but get separated and they grow up as Gora and Kala (due to some medical reasons) - Lot of sword fights, action and some good songs - managed to move this film from a flop category. This was from the banner of Raj Kumar Kohli - Rs. 2/- per ticket I funded for my 2 elder brothers and had lovely Samosas during interval that came from Gurukripa famous for their Samosa offerings. Well, it tasted sublime and here are some songs for you.

https://www.youtube.com/watch?v=JoYBPf6jOJo; (all songs)

Cheers

Laksh

Feb 14 1969 (54 Years ago)

DUNIYA

Time Films - Duniya *ing Dev Anand, Vyjantimala, Balraj Sahani, Prem Chopra, Nana Palsheekar, Lalita Pawar & Johny Walker; was released at Apsara Cinema today ie on February 14 1969. Amitabh Nigam, Google says it was released on Dec 28 1968 (which was a Saturday & movies normally do not release on Saturdays those days in Bombay).

My memory of this movie is that this movie replaced "Teesri Kasam" at Apsara which was released on Jan 10th the same year and was a flop. The joke going around was that - there was a person who saw "Teesri Kasam" - Last Day Last show and then saw on the very next day "Duniya" - First Day First show and he was so disappointed seeing the colour movie that replaced a B&W one and came out singing 'DUNIYA BANANEWALE KYA TERE MAN MEIN SAMAYEE KAHAKO DUNIYA BANAYEE TOONAY"? Needless to say this movie was quite a pain for people and was dragged for 15 weeks and was certified "Not a Flop" movie. It was some kind of an exception for me as to how our strict Amma herself booked 3 tickets for we brothers for a Saturday show ie on Feb 15 1969. We brothers were thrilled to see the movie and since it was out of turn we loved it not so much the movie but the experience - more interesting for us was the trailer during the interval of the movie that launched the Dream Girl Hema Malini "Sapnon Ka Saudagar" that was to release 2 weeks later. The regular movie started immediately after the trailer and I still kept thinking the trailer was on and told my brother... arrreee - how come Johny Walker is playing 009 James Bond in this movie too. Then I was corrected saying the movie has started post interval. We saw the movie at Rupam our most frequently visited hall.

My current memory of the movie was Nana Palsheekar the least suspected person is the one who kills Prem Chopra and that is the suspense - my cousin KS Lakshminarayanan (unable to tag) brother of KS Sivaramakrishnan and dad of Ravi Lakshminarayanan informed us that when the murder happened one could see the DHOTI worn by Nana Palsheekar - some editing would have helped I guess. Major court drama follows in the movie post this murder and our ever-green

Hero does a great job delivering in style. Some good songs by SJ is the highlight of the movie - Vyjantimala looks huge in front of a slim Dev Anand but they still made a good pair. Here are some songs of the movie.

https://www.youtube.com/watch?v=n-W9CtRlkiU;

The same banner announced the launch of their next movie "Gold Medal" *ing Dharmendra Rakhee and Shatrughan Sinha - but remained in the cans for a long time - I gathered that it was later released in 1984 but I have no recall - my friends can add value to this post with information of both the movies.

Cheers
Laksh KV

February 13 1970 (53 years ago)

RAHAGEER

The movie Rahageer was released on this day - it did not do much business but the radio ad I still recall that said "RAHAGEER - BENGALI MEIN PAINSATH HAFTHE CHAL CHUKI HI". But not much of publicity and not many saw the movie and my recall is it died a silent death. The only memory for me is what I heard on the radio and that is what I have mentioned above.

It had Biswajit in the lead that I recall besides music by Hemant Kumar - and rest of the things don't know where to go. Here are some links of the songs I recall of Hemantda ....

https://www.youtube.com/watch?v=KpUOGKouTPI;
https://www.youtube.com/watch?v=xFH0f-GwV1o;
https://www.youtube.com/watch?v=DfMydZZR8FA;

I would urge people to share more of what they know of this movie as this would be some education for all. Waiting for information from those who can contribute

Cheers
Laksh KV

Feb 07 1969 - 54 years ago

Folks:

Two movies released on this day
1. **Kanyadaan - An average grosser**
2. **Man Ka Meet - Below average grosser**

Let me talk about Kanyadan first made under the banner of Kiron Productions produced by Rajendra Bhatia and directed by Mohan Sehgal.

The story revolved around 2 men with same name creating confusion and to top it one of them had Child Marriage and the other man with the same name falls for the Heroine who was not aware about her child marriage. Some more confusion and some clarifications later the seniors in the movie decide that the child marriage was "Null and Void". Shashi Kapoor and Dilip Raj - both have the name AMAR and that is the main cause of confusion. Excellent Music by SJ is the highlight of the movie - my biggest memory of this movie is that my class-mate Subramaniam R (Chubbu)'s elder sister got married on this day that year and though he was kind to invite me, I felt odd to attend for not having proper dress for the occasion and with no gift money to give - after all I was in class IX and there was no invite for the family - just Chubbu telling "Lakshmi nee vandoodu" - To top it this movie did not release in Rupam for me to look at the posters. All I did was waiting to listen to the songs on the radio of our neighbours.

Here are some songs for you

https://www.youtube.com/watch?v=3dwzth2CJOQ;

https://www.youtube.com/watch?v=LuiTm_RL7Ac;

https://www.youtube.com/watch?v=FnSYHSxtmBM

This movie managed to run for 15 weeks - so not a flop but not a bumper hit

Now coming to the next movie - Man Ka Meet - produced by Sunil Dutt's banner Ajanta Arts where he introduced 4 stars

1. Som Dutt (Sunil Dutt's Brother)
2. Leena Chandavarkar
3. Vinod Khanna
4. Sandya Roy or Rani (I think - may be room for correction)

I wanted this movie to do well as I had loved the Tamil version of this movie called "Kumari Penn" and had seen when I was probably in class VII - the movie's plot was again a triangular one and the hero Som Dutt was a villager and the Heroine was a rich man's (Om Prakash) daughter - rich estate owner etc. The villain Vinod Khanna had his eyes on the property of old man and tries to play lot of tricks only to be thwarted by the Hero. Som Dutt vs the watchman song was a big hit sung by Mahendra Kapoor - "TU HUSN KA HAI DARBAAN TOH MAIN HOON ISHQ KA PEHREDAAR" - The movie depicts that a villager is strong though looks bhola and can have his way with his honesty and attitude that impresses the heroine's dad.

My memory this time is for a change not with Balakrishnan Narayan but with his elder bro Arun Balakrishnan aka Naseeba... He had seen the trailer of this movie and kept telling me as to how Som Dutt slowly moved his hand below the shoulder to midriff of Leena who was wearing a blouse that exposed her back close to 85%... This was probably a dream sequence in the movie. I eventually managed to see this movie at Rupam when it came in matinee at reduced rates and did not find the scene too arousing - probably Naseeba created very high expectations!!! Well, the movie ran only for 10 weeks and died a silent death those days. Here are some song links for you.

https://www.youtube.com/watch?v=tesyEQBHG_s;

https://www.youtube.com/watch?v=1kUddDm_Hso;

https://www.youtube.com/watch?v=oWCz8lhszEY;

https://www.youtube.com/watch?v=KGHb8-6TqOQ...;

Cheers
Laksh KV

February 6th 1970

PREM PUJARI

Folks

I would like to take you back by 53 years - Yes February 6th 1970 - the release of "PREM PUJARI" under the Navketan banner inaugurated in the new Cinema Hall in Mumbai "SHALIMAR". Ameen Sayani on Radio ad said "Prem Pujaari - Aaaa Rahaaa Haiiii".

The Legendary Dev Anand wore multiple hats in this movie as:

1. Hero

2. Writer

3. Producer

4. Director

As expected when the counters opened for advance booking on Feb 2nd 1970, it attracted a lot of crowd and in no time all the 9 shows of the first 3 days got over. Those selling in black had a fabulous time - chanting "2 ka 4 Bolo 2 ka 4". The cost of the tickets then for stalls used to be Rs. 2 and Balcony Rs. 3 in Rupam & most good cinema halls. The other memory was the story sessions during free period in our school days by Niranjan Pai (our Kalavati Teacher's son and Mohan Pai's Brother) who was the one in our class who had seen the movie during the week end of its release. He was particularly impressed with the background of Himalayas and with senior Burman's song - 'KAHAN HAI HIMALA AUR KAHAN AISA PAANI'...

After the initial big draw, the movie slowly slumped on the business front but as normal those days for Dev Saab's movies, females thronged the halls. Dev Saab played a peace loving person in the movie who had to lift the rifle much against his wishes as the Indo Pak war of 1965 broke out. The undoing of the movie was its length - it was almost a 'never-ending' one. Dev saab spent a lot of money by shooting part of the movie abroad & mounted the whole thing in a very lavish manner.

Waheeda Rehman played Dev Saab's sweetheart and excelled in the song "Rangeela Re". Zaheeda was introduced in this movie who, later played Dev Saab's heroine in Gambler but did not do too well in movies. A relatively new and unknown Pakistani Army officer was played by Shatrugan Sinha in this movie.

The best part of the movie was its music - SD Burman da had always given his best for Navketans & the standing out songs are:

http://www.youtube.com/watch?v=Z4iYbxFBZKQ

http://www.youtube.com/watch?v=ulG1g4FbrsE

http://www.youtube.com/watch?v=LZIqJ4VTVJs

All in all a Mile-stone movie though not very successful at the Box Office.

Happy Reading
Cheers
Laksh KV

February 05, 1971

"PYASI SHAAM"

Dear Friends:

This Day That Year, It was 52 years ago today i.e. on Feb 5 1971, this flop movie called "PYASI SHAM" released made by Kewaljit Productions who had earlier made a better movie viz "Mere Humdum Mere Dost" but this one was a disaster. All I recall is that this was curfew period for me wrt seeing movies as a class XI student and the movie did not last long enough for me to see it once my exams got over in 1.5 months after the release. So, just feel happy with the poster and envy Sunil Dutt who hugs Sharmila Tagore. The other thing I recall is the wedding of my Amma's Marathi student's brother at Tamil Sangam on this day and I did attend the Muhurtam and went to school – here I must tag my Amma's student V Narasimhan!!! Who later became my colleague in P&G. The movie and the music could not recreate the magic of the banner's earlier movie but this had a couple of hummable songs like "YE KAISA GUM SAJNA PYASA DIN PYASI SHAM", "AWARA MAAJI JAYEGA KAHAN" & "DUNIYA MEIN DILWALE HONGAY HAZARON". But a Big Box Office Disaster and here is the star cast:

- Sunil Dutt
- Sharmila Tagore
- Feroz Khan
- Om Prakash
- Manmohan Krishna
- Dhumal
- Anjali Kadam
- Kamal Kapoor &
- Birbal

Since I have not seen the movie till now, I have no option but to look up to multiple sources for the same but I will request some of the more knowledgeable folks to share about the plot and the movie. All I can say is it is a triangular plot with 2 good friends i.e. the Hero and the side Hero who get the Hero's sister married and then both fall for the same girl. Naturally there is going to be a fair amount of misunderstandings and till the side Hero realises that the Heroine too is fond of Hero ahead of him things get sorted out. Nothing much to rave about the performances I suppose. Friends – please help me with more dope on the plot. Here are the songs for you.

- https://www.youtube.com/watch?v=ljFOVuEjPJg ;
- https://www.youtube.com/watch?v=riecuME48cY ;
- https://www.youtube.com/watch?v=DD2tQ6v-Tyc ;
- https://www.youtube.com/watch?v=QQ5AYQ9g4Bk ;

Cheers
Laksh KV

February 04, 197

PAAKEEZAH

Folks

Exactly 51 years ago i.e. on February 4th 1972 saw the release of the Legendary Movie 'PAAKEEZAH' depicting "Pure" (Pak in Urdu).

There are a lot of memories with this movie like:

1. It was declared a flop on release - I remember seeing no one at the ticket counter of Rupam Cinema for the 6 PM show on the first day.
2. It took 14 years to make this movie.
3. Meena Kumari (Heroine) & Kamal Amrohi (Director) who were married and separated - the movie had to be almost shelved.
4. Songs were composed by Ghulam Mohammad who too passed away during the long gap
5. Naushad Ali stepped in to give the background music of the movie which finally hit the theatres on Feb 4th 1972.
6. The music was the highlight of this movie - all the songs were picturized on Meena Kumari with one duet with our own Jani Raj Kumar (Chalo Dildaar Chalo)
7. Despite fantastic music, the movie did not win the Filmfare award & this was not acceptable to film star Pran who refused to accept his award for his performance in the movie Be-imaan released in August 1972.
8. When the movie was released, Meena Kumari was unwell & is evident in her performance where she was lying down in many of the scenes and Padma Khanna was the one who performed the dances for the heroine as the body double.
9. Meena Kumari passed away on March 31st 1972 & the demand for the movie picked up in a big way. The movie became a very Big Hit after this - the only regret being Meena Kumari did not know how successful the movie was.

The production values were very high & had the aristocratic class in every frame of the movie. It was a great view though the current crowd may not be able to appreciate the quality of this ever-green Classic. If you have not seen it, please do - in those days when it was 35mm movies, this one was on Cinemascope i.e. wide screen.

Happy viewing - you can see some of the following songs:

http://www.youtube.com/watch?v=ubQ9hrKO6XI

http://www.youtube.com/watch?v=EDwvnOkDqSg

http://www.youtube.com/watch?v=C3LSpcw79Ys

Enjoy & Cheers
Laksh KV

Jan 31 1969 (54 years ago)

IZZAT

Dear Friends:

Jayalalita acted as a full-fledged Heroine in a Hindi movie called "Izzat". This movie was released today ie Jan 31 1969. This movie was discussed a lot on Dec 5th and 6th 2016 when death laid its icy hands on the famous "AMMA". Produced under the banner "Pushpa Films" with He-man Dharminder in a dual role (Gora Aur Kala) with Tanuja also playing the heroine along with Jayalalita. Balraj Sahani was the cause of creating 2 half-brothers!!!

Well friends, when I started the Quiz program on FB in LKFB, this was one of the early quizzes I recall way back in 2011. My memories of this movie are that I went alone to see this movie on Feb 1 1969 on Saturday 6 PM show - my late Amma allowed me to see this movie after I finished my Music Classes at 530 and I went rushing to Rupam Cinema and managed to get a ticket without paying a premium but was seated in the 2nd row from front "S 19" aisle seat and was thrilled at the fact that I was seeing a new release and annual exams were still 60 days away. Being a big Dharam fan, I had to like the movie though heart of heart I was not enjoying to the optimum. I was very disappointed with the performance of Jayalalita and the fairer and rich Dharam fell for her while the dark one impersonating the fair one wants to be honest with Tanuja - All the complications caused by Mr. Balraj Sahani as he ditched a village belle and the history was about to repeat when his son too was almost doing the same to Jayalalita who was the village belle. Mehmood too made an impact in the movie but the bigger impact was the music by LP in this movie. Good hummable numbers in the movie certainly enhanced the movie which was far from being a hit at the Box Office.

After seeing the movie, I returned home walking and on the way dropped by at Hanuman temple close to our house, thanked HIM for giving me this opportunity to see the movie and what waited for me was lovely "Khichri" prepared by my dear Amma - it gave the lovely fragrance of Garam Masala - though all other 4 members had finished the dinner, I still had the left overs but was still warm as it was pressure cooked and still inside the cooker, not to forget Amma was giving company at the table as I relished the dinner. A glass of buttermilk to cool the system was divine. Well, such memories cannot fade my friends.

Here are some of the songs from the movie:

https://www.youtube.com/watch?v=tqF1HNnub5Y

Cheers
Laksh KV

January 30 1970 53 years ago - me in class X - SIES School - 2 movies released

PAGLA KAHIN KA
PYAR KA MAUSAM

Dear Friends:

The 2 filmy brothers Shammi (my favourite then) and Shashi with Asha Parekh with both of them competed. The movies Pagla Kahin Ka and the 2nd one Pyar Ka Mausam released on the same day ie Jan 30 1970 53 years ago. I have done this quiz in my column and many cracked it - the same 2 again came with 2 movies with a common heroine earlier about 6 to 7 months on June 6 1969 - this part I will leave it for you folks to guess. It is fairly simple as many have cracked this one too.

My memories, though not seen both movies on release and in fact I saw Pagla Kahin Ka with my dear Bedi at Central in matinee show at reduced rates after I started earning while Pyar Ka Mausam till date I have only seen in bits and pieces.

On this very day during lunch break myself with my class-mates Churi (K Suryanarayanan) and LR Venkatesh went to Tequila Bar - King's Circle where there was a Music Box where we could insert a 25 paise coin and choose the song that you would like to listen to. Chury being the only child of his parents was a bit pampered and was always in funds. He gave me 25 paise besides feeding me with Samosas and sauce and told me to play any song of my choice and I played the title song of Pagla Kahin Ka. All this resulted in being a bit late to return to school. So we 3 at the door of the class asked "May I come in teacher" - teacher gave a dirty look and just showed a sign to enter and I was feeling like Shammi Kapoor and humming the song "Aashiq Hoon Main" much to the annoyance of the teacher. Then followed a lecture to me that the whole class enjoyed and heart of heart I was feeling happy that the period would get over without studies and home work. The movie was not a big box office hit but the music by SJ really was wonderful and the immortal song "Tum Mujhe Yooun Bhula Na Paaogay" has been used profitably for Mohd Rafi's death anniversary. I used to irritate everybody by singing "Mere Bhains ko Danda Kyon Maara" and would love the annoyance on their faces. Even my parents were fed up of listening to this as at every opportunity I would say "Mere Bhais Ko Dunda Tung Tung...the background music". Good acting by the main characters marked the movie but still did not appeal to the masses.

Pyar Ka Mausam was a bit more successful than PKK though I only recall my class mates Churi and Easwar seeing this movie and for a change here my langotya yaar Balakrishnan Narayan aka Bedi is not there to talk of. However, I must say that he was with me to see PKK at Central Cinema. PKM boasted of again good songs and "Tum Bin Jaaon Kahan" was the highlight - surprisingly the KK number was filmed on the lucky guy who has lip-synced the greatest Quwali in Barsat Ki Raat... Mr. Bharat Bhooshan while Shashi Kapoor had Mohd Rafi saab singing for him. Nisultana re Pyar Ka Mausam Aaya captured the audience in a big way. This movie ran for 14 weeks as against 12 weeks of PKK and both could not be termed as big hits. Incidentally RD Burman also played a role in the movie besides giving the music.

Here are some songs from both movies:

https://www.youtube.com/watch?v=bSqLxRP_qxE...;

https://www.youtube.com/watch?v=80GwLah-Aso;

https://www.youtube.com/watch?v=DqA-1K-U2G4;

https://www.youtube.com/watch?v=f0747dVKwqk...

Cheers
Laksh KV

52 Years ago

KATI PATANG

Folks:

Jan 29 1971 (52 years ago) was the release date of yet another Kaka hit movie "Kati Patang". The story was penned by Gulshan Nanda as a Novel and was made into a movie by Shakti Samanta, who for some reason decided to move to Asha Parekh from Sharmila Tagore - exactly one year later on the same Friday, the same banner released "Amar Prem".

The story of Madhu who runs away from an arranged marriage to Kamal and realizes that her boy friend Kailsah is having a rollicking affair with Shabnam. As she runs away from life, she catches up with her friend Poonam who is a widow with a child in arm but the train meets with an accident and the next thing you see is Poonam on the verge of kicking the bucket pushes her friend Madhu to take care of her baby and go and be with her in-laws as Poonam as the elders ie her parents in law have not seen her. Then what happens how Kamal comes back into her life and how Kailash too manages to reach there for his pound of flesh is the storyline - lots of misunderstandings later all ends well. Asha Parekh plays Madhu & impersonates as Poonam, while Kamal, the forest officer is played by a flamboyant Rajesh Khanna while Kailash and Shabnam are played by Prem Chopra and Bindu while the in-laws are Nasir Hussain and Sulochna. Excellent music by RD Burman made the movie a watchable one and this movie was one of the hits of Kaka in his string of some 17 odd hit movies he churned between 1969 starting with Ittefaq till 1972 when things started going down a bit for him.

Now coming to my standard personal problems in 1971 - having not done well in the prelims - movies were a big NO NO till final exams - so only solace was to see the status at Rupam Cinema and see the permanently fixed "House Full" board with my ever-dependable friend Balakrishnan Narayan aka Bedi. He being one year junior in school had the advantage of managing to see movies and he did see the movie as it released. Then it was one of our evening walks towards King's Circle, Matunga crossing Khalsa College and Don Bosco Bedi narrated the full story of the movie. Imagine he gave me the details like when the cabbie was trying to take advantage of Asha Parkeh with a kid in her arms - even that kid tried to help her by beating the driver despite crying. Another one was the girl-seeing meet for Kaka where Asha Parkeh too accompanies him with other family members. That "Bride to be" was shown as such a kid-like girl and total misfit that when sweet dish was to be ordered - Kaka orders for a "Tooti Frooti" Ice-cream. So my friend Bedi gave me such details as part of narrating the story. Kudos to you my friend for being so detailed. Lovely songs embellished the movie.

Finally, I got to see the movie (grudgingly) in March 1971 at Hyderabad with my cousin KS Sivaramakrishnan (aka Khan - I am sure he recalls our first visit when it was crowded & saw the movie at night in DILSHAD theatre). But during this trip I showed my one-upmanship to all my friends as I saw Kaka's unreleased movie "Mehboob Ki Mehandi" in Urdu which was being screened in Hyderabad while Mumbai folks could see only in May 1974 - 3 years later. I was told that Kaka managed to stall the release of a flop movie during his hit days in Mumbai!!! Well, folks - there are just too many things for me to share - but will stop here and wait for comments from friends who can relate to this.

Here is the link for some great songs from the movie

https://www.youtube.com/watch?v=7HTW1uUIIWQ

Cheers
Laksh KV

Jan 28 1972 - 51 years ago

AMAR PREM

Dear Friends:

What a classic movie Amar Prem was! It was Shakti Samanta's Baby that saw the light of the day on this very day ie January 28th 1972 – 51 years ago, and what a hit it turned out to be for the ever-popular pair of Rajesh Khanna and Sharmila Tagore who had created history with the same banner in November 1969 with Aradhana. All this I am writing as an impartial and mature man but when released, I was all of 17 (not yet) but at that time I wanted all Kaka movies to fail and my friend Balakrishnan Narayan is fully aware - one of the very few points where we had differences - the other one being Bhola and Poptalal!!!

The story of a fallen woman, a business man and a neighbour's kid - all 3 with no relationship except that of "Insaniyat" and how it develops - what are the difficulties the heroine goes thru with very bad relatives and uncles and how the business man gets drawn closer to her due to her exceptional singing prowess. Similarly how the kid is mistreated by his stepmother and he too finds a mom and dad in the lead pair who have a bit of untold love between them - When Rajesh Khanna said "Pushpa, I hate TEARS" - this line just got stuck with all and is used even today when artists perform any song of Kaka on stage. The cunning uncle played by Madan Puri with his famous line "Anand Babu, Aap Aur Is Mandir Mein?" - The way only he could say. This was exactly one week after the release of another cult movie Hare Rama Hare Krishna - this had a lot of emotion, pathos and love sublime!!! But as a dedicated Dharamendra fan, I avoided this movie when released (though secretly I wanted to see it) and happened to see it on TV on a Sunday in the 80s and loved the movie. But I recall that the "HOUSE FULL" Board was permanently placed outside Rupam Cinema in Sion.

Lot of memories and lot of nostalgia - around this time my late brother Vaidya V Raj used to give me a princely sum of Rs. 10/- as pocket money that enabled me to see movies though in college - but I did fund people those days as the cost of the tickets used to be between Re. 1 and 2 max as we did not indulge in high-end tickets. Walking to see the status of the movie towards Rupam Sion was a ritual for we friends staying in Sion. Excellent music in this movie always gave me a feeling that they were composed by SD Burman and not his son RD Burman - I know this is a very tricky subject to talk about. Well great memories and the movie did great business though I do not have the collection figures.

Enjoy some of the songs of the movie

https://www.youtube.com/watch?v=Mvb8yMqNPVM

Cheers
Laksh

January 24 1969

DIL AUR MOHABBAT

Dear Friends:

54 years back saw the release of a movie that had some good songs composed by OP Nayyar – The movie was 'DIL AUR MOHABBAT' *ing Ashok Kumar, Joy Mukherji, Sharmila Tagore, Nasir Hussain & Master Sachin.

The movie did not do well and was a flop but those money-less days meant that my friend Balakrishnan Narayan and myself had to satisfy ourselves by seeing posters at Rupam and not seeing the House Full board on the first day 6 PM show clearly indicated that the movie was not going to do well. However, we were very keen to see the movie as the posters included the heroine in swim-suit - what else will an impressionable teenager look for!!! Here was also a movie where OP Nayyar had taken the services of Mahendra Kapoor - probably had started boycotting Mohd Rafi by then.

Since I had not seen the movie, I made a bold attempt to have a dekho at it last night on YouTube and managed to last for the first 40 minutes and decided to stop. All I could see was a sincere cop Ashok Kumar succumbs to take bribe that would enable him to take care of his wife's ailing health and on her insistence returns the bribe amount and feels relieved only to also find that his wife too leaves the world. Their pampered son probably grows into Joy Mukherjee and is shown as a guy having a great night life & woos Sharmila Tagore and has support of his class-fellows that includes Johny Walker with an odd looking wig. All these actors well into their 30s then look far from convincing as college going students though to some extent Sharmila looked OK with her slim figure.

Now, I would like some of you who might have seen the movie to throw more light on the same about how it was then!!! Kindly do see it on YouTube and share your current thoughts!!!

Some of the song links are below:
https://www.youtube.com/watch?v=cOsm7mqYpNs;
https://www.youtube.com/watch?v=VNhX8uCKgTg;
https://www.youtube.com/watch?v=-pZuPpmOHZQ
Cheers
Laksh KV

Jan 23 1970

DOLI (53 Years ago)

Folks:

I take you back to Jan 23 1970 - 53 years into the past (release date of this movie called DOLI). The advertisement on the radio yelled 'HAR LADKI KA SAPNA - DOLI" followed by the hit Mahendra Kapoor song 'OH DOLI CHADKE DULHAN SASURAAL CHALI'. This movie did not help Kaka much but still it was his peak time & Rajesh Khanna managed to get the crowds for the initial draw but eventually managed just 10 weeks' run.

A typical triangular plot between Rajesh Khanna, Babita and Prem Chopra, who plays a rich foreign returned friend of the Hero. Lots of misunderstandings later and fights too - all ends well. Nothing much to talk about except that it completes 53 years of its release in Mumbai today. Overall average songs and all I recall is my walk to Rupam Cinema with my good friend Balakrishnan Narayan aka Bedi - and feeling good that the movie was not running to full house much to the disappointment of my friend.

Here are some songs for you and the best song was the duet "SAJNA SAATH NIBHANA" and when Mohd Rafi joins towards the last leg of the song, he manages to take us to a different level with his melodious rendition.

> https://www.youtube.com/watch?v=l5mmeDBcxX0 ;
>
> https://www.youtube.com/watch?v=Sj27hsBdmz0 ;
>
> https://www.youtube.com/watch?v=HglV7W27HlY ;

Cheers
Laksh KV

January 21st 1972

HARE RAMA HARE KRISHNA

Folks

Jan 21st 1972, 51 years ago saw a cult movie release that made a lot of impact on the impressionable ages – this was a movie made by none other than the "Ever-Green – Legendary" DEV ANAND Saab – yes your guess is right – it was 'HARE RAMA HARE KRISHNA' (HRHK) that hit the theaters on Friday Jan 21st 1972. And what a movie it turned out to be for Zeenat Aman who was officially introduced in this movie though OP Ralhan's "HULCHAL" & Hungama with Vinod Khanna released before this movie.

The Gossip mills were busy talking about the romance between the Brother & Sister (Zee played Dev's Sis in the movie) – well what one could clearly notice was Mumtaz having a very average role in the movie – relatively less exposure for the heroine – though, where there was chance to expose, she did !!! Prem Chopra played the villain and was called "Drona" in the movie and normally we have seen qualifications following the name of a person as – MBBS or something academic but Mr. Drona's qualification was – Owner of Large Properties. Gautam Sareen had a meaty role playing a negative character.

As usual Dev Saab had a fantastic role where he was desperate to locate his long lost kid sister – Master Satyajeet played young Dev Saab while I don't know the name of the girl who played Zee's younger version. It is very difficult to forget the words Dev Saab uttered on locating a CHARASI Zee with the Hippies towards the end of the movie 'TUMHARA BHAIYAA ZINDA HAI JASBEER' & the way he breaks the guitar hitting one of the CHARASEES.

Zeenat really arrived after this movie and Dev and Zee played lead roles post HRHK – like "Warrant", "Heera Panna" etc. Music was the Highlight of this movie with some of the best songs – a few of them are below:

https://www.youtube.com/watch?v=aKeenuBugBQ,

https://www.youtube.com/watch?v=NmS__6lBWCU,

https://www.youtube.com/watch?v=2acfBLyZXDU,
https://www.youtube.com/watch?v=SLdqaeUhu3A,
https://www.youtube.com/watch?v=29b-u4Mr3kg

A big hit then collected Rs. 7,43,000/- in the first week - next was Naya Zamana that had Rs. 7,02,000/-. My memories of this day was of not getting tickets anywhere and had to contend with seeing FARZ at Shree cinema. It was the wedding day of my cousin Krishna KRV with Kamala Krishna on this day and during the following week I saw the movie with my cousin from Hyderabad KS Sivaramakrishnan who had come for the wedding. We enjoyed the movie.

Just a point about the song Kanchi Re Kanchi Re – the higher notes of the song was a big struggle for Lata Mangeshkar – I would suggest you to listen to it and see how such a great singer struggled. I still feel they should have recorded that part again.

All said and done – this movie was a winner and did bumper business for Dev Saab – probably that kept him going till 2011 to make "Charge Sheet" that completely went unnoticed & on 3rd Dec 2011 Dev Saab breathed his last. We will miss you Dev Saab – RIP (**R**eturn **I**f **P**ossible)

Laksh KV

BHAI BEHAN

Folks:

January 16th 1970, 53 years ago, saw the release of a flop movie Bhai Bahen about which I have not much dope, for I have not seen but all I recall is that it was released on this day and it was a flop - a big one at it. I wanted it to do well as it had music of Shankar Jaikishan but that did not help.

It had Ashok Kumar, Sunil Dutt, Nutan, Padmini - Pran etc. even social media has limited data on this movie. I had to start the movie on YouTube and create the banner from the movie. Saw the first 10 mins and that had one song by Kishore Kumar which I heard for the first time and filmed on the screen brother of Sunil Dutt played by one Bhalla who dies in the movie. Ashok Kumar is the father of these 2 boys and as the disciplined Head of the Family expects discipline from all. The younger son goes off track and the elder one tries to correct him and in a matter of time the younger one dies and things are not the same as Ashok Kumar also has a daughter outside of his legitimate marriage and that is Padmini - then I thought that this could be the reason for the title of the movie where Sunil Dutt and Padmini (both late actors) play Bhai Behan. No wonder the movie flopped though SJ part kept me and pushed me to make the movie a success.

I will request the more knowledgeable people of our group to throw more light on this flop movie.

One song I liked is a Mohd Rafi one and here is the link

https://www.youtube.com/watch?v=XfUFFHpynLg ;

https://www.youtube.com/watch?v=qDr9RqX8Op0

Cheers
Laksh KV

15th Jan 1971 (52 Years)

AAN MILO SAJNA

Folks

TDTY Jan-15-1971 - i.e.

52 years ago saw the release of a very Big Hit Movie "**Aan Milo Sajna**" *ing Rajesh Khanna (Kaka), Asha Parekh, Vinod Khanna, Rajendranath, Aruna Irani & Nirupa Roy. This was made under the banner of Filmyug/Filmkunj - presented by J Om Prakash & directed by Mukul Dutt. All the J OmPrakash movies started with the Alphabet "A" - some of the movies made are:

1. AAS KA PANCHI - *ing Rajendra Kumar & Vyjantimala
2. AYEE MILAN KI BELA - *ing Rajendra Kumar, Saira Banu & Dharmendra
3. AAYE DIN BAHAAR KE - *ing Dharmendra, Asha Parekh & Balraj Sahani
4. AAYA SAWAN JHOOM KE - *ing Dharmendra, Asha Parekh & Ravindra Kapoor

Kaka was having a dream run that started with Ittefaq in Oct 1969 & went on to rule the industry till 1972 mid. His decline started with movies like Dil Daulat Duniya, Jhoru Ka Gulam etc that released after July 72. Young Randhir Kapoor was making an impact with Jawani Diwani & Rampur Ka Lakshman & a stable Dharmendra was going steady with Naya Zamana & Mera Gaon Mera Desh. Amitabh started making his presence felt with Bombay to Goa in 1972 & consolidated in May 73 with Zanjheer & there ended the era of Super Star Kaka. He continued to give hits like Aap Ki Kasam, Roti & Prem Nagar in 74.

Well coming back to Aan Milo Sajna - very standard storyline in a triangular format with Vinod Khanna the greedy man who is after property. There are some twists that are interesting. Some funny sequences by Rajendranath & his dad Sundar, though very stupid in general. Climax was interesting depicting the greed for money by the Villian - when the money flies all over, Vinod Khanna in the midst of his fight with Kaka, also tries to salvage the flying notes. The songs by Lakshmikant Pyareleal were big hits - some of the songs are:

1. Achha To Hum Chalte Hain
2. Yahan Wahan Saare
3. Palat Meri Jaan
4. Koyi Nazraana Lekar Aaya Hoon Main Diwana Tere Liye
5. Rang Rang Ke Phool Khile (Title Song)

Overall a good Masala Entertainer - makes me nostalgic of my school days.

Hope you enjoyed reading this.

Cheers

Lax

14th Jan 1972

GANGA TERA PANI AMRIT

Dear Friends:

51 years ago was the release of another abysmal failure of a movie with a long title "Ganga Tera Pani Amrit" *ing Ashok Kumar, Rehman, Pran, Nirupa Roy, Naveen Nischal, Yogita Bali and Master Satyajit and above all Shatrugan Sinha.

My recall is that there was good publicity and advertising that resulted in a good opening - the radio ad was very strong stating "Pragati Chitra International Films - Madras Ka Prastuti" - Ammen Sayani in his inimitable style announcing the title. As a college going student, I had to manage the limited money - if I should invest Rs. 2/- for this movie or keep it for the next big release "Hare Rama Hare Krishna"... I could see a very large crowd outside the Nepture Cinema Hall at Bandra. The initial opening was great but soon the movie was back to earth and ran for just 4 weeks. My cousin KS Sivaramakrishnan had come from Hyderabad to attend a family wedding and I recall he saw the movie in a cinema hall in Kalyan and said that except for Shatrughan Sinha - there was nothing in the movie and rattled some lines like "Woh Toh Bhallu Hai, Bhallu"... since I have not seen the movie I cannot comment more and I also vaguely recall from my friend Balakrishnan Narayan that Shatrugan dies in the movie and at some point his dialogues are played in the background and Bedi mentioned that the audience clapped a lot when they heard Shatrughan's voice in the background. Naveen Nischal was a big name having done well in his debut film Sawan Bhadon but in a matter of time, others took over and left him way behind.

The title song composed by Music Director Ravi was a big hit and rendered with feelings by none other than Mohd Rafi saab. Also there was a good duet picturized on Navin Nischal and Yogita Bali which was a hit too. Other songs did not make much impact.

Here are some links for you
https://www.youtube.com/watch?v=cFHFYiFW0T4;
https://www.youtube.com/watch?v=_6c2R2pfUec
Cheers
Laksh

RASTE KA PATHAR

Folks:

In TDTY series - on January 12 1973 i.e. 50 years ago released an immensely forgettable (for Big B for sure) movie that had quite a bit of hype with its promising young 2 dashing characters Amitabh and Shatrugan in the movie "Raste Ka Pathar". It turned out to be a big BO disaster - the movie introduced a new heroine called "Neeta Khayani" - where she vanished after that is unknown. Laxmi Chaya, Sudhir and Prem Chopra (PC) too had some role to portray.

The story line sounded a bit odd with the hero AB giving his flat to his boss PC to use in the nights. AB meets the heroine and falls in love with her as she is a homeless girl and gets her a job too but feels let down when he realizes that she is the "Wife to be" of his Boss. There was nothing much in the movie and most of us gave it a miss though by this time money was not an issue for me - why we gave it a miss was the input given by the only one from our gang who saw the movie - it was Arun Balakrishnan aka Naseeba who only went ga ga over Shatrugan's acting in the movie. Overall a movie best forgotten but does not get erased from my memory.

Here are some of the songs:
https://www.youtube.com/watch?v=lrzwmrXkRyc
Cheers
Lax

Jan 10 1969 - 54 years ago

PADOSAN

Dear Friends:

One week after the movie "SaraswatiChandra" was released, it was time for one of the Biggest Comedies to hit the Silver Screen. I would like to take you back to January 10th 1969 - the day "PADOSAN" was released. This movie had a star-cast that is just amazing with Mehmood at the helm, Sunil Dutt, Saira Banu, Kishore Kumar with his Pancharatna like Keshto, Mukri, Raj Kishore, Besides Om Prakash, Agha, Dulari & to top it outstanding music by RD Burman.

It was generally felt that this movie made fun of "Tamilians/Madrasees" & did not go too well with this crowd though it was a remake of a Tamil movie. However, if one looks at objectively, Mehmood played the role of Mr. Pillai a Musician to the T. He actually had his hair shaved off for the role and did complete justice to Mr. Pillai. The comedy timing was brilliant - one of the most hilarious scenes was when Bhola (Sunil Dutt) relocates to his aunt's place & sees his girl, he gatecrashes into a live play where his Guru (Kishore Kumar) & the others are in the midst of something very serious. On seeing Bhola, the Guru asks "BHOLE - US KANYA KA PATA CHALA?" and on getting a positive response from Bhola, Guru just says "CHALO HUM US KANYA SE VAARTALAAP KARTE HAIN" and the whole gang walks out of the live play. The Manager of the theatre played by Janki Das is completely lost & perplexed and so is the audience in the hall. However, those in the movie hall just kept laughing their guts out & this was all pure timing.

The Highlight of the movie was the music competition between Mehmood & Sunil Dutt with Kishore doing the playback for him - the hit song 'EK CHATURNAAR KARKE SHRINGAAR'. The musical instruments included, a comb, a broom & what not. Absoutely fascinating action in this song - but at the time of recording the film makers & music director Pancham had a tough time to convince the legendary Manna Dey as he had to lose to Kishore Kumar. A classically trained Manna Dey in real life is a far superior singer but after some good food Manna Dey agreed to lose. The coordination was so good with 3 voices (Manna, Kishore & Mehmood) & lip sync by Sunil Dutt & Mehmood was out of the world.

An out and out comedy, it did bring some tears in the end - after the climax when a dead Sunil Dutt comes back to life & gets married to Saira Banu, it is Mehmood who plays Nadaswaram with tears in his eyes - a complete loser. There is so much that one can write about this movie - but let me stop here. This movie comes at a fair frequency on Zee Classic Channel (328 of Tata Sky) - do enjoy it & myself despite being a Madrasi - am a great fan of this movie.

The radio ads started in the month of Feb 1968 with slogans like 'KHADAK SINGH KE KHADKNE SE KAHDAKTI HAIN KHIDKIYAAN AUR KHIDKIYON KE KHADAKNE SAY KHADAKTA HAI KHADAK SINGH - PADOSAN DEKH PADOSAN - PADOSAN DEKH PADOSAN' - Another jingle was with the tune of 'DHEERE SE JAANA KHATIYAN MEIN' later used by SD Burman in the DevAnand movie Chupa Rushtam.

Sadly, most of the actors are now history - good that the Heroine Saira Banu is still around and doing well.

All I could do is to envy my good friend Narayan Balakrishnan aka Bedi who manged to become kabab mein haddi of his then recently wed Maasa and Maasi and I had to wait till I was in college to see this hilarious comedy and again with Bedi at Kohinoor Cinema Dadar.

Good Luck and enjoy folks

Cheers

Laksh KV

Jan 10 1969 - 54 years ago

TEESRI KASAM

Dear Friends:

Along with Padosan ie January 10th ...well TDTY 1969 was also the release of this B&W movie called "**Teesri Kasam**". Though it says 1966 release, I recall very well that in Mumbai it hit the theatres only in 1969 though it was colour era - this was a B&W movie. While it is believed that, the movie caused the death of the great lyricist Shailendra who produced the movie - I would avoid getting deeper into that area. Here I am only sharing my memories of the movie.

It was a critically acclaimed movie but a financial disaster at the Box Office. The story revolved around an innocent "Bail Gaadi" guy who transports things from one place to another till he realizes that something is not OK and takes the first promise that he would not do anything illegal - takes a second promise on transporting Bamboos and then situation demands that he stop it too. Then he transports a Nautanki artist and entertains her by singing and develops a fondness for her and she too reciprocates. The innocent guy thinks that she is a paragon of virtues and gets free passes for seeing the shows of this Nautanki group and here he realizes that people are looking at the artist as a business woman and she herself tells that she is not "Pure" or "Paak" and that is when he takes his Teesri Kasam not to transport Nautanki artists.

Outstanding characterization and shot in villages of Bihar outskirts to give the right effect of the earthy feelings. Raj Kapoor and Waheeda Rehman were brilliant in this movie and the music by SJ - just wow... outstanding indeed. My oft repeated situation during school days continue of not having funds to see the movie but just look at the posters and appreciate the lucky ones who came out of the hall and assess what they felt without asking them about the movie. Released on Jan 10th at Apsara - ran exactly for 5 weeks and on Feb 14th 1969 saw Time Films Duniya *ing Dev Anand and Vyjantimala take over which too was not a big hit movie. But there is one thing that I recall reading those days and I am reproducing that below:

There was someone who saw the last show of Teesri Kasam at Apsara and saw the first show of Duniya at the same venue on the very next day on release of the new movie. But when he came out of the 2nd movie - fully disappointed he was heard singing

"DUNIYA BANANEWALAY KYA TERE MAN MEIN SAMAAYEE, KAHAYKO DUNIYA BANAAYEE TOONAY?"

This was questioning the makers of Duniya as to why such a movie was made and that too, to take over from a good movie like Teesri Kasam!!!

Here are some links of the good songs from Teesri Kasam:

https://www.youtube.com/watch...

Enjoy friends

Cheers

Lax

Jan 9 1970 - 53 years ago

TALASH

Folks:

On January 9th 1970 - 53 years ago was the release of OP Ralhan's **Talash** *ing Rajendra Kumar, Sharmila Tagore, Balaraj Sahani, Jeevan, OP Ralhan himeself. Then banners yelled 1 Crore Color Colossus - whatever it meant - did not know then. All I realized was this was a movie where the producer invested Rs. 1 crore to make it. All of us as school boys were overwhelmed with such a huge number as we did not have even Rs.2/- to see the movie. My late class mate PV Ramachandran with half knowledge said that the movie is not Eastman Color but it is Color Colossus!!! That was the level of understanding. Radio ad yelled "TALAASH KAHANI HAI US LADKI KI JISAY ZINDAGI MEIN TALASH THI"

Now coming back to the movie, with all the hype and money spent and with excellent music of Senior Burman it had all the promise. On release the movie came up with mixed reactions from those who were fortunate to see the movie. As usual my friend Bedi and me would go to Rupam Cinema to see the posters but the lucky guy that he was, he managed to see the movie and then told me the story of the movie. The plot revolved around an honest man from very middle class background who wants to do well in life and finds in Balaraj Sahani a man who gets impressed by his honesty. He does well in his organization but then now the Hero is confused regarding the village girl he fell for and a look alike but very hep who happens to be his boss's daughter. The movie also was talked about and not in very good taste about the hug scene between mother "Sulochana" and son "Rajendra Kumar" - still audience took it - OP Ralhan played the Hero's friend and a confused Rajendra Kumar was telling his Dil Ki Baat to his friend

"KAAM PE DIL NAHI LAGTA, BOSS NE MUJHE WARNING DEE HI" - Now OP Ralhan responds: " KAAM PE DIL NAHI LAGTA, BOSS NE WARNING DEE HI, WARNING NAHI TOH KYA DARLING DEGA?".

I managed to see the movie during my college days when I had some money and that too in reduced rates matinee show at Rupam Sion and was not very impressed with the movie. As my friend Dilip Apte said the other day, some movies were artificially made hits and this one belonged in that category.

Here are some songs for you to enjoy the genius of SDB

https://www.youtube.com/watch?v=SJ0nBUdrnVA ,

https://www.youtube.com/watch?v=eoVQg9rQCJs ,

https://www.youtube.com/watch?v=jxCJYNim380 ,

https://www.youtube.com/watch?v=W8-aWu33lGc

Cheers
Laksh

January 8th 1971

JOHAR MEHMOOD IN HONG KONG

Dear Friends:

In this series of TDTY (This Day That Year), I am touching January 8th 1971 ie 52 years ago - a movie released that was not a big hit and was called "Johar Mehmood in Hong Kong". In the mid-60s this combination of IS Johar and Mehmood did well with the movie JM in Goa but then there was a disaster in Namasteji and later ISJ made a movie without Mehmood called Johar in Kashmir. But overall both the guys were highly gifted actors and capable of playing good comic roles just by their sheer timing.

Now coming to this movie JM in HK, the story revolved around these 2 guys who are con men and ever ready to cheat each other and other people. They continuously play the game of one-upmanship with each other and at some point realize that it is futile fighting against each other and it would be better to join hands. By turn of events they land up in Hong Kong where the Chief Villain (Kamal Kapoor) of the movie resides and is working towards destroying India. These two work towards stopping the evil guys and protect India. In the bargain there are a lot of comedy sequences and the one that was outstanding sequence was the overnight conversion of Morgue into a Bank and with all the dead bodies working as the staff of the Bank - all for the secret formula that is in the locker of the bank. Needless to say things look very stupid but despite that it evokes laughter. Interesting songs in the movie makes it an OK watch for once - well the highlight being the song of Sadhu Aur Shaitan filmed on Jr. Mehmood while the Senior Mehmood without his knowledge does the lip sync & the Aayo Aayo Navrathri Tyohar filmed to fool the Villain gang - tough to do repeat watching but still I have done it all on TV and DVD. Needless to say, or me repeating that while in class XI, from Jan 1971 till March 20 1971 – till the day the exams got over "NO MOVIES" was the way of life. So, me and my good friend Narayan Balakrishnan aka Bedi would just gaze at the posters and assume things and show off as if we had seen the movie post reading the Sunday review in TOI. Woh bhi kya din thay!!!

Some songs of the movie:

https://www.youtube.com/watch?v=tM0EZsfAP9Y,

https://www.youtube.com/watch?v=jt-cT72alOQ,

https://www.youtube.com/watch?v=g2VC70IiB4o,

Cheers
Laksh

January 7ᵗʰ 1972

DUSHMAN

Dear Friends:

Good day folks - me casting my memories back - 51 years - 7th Jan 1972 - This Day That Year....was the release of the hit movie "Dushman" *ing Rajesh Khanna Mumtaz Meena Kumari Rehman Abhi Bhattacharya Bindu and others. Produced by Premji and directed by Dulhal Guha - this had a theme that was quite an off-beat one with respect to the judgement given by the Judge Rehaman. Kaka plays a truck driver who after the famous Qawali with Bindu (Vaada Tera Vaada) and night out, rushes in his truck and due to the mist ends up killing a poor farmer. As an honest person he does not run away but goes thru the court process and instead of imprisonment is given the task of playing the role of a bread-winner for the impacted family. This is a tough task as everyone in the family that includes parents of the deceased, widowed wife, young sister and kid brother have nothing but hatred for the hero and is referred to as "Dushman" by all including the villagers. Rest of the movie is how Mr. Dushman gets reformed and one by one wins them over but the tough nut to crack is the widow who is the most impacted. Dushman sings 'SUB NE MAAF KIYA MUJHKO PAR

> MAIN HOON JIS KAA DOSHI
>
> KAB TOOTEGI UNKI GHAAYAL
>
> HONTON KI KHAAMOSHI
>
> WOH BHI MAAF KARE TOH JAANU'

The movie deserved all the accolades for being so different. Good news for me now was - money was no more a scarce thing as my late bro who had started working from June 1971 used to give Rs. 10/- as pocket money and the cost of the ticket was only Rs. 2/-. Now was the conflict for me, I was not a Rajesh Khanna fan as was a loyalist of Dharam Paji. So kept avoiding the movie but used to feel "J" that the movie had the constant "House Full" board at Rupam Cinema. My best friend Balakrishnan Narayan aka Bedi was a great fan and he suggested to me prejudice chodo and see a good movie. So it was one day from the college I went directly to Nandi Cinema in Bandra and enjoyed the movie. I still had to find fault and was happy when I found one flaw and that was the limping Nana Palsheekar who played the role of the Bapuji of the family throughout the movie had his right leg hanging in the air except in the climax when he decided to lift the left leg. Bedi told me "Tu kya kya notice karta hi - in Caravan movie you found the Toffan mail's number plate changing and here this Langda Leg!!!" Well, I look for some familiar areas where one can go wrong.

Some song links for you to enjoy –

https://www.youtube.com/watch?v=Y5OerY3wLcM,

https://www.youtube.com/watch?v=xNcHdxov0nU,

Cheers - hope you read this and do not get bored
Laksh KV

January 03 1969

SARASWATICHANDRA

Dear Friends:

When the movie Sangam (Technicolor) released in June 1964, I thought that was the beginning of colour era - though there were a few before that and some were partially in colour like Mughal-e-azham. A few B&W movies too released post Sangam like Teen Deviyan, Juari, Khamoshi etc.

But on This Day That Year - 1969 on January 3rd released a big hit B&W movie called "Saraswatichandra" 54 years ago - It had Nutan playing the central character who felt her Piya Ka Ghar was better than her Babul Ki Galiyan... In reality it is not so in my view!!! Be that as it may - it had an unknown Manish playing the Hero and some people compared him to Guru Dutt those days - But he was an unsung hero. Out of context but another Hero who was thought to be a future Guru Dutt came in the movie "Uphaar" called Swaroop Dutt but far from Mr. Padukone.

Coming back to Saraswatichandra - hit movie, good songs by Kalyanji Anandji - female-centric movie that we were not allowed to see due to lack of money and school going kids are supposed to see movies only during vacation - so wait till April when the movie runs only at Opera House... ufff take a 66 number bus and go all the way... well, No way said our parents... So had to wait till I was well into my 30s when DD kindly showed the movie on a Sunday evening and I said to myself how come Nutan who looked easily 35 + had such a young kid bro... Then I said yes even Mumtaz had Master Alankar as her bro in "Dhadkan" - sub chalta hai. But overall I love going back to my school and Bachpan - hence this post.

Some more amplification

Those days for most of the people my age could see movies only during vacations. Needless to say, we had to satisfy ourselves by seeing the postures at Rupam Cinema (Sion) or Aurora (King's Circle) & assume/derive the story of the movie on the basis of what we could read on Sunday Times in the review column.

The movie "SC" was a very big hit and ran for over 25 weeks at Opera House those days - Nutan had a plum role and she did very well. Manish - the hero was comapred to Guru Dutt for his acting capabilities - however, he remained a one film wonder. Kalyanji Anandji's music was a real highlight of this movie with the following songs:

1. Chandan Sa Badan sung solo by Mukesh & solo Lata Mangeshkar – in the current parlance known as Tandem Song
2. Main To Bhool Chali Baabul Ka Des Piya ka Ghar Pyara Lage by Lata
3. Phool Tumhe Bheja Hai Khat Mein - duet by Mukesh and Lata
4. Chod De Saari Duniya Kisi Ke Liye by Lata
5. Humne Apna Sub Kuch Khoya Pyar Tera Paneko by Mukesh

Overall a well made movie directed by Govind Saraiya

Here is a link with some very popular numbers

https://www.youtube.com/watch?v=WtU389r6uys...

Cheers
Laksh KV

Jan 2 1970 - 53 years ago

DO BHAI

Folks:

This Day That Year... 2nd Jan 1970 - 53 years ago this movie "**Do Bhai**" was released in Mumbai. It was not a hit movie but had the story line to be remade in 3 South Indian languages - Despite Ashok Kumar and Jeetendra, the outstanding character was that of Sheikh Mukhtar in this movie.

I have some memories of this movie though not seen when released but it was just yesterday I managed to reach out to a batchmate who passed out with me in 1971 K Sundaram by name. He had seen the movie and during one of the free periods was narrating the story to me of this movie and I so much wanted to see it ... but where was the money!!!

Finally, one day during my working days in the year 1988 it was shown on DD and I had a flight to catch in the evening but luckily it was beamed in the noon and I kept telling people at home - DO Bhai the movie Sundaram had seen... Strange nostalgia but that is reality.

Cheers
Laksh KV

Jan 1 1971 - 52 years ago

AANSOO AUR MUSKAN

Dear Friends:

Jan 1st 1971 (52 years ago) a movie was released called **Aansoo Aur Muskan**. The movie *ing Hema Malini, Ajay (Parikshit) Sahani, Wonder Child Bobby and Kishore Kumar in a cameo but it was a big disaster. I do not have fond memories as the year began in a disastrous way for me as I had failed in one subject in school though I was given the go ahead to appear for the final exam of class XI. The condition laid was that I will not see any movies till my SSC exams got over on March 20 1971. Every one took a dig at me for the rare failure I had - so much so I was not even allowed to enjoy the KK hit song of the movie - the radio would be switched off saying "go study"... Tough days... But once March 20 happened, though I could not see this movie as it had failed and gone... I did not look back as in the next 85 days saw some 26 movies!!!

The plot was regarding an abandoned girl child born out of wedlock who has no one except a blind man who shows sympathy towards the child. They take care of each other and one day, this girl wins a lottery and now there are multiple claimants and eventually the real parents get her back, who had earlier separated. There is nothing much to the story line.

Highlight of the movie was the song 'GUNI JANO BHAKT JANO" - https://www.youtube.com/watch?v=Etx0Y5YmACs

Have a great year all
Cheers
Laksh

www.ingramcontent.com/pod-product-compliance
Lightning Source LLC
LaVergne TN
LVHW091653070526
838199LV00050B/2161